SECOND EDITION

Group Politics and Social Movements in Canada

Edited by MIRIAM SMITH

UNIVERSITY OF TORONTO PRESS

Library and Archives Canada Cataloguing in Publication

Group politics and social movements in Canada / edited by Miriam Smith.—Second edition.

Includes bibliographical references and index.
Issued in print and electronic formats.

ISBN 978-1-4426-0817-7 (bound).—ISBN 978-1-4426-0695-1 (pbk.).
—ISBN 978-1-4426-0696-08 (pdf).—ISBN 978-1-4426-0697-5 (epub)

        1. Social movements—Political aspects—Canada.   2. Social movements—
Political aspects—Canada—Case studies.   I. Smith, Miriam Catherine, editor of
compilation

HM881.G76 2014   322.4'40971   C2013-906797-3   C2013-906798-1

We welcome comments and suggestions regarding any aspect of our publications—please feel free to contact us at news@utphighereducation.com or visit our Internet site at www.utppublishing.com.

North America	UK, Ireland, and continental Europe
5201 Dufferin Street	NBN International
North York, Ontario, Canada, M3H 5T8	Estover Road, Plymouth, PL6 7PY, UK
	ORDERS PHONE: 44 (0) 1752 202301
2250 Military Road	ORDERS FAX: 44 (0) 1752 202333
Tonawanda, New York, USA, 14150	ORDERS E-MAIL: enquiries@nbninternational.com

ORDERS PHONE: 1–800–565–9523
ORDERS FAX: 1–800–221–9985
ORDERS E-MAIL: utpbooks@utpress.utoronto.ca

Every effort has been made to contact copyright holders; in the event of an error or omission, please notify the publisher.

This book is printed on paper containing 100% post-consumer fibre.

The University of Toronto Press acknowledges the financial support for its publishing activities of the Government of Canada through the Canada Book Fund.

Printed in Canada

RECYCLED
Paper made from
recycled material
FSC
www.fsc.org   FSC® C103567

Contents

Preface

This book evolved from my own need for a teaching text that would provide a comprehensive overview of the recent evolution of social movement and group politics in Canada. The main challenge in developing this volume was to locate authors who could write about all of the movements that would ideally be included in such a text. With help from many colleagues, I succeeded in developing a team to write on most of the main topics.

The book provides an introductory theoretical chapter, adapted with permission from my book *A Civil Society?: Collective Actors in Canadian Political Life* (University of Toronto Press Higher Education, 2005) and updated to reflect recent developments in social movement theory. Each contributor was asked to provide an overview of the main organizations and political issues for each group or movement and an evaluation of the success or failure of the group or movement in exercising influence in Canadian politics. Most of the chapters focus on the activities of groups and social movements in federal politics, and many of them provide an overview of trajectories of influence and political mobilization over time. All of the chapters were written by authors who have a long-standing interest in the area and, therefore, they reflect a broad and deep expertise and familiarity with the subject matter. Many of the movements and groups included here are relatively understudied in the Canadian context (e.g., health, disability and queer politics) while others are rarely approached through the lens of social movement mobilization (e.g., First Nations and Quebec nationalism). Other chapters deal with enduringly important areas such as the women's movement, the labour movement, the environment, and populist and evangelical movements; they provide authoritative overviews that will be of interest in teaching and scholarship. As the volume extends to "group politics," I have included a chapter on business organizing as the business community in Canada has been very successful in using the tools of collective action and in exercising political influence. Similarly, a new chapter on farmers rounds out the consideration of group politics. The result is a volume that provides a strong synthetic overview of a wide range of empirical material from different theoretical perspectives. The texts reflect the diverse theoretical interests and approaches of their authors.

I believe that this theoretical pluralism best represents the state of the field and will prove most useful in providing an introduction and overview of this rich material for political science and sociology courses. In addition, each contributor was asked to provide a list of references to assist further reading on each group or movement.

All in all, I hope the book fills a gap in the existing literature in Canadian politics and that it focuses our interest and attention on the possibilities, potential, and pitfalls of collective political agency. I would like to thank the contributors for their excellent work in making this book possible.

Key Acronyms

9/11	symbol for the terrorist attacks on New York's World Trade Center and the Pentagon in Washington, DC on September 11, 2001.
ADQ	Action démocratique du Québec (Quebec Democratic Action)
AFN	Assembly of First Nations
BQ	Bloc québécois
CACSW	Canadian Advisory Council on the Status of Women
CAP	Canada Assistance Plan
CAW	Canadian Auto Workers
CCF	Co-operative Commonwealth Federation
CCSD	Canadian Council on Social Development
CDC	Centers for Disease Control (US)
CHRC	Canadian Human Rights Commission
CHP	Christian Heritage Party
CHST	Canada Health and Social Transfer
CLC	Canadian Labour Congress
CPC	Communist Party of Canada
CUFTA	Canada-US Free Trade Agreement
CUPE	Canadian Union of Public Employees
CUPW	Canadian Union of Postal Workers
CWC	Canadian Welfare Council
EPF	Established Programs Financing
FFQ	Fédération des femmes du Québec (Quebec Women's Federation)
FLQ	Front de libération du Québec (Front for the Liberation of Quebec)
FTAA	Free Trade Area of the Americas
GATT	General Agreement on Tariffs and Trade
GPC	Green Party of Canada
GST	goods and services tax
HBC	Hudson Bay Company
HRDC	Human Resources Development Canada

ILPs	Independent Labour Parties
IMF	International Monetary Fund
LEAF	Women's Legal Education and Action Fund
LGBT	lesbian, gay, bisexual, and transgender
LGBTQ	lesbian, gay, bisexual, transgender, and queer
MLA	Member of [provincial] Legislature
MNA	Member of the National Assembly (of Quebec)
MNC	Métis National Council
MP	Member of Parliament
NAC	National Action Committee on the Status of Women
NAFTA	North America Free Trade Agreement
NCC	Native Council of Canada
NCW	National Council of Welfare
NDP	New Democratic Party
NFU	National Farmers Union
NGO	non-governmental organization
NSM	new social movements
OECD	Organization for Economic Development
OPEC	Organization of Petroleum Exporting Countries
OPSEU	Ontario Public Service Employees Union
PLQ	Parti libéral du Québec
PQ	Parti québécois
PSAC	Public Service Alliance of Canada
RCMP	Royal Canadian Mounted Police
RMT	resource mobilization theory
RN	Ralliement national (National Movement)
SDP	Social Democratic Party of Canada
SPC	Socialist Party of Canada
SWC	Status of Women Canada
UAW	United Auto Workers of America
UK	United Kingdom
UN	United Nations
US	United States of America
USWA	United Steelworkers of America
WTO	World Trade Organization

INTRODUCTION

Theories of Group and Movement Organizing[1]

MIRIAM SMITH

This book provides a set of case studies of the role of social movements and interest groups in Canadian politics. Such groups provide a vehicle for public participation in collective decision-making in a democratic society. Collective action is an alternative to voting and participating in the electoral system and enables people to pursue and express a broad range of political interests and identities. Participation in collective action is central to democratic political life. The right to assemble freely was one of the first freedoms of the democratic revolution and remains a core element in democratic practice. Historically, the central framework of democratic group politics has been provided by the nation-state. As many of the chapters in this book show, there are a broad range of issues on which the domestic nation-state is still central to decision-making and to political outcomes. However, the declining role of states and the rapid growth of new communication technologies have led to the rise of transnational and international forms of organizing such as the global justice and indigenous rights movements epitomized in Canada by Occupy and Idle No More.

The chapters in this volume cover a broad range of organized group and movement activity, ranging from business and labour to health and disability. The authors deploy a broad range of theoretical perspectives in describing the evolution of organized groups and movements in their sector and in evaluating the success of organized groups in exercising influence in Canadian politics. The diversity of approaches is one of the strengths of the volume as the chapters provide concrete examples of groups and movements in action in the Canadian context. Some chapters evaluate several approaches to understanding he sources and effectiveness of group political mobilization. For example,

Peter Clancy's chapter on business organizing includes discussion of Canadian political economy as well as neopluralist approaches to understanding the role of business in Canadian politics. Trevor Harrison's chapter on populism and Christian evangelical organizing evaluates different explanations of the evolution of populist movements. Other chapters concentrate on developing a particular theoretical perspective. For example, Alexandra Dobrowolsky's chapter on the women's movement argues for specific developments in social movement theory while Pascale Dufour and Christophe Traisnel's chapter examines the sovereignist movement in Quebec from a social movement perspective.

The purpose of this introduction is to set the stage for a presentation of these case studies by providing an overview of the main theoretical approaches to explaining and understanding the role of interest groups and social movements in Canada. There is no agreement among political scientists specifically or social scientists in general about the best ways to study group and social movement politics. Rather, there are a plethora of theories that draw our attention to different facets of collective action (Baumgartner and Leech, 1998). Each of these theories have clear normative and ideological implications. Some tend to legitimate the existing political system while others provide a critical stance toward existing democratic institutions. In the sections to follow, we will canvass several of these theoretical approaches for studying social movements and groups in comparative and Canadian politics and explore their normative implications. The main approaches that will be explored are pluralism, Marxism, political economy, historical institutionalism, social movement theory, and rational choice theory.

PLURALISM

For pluralists, society is composed of individuals. This may not seem like a controversial assertion; however, there is a key difference between pluralism and rational choice theory, which gives methodological primacy to the role of the individual in politics, and Marxism or Canadian political economy, which emphasize the importance of groups and structures of power. Pluralists begin with the individual who, in their view, has multiple loyalties, representing his or her diverse interests and preferences. Any of the individual's interests may form the basis for participation in a group that seeks to influence politics.

In Canadian society, for example, class, language, religion, region, socioeconomic status, gender, and ethnicity might all be considered important lines of political cleavage. Groups form when like-minded individuals join together in pursuit of their common interests and pressure or lobby government for policies that will favour their group. Pluralists usually describe such groups as interest groups or pressure groups. Many of the groups discussed in this volume might be categorized as interest groups, ranging from the Canadian Council of Chief Executives described in Peter Clancy's chapter to some of the environmental organizations discussed by Robert Paehlke. Because there are many potential political cleavages in complex societies, pluralist theory argues that no one group ever dominates politics for long. If one group becomes too powerful, another will often rise to counterbalance its power (Bentley, 1908). The multiple interests of individuals mean that there are many possible groups and that society is characterized by cross-cutting cleavages along different lines. However, society is not divided by class cleavages alone, but is also characterized by cleavages based on other definitions of the interests of the individual. Because of this, it is not likely that one cleavage will become dominant or that strong groups will go unchallenged.

According to pluralist theory, political scientists should be interested in group politics because public policy is a reflection of the struggle between groups to secure advantage (Dahl, 1961; Polsby, 1963). For pluralists, manifest and open conflict between groups is the key to political conflict; cases in which conflicts are submerged or marginalized or in which power is exercised by structural forces cannot be subsumed under the rubric of pluralism (Gaventa, 1982; Lukes, 2004 [1974]). In this respect, state actors, such as politicians and bureaucrats, do not play an independent role in the development of public policy as they are influenced by the contestation of groups (although, see Almond, 1988). Pluralist theory is analogous to Adam Smith's idea of the "invisible hand" of the market economy in which economic growth for the good of all is the end result of the self-interested struggle of individuals. Pluralist theory suggests that there are multiple access points to the political system for all citizens through group politics.

However, in the 1960s and after, pluralist theory was found wanting on several fronts. The social conflicts of the period suggested that not everyone has access to the political system. Some groups may be permanently marginalized, and some may indeed have more power than others. This point was brought home forcefully by the race riots of the 1960s, the anti-war movement, and the student movement in the US. In Canada, the rise of more powerful Quebec and Aboriginal nationalisms and the resurgence of anti-Americanism among youth in English-speaking Canada deepened the critique of a happy and benign group politics. Developments in these movements are discussed in the chapter by Charlotte Yates and Amanda Coles on the evolution of the working-class and trade union movements in Canada, Kiera Ladner on Aboriginal politics, Pascale Dufour and Christophe Traisnel on the evolution of Quebec nationalism as a social movement, Miriam Smith on the lesbian and gay movement, and Alexandra Dobrowolsky on the women's movement. These movements and the accompanying counterculture of the period suggested a more profound appraisal of democratic capitalism and called attention to structures of power in society such as racism and sexism. Just as the US was under internal siege from within during the late 1960s and early 1970s, so too the dominant pluralist approach in political science came under fire. The response to these critiques was the development and revival of other approaches, including neo-Marxism, Canadian political economy, and neopluralism. The neo-Marxist critiques of pluralist theory in political science helped to spawn the neopluralist amendments to the original theory. Therefore, it is to neo-Marxism that we will now turn.

MARXISM AND NEO-MARXISM

In contrast to pluralism, structural theories of the role of social forces in the political process stress that power relations are not the result of individual choices but of socially patterned behaviour, collective action, and institutional and organizational configurations. Individual choices are overwhelmed by the structural forces that shape behaviour. The pattern of group formation is affected by economic and social inequality, which create systemic obstacles for marginalized groups in the political system. While there are several such structural theories, the most elaborated by far is Marxism and its neo-Marxist variants (Seidman, 2004).

Unlike the pluralists and neopluralists who see social forces as individuals organized into groups or interest groups, Marxists understand social forces as organized into classes. Classes are not merely socio-economic groupings, such as "middle class" or "lower class," but are specifically defined by their relationship to the means of production. In the chapters in this volume, Charlotte Yates and Amanda Coles discuss the evolution of organized labour in Canadian politics in relation to the socialist political project; and Trevor Harrison considers class as a factor in the rise of right-wing populist movements. These chapters provide concrete examples of the use of class analysis in understanding political mobilization in Canada.

For Marxists, the economic organization of society determines class relationships. In a capitalist economic system such as Canada's in which property is privately owned, the means of production (land, labour, and capital) are owned by the capitalist class or bourgeoisie, and the working class or proletariat, which does not own the means of production, is forced to work to live. The capitalist class attempts to extract as much value from the labour of the working class as possible, and the working class, in turn, struggles to resist this exploitation. The conflict between capitalists and workers in a capitalist economy is termed the class struggle. In the Marxist view, political conflict centres on the class struggle between workers and capitalists (Panitch, 1995). This perspective constitutes a profound critique of the pluralist idea of the role of interest groups. It suggests that the main cleavages in society are based not on multiple group memberships but on economic divisions rooted in the capitalist economic system. Groups are not all able to access the political system; rather, the system is profoundly unequal, and the subordinated classes face structural barriers to political influence and participation.

In the analysis of collective actors in the political process, then, neo-Marxism and pluralism begin at very different starting points. Pluralists view society as composed of individuals who have multiple interests that give rise to cross-cutting cleavages. Neo-Marxists view society as composed of classes in which the dominant class exploits the subordinated class, thus giving rise to class struggle. Pluralists have a benign interpretation of the ends of power: in the long run, the struggle between groups will even itself out, and no group is presumed to dominate politics in a democratic political system. The neo-Marxist views democratic political institutions as a cover or tool for capitalist class power and as an arena of class struggle. The pluralist does not inquire into the source of the individual's interests and preferences, while the neo-Marxist emphasizes the ways in which the commonsensical consciousness of everyday life is shaped by the class system. What these two perspectives do have in common, though, is their view of the state and of state institutions as relatively passive in relation to organized collective actors. While there are many different interpretations of the role of the state within Marxist theory and within the middle-range empirical studies of the pluralists, both perspectives tend to downplay political institutions and their effects on group politics and policy development. The pluralist sees the state as vulnerable to group influence, an unsurprising conclusion given that pluralist analysis has most often been applied to the American political system, a system that provides multiple points for group access. Neo-Marxists see the state as fundamentally capitalist and its actions as structurally circumscribed by class power, the capitalist economic system, and even the consciousness of citizens, who may be taught to consent to their own exploitation.

CANADIAN POLITICAL ECONOMY

While pluralist approaches to the study of pressure groups existed in Canada during the 1960s, the approach was not as dominant as it was in the US. Nonetheless, its assumptions about the nature of political power in capitalist democracies also came under fire in this country. However, the Canadian critique took on a particular flavour. As Peter Clancy discusses in his chapter on business organization, students of Canadian politics of this period were influenced by the political economy tradition. During the 1970s, political economy approaches were revived by a new generation of political economists, led by Mel Watkins (1977). The new political economy took up the theme of colonialism, specifically, the colonial position of Canada in relation to American political and economic power. However, it had an ambiguous relationship to capitalist class power. Some analysts in this tradition, such as Tom Naylor (1972), viewed the Canadian state as the instrument of capitalist class power, much as in the instrumentalist Marxist view outlined in the previous section. Others bemoaned the weak position of Canadian capital as undermining Canadian sovereignty and economic independence (Levitt, 1970). Much of the new political economy was concerned with structures of economic power in Canada and Canada's position of relative underdevelopment compared to other similar political systems (e.g., Laxer, 1989; Marchak, 1985) and did not have much to say about collective actors in politics. For example, a new political economy analysis of why Canada adopted free trade would focus on the position of Canada as a region or series of regions in the North American political economy and the role of the Canadian state in reinforcing north-south economic linkages following the demise of the Keynesian welfare state. Similarly, recent attempts to bring gender and race into Canadian political economy explore such issues as the ways in which the labour market is gendered or racialized but not the role of collective actors as agents in the political process (Vosko, 2000; Abele and Stasiulis, 1989). The new Canadian political economy, then, is mainly a structural approach that focuses on the social and economic forces that limit the actions of political actors, but does not suggest an approach to the study of such actors.

HISTORICAL INSTITUTIONALISM

Historical institutionalists argue that the main problem with both pluralist and neo-Marxist theories of state–society relations was that both assumed that the state's actions were driven by social forces, that state decisions reflected the power of the dominant forces in society, and that political institutions played almost no independent role in shaping policy and political outcomes. Pluralists and neo-Marxists disagreed over the nature of society and over the nature of the collective actors or groups that comprised the social forces driving the state. As we have seen, for pluralists, groups are the most important social actors, and their conflicts drive politics. For neo-Marxists, the pluralist emphasis on the group is an ideology that masks the importance of classes, whose conflicts drive politics. Pluralist analyses tended to legitimate American democracy (and, hence, indirectly, American power in the world), while neo-Marxist analysis tended to de-legitimate American democracy and power.

But, despite the profound theoretical, normative, and ideological differences between pluralists and neo-Marxists, they shared an important theoretical similarity in their lack of attention to the independent causal power of states and state institutions (Skocpol, 1979).

In contrast, historical institutionalists argue for a return to the Weberian tradition in social science, meaning a return to the work of German sociologist Max Weber, who pioneered the study of the rationalities of a variety of large-scale social institutions such as religion, bureaucracy, and the state. Weber developed a critique of bureaucracy as the "iron cage" of modern industrial society as well as taxonomies of states and the implications of their differences for political styles and outcomes (Seidman, 2004). Weber's importance rests on his systematic attention to the understanding of states as independent and internally differentiated, an attention that institutionalist critics found to be lacking in American political science scholarship during the pluralist period. As we have seen, pluralists largely viewed the state in terms of government, hence neglecting the state's permanent apparatus, most importantly, the bureaucracy. According to the institutionalist critique, pluralists tended to view government as the "cash register of group demands" rather than an independent player, while the neo-Marxists were unable to offer any explanation of the capitalist state beyond their claim that it *was* capitalist and that it would enact policies that protected the capitalist system. As historical institutionalists rightly pointed out, a theory of the capitalist state that rests on the assertion that such a state will always protect capitalism and/or capitalists cannot explain the myriad of interesting differences between capitalist states, such as the low rate of American social spending compared to other capitalist democracies (Skocpol, 1985).

Compared to the other approaches that have been described so far, historical institutionalists share with neo-Marxists the idea that the beliefs and values of collective actors are shaped through social processes. Unlike neo-Marxists, however, historical institutionalists open up the possibility that the values and preferences of collective actors are shaped by contingent policy processes (policy legacies) as much as by macro social forces (the capitalist economic system). While a neo-Marxist might ask why workers believe in and consent to a capitalist economic system, the historical institutionalist would explore why workers in one context argued for industrial policies while workers in another ignored industrial policies and demanded Keynesian macroeconomic stabilization (e.g., Hattam, 1993). Precisely because historical institutionalism focuses on the mid-range level, it does not have a theory of history or an overall theory of social power. Therefore, in historical institutionalist analyses, class-based politics arising from capitalist exploitation may be acknowledged at the same time as group-based interests are also recognized.

NEOPLURALISM

In response to the critiques of their approach by both neo-Marxists and historical institutionalists, pluralists amended their theory. They developed a new perspective, often called neopluralism (Lukes, 2004 [1974]). In this approach, more attention was paid to the idea that government may influence the public agenda. The neopluralists conceded two important points to critics of the original pluralist theory. First, they acknowledged that democratic capitalist societies, such as Canada, might be characterized by persistent social inequality that would create barriers to the formation and influence of interest groups. For example, poor people are unlikely to have the economic and social resources to form effective interest groups, and their interests will not be reflected in the political system. Jonathan Greene's chapter on the anti-poverty movement emphasizes the ways in which anti-poverty organizations do not have the resources to exercise substantial influence. The political system itself may mobilize bias; that is, certain types of political issues may be mobilized out of political consideration and debate. Another example is that of race. Until recently, the idea that Canadian society might be characterized by pervasive racism was not a subject of political debate. As Audrey Kobayashi's chapter discusses, until recently, political debate was biased against consideration of the problem of racism in Canadian society and of how public policies could be designed to address it.

Second, in a variant of institutionalist analysis, neopluralists recognized that governments themselves could play an important role in the development of public policy. Governments were not simply carrying out the wishes of the strongest group; instead, politicians and bureaucrats were actively involved in the development of public policy and often used groups to communicate with particular constituencies of citizens to legitimate these policies. Groups might advocate their interests to government, but the bureaucracy also might develop institutionalized links with key groups and consult them regularly in the formation of policy, as Grace Skogstad's chapter on farmers discusses. This type of analysis draws on historical institutionalism and relies more on public policy analysis than on the grand questions of comparative politics. Studies of policy communities and policy networks are important in the studies of Canadian public policy.

SOCIAL MOVEMENT THEORY

Another approach to the analysis of groups in the political process is provided by social movement theory, which was mainly developed by sociologists. In part, it is based on the experiences of the 1960s when several new movements arose that posed profound challenges to the status quo. The women's, environmental, gay liberation, peace, student, and civil rights movements suggested that all was not well with capitalist democracies. New Left movements, as they were sometimes termed, engaged in mass protests and demonstrations and generated a culture of transformative and liberation politics. These spontaneous mass protests seemed to be fundamentally different from the well-organized and institutionalized interest groups of pluralist theory and from the class politics of neo-Marxist theories.

New social movement theory, developed mainly in Europe, and resource mobilization theory, developed mainly in the US, evolved to explain the rise of the social movements of the 1960s and after. A third approach—the political process model—synthesizes these two theories (Della Porta and Diani, 1999; Staggenborg 2012: ch. 1). The political process model deals with many of the same issues as political science models of group behaviour, as we will see below.

We will begin by looking at some of the common elements in the analysis of social movements across the three most recent theories—new social movement theory, resource mobilization, and the political process model—followed by a look at some of the distinctive features of each of the three approaches in the order in which they arose.

What is a social movement? The broadest definition, offered by Manuel Castells, is: "purposive collective actions whose outcome, in victory as in defeat, transforms the values and institutions of society" (Castells, 1997: 3). For political scientists and sociologists who encountered the social movements of the 1960s, a series of traits was thought to distinguish the "new" social movements from organized interest and advocacy groups. First, social movements challenge the traditional boundary between state and society, public and private. In pluralist and neopluralist theory, there is a clear distinction between state and society; societal groups form and then attempt to influence government. Although groups may develop institutionalized links to government, there is still a clear distinction between public and private. Social movements challenge this distinction, arguing that "the personal is political" and bringing issues that were once defined as private into the sphere of public debate. Social movements may also challenge the public/private divide by demonstrating how the private sphere is imbued with power relationships or politics. Chapters by Alexandra Dobrowolsky on the women's movement, Lisa Vanhala on the disability movement, Michael Orsini on health social movements, Miriam Smith on the lesbian and gay movement, and Robert Paehlke on the environmental movement exemplify this challenge to the conception and definition of the private sphere.

Second, social movements may emphasize the creation and reinforcement of identity and the promotion of certain values over the pursuit of material interests. As such, social movement goals may be primarily aimed at society rather than the state. Alexandra Dobrowolsky provides a strong discussion of the role of identity in the women's movement and the ways in which its claims are framed. The second wave of the women's movement often engaged in consciousness-raising in which small groups of women would meet to share their experiences. In the process, women realized that their problems and experiences were not unique, that many women had had similar experiences, and that their problems had social and political causes. In this way, a common bond of solidarity was created among feminist women, and a new identity was formed that, in turn, provided the base for women's mobilizing. Lisa Vanhala highlights the social construction of "disability" and points to the role of disability activism in challenging the dominant constructions of ability and disability. Similarly, Michael Orsini demonstrates how social movements may challenge dominant definitions of knowledge and science in the health field. In this way, as Alberto Melucci has put it, social movements challenge the dominant "codes" of society (Melucci, 1996). Although state policies may also be targeted, state policy alone cannot effect changes in social behaviour. Movements aim to achieve cultural and knowledge shifts and not just shifts in policy.

Third, social movements are often said to engage in strategies and tactics that are more radical than those used by interest groups. While interest groups may attempt to influence government policy through the conventional means of lobbying in one form or another, social movements often engage in direct action tactics. For example, the environmental movement has often chosen to confront its opponents directly rather than to work with government— environmentalists have spiked trees and chained themselves to trees to prevent clear-cut logging. Such direct action tactics are often particularly useful because they create dramatic media footage that can be used to promote the values of the movement. Large-scale disruptive demonstrations and protests may also be used to force government action and to capture media attention, as Jonathan Greene discusses in his chapter on anti-poverty organizing in Canada.

Social movements are also said to have a more decentralized and democratic organization than interest groups. They often form as networks of activists, with little formal organization, and even where formal organizations exist, they are often highly decentralized. The New Left explicitly rejected bureaucratization and majority rule as oppressive and often operated by direct democracy, task rotation, and consensus decision-making in which each member of the group could veto group decisions and in which tasks were rotated among members.

In reality, social movements may not conform to this ideal typical picture. Some have been quite well-organized, at least during certain periods, and may seek to influence government through participation in consultative exercises or policy communities. Unlike traditional interest groups, social movements usually form networks of smaller groups instead of well-organized and hegemonic organizations. Rather than conforming to the ideal type of social movement political behaviour, many may follow a dual strategy of influencing the state and influencing society. For example, environmental groups may lobby government while engaging in activities that are designed to influence public opinion and to change social attitudes (Wilson, 1992). In practice, social movements pursue diverse strategies. Further, distinguishing collective actors on the basis of their regard for their own material interests is also problematic. As we shall see, the tools of social movement analysis work well for understanding business militancy of the 1980s and 1990s, despite the fact that such groups pursue the material interests of their members. Social movements that are thought to be part of identity politics—ethnocultural groups, gay and lesbian groups, or women's groups—may also have important material interests at stake in their organizing.

Why do social movements arise, and what are the most important factors that influence their success and failure? The three theories of social movements have different answers to these questions. According to resource mobilization theory, social movements mobilize pre-existing grievances. For example, African Americans living under segregation evidently had grievances; however, systematic political mobilization around these grievances did not emerge until the 1950s. Thus, according to resource mobilization theory, it is not the grievances that are new but the resources that movements can bring to bear to press their demands (Jenkins, 1983). Audrey Kobayashi's article on ethnocultural organizing also highlights the historical and material obstacles and barriers to organizing. According to resource mobilization theory, the success and failure of social movements is determined by their ability to bring diverse resources—money, organization, sympathetic allies, and expertise—to bear in their struggles. Resource mobilization is analogous to pluralist theory in political science because it focuses on organized groups that attempt to influence government and that are viewed as competing on a relatively level playing field (Mayer, 1995). In fact, many of the same critiques that were made of pluralist theory have been made of resource mobilization, particularly with respect to the extent to which the theory ignores both preference and value formation and structural sources of social power.

The new social movement approach argues that social movements are increasingly a feature of developed capitalist democracies as the older class-based politics has declined. According to this view, the developed democracies are increasingly post-material; that is, their political cultures are increasingly oriented around non-material political issues such as identities and values.

Post-materialist values emphasize issues such as quality of life and political participation rather than the material questions of who gets what, when, where, and how. This political cultural change sets the stage for the rise of movements that stress identity and non-material goals (Inglehart, 1997), which are associated with a particular class politics. The new social movement approach is post-Marxist in that it argues that the traditional class struggle is no longer dominant in the politics of advanced capitalist societies; instead, it stresses the rise of the new middle class of professional knowledge workers, who break with the old division between worker and capitalist and who are carriers of post-materialist values. Michael Orsini's chapter on health social movements in Canada illustrates another theme in this debate by pointing to the ways in which health and risk have become increasingly important markers of political mobilization and identity.

The political process model brings together elements of resource mobilization and the new social movement approach, drawing from the former a focus on the social movement organization and the organizational networks that underpin such groups and from the latter the focus on identity and on the cultural processes through which movements construct their activism. However, in addition to this, the political process model, found in the work of scholars such as Sidney Tarrow (1998), brings together these elements with a focus on the broader political environment within which social movements operate. The broad context of politics in relation to the goals of the social movement is what Tarrow terms the "political opportunity structure," which he defines as "consistent—but not necessarily formal, permanent or national—dimensions of the political environment which either encourage or discourage people from using collective action. The concept of political opportunity structure emphasizes resources external to the group" (Tarrow, 1998: 18). The concept of political opportunity encompasses the institutions of the state and the ways in which political institutions provide points of access to social movements or block them. For instance, Audrey Kobayashi includes a case study of the Japanese–Canadian redress movement, emphasizing the ways in which a constellation of political opportunity external to the movement helped facilitate success for redress claims at a particular historical moment. Similarly, Miriam Smith's chapter on the lesbian, gay, bisexual and transgender movement emphasizes the opportunities provided by the Charter of Rights and Freedoms as influencing the direction of the movement and its recent successes in securing public policy change.

RATIONAL CHOICE THEORY

The contributors to this volume largely reflect the lack of interest in Canadian scholarship in the area of rational choice theory. However, this approach is worth mentioning because it has become one of the dominant approaches to the study of collective action outside this country. To date, there have been very few works that have attempted to apply this perspective to the study of group behaviour in the Canadian context, and those that have appeared are not the strongest exemplars of the rational choice tradition (e.g., Flanagan, 1998). Despite the weaknesses of Canadian work on rational choice, the approach has important implications for the study of group politics.

The seminal work in the development of rational choice theory and group politics is Mancur Olson's *The Logic of Collective Action* (1971 [1965]). Drawing from economics, Olson based his theory on the individual as a rational self-maximizer. Each individual seeks to maximize their own "utility" or seeks benefits for themselves. Economic theory is based on the assumption that the individual—whether a consumer or a firm—will seek to maximize utility. For example, a consumer is more likely to make a purchase if the price of the desired item drops. Firms are less likely to hire if the price of labour increases. Rational choice theory, then, is based on the idea that society is composed of individuals who seek their own advantage. Moreover, they seek advantage based on rationality; that is, there is a logical relationship between the ends sought and the means used to reach the ends. The ends sought by the individual are labelled "preferences" by rational choice theorists. Preferences are rank ordered, meaning that some are considered to be more important than others. The focus on the collective as the sum of the individual is quite different from the neo-Marxist, political economy, and institutionalist traditions, which are structuralist in their interpretation of individual action.

The individual's pursuit of her own best interests through rational self-maximizing behaviour makes collective action difficult. A goal or a "good" (in rational choice parlance) may be such that the benefit cannot be restricted to the individual. One example of such a good would be clean air: the benefit of clean air cannot be restricted to a single individual. The same applies to many other types of goods, which, by definition, benefit a group of individuals. Higher wages, for example, benefit all workers in a given workplace. Resources for student activities and clubs on a university campus benefit all students. Rational choice theory labels these types of goods "public goods." In contrast, "private goods" are the property of the individual and the benefit accrues to the individual alone.

Much of politics is about the pursuit of public goods. According to Olson, the problem of collective action arises from the fact that the individual has no incentive to pursue a public good. The individual will benefit from the achievement of the goal (cleaner air, higher wages, better student activities on campus) as long as she is a member of the class affected by the public good (human beings, workers, students). Therefore, why should the individual waste her time in pursuing these public goods? Why should the individual join together with other individuals in pursuit of the goal? Why should workers join a union to push for higher wages when they will receive the benefit of the higher wages regardless of their contribution to the collective effort? Why should students push for better student activities or student services when all students will benefit from any gains that are made? Why not let someone else do the work and run any risks that may be entailed? This behaviour is called "free riding" in rational choice parlance.

According to Olson, the rational self-maximizing individual will tend to free ride on the efforts of others in the pursuit of public goods. This, for Olson, is the "problem of collective action," which is the central contribution of rational choice theory to the study of group politics. According to this view, individuals are not naturally inclined to sociability and group life. Such behaviour must be explained, rather than assumed, by the analyst. Here, rational choice theory parts ways very fundamentally with pluralist analysis. The pluralists saw society as composed of groups, which, in turn, were made up of individuals with diverse interests. Rational choice theory views society as composed of individuals with diverse interests. The pluralists never gave a thought to the process by which groups form. They assumed that, by default, people with common interests would form groups. Rational choice theory assumes that, by default, individuals will not form groups.

How then do groups come into being in society, according to rational choice theory? The solution to the problem of collective action is "selective incentives"—benefits that are restricted to members of the group. You must join the group to receive information from the group, to receive access to governmental decision-makers who may affect your business, or to receive insurance benefits through a group scheme. All of these are examples of selective incentives.

According to rational choice theory, the groups that are most likely to be able to offer selective incentives are those that are most likely to form. These will be groups that are able to offer economic incentives of some kind. Some rational choice theorists (including Olson) argue that politics will tend to be dominated by narrowly defined group interests because these are the groups that will be able to organize themselves successfully by using selective incentives (Olson, 1982). Rational choice theory is particularly concerned about groups that are very large, such as taxpayers and consumers. It is difficult for such broad groups to form because of the problem of offering selective incentives to encourage organization. In the view of rational choice theory, all taxpayers would benefit from lower taxes, but it is unlikely that taxpayers will be able to organize to achieve this because of the problem of collective action. Similarly, although consumers would benefit from lower food prices, it is unlikely that consumer interests will be represented in debates over farm policy. Farmers' groups are much better able to organize and to offer selective incentives. In Europe, Canada, and the US, farmers' organizations have succeeded in negotiating important subsidies and tax breaks that greatly enhance profitability at the expense of consumers.

Just as pluralist theory implies liberalism and neo-Marxist theory implies socialism, so too there are important ideological implications to rational choice theory. It tends to lend very strong support to the neoliberal political project, that is, the restructuring of state–society relations around the rolled-back state, the retrenchment of social programs and social obligation, and the primacy of the choice and responsibility of the individual. By placing the self-maximizing individual at the heart of the analysis, rational choice theory supports the central tenet of neoliberalism—the primacy of the individual in the market. Rational choice theory's pessimistic view of collective action mirrors the neoliberal distaste for groups and provides a justification for skepticism toward group claims. Rational choice theories suggest that group claims are undemocratic.

NEW THEORETICAL DIRECTIONS

Other chapters in this volume also point to themes that are underdeveloped in the literatures on group politics and social movements in Canada, as well as to the ways in which existing approaches need to be expanded to take account of new forms of collective action and new theoretical developments. This expanded theoretical agenda includes the exploration of the links between nationalism and social movement politics, the role of legal mobilization, the turn to constructivism in social movement studies, the impact of new communications technologies such as social media and the changing nature of targets in social movement and group activism. In this section, I will deal with each of these in turn.

NATIONALISM AND SOCIAL MOVEMENT POLITICS

Two of the chapters offer original explorations of the links between nationalism and social movement politics in Canada. Pascale Dufour and Christophe Traisnel provide an ambitious overview of the sovereignist movement in Quebec and demonstrate the ways in which it has been based in a broad range of networks and organizations, including political parties but also the trade union movement, the women's movement, artistic and cultural networks, and other organizations. Kiera Ladner tells the stories of Aboriginal resistance to colonialism in Canada over time and provides a useful corrective to the view that Aboriginal movements only emerged in the 1960s. Audrey Kobayashi explores the evolution of organizing among racialized minorities in Canadian politics and, especially, the emergence of "third force" and ethnocultural organizing in Canada in response to the constitutional politics of the 1970s and 1980s. Kobayashi's case study of the redress movement of Japanese Canadians demonstrates both the importance of racialization in Canadian social movement politics and the emergence of collective action around new issues. For example, the idea of redress or compensation for past state actions has emerged relatively recently and extends to other cases of ethnocultural organizing such as the Chinese Canadian head tax case as well as to cases of compensation for medical injury and "natural" disasters such as hurricanes (James, 2007). These chapters suggest that existing frameworks on collective action and political mobilization in Canadian politics have not paid sufficient attention to the structuring impact of colonialism and racialized power relations in Canadian society. A next step from these analyses would explore the ways in which other forms of organized political action, such as business organizing, or other social movements, such as the environmental movement or the lesbian and gay rights movement, enact, reinforce, or challenge existing structures of gendered and racialized power.

Legal Mobilization

The chapters by Miriam Smith and Lisa Vanhala also demonstrate the increasingly important role of courts and legal mobilization in social movement politics. In the case of both the lesbian and gay movement and the disability movement, litigation under the Charter has been an important strategy for social movement organizations. Legal mobilization is not only a particular strategy for social movement and group politics, but also a mechanism for framing movement and group demands. As Vanhala discusses, legal mobilization is an extension of the political process model, and courts may be seen as providing an opportunity for contesting groups within Tarrow's political opportunity structure. However, movement activists perceive opportunities differently, and, as Vanhala argues, they must perceive opportunities to act on them. Further, she emphasizes that social movement mobilization may itself shape political opportunities. Similarly, my chapter on the lesbian and gay movement demonstrates how the legal opportunity of the entrenchment of the Charter was effectively used to extend lesbian and gay, as well as bisexual and transgender, rights protections.

Constructivism

The chapters also shed light in various ways on new strands of constructivism in social movement theory. In addition to Vanhala's discussion of the importance of activists' interpretation and framing of political opportunity, Alexandra Dobrowolsky's chapter on the women's movement also emphasizes the importance of the framing process. Further, Michael Orsini's chapter on health social movements points to the importance of emotions in the context of mobilization around illness identities.

These strands connect to a wider discussion in the recent literature on social movements that emphasizes the role of emotions in social movement politics and the importance of the construction of meaning in political mobilization (Staggenborg 2012: ch. 2). This turn is consistent with the rise of constructivism in many different areas of social science, especially international relations theory. The constructivist approach sees power in meaning; that is, it explores how activists mobilize through ideas, interpretation, and framing. As Manuel Castells (2012) argues in his exploration of the networked politics of contemporary social movements, power is mobilized through communication and meaning and not solely through the violence of the state. Castells (2012: 13) sees emotions mobilized into action as the "big bang" of social movement politics, that is, the trigger that causes movements to spark, form, and contest. Similarly, a new literature in sociology is explicitly focused on examining the role of emotions in social movement politics (Gould 2009). This focus on the importance of emotion in social movement politics forms a stark contrast with the main theories of political science, which, even if they are not explicitly engaged with rational choice theory, tend to assume a rational actor model of individual action and motivation. While constructivists do not believe that social movement contestation is "irrational," they seek to understand how the meanings of rationality are constructed in a given context, rather than assuming a universal and uniform definition of costs and benefits.

Networked Movements?: The Role of the Internet

The rise of the Internet and its role in social movement and group networks is increasingly seen as a deep social and political development that is contributing to the displacement of the power of nation-states. While we can see many cases of Canadian groups and movements that participate in transnational and global activism (and are influenced by them), the Internet is also more than a means of communication. According to some analysts such as Castells (1997; 2012), it also represents the rise of the network society and an entirely new form of social movement politics. While Castells (2012: 4–14) sees the Internet as a free and autonomous space for the creation of new forms of activism, he also emphasizes its links to movements such as Occupy that are based on the physical occupation of local space.

Both Matt James's chapter on Occupy and Kiera Ladner's chapter on Aboriginal politics touch on these themes. Like Castells, James calls our attention to the ways in which Occupy prefigures the changes it wants to see through creating communities and assemblies that function democratically. James emphasizes the extent to which Occupy rejects traditional politics, which are centred on the state and parties, and draws on web-based networks for organization. Similarly, Ladner's discussion of the new wave of contestation in Canadian Aboriginal politics argues that social media provided the space for the original launch of Idle No More as well as a means by which the various actions of the movement have been communicated throughout both Aboriginal and mainstream media and communities.

This work, along with other recent empirical studies of the role of the Internet in social movement organizing (Earl and Kimport, 2011), suggests that there are several potential ways in which we can theoretically approach the role of the Internet and the rise of the network society in relation to group and movement activism. On the one hand, as Earl and Kimport (2011) point out, we can view the Internet as a simple tool that adds to the resource kit of social movement activism. This makes sense for organized interests such as business, farmers, and even trade unions, for whom the use of this new tool may not make a fundamental difference to the goals, targets, or nature of their political activity. However, Earl and Kimport also argue that the Internet can be viewed as a new space of social movement contestation and as generating new forms of activism. Similarly, Castells's (2012) work also points to the Internet as autonomous space for the emergence of global networks as well as for mobilizing face-to-face societal networks for political change. According to these views, the Internet is more than simply a tool or resource for social movements and groups; rather, it entails a profound societal shift that requires the development and extension of social movement theory. This debate is still very much in process.

CONCLUSION

Taken together, the chapters in this volume highlight both traditional political actors such as business and labour and new political actors such as the disability movement and health social movements. Many of the contributors point to the emergence of new political cleavages in Canadian society that have not traditionally been the focus of attention by political scientists and sociologists who have studied interest groups and social movements. It is only very recently that scholars in Canada have even paid serious scholarly attention to the women's movement or to the emergence of movements and groups that politicize gender relations and sexuality such as the lesbian and gay movement. The study of disability movements and health social movements in Canada is in its infancy. These themes in the study of collective action indicate that a new set of political actors has arrived on the scene, emphasizing a new set of issues in the process of political mobilization.

In doing so, *Group Politics and Social Movements in Canada*, second edition, draws attention to the question of how these movements interact and how they reflect the structuring of economic, social, and political power in Canada in the global era. It does not provide a systematic answer to the question of which theory or theoretical approach best helps us to make sense of social movement and organized group politics in this country. However, it does point to a broad range of civil society activity that must be taken into consideration in thinking about and theorizing the role of collective actors in Canadian political life.

NOTE

1 This is an adapted, abridged, and updated version of the first chapter of my book *A Civil Society? Collective Actors in Canadian Political Life* (University of Toronto Press, 2005).

REFERENCES AND FURTHER READING

Abele, Frances, and Daiva Stasiulis. 1989. "Canada as a White Settler Colony: What About Natives and Immigrants?" In *The New Canadian Political Economy*, ed. Wallace Clement and Glen Williams, 240–77. Montreal, Kingston: McGill-Queen's University Press.

Almond, Gabriel. 1988. "The Return to the State." *American Political Science Review* 82 (3): 853–74.

Baumgartner, Frank R., and Beth L. Leech. 1998. *Basic Interests: The Importance of Groups in Politics and in Political Science*. Princeton: Princeton University Press.

Bentley, Arthur F. 1908. *The Process of Government*. Chicago: University of Chicago Press.

Castells, Manuel. 1997. *The Power of Identity*. Oxford: Blackwell.

Castells, Manuel. 2012. *Networks of Outrage and Hope: Social Movements in the Internet Age*. Cambridge, UK: Polity.

Dahl, Robert A. 1961. *Who Governs?: Democracy and Power in an American City*. New Haven: Yale University Press.

Della Porta, Donatella, and Mario Diani. 1999. *Social Movements: An Introduction*. Oxford: Blackwell.

Earl, Jennifer, and Katrina Kimport. 2011. *Digitally Enabled Social Change: Activism in the Internet Age*. Cambridge, MA: MIT Press.

Flanagan, Thomas. 1998. *Game Theory and Canadian Politics*. Toronto: University of Toronto Press.

Gaventa, John. 1982. *Power and Powerlessness*. Urbana: University of Illinois Press.

Gould, Deborah. 2009. *Moving Politics: Emotion and ACT UP's Fight Against AIDS*. Chicago: University of Chicago Press.

Hattam, Victoria C. 1993. *Labor Visions and State Power: The Origins of Business Unionism in the United States*. Princeton: Princeton University Press.

Inglehart, Ronald. 1997. *Modernization and Postmodernization: Cultural, Economic, and Political Change in Forty-Three Societies*. Princeton: Princeton University Press.

James, Matt. 2007. "The Permanent-Emergency Compensation State: A 'Postsocialist' Tale of Political Dystopia." In *Critical Policy Studies*, ed. Michael Orsini and Miriam Smith, 321–46. Vancouver: University of British Columbia Press.

Jenkins, J. Craig. 1983. "Resource Mobilization Theory and the Study of Social Movements." *Annual Review of Sociology* 9: 527–53.

Laxer, James L. 1989. *Open for Business: The Roots of Foreign Ownership in Canada*. Toronto: Oxford University Press.

Levitt, Kari. 1970. *Silent Surrender: The Multinational Corporation in Canada*. Toronto: Macmillan.

Lukes, Stephen. 2004 [1974]. *Power: A Radical View*. 2nd ed. London: Macmillan.

Marchak, Patricia. 1985. "Canadian Political Economy." *Canadian Review of Sociology and Anthropology. La Revue Canadienne de Sociologie et d'Anthropologie* 22 (5): 673–709.

Mayer, Margit. 1995. "Social Movement Research in the United States: A European Perspective." In *Social Movements: Critiques, Concepts, Case-Studies*, ed. Stanford M. Lyman, 168–95. London: Macmillan.

Melucci, Alberto. 1996. *Challenging Codes: Collective Action in the Information Age*. Cambridge: Cambridge University Press.

Naylor, R. Tom. 1972. "The Rise and Fall of the Third Commercial Empire of the St. Lawrence." In *Capitalism and the National Question in Canada*, ed. Gary Teeple, 1-41. Toronto: University of Toronto Press.

Olson, Mancur. [1965] 1971. *The Logic of Collective Action: Public Goods and the Theory of Groups*. Cambridge, MA: Harvard University Press.

Olson, Mancur. 1982. *The Rise and Decline of Nations: Economic Growth, Stagflation, and Structural Rigidities*. New Haven: Yale University Press.

Panitch, Leo. 1995. "Elites, Classes, and Power in Canada." In *Canadian Politics in the 1990s*, ed. Michael S. Whittington and Glen Williams, 152–75. Toronto: Nelson.

Polsby, Nelson W. 1963. *Community Power and Political Theory*. New Haven: Yale University Press.

Seidman, Steven. 2004. *Contested Knowledge: Social Theory Today*. 3rd ed. Oxford: Blackwell.

Skocpol, Theda. 1979. *States and Social Revolutions: A Comparative Analysis of France, Russia, and China*. Cambridge: Cambridge University Press.

Skocpol, Theda. 1985. "Bringing the State Back In: Strategies of Analysis in Current Research." In *Bringing the State Back In*, ed. Peter B. Evans, Dietrich Rueschmeyer, and Theda Skocpol, 3–37. Cambridge: Cambridge University Press.

Staggenborg, Suzanne. 2012. *Social Movements*. 2nd ed. Don Mills: Oxford University Press.

Tarrow, Sidney. 1998. *Power in Movement: Social Movements, Collective Action, and Politics*. 2nd ed. Cambridge: Cambridge University Press.

Vosko, Leah. 2000. *Temporary Work: The Gendered Rise of a Precarious Employment Relationship*. Toronto: University of Toronto Press.

Watkins, Mel. 1977. "The Staples Theory Revisited." *Journal of Canadian Studies / Revue d'Etudes Canadiennes* 12 (5): 83–95.

Wilson, Jeremy. 1992. "Green Lobbies: Pressure Groups and Environmental Policy." In *Canadian Environmental Policy: Ecosystems, Politics, and Process*, ed. Robert Boardman, 109–25. Toronto: Oxford University Press.

Group Politics and Social Movements in Canada

PART ONE

Political Economy

ONE

Business Interests and Civil Society in Canada

PETER CLANCY

This chapter explores the many shapes of business influence in Canadian civil society. In the pages below we consider the structure of capitalist interests, their organizational expressions, the political issues that top the business agenda today, the processes and instruments of exercising power, and the ramifications for group and movement theory. Special attention is devoted to the events and impacts of the 2008 financial crisis. This discussion will show that there is a striking variability in the political orders and relationships involving capital, which vary over time, space, and function. The structure of markets makes a difference here, as does the structure of state institutions. Thus, there is a value to distinguishing periods—and generic "types" and "styles"—of political representation and intervention. A central question in this chapter is how does organized capital relate within itself and to other social interests in the democratic context? This theme figures strongly in contemporary political debate, where the power of national and international capital is widely considered as hostile to both public interests and popular politics. A corollary question, of more than passing interest, is whether business and market players should be conceptualized as a part of civil society or outside of it. This is a matter of theoretical and also tactical significance. The discussion below suggests some difficulties in demarcating a firm boundary between market and civil space.

There is a tendency to see capital as a powerful but "traditional" block of interests in politics, the prime beneficiaries and the great defenders of the processes of capitalist democracy. It is certainly true that firms and trade associations have functioned as the interest groups of the marketplace. The same qualities enabled the business bloc to penetrate centrist and rightist political parties by furnishing leadership talent and financial resources critical to the ministerial, parliamentary, and electoral processes. It would be a mistake, however, to assume that business power starts and ends in this way. Given the extraordinary financial and informational resources that are controlled by business firms, they can wield power in many domains. This capability has been applied to new and innovative effect in recent decades.

HISTORICAL CONSIDERATIONS

Several preliminary points can be made. First, as a capitalist economy expands, the range of business interests diversifies, and the political structure of business interests tends to be cumulative. Over time this creates complex fields, revealing considerable variation. This opens the way for political difference and tension as well as a potential for cooperative or collective action. The understanding of these webs of class and group alignments of course will vary according to the theoretical perspective that underpins the analysis. As the Introduction to this book points out, each framework highlights a particular set of relationships.

In Canada, business politics has shaped public life from the historical outset. It started in the 1500s, when European merchant syndicates encountered Aboriginal peoples in the New World. As colonial settlement progressed, the range of staple commodities broadened, and French and English export networks for fur, fish, timber, and grains dominated business politics. Imperial trade policy was, in many ways, the wellspring of business viability, and decisions made in London (and later Washington) could create or destroy the prospects for profitable accumulation. In addition, the local markets that sprang up along transport corridors—first the rivers and ports and later the railways—made possible new domestic business sectors that were ultimately consolidated in the post-Confederation market. Pioneer manufacturing was followed by factory production under the National Policy protective tariff regime installed in Ottawa in 1879 (Williams, 1983). Advancing technologies made possible successive waves of new industries: from textiles and food processing to coal, rail, and steam; steel and autos; electricity and petroleum; aeronautics and chemicals. The most recent innovations derive from microelectronics, telecommunications, and biotechnology. The rise of the service business sector marked another historic shift. The traditional services in the legal, financial, and transport sectors were joined, in the second half of the twentieth century, by a burgeoning public or government service sector including medical, hospital, education, and social services.

This diversification of business interests by sector, industry, and geography means that affinities and rivalries within the capitalist bloc can be pivotal in determining its power. Pluralist perspectives view this principally as a problem of representation or the distillation of pressure vectors within issue areas. Neo-Marxists have been particularly sensitive to the impact of fractional tensions on the overall coherence of capital in politics.

A second point refers to the relationships between capital and the state. It is not simply a matter for the business bloc to manage its own differences. State authorities can play crucial roles in ordering priorities, fashioning compromises, and securing coherence among the disparate political tendencies of capital. This is not to say that government could or would satisfy all business demands. The state, however, does have the capacity to shape the playing field of the market through political intervention, sometimes in decisive ways. This is acknowledged in both neo-Marxist and neopluralist paradigms. The former view the state as playing crucial roles in ordering the relationships between classes and within them, thus formalizing and stabilizing hierarchies of class power. This can be achieved, for example, by implementing policy strategies to underwrite long-term investment and profitability. Neopluralists also acknowledge the complexity of business-state relations, though they tend to concentrate on the importance of linkage processes in shaping outcomes.

In Canada, several crucial public policy bargains were struck over the years. So fundamental were some of these that they underwrote normal politics for generations at a time. The mercantile colonial era of staple resource exports was the first such framework regime. The National Policy tariff, already mentioned, was another. By simultaneously facilitating natural resource exports (at low or zero tariff rates) and domestic manufacturing (at medium to high tariff rates), the 1879 system anchored Canadian economic growth (and business prosperity) for the next half century. Following the upheaval of the 1930s Depression and World War II, the federal government fashioned a new political settlement. This involved the application of fiscal (budgetary) policy along Keynesian lines to promote full employment and economic growth, together with the income redistribution measures of the welfare state. This post war settlement flourished for a generation, but came under significant political pressure by 1975. Yet another basic policy bargain has emerged in the decades since (McBride, 2001). Known as neoliberalism, its hallmarks include continental free trade, budget constraints, and deregulation of financial markets. In pursuing these aims, Western states have, once again, had to alter some basic operational contours. The new governing challenge was to stabilize national societies against global pressures while operating on neoliberal foundations. The most recent of these grand bargains was fashioned, under crisis conditions reminiscent of the 1930s, in response to the international bank failures and global credit collapse of 2008 (Roubini and Mihm, 2010). Under the leadership of the US, leading nations took unprecedented steps to stabilize their financial sectors by means of bank takeovers or capital transfers along with gigantic, multi-year fiscal stimulus strategies and money supply injections of unprecedented magnitude. The emergence of this guarantor state marks a new phase of capital-state relations.

A third and final point here is a caution against easy assumptions about business power. Business interests seldom enjoy absolute dominance, particularly in contexts of democratic politics. Issues are almost invariably contested by non-business interests, which frequently prevail. While politicians can be disciplined by market forces—such as currency runs, capital strikes, and adverse bond ratings—corporations also can be disciplined by commercial scandals, populist electoral outcomes, and consumer boycotts. On another level, existing state institutions and policies may be regarded as the distillation of past political struggles, exerting an independent impact on the shape and prospects for politics today. The neo-institutional concept of path-dependence (the notion that historically earlier choices serve to shape the range of available opportunities and choices in the future) is insightful here as well. Not only can it explain how state agencies and programs can enjoy significant political autonomy but also how state-based actors can acquire an independent standing as "interests of state" (Pal, 1995).

Canadian researchers in the political economy school have long debated the range and ordering of capitalist class fractions and the seat of business dominance. Not surprisingly, the answers have varied over time. One influential interpretation, put forward by R.T. Naylor, held that an alliance of merchant and finance capitalists, rooted in the colonial era, managed to subordinate indigenous (Canadian) manufacturing following Confederation (Naylor, 1972). According to this argument, the profit terms of commercial capital (short investment horizons, low fixed capital, open borders) were incompatible with those of domestic manufacturing (long-term horizons, high fixed investment, tariff protection). Consequently, the primacy of commercial capital served to relegate the manufacturing fraction to a subordinate and truncated form. Wallace Clement took a somewhat different line. Emphasizing compatibility rather than antagonism, he argued that the indigenous or Canadian-owned fraction of finance capital anchored an alliance with a comprador or foreign-dominated industrial fraction, particularly by underwriting the expansion in Canada of American corporate capital (Clement, 1983).

Rianne Mahon drew attention to the critical role of state institutions in ordering and adjusting the hierarchies of business interest. For Mahon, the alliance of indigenous finance and staple resource export fractions was anchored by the federal Department of Finance. Its strategic place atop Ottawa's bureaucratic state, and its commitments to liberal trade and investment flows as prerequisites for Canadian economic growth, allowed the department to indirectly "represent" the core fraction's interests in strategic policy. Indeed, a more elaborate inter-agency "structure" of representation provided voices for all significant factions and classes. Mahon's study of strategic efforts to revive the declining textile manufacturing sector illustrated both the constraints and opportunities available within the larger structured state (Mahon, 1984).

There are further questions to consider. For example, does capital benefit from several structural mechanisms that confer privileged political leverage on business interests? Structural dependence points to mechanisms that enable business to entrench its interests despite government opposition. These must be fixed relationships and mechanisms that routinely prevent anti-business policies or activities from taking place. Charles Lindblom describes this as the market behaving as a "prison." Formally, of course, governments remain free to enact any policy they see fit. However, they discover that certain types of non-business or anti-business initiatives result in an automatic "recoil" effect, a dramatic reaction from the business system that punishes the political authors of the offending policy. Repeated experience with the recoil tends to discourage politicians from pursuing such policy initiatives. Since no other social institution enjoys similar power to the market in this respect, the capitalist interest is said to enjoy a privileged position (Lindblom, 1982).

A powerful example of this is the mechanism of modern global finance. In recent decades, capital has become highly mobile and volatile. Trading in currencies, commodities, bonds, and shares takes place around the clock and around the globe. Extraordinary amounts of money are at stake, and one of the key stimulants of speculative business moves is political. Put simply, the markets can "vote" with their wallets, expressing approval or hostility to government policy by deciding to invest or disinvest. While this business "confidence" is an elusive notion, its effects are clear to see.

When left-of-centre parties take power, the financial markets slump as a signal of suspicion or disapproval. When tax rates are raised, or budget deficits increased, the markets give out negative signals. In extreme cases, currencies go into free fall, capital strikes occur, and business shifts its operations elsewhere. Even right-of-centre governments can be affected. In 1974, the Alberta oil industry was so enraged by Progressive Conservative Premier Peter Lougheed's new tax and royalty policies that exploration activity dried up (Richards and Pratt, 1979: 227). Companies hauled their rigs into Saskatchewan or neighbouring Montana, where they sat idle as pressure built on Lougheed to revise his position.

Another powerful mechanism is the debt relationship between private lenders and government borrowers when budget shortfalls occur. After 1980, Western governments were swept up in a fiscal crisis that left them facing persistent budget deficits. These could only be met by borrowing from private sources in financial centres such as New York, London, and Toronto. Corporate lenders acquired leverage over prospective borrowers, and differing levels of risk were reflected in interest rates. Bond rating services such as Moody's Investors Service, Standard & Poor's, and the Dominion Bond Rating Service weighed government fiscal policies and graded them on a scale of credit worthiness. Finance ministers made annual treks to New York to outline their fiscal plans and pitch for positive ratings. In effect, the financial markets became a key arbiter of government policy choice.

The 2008 crisis carried the potential to transform a political relationship that many would argue had become harmfully distorting. With most of the world's largest investment banks collapsing or on the brink of collapse as a result of years of largely unregulated and unmonitored financial speculation, it seemed that the financial casino had, in only two decades, sown the seeds of its own destruction. At one point, newly elected President Barack Obama summoned the top American bankers to a White House meeting and reminded them that he was the only thing standing between them and the pitchforks. While nation-states intervened to stabilize financial institutions deemed too big to fail, the price of such extraordinary rescues was expected to involve re-regulation and restructuring of the global financial sector (McLean and Nocera, 2010; Sorkin, 2009; Tett, 2009).

MAIN ORGANIZATIONS AND NETWORKS

Any exploration of business politics involves knowledge of the actors. The literature on political conflict (and the chapters in this book) utilize a variety of terms in identifying the political players: interest groups, organizations, associations, social movements, coalitions, and networks. Such terms tend to be associated with different theoretical traditions and derive some of their core properties from these traditions. Interest or pressure groups, for example, are the preferred analytic unit of pluralism, which holds that decisions in any policy field or issue area will be determined by the balance of forces among organized groups that are policy-specific. This was later reformulated as "post"- or "neo"-pluralism, with the recognition that state authorities were normally entangled with groups in policy networks that jointly shaped decisional outcomes. Organizations and associations have been treated, at times, as synonyms for interest groups, acknowledging, for example, that groups must achieve a level of "organization" to achieve longevity or that most groups involve a membership that is "associated" with a particular interest. On the other hand, there are many organizations in modern life (formally structured social bodies such as churches, corporations, and universities) that are not, first and foremost, dedicated to political intervention. They do, however, assume political roles when their underlying interests are at stake in the policy process. Social movements refer to political bodies that are based often on shared identities (as opposed to material interests) and that promote both social and political change.

In this chapter, we will consider the full range of prospective business actors described above. First, though, it is useful to survey the bloc of business interests as an action universe. How can business interests organize politically? This reveals a continuum of levels on which interests can be mobilized. At the most general level, there are certain common interests of capital that are shared by virtually all commercial enterprises. Somewhat less inclusive, but still expansive, is the sectoral political interest, where firms sharing some decisive property (big or small scale, manufacturing or service activity, national or global operations) come together on that basis. On the next scale we find that each industry, or even sub-industry, constitutes a shared interest that member firms must advance or defend politically. Finally, there are the political interests of the specific firm, which are asserted against those of business rivals.

If political interests can spring from such distinct levels, then we can expect organizations to be formed to articulate each in turn. At the most general level, it is often the market mechanism itself that exerts pressure, through the "automatic recoil" mechanism described by Lindblom. Here currency, commodity, or share markets react adversely to state policies deemed negative to "business," signalling their opposition and bringing pressure to bear on the political class. In the 1963 budget, federal Finance Minister Walter Gordon announced a new "takeover tax" to discourage foreign acquisitions of Canadian firms. This triggered a major sell-off on the stock markets and the proposal was subsequently dropped. The very prospect of such policy recoil by markets, and their subsequent political costs, can be sufficient to nullify policy choices in advance.

A series of studies has highlighted the multidimensional spectrum of business interest groups or associations. Some of these operate at the peak association level, where particular capitals and industries are gathered together. In some nations, a comprehensive umbrella voice speaks for propertied interests on general issues. In Canada, there is no single peak business group, but there are several contenders with impressive though less than comprehensive scope. For example, the Canadian Council of Chief Executives (CCCE; formerly, the Business Council on National Issues) speaks for big corporate capital and the staple resource faction, drawing its membership from the 150 largest firms (Langille, 1987). The Canadian Manufacturers & Exporters Association (CME) represents secondary industry, much of it made up of foreign-owned subsidiaries. The increasing export orientation of this faction during the 1970s and 1980s culminated in the amalgamation of the hitherto separate voices of manufacturers and exporters. The Canadian Chamber of Commerce (CCC), a federation of local and provincial bodies, tends to reflect the concerns of small and medium-sized business, including service and retail capital. Finally, the Canadian Federation of Independent Business (CFIB) claims 100,000 small and often independent operators and proprietors as members. Despite this institutional separation, the peak voices of Canadian business are not necessarily at odds on important issues. In some situations, such as the continental free trade campaigns of 1985–93, the peak groups have been known to form issue-based alliances to extend their leverage.

At the industry and sub-industry level, hundreds of national "trade associations" represent member firms for political advocacy at a more restrictive level (Coleman, 1988; Atkinson and Coleman, 1989). By contrast to the visibility of the peak lobby groups, which tend to assume a high media profile, trade associations operate more commonly within the policy orbits of government bureaus and agencies where information exchange and clientelistic access can translate into policy leverage (Litvak, 1984). Indeed, the micropolitics of business is a fertile field for industry and sub-industry advocates (Clancy, 2004).

In one sense, business power is constituted by the continuing networks of interest operating within and between such associations. There are moments, however, when the extraordinary scope and depth of these formations are evident in campaigns of joint action. During the 1970s, for example, the federal government launched a comprehensive revision of Canada's competition policy. There was widespread recognition that this long-standing statutory framework to enforce competitive market behaviour suffered from fundamental flaws. In response, the federal government commissioned a series of technical reviews aimed at renewing the competition regime, and new draft legislation was tabled. The negative reaction from the corporate sector was overwhelming, and a decade-long struggle ensued between successive Ottawa governments advancing policy renewal and the corporate opponents (and potential targets) of an invigorated competition mechanism (Stanbury, 1977).

Finally, there is the situation where specific firms define and advance political interests against their rivals in a shared marketplace and lobby accordingly. This is the most fine-grained level of business politics. What is the place of individual firms in this political environment? Do they possess irreducible interests that cannot be merged with rivals or realized through collective association? In fact there are many respects in which adroit political intervention can confer strategic advantage on the single firm. Government procurement, in which rival firms bid competitively for public tenders, is one such field. Regulated industry politics, in which statutory agencies control key business variables by licence or permit, is another. Defensive trade tactics, aimed at blocking import competition or dumping by offshore rivals, is a third example.

Operationally, such firm-specific advocacy can be handled by in-house government relations specialists (often the case for top-tier corporations). It may also be handled by political affairs consultants for hire, a more viable option for small and medium-sized firms (Gollner, 1983).

MAIN POLITICAL ISSUES TODAY

Is there a consensual business policy agenda in contemporary Canada? Or are there rival agendas, advanced by separate coalitions, vying for the limited attention of executive political elites? Part of the literature on business politics holds that a tight core of market-centred values propels a largely unified business political agenda (Clarke, 1997; Dobbin, 1998). This right-wing agenda is seen as deeply rooted in the shifting international economy following 1980. Sometimes known as the "Washington consensus" and also labelled the "neoliberal agenda" or "market-driven politics," it includes initiatives to curtail state spending, privatize state enterprise, deregulate markets and industries (including the labour market), and promote a culture of individual as opposed to collective interest (Leys, 2001). Underlying such actions is a theory or philosophy of economic rationality (the rational choice theory discussed in the Introduction to this book). Either way, however, it unleashes a blistering logic of programmatic change (Edwards, 2002). However, while the neoliberal consensus might offer a template or wish-list for business-friendly governance, there is no guarantee that any right-of-centre government will fully subscribe. Even if it did, there is no further guarantee that the measures will emerge intact from the issue definition and agenda-setting stages of the policy process.

In sorting out these difficulties, one useful distinction is between a category of fundamental policies that define a generalized framework or regime and a category of normal or routine policies that can be addressed from within the regime. Stephen McBride elaborates on the notion of the "conditioning framework"—a set of institutions (often embedded by international agreement) whose "provisions foreclose certain options that the populations of nation-states may want to preserve or adopt in the future" (McBride, 2001: 103).

An interesting aspect of framework-setting policies is that they impose, either through their design logic or their operational biases, powerful consequences for future action. The Canada-US Free Trade Agreement (CUFTA) and the North American Free Trade Agreement (NAFTA), embedded in international agreement, are no longer under the strict control of a national legislature to alter. The ill-fated Multilateral Agreement on Investment, sponsored by the Organization for Economic Development (OECD) is another example (Jackson and Sanger, 1998). When the agreement further restricts the unilateral capacity of either partner to act, by prohibiting lines of policy action that were hitherto used, the follow-on consequences are evident. A conditioning framework sets the rules for future exercise of normal policy and the more basic the constraints, the more significant is the framework policy.

Another example of an emerging framework policy, this time in the domestic setting, is Ottawa's war on the deficit in the 1990s. Curiously, meaningful "fiscal restraint" had been central to the business agenda for a decade or more. Yet, despite their neoliberal credentials on other issues, ranging from continental trade to financial deregulation to tight monetary policy, the Mulroney Progressive Conservatives were unable to deliver results on the fiscal front during their tenure in government from 1984 to 1993. This contrasts with the record of the Chrétien-Martin Liberals after 1993. Despite campaigning for a rollback of the Mulroney agenda, the Liberals managed to consolidate this program in almost all key respects. Indeed, when it came to budget balancing, Finance Minister Paul Martin was able to achieve in four years what Mulroney had failed to deliver in eight. Ottawa's "program review" exercise, which aimed to roll back federal expenditures by an average of 19 per cent, imposed draconian cuts on national programs and intergovernmental transfers (Lewis, 2003). In the process, Martin successfully presented the drive for fiscal surplus as a public virtue, which was confirmed in two subsequent elections. So deeply embedded is this standard, after nine successive budget surpluses (at time of writing), that a market recoil and perhaps even a popular recoil can be expected to attend any significant return to deficit.

One final example of framework-oriented policy-making involves responses to the 2008 financial crisis. The breadth and depth of the economic collapse had the effect of shattering the credibility of unregulated financial firms as masters of the universe. However the shape of a replacement was difficult to discern, and several years were devoted to efforts to reflate capitalist economies then on the point of collapse. An effective policy fix has proven elusive—it includes some national reregulation such as the American Dodd-Frank Act along with experimental monetary policies such as quantitative easing. But marked fiscal policy differences have opened up between an Anglo-Saxon (including Canadian) inclination for budget balancing and a European inclination toward stimulative deficits. Moreover, as international markets turned their attention from vulnerable banks to vulnerable states, the focus shifted from New York and London to the peripheral nations of the Euro-currency bloc.

For Canadian business, the notion of the continuum of priorities arises again. If business seldom speaks with one voice, we would not expect an easy or spontaneous consensus to emerge. Still, certain issues, by their scope, extent of support, or persistence, may come to typify an era. For Canadian business, the 1985–95 period was dominated by engagement on two overriding issues—continental trade ties with the US and Mexico and fiscal deficit elimination at home. In the decade that followed, there was less focus. Issues rose and fell. Quebec sovereignty has moved on and off the agenda. Canada-US sectoral trade disputes—in softwood lumber, cattle exports, wheat, steel, and others—rotate through the action list. The corporate sector advanced a productivity agenda that attracted rhetorical support from ministers of finance and industry. However, the concrete policy outputs remained thin. A round of tax cuts preceded the November 2000 election, but expenditure priorities have absorbed the lion's share of the fiscal dividend in the period since. Part of this was directed to security and border policing upgrades following the 9/11 terrorist attacks. Indeed, for the Canadian business sector, the threat of draconian post-9/11 security measures from Washington constituted the greatest single threat to continental trade. In 2012, the business lobby for Pacific trade scored major advances when the Harper Conservative government signed a new investment treaty with China and joined the negotiations on the Trans-Pacific Partnership.

Another significant issue was the "standstill" character of Canada's three minority governments between 2004 and 2011. Normally the fragility of government that is continually vulnerable to defeat in Parliament is deplored by organized capital as an impediment to hard and determined political choice. However in Canada, somewhat ironically, minority politics may have dampened Ottawa's capacity for single-minded pursuit of the market-driven agendas in the critical 2004–08 period and thereby buffered the economy from extreme financial imbalances. Canada avoided the sub-prime mortgage meltdowns that marked the first phase of the financial crisis, and Canadian banks were not as free to participate in the new speculative world of consolidated debt obligations and credit default swaps. Also, when the Harper Conservative government completely misperceived the onset of the crisis, as evidenced by the November 2008 fiscal update that triggered an opposition non-confidence coalition, it was able to pivot in a matter of months to offer a massive fiscal stimulus that was more in keeping with the scale of the emergency. Since the Harper Conservatives achieved a modest majority in the 2011 election, the question is whether the flexibility of minority parliaments will be lost to the rigidity of ideological rule.

MEANS OF ACTION

Given the multiple dimensions of business interests, and the varying forms of political representation, it is not surprising that a wide choice of mechanisms is available for political action. Well-resourced organizations have access to a range of political weapons. This section explores eight of the most prominent forms: the businessman-politician, the party system, the business interest group, the coalition or alliance of groups, the populist movement, the policy think tank, judicial litigation, and public propaganda. Each form is illustrated by a brief case study. It is important to remember that issue conflicts will normally include more than one line of action. Part of the art of issue campaigning is to recognize the strengths and weaknesses and the optimal applications for these respective techniques.

Businessman-Politician

The phenomenon of the politically engaged businessman is as old as Western commercial society. It refers to the migration of capitalists into government, as an extension of their market interests. By this logic, the best way to influence critical decisions of state is from the inside. There are many examples in Canadian history. For example, Prime Minister R.B. Bennett (1930–35) came to politics from a dense world of corporate directorships (Finkel, 1979). Liberal minister C.D. Howe (1935–57) enjoyed perhaps the widest-ever network of Canadian business contacts, dating from his responsibilities for wartime production (Bothwell and Kilbourn, 1979).

While no cabinet is entirely without business-affiliated ministers, their prominence declined after the 1950s. This became a cause for concern in business circles, where it was argued that a lack of champions around the cabinet table left corporate Canada in a politically vulnerable position (Gillies, 1981). In the Mulroney and Chrétien eras, there was no shortage of businessman-politicians. Mulroney himself sprang from the Montreal corporate network while Chrétien's cabinet included the Three Ms—Paul Martin, Roy MacLaren, and John Manley. Indeed Martin, who became prime minister in 2003, sported the strongest business credentials since Howe, even to the point of his alumnus status with the CCCE. Yet, there are grounds to question the assumption that career businessmen ensure effective cabinet representation. At senior levels of influence, politicians speaking for only Bay Street have extremely limited potential. Besides, a variety of ancillary channels provide means of political leverage.

Party System

When elite social connections no longer sufficed to guarantee access to state power, new channels rose to prominence. The nineteenth-century emergence of elected legislatures and responsible government marked a new stage in liberal politics. Political parties, first as legislative caucuses made up of like-minded representatives and later as mass membership associations grouped around shared values, ideology, or patron-client networks, began to play a crucial linkage role.

Jesse Unruh, the speaker of the California Assembly in the 1960s, made the famous observation that "money is the mother's milk of politics." Nowhere is this more true than in the case of political parties. While business leaders seldom make the most effective politicians, business interests have recognized the need to have an influence at the party and electoral levels. One way of making meaningful contacts, and ensuring access when necessary, is through financial contributions. In the lore of party politics, an omnipresent figure is the party "bagman," the broker who approaches wealthy firms and businessmen for voluntary donations to electoral war chests. In times past, political leaders might have served as their own fundraisers, though this was not without serious risk. In the years immediately following Confederation, Conservative leader John A. Macdonald was often in this position. In an ill-considered moment in the heat of the 1872 election, Macdonald wired Sir John Abbott, the legal advisor to the Canadian Pacific Railway, stating "I must have another ten thousand: will be the last time of calling; do not fail me; answer today." Abbott's reply ("Draw on me for another ten thousand dollars") was later publicly revealed, and Macdonald was forced from office by the so-called "Pacific Scandal" (cited in Creighton, 1955: 141). In more modern times, leaders have sought to distance themselves from direct fundraising. Nonetheless, the "$5,000-a-plate" dinner or cocktail party is a familiar modern fixture, where donors are invited to a social evening with elite leaders.

Business interests often adopted hedging financial strategies to manage the uncertainty of voter choice. It has been common for corporate donors, as a matter of formal policy, to split their party contributions between the leading contenders advancing business-oriented agendas. For example, the party of government might win a 60 per cent share while the leading opposition party receives the remaining 40 per cent. More generally, the party system alignment may work to the benefit of vested commercial interests. Canada's party system has long been described as a "brokerage system" in which the leading parties (Liberal and Conservative) follow strategies that appeal across major social cleavages in efforts to defuse potential tensions. This is best done through a pragmatic form of decision-making, often aimed at accommodating group elites and avoiding firm doctrinal or ideological commitments. Such brokerage politics often leads to a convergence between the contending parties as they compete to build the largest voter coalitions. Whether campaigning or governing, this can result in rather shallow differences between the competitors. Populist democrats have long condemned such arrangements as a democratic sham, depriving voters of real choice and protecting vested interests by the faux displacement of "Tweedledum" by "Tweedledee."

In 2003, the federal laws governing national campaign finance were revised, with potentially significant consequences for corporate participation. Effective the following year, a ban took effect on contributions by corporations, associations, and trade unions to registered political parties and party leadership campaigns. (Individuals may contribute up to $5,000 annually.) This was part of a new electoral finance regime that saw expanded public (state) financial support to parties. Corporations and unions could still contribute a maximum of $1,000 per year to constituency associations and nomination contestants (combined) and to non-registered candidates for election. Furthermore, so-called "third parties" (which refers, somewhat paradoxically, to non-political party actors) could sponsor election advertisements up to almost $170,000 in total, thereby providing a significant continuing outlet for corporate and union interests. The constitutionality of regulating "third-party" participation was itself politically contested and was confirmed by the Supreme Court of Canada in 2004 in the *Harper* case.

In 2011, the new Harper majority government eliminated the per-vote subsidy, a step widely seen as intended to weaken the financial base of non-Conservative parties. The subsidy to private contributions (subsidized by tax incentives) remains. Thus, a system by which all citizens contributed to party finance has been replaced by a system where only several hundred thousand citizens, amounting to less than 2 per cent of registered voters, contribute. If recent patterns continue to hold, the majority of private contributions will flow to the Conservative Party.

Thomas Ferguson offers an alternative perspective on business involvement in politics. He contends that electoral contributions can be viewed as investments by firms and industries in the party that offers the greatest policy fit with corporate interests. Even in brokerage systems, it is argued, key issues will arise (often in crisis conditions) that will polarize the business sector and differentiate the contending parties. Corporate coalitions gather behind the respective parties at such moments. Once a crisis passes, new business coalitions can enjoy dominance within the party system for an extended time (Ferguson, 1995). There have been many arguments about the decline of political parties as policy engines in the face of contemporary rivals such as the bureaucratic state, the new mass media, and the deepening networks of civil interests. While this may indeed be the case, it does not invalidate Ferguson's notion of parties as vehicles for business strategy, under particular conditions.

Business Associations

There have always been business lobbies in Canada. The Canadian Manufacturers & Exporters (formerly the Canadian Manufacturers Association) and the Chambers of Commerce trace their roots to the pre-Confederation period (Clark, 1939). With industrialization, trade associations grew in number to represent member firms in policy matters involving trade, employment, and transport. Following World War II, however, and the rise of the bureaucratic state, business groups further proliferated as instruments of influence with the administrative state. One study identified more than 750 national associations in the modern period (Litvak, 1984). Another study reports that the majority of these originated in the post-World War II era (Coleman, 1988). It is not by coincidence that the rising profile of trade group representation paralleled the expanding reach of the state.

The target of business influence shifted from legislatures (and to some degree, cabinets) to the professional civil service. It was here that policy problems were being identified and policy responses were being formulated. Effective group influence depended upon early involvement. This, in turn, required new forms of advance scanning, deliberation, and intervention. The technical and professional expertise that business lobbies bring to the table is a valued policy commodity, which can open the way to the inner reaches of many consultative networks.

None of this can guarantee success, of course, in particular political battles. While the classic confrontations are often seen between financiers and farmers, or between manufacturers and workers, a surprisingly high proportion of business political encounters pit one industry or block of industries against another. In such situations, several additional determinants arise. For one, the respective mobilizing capacities of the rivals are put to the test. For another, the wider coalitions of interest attached to the principals can play a decisive role. In addition, the protagonists may be aligned with separate parts of the state, which can be drawn into the struggle as proxies.

Consider the following situation. Until recently, the four "pillars" of Canadian finance were defined as separate sectors: the chartered banks, insurance companies, trust companies, and stockbrokers. Each was separately regulated in law, with rules against operating in more than one sector. The walls between these pillars began to dissolve in the 1980s, as finance was progressively deregulated around the Western world. In 1995, the federal government turned its attention to new rules for the insurance market, and two rival business associations appeared before the Liberal Party caucus (the body of Liberal members of Parliament and senators) in Ottawa to make their case.

Representing the chartered banks, the Canadian Bankers Association (CBA) mounted an aggressive argument for gaining access to insurance sales. For its part, the Insurance Bureau of Canada (IBC) pushed strongly for the status quo, fearing that the huge banks would carve up the insurance market through mergers and takeovers. At the Liberal caucus meetings, the CBA received a cold and critical reception. Reflecting the public's resentment of the chartered banks, which were reporting record profits despite a poor record of lending to small business, parliamentarians responded in kind. By contrast, and perhaps surprisingly, the IBC gained a sympathetic ear in the caucus. One key factor flowed from the contrast in the membership structures of the two industry groups. The highly centralized banks spoke from their corporate headquarters, with little local input to their campaign. In contrast, the insurance sector mobilized thousands of affiliated brokers in towns and cities across the nation. This registered strongly on Liberal members of Parliament (MPs) and was instrumental in swinging government opinion. In the end, the IBC prevailed (Howlett et al., 1996).

Alliances

In some cases, formal coalitions of groups are marshalled behind an advocacy campaign. Here the logic is that a broad common front can signal a virtual consensus position on an issue. Not surprisingly, such interest group alliances are likely on issues of general business salience, which affect firms and industries regardless of size or product. For example, in the late 1960s, corporate Canada mobilized with determination to oppose a proposed revision of the income tax regime that stood to increase business exposure and burden. Acknowledging a business *force majeure*, Ottawa backed away from corporate tax reform. Less than a decade later, another broad front was forged to resist revisions to the competition policy law, whose effects would stiffen the policing of collusive behaviour and mergers. For months, business representatives deluged a parliamentary committee with criticism and prognostications, until the Trudeau government buckled under the pressure.

More recently, three dramatic instances of broad-scale corporate advocacy coalitions come to mind. The first of these coalesced in 1987, as the Canadian Alliance for Trade and Job Opportunities (CATJO). In its first year of operation, CATJO advertised extensively in newspapers across the country and participated in over 500 conferences, meetings, and press conferences to the tune of $3 million (Doern and Tomlin, 1991). However, it was during the 1988 federal election campaign, when support for the Mulroney Progressive Conservatives (and the free trade agreement) plummeted, that CATJO made its most forceful impact. Mounting the largest third-party advertising campaign in modern Canadian history, the pro-free trade CATJO spent more than $2.3 million during the election period (Hiebert, 1991: 20). Given that this was directed toward a single issue in a nation-wide context, it has been credited with staunching the Tory decline and, ultimately, contributing to the rescue of the free trade agreement.

The second example involves the business campaign to secure broad-scale tax cuts in the wake of Ottawa's 1998 balanced budget achievement. This marked the beginning of a new political era and a new political debate over how to dispose of Ottawa's mounting "fiscal dividend." Almost immediately, advocates for restored public expenditures (to fill the voids left by the program review) squared off against proponents of continued debt pay-down and champions of tax relief. In the February 1999 budget, Finance Minister Martin set out a formula for a 50/50 "balance" of expenditure and tax cut measures within the envelope of fiscal surplus. For the first time since the free trade campaign, more than a decade earlier, the CCCE, CCC, and CME joined together in the autumn of 1999 to emphasize their conviction. While their specific tax agendas varied, the three peak associations made common cause out of fear that tax relief was losing out (Toulin, 1999).

The third and most recent case arose after 9/11, when the US undertook an urgent review of its border security arrangements. There were serious prospects that, in its bid to clamp down on cross-border terrorist movements, Washington would impose a chokehold on Canadian exports to the south. With more than 80 per cent of its exports taking this route, Canadian business struck a Coalition for Secure and Trade-Efficient Borders. Directed by the four peak business associations, this encompassed more than 45 trade associations and companies. Its first statement was released less than two months after 9/11 and was followed by four years of work aimed at protecting the border passage of low-risk goods, strengthening Canadian border management, and ensuring border cooperation in the future (Coalition for Secure and Efficient Borders, 2001).

Property Rights Populism

Social movement politics is not often associated with business campaigns. However business populism, once triggered, can be a formidable force. The identity at the root of many such campaigns is that of property owner or middle-class taxpayer, whose hard-won assets and earnings are vulnerable to the reckless appetites of the state. Sometimes these are labelled the "blue" movements to distinguish them from the green (environmental) and the red (socialist) social movements (see also the discussion of populism in chapter 9).

Perhaps the most graphic modern example of such a movement is the California property tax revolt of the late 1970s (Sears and Citrin, 1985). In a series of citizen-driven referendum initiatives, state voters decisively reined in California budget leaders. The first of these, Proposition 13, was approved by a two-to-one margin and required property tax cuts together with limits on their future growth. A new era of "plebiscitary budgeting" had begun, and the tactics spread to new arenas, including Canada.

Several groups have driven the Canadian experience with grassroots tax protest. A right-wing think tank, the Fraser Institute, has been highlighting tax trends for 30 years or more. This began with the calculation of a Canadian consumer tax index, after the fashion of the consumer price index and intending to highlight the inexorable growth of average family tax burdens. Several years later, the Fraser Institute launched a simpler but more visceral campaign. Following the lead of the American Tax Foundation, it began to calculate an annual calendar setting of "tax freedom day." This aimed to capture the point when the average family had earned sufficient income to pay its tax dues and could thereby begin to earn for themselves. For example, in 1981 the national tax freedom day was May 30. By 2005 it had retreated to June 22, though the recession shifted the date forward to June 11 in 2012 (Palacios et al., 2012). While tax freedom day, as applied by the Fraser Institute, may indeed amount to a "flawed, incoherent and pernicious concept" (Brooks, 2005), it nevertheless offers a ready frame of reference for resentful taxpayers.

The organizational catalyst for taxpayer resistance lies elsewhere, however, with the Canadian Taxpayers Federation (CTF). With roots going back to 1989 and the appearance of the Association of Saskatchewan Taxpayers, this group advanced the cause through newsletters and field representatives across Western Canada (Lanigan, 2000). Its energy level and organizational acumen jumped in 1991, when Jason Kenney (later a Reform MP and later still a Conservative MP) came on the scene. The CTF combined attacks on legislator perks (benefits and pensions for members of provincial legislatures), protests on the goods and services tax (GST), and petitions for referendums on balanced budget laws. By 1993, offices were open in all four western provinces. Another turning point was the national "tax alert" campaign opposing revenue hikes as part of the federal Liberal Party's war on the deficit. In 1995, a petition bearing a quarter million signatures was presented to Finance Minister Martin.

Perhaps the CTF's most original and lasting policy contribution was its campaign for balanced budget laws. The model statute called for a requirement to balance the budget, a salary penalty on legislators who failed to achieve it, and plebiscitary approval for any new or increased tax measure. The first major success came in Manitoba, where Progressive Conservative Premier Gary Filmon put in place a Taxpayer Protection Act following the 1995 election. The remaining three western provinces followed, in varying degrees, as did Ontario Progressive Conservative Mike Harris in 1999. Today, this taxpayer advocacy group claims 65,000 members (Canadian Taxpayers Federation, 2013).

While there has been no Canadian taxpayer revolt along American lines, a distinct discourse of small property rights runs through the past several decades. Occasionally it intersects with another vector that stresses corporate tax cuts as part of big business's productivity agenda. Interestingly, it is at the provincial level that CTF-style advocacy has drawn the greatest response.

Populism is seldom a steadfast ally to organized business. In the wake of the 2008 crisis, two lines of populist politics emerged in the US. Their presence in Canada has been mixed. First, the American Tea Party movement came to life barely months after Obama's inauguration. Driven by a complex interplay of grassroots social distress, conservative interest groups, and blanket coverage on Fox News, it began in resistance to Obama's economic stimulus and health reform agenda but soon evolved into a focus on the 2010 mid-term elections. The Tea Party was less a single movement than an amalgam of loose umbrella networks, shifting themes, and personalities. (Skocpol and Williamson, 2011) The iconography blended imagery of the flag, the Constitution, and the Boston Tea Party of 1773 (seen as the first American grassroots tax revolt). The Republican Party found itself playing catch-up to a movement that quickly pre-empted the right wing of the party's support coalition while advancing an anti-government agenda that posed problems even for the Republican congressional leadership. The Tea Party's "Contract From America," composed by online vote in February 2010, threatened a variety of organized big business preferences including free trade, a basic welfare safety net, monetary stability and fiscal moderation, a market-based climate change strategy, and American diplomatic leadership in the world. While efforts were made to launch a parallel Canadian version of the Tea Party, it has never amounted to more than a fringe presence, perhaps not surprising given the range of political cultural differences between the two countries.

The second movement, emerging in 2011, is Occupy Wall Street (also covered in chapter 5). Here the formative event was the tenting occupation of Zuccotti Park in Lower Manhattan. The signature slogan for the Occupy Movement is "We are the 99 per cent," referring to the portion of Americans who lost ground during the massive income shift to the wealthy in recent decades. Within weeks, hundreds of Occupy actions sprang up across North America and Europe. The small nylon tent, pitched in public space, became a powerful expression of the desire to reclaim a popular interest against business privilege. As other slogans put it, "bankers have broken our world" and "capitalism as we know it is finished." Though some observers criticized the Occupy movement for the lack of a substantive program, the slogans were neither empty nor simplistic. Moreover, Occupy encampments drew significant public support and outpolled the Tea Party in one Rasmussen poll in early October 2011 (Weigel, 2011). Ironically, given that they were often Wall Street victims along with mainstreet Americans, municipal authorities began to evict the occupiers as the autumn wore on. While the campaign epicentres had largely disappeared by year's end, the left populist critique did not. Indeed the contrast between Occupy and the Tea Party are evident in both values and outlooks.

Litigation

In the era of the Charter of Rights and Freedoms (the Charter), the judicial system is an increasingly prominent avenue of political dispute. For business, however, this was the case long before the entrenchment of the Charter in 1982. Indeed, capital has resorted to the courts to resist unfavourable state policies throughout Canadian history. A biting aphorism, attributed to Justice Darling, holds that "the law-courts of England are open to all men, like the doors of the Ritz Hotel." Not all, of course, enjoy the means to take advantage of that open door, and so it has been in politics.

Litigation is the process of contesting a claim in law. As a political weapon, it plays several functions. In the early stages of a policy process, when issues are still being defined, a favourable judicial ruling can set the limits of substantive content. Rulings can also reorder the political agendas of ruling governments, either elevating or diminishing the priority of an issue. In this way, courts can either block or facilitate government intentions. Litigation may also be effective in the latter stages of policy-making, when formal decisions have been made and attention turns to implementation. Here we consider three bases for strategic litigation in corporate politics.

For Canada's first century, the most important of these was the challenge based on federalism, which means challenging the constitutional competence of the originating jurisdiction. If a statute posed a threat to a powerful interest, it could be resisted by asking the court to declare the law *ultra vires*, or beyond the powers of the sponsoring legislature. Since the Constitution sets out a division of jurisdictions between national and provincial authorities, judges are asked to consider the disputed subject against the constitutional division of federal and provincial powers and determine whether the sponsoring legislature had exceeded its authorized powers. For example, when the government of Ontario prohibited the export of raw pulp logs to the US to build up a forest processing industry within the province, log exporting firms challenged this measure by arguing that only the Government of Canada could regulate such matters of international trade.

Notice the distinctive logic of a federalism challenge: a statute or program is questioned only for being enacted by the "wrong" government. If the appeal courts agree, that law is struck down, creating a policy vacuum. However, there is nothing to prevent the other level of government from enacting the identical measure with complete constitutional propriety—nothing except the vigorous lobby that would undoubtedly be mounted by the judicial victors. In the pulp-wood case, the courts upheld the Ontario regulation (Armstrong, 1981).

A second basis of challenge involves procedural grounds. An important part of English common law is the notion of due process, which holds that state authorities must follow fair and proper channels as they conduct their business. Due process is particularly important in relations between citizens and the police and courts and to the field of administrative law, which involves relations between citizens and state bureaucracies. The need to follow fair procedure is central to this. Has there been adequate public notice where the law requires? Are officials free of bias or conflict of interest when they rule on important allocations? These are the staples of procedural challenge, since serious defects of process are sufficient to invalidate the results.

This provides interest holders with another potential lever for avoiding or evading adverse measures. In fields where government moves to regulate industry, it is common for the regulated firms to spend years in the courts testing the mandate, procedures, and personnel of newly established regulators. Even if the substance of such challenges fails, advantages are gained by postponing the application of the adverse policies for years. Quite apart from the time gains, political will may ebb in the face of persistent litigation and policy regimes may be transformed as a result. When the government of Nova Scotia created a Pulpwood Marketing Board in 1970, against unanimous opposition from the pulp and paper industry, the lead firms engaged in procedural challenges to delay agreement on the first supply contract for a full decade (Clancy, 1992).

A third type of challenge is based upon possible violation of constitutional rights. Prior to 1982 this was not a significant option. However, the enactment that year of the Charter opened a dramatic new field of rights-based judicial review of legislation. The Charter sets out categories of fundamental freedoms, democratic rights, legal rights, equality rights, language rights, and others. It is fair to say that it has revolutionized the practice of strategic litigation. The past 20 years have brought new prominence to the Supreme Court and heightened the "rights holding" theme in Canadian political culture. The National Citizens Coalition case on third-party electoral advertising, discussed below, is a case in point.

Civic Propaganda

In essence, propaganda connotes schemes to propagate a doctrine or idea to a mass public. This becomes especially salient in democratic societies where the mass public plays an active political role. Not by accident, modern propaganda coincides with the emergence of electoral democracy, which occurred in the period 1880–1920. During this time, the extent of the franchise grew from 10 to 15 per cent to 40 to 50 per cent of liberal societies.

For capitalist interests, this was a transition fraught with danger. Under far more intense pressure from populist and working-class interests, the state more assertively challenged market prerogatives. Alex Carey argues that American corporate interests pioneered a most effective response, refining a set of propaganda techniques to shape public and cultural values in favour of private property and markets and thereby "taking the risk out of democracy" (Carey, 1995). This involved a convergence of new advertising and public relations techniques, new media of dissemination (in print and electronic forms), and a firm will on the part of organized business to use them. These are indirect techniques of political influence in that they seek to shape underlying social expectations and perceptions, largely through the manipulation of powerful symbols—religious, national, and patriotic. In the twentieth century, this included sustained efforts aimed at the assimilation of immigrants, the prospects for trade unions and social democratic parties, and the contours of the anti-Soviet Cold War alliance. The most recent cultural discourse to be promoted in this way is that of neoliberalism.

Carey contends that business propaganda efforts can function on parallel tracks, for "treetops" influence (with political elites) and mass influence (with the public at large). The first is the domain of the think tanks and peak associations. Policy research institutes or think tanks have become an increasingly prominent part of the policy landscape over the last quarter-century or so. Prior to 1970 there were few stand-alone research and advocacy centres in Canada. Since then, however, a series of primarily business-sponsored voices, such as the C.D. Howe Institute, the Fraser Institute, and the Atlantic Institute for Market Studies, have assumed public prominence. William Carroll points out that a series of shared directors links these groups into a corporate-sponsored network. Together, they advance a comprehensive neoliberal policy discourse while displaying a division of labour that "offers possibilities for a nuanced debate and diverse action repertoires, all within the perimeter of neoliberal discourse" (Carroll, 2004: 170).

The second, or mass influence strategy, aims directly at the civic public by means of alternative communications campaigns. This is the domain of the CTF, for example, whose creative publicity and grassroots networking was noted in sections above. The National Citizens Coalition is interesting in this regard. Founded in the 1970s by right-wing businessman Colin Brown, it is funded by anonymous donors and is directed by a select group of voting members and a core staff group. Murray Dobbin sees a leitmotif in the generalized attack on publicly delivered programs and a corresponding preference for the personal and the private. Conservative Party leader Stephen Harper served briefly as president of the Coalition in the 1990s, between stints in Ottawa. Despite the grassroots nomenclature, the operative style is more commercial lobby than citizen democracy. "What the [Coalition] does do . . . is commission opinion polls, try to generate public pressure on politicians through opinion pieces and mass media advertising, cultivate political friends who will push its policies to the forefront, and make submissions to governments" (Dobbin, 1998: 205).

The breakthrough event for the Coalition came in 1984, when it won a court challenge to Ottawa's third-party advertising ban during election campaigns.

The Alberta Supreme Court held that, short of evidence that it undermined the democratic process, any ban on third-party interventions violated the Charter right of freedom of expression. The practical consequences of this victory became clear four years later with the unprecedented third-party business intervention in the free trade election of 1988. This case captures the continuing dimensions of political victory on such framework-setting issues. Once objectives are achieved, they are embedded in the values or procedures by which future politics will be waged.

One further dimension of the propaganda battle deserves note, as it highlights the ways in which the rules of public advocacy can be shaped for political advantage. This involves the corporate use of lawsuits to suppress critical discourse. A SLAPP suit (or strategic lawsuit against public participation) is normally a civil action by a plaintiff seeking monetary damages against individuals or groups raising issues deemed in the public interest. Whatever the alleged grounds—libel, negligence, and bad faith are common ones—the goal is to silence political critics. The respondents face multiple burdens in the costs of defending themselves, the diversion of public attention, and the discouragement, by implication, of future criticism (Valentin, 2011). Although "anti-SLAPP" remedies have been debated widely in Canada in the 2000s, only Quebec has enacted a law that authorizes judges to identify and dismiss cases aimed at discouraging public participation.

THEORETICAL IMPLICATIONS

In the discussion above, we have seen that capital can mobilize politically across a wide range of issues and act within a variety of arenas. These include embedded structures such as market recoil, active agents such as trade associations, formative mechanisms for mass beliefs and values, and populist movements. There are no grounds, theoretically or empirically, to expect universal business hegemony. Nonetheless, a pronounced tilt may affect the business-government relationship within national or local, sector or industry settings. To conclude, we will return to the question posed early in this chapter, as to whether business politics should be considered within or outside of civil society proper. That this question is posed at all reflects diverging perspectives on the constitution of society.

The very notion of civil society springs from the recognition of an autonomous political space that is outside of the state while related to it. It parallels the historical processes in the West that established first the liberal state and later the democratic state. While the liberal state emerged as a limited authority that guaranteed not only a private social space but also a public social space outside of its immediate control, the democratic state acknowledged that its authority sprang from a mass political mandate conferred and renewed by public consent. This involved citizens in a dual fashion, as voters in elections and as activists between them. Not only is the state–society dichotomy fundamental, but the quality of societal autonomy is critical. If organized capital furthers the cause of holding accountable the burgeoning modern state, it enhances the quality of civil society. Even while acting in defence of its immediate interests, the institutions of capital may contribute to the maintenance of that vital public space outside of the state where civil politics can be realized.

The alternate perspective, however, focuses on the capacities of these powerful market interests not to enhance but to erode civil society. It seems to prefer a more restricted version of civil society that would leave capitalist market interests on the outside, for the most part. It begins with the recognition that commercial markets constitute immensely powerful allocative systems. Not only are they capable of standing on their own for purposes of material production and exchange, they can also rival and even predominate over state systems (the only other allocative system of comparable scale). It is true that markets involve social relationships at various levels—buyers and sellers, employers and employees, lenders and borrowers. Furthermore, these relationships have given rise to collective bodies in the form of groups and movements to represent these commercial interests. Just as the institutions of the market depend on political authorities for validation and sanction, the social interests created by markets look to politics as a means of fulfilling their needs. However, capitalist interests differ from other civil interests in their capacity to eclipse the public realm (Bakan, 2004).

This question of whether a preponderance of capitalist power serves to distort the shape and capacities of a civil society is another question entirely and has taken on growing urgency as capitalism matures. Indeed, it is the latter concern that underlies the civil sector's challenge to neoliberal politics and globalization, whether at World Trade Organization (WTO) conference sites, International Monetary Fund (IMF) governing meetings, United Nations (UN) Conferences on Sustainable Development, or G-7 summits. These battles will continue to shape the contexts of business politics for years to come.

REFERENCES AND FURTHER READING

Armstrong, Christopher. 1981. *The Politics of Federalism: Ontario's Relations with the Federal Government.* Toronto: University of Toronto Press.

Atkinson, Michael M., and William D. Coleman. 1989. *The State, Business, and Industrial Change in Canada.* Toronto: University of Toronto Press.

Bakan, Joel. 2004. *The Corporation: The Pathological Pursuit of Profit and Power.* Toronto: Penguin Canada.

Bothwell, Robert, and William Kilbourn. 1979. *C.D. Howe: A Biography*. Toronto: McClelland and Stewart.

Brooks, Neil. 2005. *Tax Freedom Day: A Flawed, Incoherent, and Pernicious Concept*. Ottawa: Canadian Centre for Policy Alternatives. June.

Canadian Taxpayers Federation. 2013. http://www.taxpayer.com

Carey, Alex. 1995. *Taking the Risk Out of Democracy*. Ed. Andrew Lohrey. Sydney: University of New South Wales Press.

Carroll, William K. 2004. *Corporate Power in a Globalizing World*. Don Mills: Oxford University Press.

Clancy, Peter. 1992. "The Politics of Pulpwood Marketing in Nova Scotia." In *Trouble in the Woods*, ed. L. Anders Sandberg, 142–67. Fredericton: Acadiensis Press.

Clancy, Peter. 2004. *Micropolitics and Canadian Business: Paper, Steel, and the Airlines*. Peterborough: Broadview Press.

Clark, S.D. 1939. *The Canadian Manufacturers' Association: A Study in Collective Pressure and Political Action*. Toronto: University of Toronto Press.

Clarke, Tony. 1997. *Silent Coup: Confronting the Big Business Takeover of Canada*. Toronto: James Lorimer.

Clement, Wallace. 1983. *Class, Power, and Property: Essays on Canadian Society*. Toronto: Methuen.

Coalition for Secure and Efficient Borders. 2001. *Rethinking Our Borders: A Plan for Action*. (December). http://www.cita-acti.ca.

Coleman, William. 1988. *Business and Politics: A Study of Collective Action*. Montreal, Kingston: McGill-Queen's University Press.

Creighton, Donald. 1955. *John A. Macdonald: The Old Chieftain*. Toronto: Macmillan.

Dobbin, Murray. 1998. *The Myth of the Good Corporate Citizen*. Toronto: Stoddart.

Doern, G. Bruce, and Brian W. Tomlin. 1991. *Faith and Fear: The Free Trade Story*. Toronto: Stoddart.

Edwards, Lindy. 2002. *How to Argue with an Economist*. Cambridge: Cambridge University Press.

Ferguson, Thomas. 1995. *Golden Rule: The Investment Theory of Party Competition and the Logic of Money-Driven Political Systems*. Chicago: University of Chicago Press.

Finkel, Alvin. 1979. *Business and Social Reform in the Thirties*. Toronto: James Lorimer.

Gillies, James. 1981. *Where Business Fails*. Montreal: Institute for Research on Public Policy.

Gollner, Andrew. 1983. *Social Change and Corporate Strategy: The Expanding Role of Public Affairs*. Stamford: Issue Action Publishers.

Hiebert, Janet. 1991. "Interest Groups and Canadian Federal Elections." In *Interest Groups and Elections in Canada*, ed. F. Leslie Seidle, 3–76. Toronto: Dundurn Press.

Howlett, Karen, Barrie McKenna, and John Partridge. 1996. "How the Banks Lost Big." *Globe and Mail* (March 9: B1).

Jackson, Andrew, and Matthew Sanger. 1998. *Dismantling Democracy: The Multilateral Agreement on Investment (MAI) and Its Impact*. Toronto: Canadian Centre for Policy Alternatives.

Langille, David. 1987. "The BCNI and the Canadian State." *Studies in Political Economy* 24 (Autumn): 41–85.

Lanigan, Troy. 2000. *The Canadian Taxpayers Federation: A Ten Year Retrospective (1989–2000)*. http://www.taxpayer.com

Lewis, Timothy. 2003. *In the Long Run We're All Dead*. Vancouver: University of British Columbia Press.

Leys, Colin. 2001. *Market-driven Politics: Neoliberal Democracy and the Public Interest*. London: Verso.

Lindblom, Charles. 1982. "The Market as Prison." *Journal of Politics* 44 (2): 323–36.

Litvak, Isaiah. 1984. "National Trade Associations: Business-Government Intermediaries." *Business Quarterly* 49 (3): 35–42.

Mahon, Rianne. 1984. *The Politics of Industrial Restructuring: Canadian Textiles*. Toronto: University of Toronto Press.

McBride, Stephen. 2001. *Paradigm Shift: Globalization and the Canadian State*. Halifax: Fernwood.

McLean, Bethany, and Joe Nocera. 2010. *All the Devils are Here*. New York: Portfolio.

Naylor, R.T. 1972. "The Rise and Fall of the Third Commercial Empire of the St. Lawrence." In *Capitalism and the National Question in Canada*, ed. Gary Teeple, 1–36. Toronto: University of Toronto Press.

Niosi, Jorge. 1985. "Continental Nationalism: The Strategy of the Canadian Bourgeoisie." In *The Structure of the Canadian Capitalist Class*, ed. Robert J. Brym, 53–65. Toronto: Garamond Press.

Pal, Leslie A. 1995. *Interests of State: The Politics of Language, Multiculturalism, and Feminism in Canada*. Montreal: McGill-Queen's University Press.

Palacios, Milagro, Niels Veldhuis, and Charles Lammam. 2012. "Canadians Celebrate Tax Freedom Day on 11 June 2012" *FraserAlert* (June).

Richards, John, and Larry Pratt. 1979. *Prairie Capitalism: Power and Influence in the New West*. Toronto: McClelland and Stewart.

Roubini, Nouriel, and Stephen Mihm. 2010. *Crisis Economics*. New York: Penguin.

Sears, David O., and Jack Citrin. 1985. *Tax Revolt: Something For Nothing in California*. Cambridge, MA: Harvard University Press.

Skocpol, Theda, and Vanessa Williamson. 2011. *The Tea Party and the Remaking of Republican Conservatism*. New York: Oxford University Press.

Sorkin, Andrew Ross. 2009. *Too Big to Fail*. New York: Viking.

Stanbury, W.T. 1977. *Business Interests and the Reform of Competition Policy in Canada*. Toronto: Methuen.

Tett, Gillian. 2009. *Fool's Gold*. New York: Free Press.

Toulin, Alan. 1999. "Business Groups Unite to Battle for Tax Relief." *National Post* (September 28).

Valentin, Candice. 2011. "Code of Silence." *The Walrus*. (November).

Weigel, David. 2011. "Poll: Occupy Wall Street Starts Off with Favorable Ratings." *Slate* (October 5). http://www.slate.com/blogs/weigel/2011/10/05/poll_occupy_wall_street_starts_off_with_favorable_ratings.html (accessed September 25, 2013).

Williams, Glen. 1983. *Not For Export: Toward a Political Economy of Canada's Arrested Industrialization*. Toronto: McClelland and Stewart.

Young, Brian. 1981. *George-Etienne Cartier: Montreal Bourgeois*. Montreal: McGill-Queens University Press.

TWO

Party On or Party's Over?: Organized Labour and Canadian Politics

CHARLOTTE YATES AND AMANDA COLES

Canadian labour markets have undergone an enormous transformation over the past three decades. More people are doing more work, for longer hours, over more of their lives, and for less money. Permanent, full-time employment with benefits and a pension is no longer the norm. Precarious employment—contract, freelance, temporary work, or self-employment—is on the rise. Unionized jobs that protect job security, wages, benefits, working hours, health and safety provisions, vacations, sick days and pension benefits are in serious decline. Collective bargaining is under attack by governments and employers.

Traditionally, unions, as representatives of working people, have fought for and won major gains for workers through collective bargaining in the workplace as well as political advocacy. Since the late nineteenth century, working people have organized their own political parties in attempts to redress the inequities and indignities of work and life in a capitalist economy. In reaction to their exclusion from the bourgeois politics of property ownership and privilege that dominated nineteenth-century political parties, workers formed socialist, communist, and social democratic parties to gain representation in and influence the political process. These political parties distinguished themselves with their mass membership base, their critique of exploitation under capitalism and oppression by the state, and their advocacy of the transformation of the capitalist system.

In Canada, the labour movement has influenced the quality of life for the working class through workplace activism and collective bargaining, broadly based political advocacy, and party politics via support for the New Democratic Party (NDP). Throughout the postwar period from 1948 to the 1980s, the labour movement in Canada advanced an egalitarian vision of society and the economy that relied heavily upon the state for the protection of rights and the redistribution of wealth. Over the past 20 years, however, union political activism has been undermined by the lack of a unifying, alternative vision for the future of political and economic life that wrestles with the problems of growing economic inequality and diversity among the working class. We argue that this lack of a unifying alternative vision, aggravated by growing hostility and opposition to unions by employers and governments, is reflected in labour's pursuit of a defensive "politics of pragmatism."

Throughout this paper, we use the term ideology to reflect an underlying set of ideas, principles, and values that underpin and shape the ways in which political actors identify, understand, and propose solutions to political, economic, and social issues. A politics of pragmatism is not grounded in a broader ideological understanding of power relations between the state, workers, citizens, and capital but is a defensive approach to union political activism that focuses on narrowly defined vested interests of specific union memberships. It is about pursuing strategies that respond to immediate, short-term issues and goals which, albeit important, fail to recognize the structural or systemic constraints and opportunities arising from capitalist social relations. It has no broader transformative agenda in pursuit of a larger collective good.

We argue that a politics of pragmatism is deeply problematic for three reasons. First, the expression of political pragmatism through, for example, strategic voting, wherein unions advocate voting for "anyone but the Conservatives" does not work. It has consistently failed to produce positive political results for the Canadian working class. Second, by adopting a political strategy based on the interests and actions of specific union memberships, a politics of pragmatism exacerbates deep fractures in solidarity within the labour movement and weakens the appeal of unions to non-union members. Third, the consequences of a politics of pragmatism within the Canadian labour movement means that unions have failed to offer a comprehensive alternative vision rooted in collective social justice principles. Neoliberalism and the politics of austerity remain unchallenged and social and economic inequality persist.

The chapter is divided into three sections. The first explains what we mean by the labour movement and why we need to understand its significance in the context of group politics and social movements in Canada. We briefly review the relationship that unions, as key organizational actors in the labour movement, have had with the NDP and the Liberal Party in Canadian politics. In the second section, we examine the emergence of a politics of pragmatism that is expressed through an issues-based approach to policy advocacy and strategic voting. The complex relationship between unions, political parties, and other social movements varies between provinces. Our analysis focuses on the relationship between unions and governments primarily in Ontario and federal politics. In the third section, we examine the changing nature of work and workers in twenty-first-century Canadian labour markets as a step to understanding why it is more important than ever that the Canadian labour movement develop and mobilize collective support for an alternative inclusive vision of Canadian society.

UNDERSTANDING THE LABOUR MOVEMENT

Understanding what we mean by "labour movement" is complicated. Generally speaking, unions are the key organizational actors in the labour movement whose goal is to advance the collective interests of working people at work and in society at large. Because of this mandate, labour movements are actively engaged in politics as a means for advancing working-class interests. In countries around the world, including Canada, this has manifest itself in the formation of worker-based political parties, most of which have been ideologically oriented toward socialist, communist, or social democratic ideas and strategies. Yet, unions, and hence labour movements, share an uncomfortable and often contradictory relationship to capitalism insofar as they are tied to the perpetuation of capitalism and the labour-management relationship. They represent the interests of working people whose livelihood depends upon capital investment and profits. These constraints curb the enthusiasm of organized labour for radical solutions to political economic problems. Unions in Canada have been further constrained in their political imagination and activism as a result of the Canadian system of industrial relations; labour laws configure unions' primary purpose to be collective bargaining with employers. Operating in highly formalized, institutionally structured environments creates lasting tensions for unions between their capacity to mobilize class interests as social movements and the accommodation of class interests within institutions (Fairbrother and Webster, 2008: 3).

Also important for our purposes here is the degree to which the labour movement must be understood as needing to represent the working classes as a complex constellation of diverse identities. As Garton and McCallum argue,

> [Labour] can be variously discussed as a material activity, a political ideology, a representative political actor, an institutionalized and organized movement, and a broader social class. Equally, labour as a social and political force is a product of material relations

but also as an "imagined community"[1] . . . constantly reimagined
in diverse ways, with particular factions, groups, and constituencies drawing the signifying boundaries in different ways. And
each of these processes—material and ideological—is the site of
contest and struggle. (Garton and McCallum, 1996: 117).

Understanding who and what is the labour movement has become more
complex as the nature of the working class changes and as women, in particular, have challenged the labour movement's distinction between paid work
and unpaid work. Understanding the intersection of paid work to questions
around access to employment and value of non-paid work (i.e., caring for
children or the elderly, housework, and so forth) has produced both synergies
and tensions between the labour movement and women's social movements
over time in articulating inclusive political alternatives. Actors in other social
movements making claims for social justice and equity rights have also had
a significant impact on labour and employment relations. Examples include
the LGBTQ (lesbian, gay, bisexual, transgender, and queer) rights movement
around the question of same sex partner benefits and ethnocultural groups
advocating for anti-discrimination legislation. As the demographic profile of
the Canadian working class becomes increasingly diverse, and as other social
movements open up political space for a greater range of social groups to
articulate their issues, union politics are transformed—both in the workplace
and as political actors.

Historical Overview

Unions, as the primary organizational actors that constitute the labour movement both in the workplace and in political advocacy, have played a major
role in advancing industrial citizenship and social citizenship for working-class
Canadians. Unions promote industrial citizenship through collective bargaining,
which allows unionized workers to participate in shaping the terms and conditions of their employment. Yet unions also benefit non-unionized workers
by increasing wage rates, benefits, and workplace entitlements for workers
throughout the labour market. We now turn to a brief overview of the ways in
which Canadian unions historically have engaged in formal party politics and
broadly based political advocacy to advance the interests of the working class
as a whole.

The decentralized nature of Canadian federalism produces a political landscape where legislative and policy-making powers are either the responsibility
of or shared between federal government and provincial governments. For
example, the federal government has exclusive jurisdiction over international
trade, employment insurance, the Canada Pension Plan, and Old Age Security.

Provincial governments have exclusive jurisdiction over education and social assistance programs. Jurisdiction over pensions, immigration, and health care is shared between the federal government and provinces. The federal and provincial governments also share jurisdiction over labour law and collective bargaining. Public service workers for the federal government, as well as some workers in a few key sectors that fall under federal jurisdictions—such as banking, broadcasting, railway, shipping, and aviation—are covered by federal labour law. The majority of workers, however, are covered by provincial labour laws that determine hours of work, minimum wages, health and safety regulations, workers compensation, and collective bargaining rights. Consequently, the division of federal-provincial powers under Canadian federalism means that unions engage in electoral and extra-parliamentary political advocacy at both levels of government.

After a brief period of syndicalist politics around World War I, it was the Depression of the 1930s that laid the conditions for a more sustained socialist politics among Canadian workers and their allies. The Communist Party played a critical role in organizing workers into unions throughout Canada in the 1930s and 1940s; it also played a decisive role in political debate within the labour movement until the Cold War.

The only lasting left-wing political alternative formed out of this period was the Co-operative Commonwealth Federation (CCF), which was established in 1932 out of an alliance of farmer groups, unions, and progressive academics. Initially espousing a socialist agenda, the CCF quickly moderated its political stance and advocated a blend of populist, farmer cooperative politics with social democratic state intervention in the economy to achieve redistribution of political and economic power. The CCF experienced a surge of success during World War II. In 1943, it became the official opposition in Ontario and in 1944 formed the government of Saskatchewan, with Tommy Douglas as premier. The CCF remained in power in Saskatchewan from 1944 until 1964, introducing the first public medicare program in Canada and being the first government to accord public sector workers the right to organize into unions and strike. But the Cold War took its toll. The 1958 federal election, when the CCF elected only eight MPs, marked a turning point for the party. This coincided with a period of reorganization of the Canadian labour movement, which in 1956 forged an alliance between two competing national federations of labour to create the Canadian Labour Congress (CLC) in 1956.[2] This merger in part reflected a political shift within unions and a greater willingness among unions to follow the British and European traditions of affiliation with a political party. In 1958, the CCF and the newly formed CLC initiated a three-year period of negotiation, at the end of which was the formation in 1961 of the NDP (Avakumovic, 1978; Horowitz, 1968). Unions were given a privileged position within party affairs through special affiliation procedures, representation on party bodies, and eventually informal guarantees of a position on the party executive.

During this same period, many unions, especially the growing industrial unions, established political action committees in recognition of the new-found importance attached to ongoing political engagement, particularly in partisan activities. The NDP won power from 1969 to 1977 in Manitoba, resumed power in Saskatchewan in 1971 until 1982, and won the 1972 election in British Columbia. Through the 1960s and 1970s, the NDP advocated expansion of the welfare state, the use of public ownership to pursue Canada's national economic interests, and the use of the tax system to redistribute wealth from the rich to the poor.

Organized labour, in particular large industrial unions such as the United Steelworkers of America (USWA), the meatpackers, and the United Auto Workers (UAW-Canada, now the Canadian Autoworkers Union—CAW), had greatly increased their partisan influence with the creation of the NDP. Yet, the history of union-party relations was fraught with tension. The NDP saw itself as an alliance of labour, farmers, and progressively minded liberals and resisted granting unions too much control over party decision-making. For their part, many in the labour movement felt that their financial and organizational support for the NDP, especially during election times when unions would donate staff time and office resources as well as cash, should grant them even greater leverage over party decisions and policy.

Although much scholarly attention has been paid to the elaboration of union-CCF/NDP relations, little attention has been paid to union relations with the Liberal Party. The Liberal Party's support from workers was built when national Liberal governments constructed the welfare state: Mackenzie King introduced unemployment insurance; Lester Pearson introduced the Canada Pension Plan as well as national medicare; and Pierre Trudeau repatriated the Constitution with the Canadian Charter of Rights and Freedoms. Organized labour's political pressure was critical for securing such national social policies as unemployment insurance, public pensions, medicare, and universalistic social welfare benefits (Yates, 1990). Labour federations at both the national and provincial levels were especially prominent in lobbying activities, mandated as they were by constituent unions to advance labour's interests in the political arena between elections. Until the late 1980s, the CLC nominated representatives to several government advisory boards and commissions, such as the Unemployment Insurance Advisory Committee. Labour's lobbying efforts secured organized labour "a junior insider role in the policy process" (Jackson and Baldwin, 2005: 3). Organized labour's lobbying strategies thus developed hand-in-hand with the consolidation of the Liberal Party's hold over national politics in the postwar period. Notwithstanding the fact that many Keynesian policies were first articulated by the NDP, the repeated translation of these ideas into policy by Liberal governments built this party's long-standing support among working people. At election times, working people were more likely to vote Liberal than NDP. The almost uninterrupted tenure of the Liberal Party as the government of Canada in the postwar years cemented these ties.

As we will return to shortly, strategic union relationships with the Liberal Party play a key role in the politics of pragmatism in its contemporary form. To understand the shift in labour movement politics away from a broader collective agenda for social change to a politics of pragmatism, it is useful to examine union politics and their relations to political parties in three key time periods after the end of World War II.

Late 1940s—1980s: The Postwar Compromise

From the end of World War II through to the early 1980s, unions used grass-roots mobilization tactics, formal policy advocacy, and their formal relations with the NDP to advance a clear vision of a Canadian state rooted in social democracy and social justice principles. By the late 1970s, the struggles by the labour movement and political allies resulted in the consolidation of a Canadian welfare state that included universal health care; public housing; the minimum wage; employment standards and collective bargaining; a social wage through unemployment insurance, social assistance, workers compensation, child welfare/family allowances, parental leave, and public pensions; and primary, secondary, and post-secondary public education (Garton and McCallum, 1996: 121; Yates, 1990).[3] These were important developments that reflected labour's commitment to advancing a progressive political agenda, often in association with other social movement groups, such as the feminist movement (Coles and Yates, 2012).

It is important to note that the Canadian welfare state was built largely around the concept of a male breadwinner wage in support of a nuclear family. When welfare supports for marginalized groups of workers, such as women and racialized minorities, were advanced by unions, it was largely to protect union wages from downward pressure by cheaper sources of labour (Luxton, 2001). By the 1970s, however, the labour movement like the rest of society became subject to pushes from within its own ranks as well as from outside for the embrace of a more radical politics. The women's movement demanded access to better jobs, taking on union rules and practices that protected these jobs for men (Corman et al., 1993; Briskin and McDermott, 1993). The civil rights movement similarly found its mark in the labour movement as temporary foreign farm workers demanded basic human and union rights as well as access to good union jobs, something that the CLC quickly supported. Unions responded differently to these pressures. Public sector unions, themselves dominated by women memberships, advanced a politics of change within the labour movement, often demanding better representation for women and gender issues within unions. As a whole, this period saw the labour movement pushed to the left by its own rank and file as well as by broader social developments.

As a decade that posed considerable opportunities and threats to the labour movement, the 1980s marked a key transitional period for labour politics in Canada. Overall, while a recession foreshadowed major changes ahead for the global economy and the future of unions, union politics held out hope that labour was to be a central player in mobilizing support of an alternative agenda. The 1982 repatriation of the Canadian Constitution and the entrenchment of the Charter of Rights and Freedoms signalled a Canadian state that was committed to a rights-based approach to equality and a means by which an expanded group of workers—in their diverse identities—could make claims on employers and the state. The expansion of the welfare state, especially health care and education, created a growing source of good quality, unionized employment, particularly for women. The 1984 Abella Commission put employment equity on the political map, and human rights and equity committees were common within unions.

Union memberships became increasingly diverse, and broad engagement with equity issues meant that unions began to articulate an inclusive political agenda that represented the interests of the working class as involving questions of equality based on citizenship, gender, racialization, sexuality, age, and ability. This period was also key for unions in developing strategic alliances with other social movements in Canada. Driving many of the alliances was the fact that, while equity politics and public sector growth produced gains for many equity-seeking groups, the emergence of neoliberalism as a political economic strategy and a response to economic recession challenged the foundations of the welfare state and, indeed, the labour movement itself.

McBride and Whiteside argue that as a political strategy, neoliberalism is designed "not to contain labour, but to roll back the gains it made in the postwar period" (McBride and Whiteside, 2011: 44). Neoliberalism is an ideological approach to public policy and public management that emphasizes individualism, free-market rationale, international trade liberalization, privatization, and deregulation. In early 1981, Canada entered into a deep recession with double-digit unemployment, inflation, and interest rates. Factories closed and working-class families lost their houses, wages, and benefits. Union rules governing work and employment relations were blamed for contributing to Canada's high costs of production, declining competitiveness, and high rates of unemployment. Governments of all stripes exhorted Canadians to tighten their belts in a collective effort to share the pain of restraint needed to turn around the economic crisis. The federal and provincial governments introduced restraint packages that limited or rolled back wage increases for public servants and unilaterally imposed collective agreements. Governments also embarked on a dramatic restructuring process aimed at reducing costs, seen in program closures, contracting out, and privatization (Panitch and Swartz, 2003). These government actions fed the overall climate of crisis to which private employers responded with demands for concessions from unions and workers and heightened resistance to unionization. Although by the mid-1980s the economy had recovered in terms of rates of growth, high rates of unemployment persisted, real wages fell throughout the decade, and economic restructuring by companies and governments continued unabated (Burke and Shields, 2000). Governments, employers, and world economic organizations promulgated neoliberal ideas and policy solutions as the only viable ones for addressing economic woes and the costs associated with a "bloated" welfare state.

Unions have a unique capacity as a social movement for mass mobilization that stems from the broad base of their membership and the institutional resources and formalized networks that link individual locals with parent unions, who are connected to other unions through provincial and national labour federations. Union resistance to downward economic pressures in the early 1980s provides several excellent examples of the mobilization capacity of the Canadian labour movement. In 1981, unions organized a mass protest that saw 100,000 workers and citizens arrive on Parliament Hill to protest high interest rates. In response to the announcement of several factory closures beginning in 1980, Canadian members of the UAW occupied factories and engaged in sit-downs to demand better severance, advance notice of plant closures, and government action to protect workers against the ravages of high unemployment and widespread recession (Yates, 1993: 200–201). In British Columbia in 1983, the Social Credit government introduced 26 bills that attacked the rights of unions and stripped away all but the bare essentials of such institutions as the Human Rights Commission. A coalition of unions, social movements, and citizen groups responded by organizing Operation Solidarity with the goal of using a general strike to force the government to retract these bills. Widespread demonstrations and strikes seemed to promise a new day of worker-citizen coalition and power. But the end to the story of Operation Solidarity also pointed to emerging tensions over this political strategy within the labour movement and in its alliances with other progressive social movements. On the verge of a general strike in 1983, key labour leaders negotiated a settlement with the provincial government, winning the withdrawal of some of the worst changes to labour law but leaving unchanged many of the attacks on human rights and social welfare. To many social justice activists, it appeared that labour had sold out its allies (Palmer, 1987).

Despite these tensions, throughout the 1980s Canadian unions continued to embrace mass mobilization strategies to contest the emergence of neoliberal economic and political solutions. Key to the triumph of neoliberal ideas in Canada was the negotiation of free trade agreements that opened up Canada's economy to low wage competition and waves of deregulation, also narrowing the scope of action for the state in protecting Canadian interests and resources. It was in this context of a determination to fight back against what unions dubbed "the corporate agenda" of neoliberal restructuring that unions opposed the free trade agreement. As the free trade debate heated up between 1986 and 1988, a new coalition of labour and social justice activists, nationalists, and environmentalists, entitled the Pro-Canada Network, was formed to put forward an alternative industrial policy in which governments would continue to play important roles in regulating the economy and protecting Canadians. And it was the federal election fought over free trade that exacerbated existing cracks in the relationship between the NDP and organized labour (Whitehorn, 1993: ch. 8).

During the 1988 federal election, two dynamics strained relations between the NDP and parts of organized labour. First, the NDP was outflanked by the Liberal Party, which presented itself as the true opponent of free trade. Second, political parties often took the back seat in public debates over free trade, with Bob White, leader of the CAW, often usurping the role of the NDP as the spokesperson for opponents to free trade. To many, the NDP's failure to focus its campaign on free trade was evidence that it was no longer capable of articulating the alternatives to neoliberalism demanded by workers and their unions. The victory of the Progressive Conservatives and the signing of CUFTA in 1988 marked a significant shift in Canadian politics in favour of neoliberalism, the primacy of the market, and greater vulnerability to the influence of neoliberal policies.

THE 1990S AND ON: THE POLITICS OF PRAGMATISM

By the end of the 1980s, labour politics looked considerably different than throughout much of the postwar period. While the early 1980s saw many unions continue their militant strategies in the face of corporate and government attacks, by the end of the decade strike rates and union memberships were down in Canada, many unions were engaged in partnership arrangements with employers, and unions found themselves on the defensive in the face of economic and welfare state restructuring. Despite changes within unions that led to a more inclusive labour movement with a more diverse membership, by the mid-1990s the labour movement in Canada was driven to a defensive politics of pragmatism. Economic uncertainty, exacerbated by the competitive pressures of globalization and periods of high unemployment, left unions scrambling to articulate an alternative to neoliberal politics and conservative media. Unions were framed as relics of the past, primarily interested in protecting their own memberships at the expense of the economy more broadly, and defending a "nanny state" whose commitment to social welfare was criticized as expensive and intrusive. The collapse of the Soviet Union further delegitimized socialist principles and ideas, instead venerating individualistic merit-based principles and the triumph of capitalism. As markets increasingly opened up on a global scale, and in doing so, undermined the manufacturing base of the Canadian economy, unions were blamed for creating uncompetitive economic conditions, and unionized wages were blamed for lost investment.

By the 1990s, consolidation of neoliberalism eroded both the foundations for social democratic policy and political support for state intervention in the economy. The state's primary role became one of facilitating the market and enhancing national or regional competitiveness. As North American employers became increasingly hostile to unions, governments introduced regressive labour laws that restricted unionization, weakened regulations that protected the minimum wages and working conditions of all working people, implemented tax cuts that compromised the ability of governments to fund social security programs, and instituted major cutbacks to the public sector workforce. NDP governments across the country also adopted neoliberal solutions, often restricting collective bargaining and the right to strike (Evans, 2011). Arguing that there was no alternative to wage restraint and government-facilitated economic competitiveness, NDP governments began to look very much like their Liberal opponents. This contributed to the decline in alternative visions for left-wing politics in Canada. The resulting loss in credibility for the party was seen in the 1993 federal election when the federal NDP lost official party status with its drop to nine elected representatives. This cleared the way for a Liberal majority government that, in 1995, delivered a federal budget that is widely understood to be a key moment in the dismantling of the Canadian welfare state. Deficit reduction took priority over the social safety net. The federal government redesigned and rebranded unemployment benefits as "employment" insurance aimed at tightening workers' ties to labour markets. The provinces received less funding from the federal government, with fewer conditions attached, which allowed them to impose what McBride and Whiteside describe as a "harsh regime of austerity on recipients of social assistance" (2011: 47).

On the Ropes and to the Polls! Unions and Strategic Voting

Under attack, and with their postwar vision and strategy for social and economic transformation in shreds, unions began to retreat into a politics of pragmatism. While some unions continued to mobilize their members in resistance
to government policy, they did so without a clear vision and alternative strategy for change. The events of the 1990s in Ontario revealed the emergence of
deep divisions within the labour movement over political strategy and laid the
conditions for labour becoming trapped in a politics of pragmatism.

The NDP won its only victory in Ontario in 1990. Upon taking office,
and in the midst of a deep recession, the NDP sought to reduce government expenditures through the 1993 Ontario Social Contract, a package of
measures that cut $2 billion from public service costs through a wage freeze
and mandatory unpaid days of holidays (McBride, 2005). The labour movement was deeply divided over its response to this policy. The Canadian Union
of Public Employees (CUPE) passed a resolution that withdrew electoral support for any member of the Ontario NDP caucus who supported the social
contract legislation, and the Ontario Federation of Labour passed a resolution
to withdraw all support from the NDP in the next provincial election unless
the legislation was withdrawn (McBride, 2005: 39). Several major private sector unions continued their support for the NDP, arguing that this was the only
viable political strategy for the labour movement.

When the Progressive Conservatives crushed the NDP in the 1995 Ontario
provincial election, they used the rationale of deficit reduction to implement
ideologically driven and deep cuts to social programs and government services that disproportionately impacted society's most vulnerable populations.
Labour played a key organizational role in the broadly based opposition to
these cuts known as the Days of Action, which peaked in Toronto in 1996
when more than 200,000 people marched through the city to protest government cutbacks by the Harris government. This was followed in 1997 by a
two-week illegal work stoppage by public school teachers protesting cutbacks
to school funding and increased class sizes (Camfield, 2000). Although tens
of thousands of union members marched in Days of Action across Ontario,
unions were divided between those who saw this as a broadly based mass
mobilization that would force the hand of the Progressive Conservative government to reverse many policies and those who saw the ballot box as labour's
only avenue for changing government policy through support for the NDP.
When electoral politics ultimately prevailed, protests halted, leaving many social activists, including union members, estranged from the labour movement.

The decision to embrace party politics through support of the NDP
rather than a strategy of mass mobilization deepened divisions within the labour movement. The teachers' unions, the CAW, the Ontario Public Service

Employees Union (OPSEU), the Ontario Nurses' Association, and the building trades formed the Ontario Election Network (OEN), which "took the position that defeating the Harris Conservatives was labour's first electoral priority" (Savage, 2012: 78). This group endorsed strategic voting, whereby the unions endorsed either Liberal *or* NDP candidates in key ridings based on their likelihood of defeating the Progressive Conservative candidate. In the 1999 Ontario provincial election, the OEN supported strategic voting in 26 ridings, endorsing 14 Liberals and 12 NDP candidates (Savage, 2012: 78). The strategy was a failure; the Progressive Conservatives returned to power with a stronger majority government and the NDP lost official party status in the province (Savage, 2012: 79). Despite this, strategic voting continues to dominate Ontario labour electoral politics through the Working Families Coalition, formed in 2003 and funded by the CAW, teachers, nurses, and building trades unions. The Coalition has clearly distanced itself from an ideologically driven, alternative vision for Canadian politics and describes itself as "an independent non-partisan organization raising awareness about issues that are important to families" (Versace, 2007). The Coalition's ad campaigns are credited with playing a key role in defeating the Progressive Conservatives in 2003 (Benzie, 2011). Working people in Ontario benefited from many Liberal government initiatives such as investment in the education sector, including full-day kindergarten, and significant increases in the provincial minimum wage. Notwithstanding more recent attacks on collective bargaining by the Liberal government, the Ontario Liberal Party continues to advance policies that are at least as favourable to working Ontarians as those of the NDP, the supposed labour party of Canada. For many, strategic voting seems to work, if for no other reason than to keep out the Progressive Conservative Party, which has proposed sweeping changes to labour law that would curb the rights of unions to represent workers through collective bargaining.

A politics of pragmatism was also an increasingly prominent feature in national union politics. At the federal level, the 2006 election underscored the increasingly contradictory relationship of organized labour to the federal NDP. Its tone was set early when, in December 2005, Buzz Hargrove, leader of the CAW, sent shock waves through the Canadian media, labour supporters, and analysts with the announcement that his union was recommending to its members that they vote Liberal, except in ridings it designated as winnable by the NDP. Even though the CAW had recommended strategic voting in the previous federal election and had a long history of uneasy relations with the NDP, these events suggested a shift in CAW partisan politics and revealed the depth of ambiguity in labour politics in Canada more generally. When the NDP threw Buzz Hargrove out of the party for advocating strategic voting, this action reflected the fundamentally changing nature of NDP-union relations and the growing ambivalence about which political party best serves the interests of working people and their families.

Although many unions continued their long-standing policy of support for the NDP during the 2005–06 federal election campaign, it would be a mistake to see the CAW's recommendation for strategic voting as an outlier political strategy among Canadian unions. The Public Service Alliance of Canada (PSAC), which represents large numbers of federal government employees, also endorses strategic voting, as does OPSEU (Savage, 2012). What was striking about the continued endorsement of strategic voting by unions was its failure to deliver during the federal election. Out of 50 strategic voting ridings identified by the CAW in the 2011 federal election, the Conservatives *gained* 12 seats. The Liberals lost a total of 17 seats, suffering their worst electoral defeat ever, and winning only 35 seats overall. Although the federal NDP, under the leadership of the late Jack Layton, won a record number of seats, it did so through enormous electoral success in Quebec and in spite of many unions' decisions *not* to support the NDP (Graefe, 2012; Savage, 2012).

The foundation for strategic voting is rooted in a politics of pragmatism and manifest in an approach to politics. For example, the CLC's Better Choices campaign in the 2006, 2008, and 2011 federal elections identified key issues for union members to consider when deciding which party or candidate to support. In the 2011 federal election, these key issues were child care, pensions, health care, and jobs. Part of the problem with this approach was that job creation, for example, was a central focus of Conservative, Liberal, and NDP platforms. The CLC's political strategy failed to provide working people with a critical lens through which to understand how the distinctive ideological and policy approaches of different political parties to an issue such as job creation, could have potentially negative effects on working people and their families. An issues-based approach to voting fails to explain how important ideology continues to be in understanding state–society relations and the roots of social and economic inequalities and, hence, the policy solutions proposed by political parties. Issues-based politics also ignores the root of labour's political power, namely, its large membership base, which, if mobilized, constitutes a source of social, economic, and political power. Finally, issues-based politics of pragmatism tends to narrow union political influence by focusing its demands on the interests of their specific memberships, rather than those of the broader working class. The consequences of an issue-based approach to politics have resulted in three consecutive federal electoral victories for the Conservative Party to the serious detriment of the working class in Canada. As the labour movement steers away from a politics of ideology, not so the Conservative Party of Canada. Since its re-election, it has quickly cut the ground from under unionized workers. In 2011–12, the federal government was swift to undermine free collective bargaining in response to labour disruptions at Canada Post, Air Canada, and CP Railway, using legislative means to suspend workers' right to strike and to arbitrate collective agreements. It gutted employment equity guidelines for federal contractors (PSAC, 2012), raised the age of eligibility to qualify for Old Age Security, and introduced a two-tier wage system that allows employers to pay temporary foreign workers 15 per cent less than the average wage (Goar, 2012). Most recently, the federal government has been considering the introduction of right-to-work legislation that would cut deeply into union membership and resources. Yet, many labour unions are responding to these conditions with attempts to build new membership, which has in turn increased membership diversity and opened the door to a new politics based more on alliances with social movements.

LIFE OF THE PARTY: EQUITY, ORGANIZING, AND ADVOCATING FOR A BETTER FUTURE

As a consequence of economic restructuring and regressive labour legislation, unions in Canada have experienced a slow but steady attrition in membership, with union density dropping from 37.6 per cent in 1981 to 29.6 per cent in 2010. Statistics Canada reports unionization declined across several occupations groups in 2010, including health and management, processing, manufacturing, utilities, trades, transport, and equipment operator occupations. A decline in union density reduces bargaining leverage in industries that once set the standard for wages and benefits. Most analysts agree that recent membership decline is related to shifts in employment away from these areas in which unionization rates were high and shifting work from unionized to non-unionized establishments (Uppal, 2010).

Since the 1990s, some unions in Canada have placed strategic priority on organizing the unorganized, particularly in the health and service sectors. Although breakthroughs in retail and restaurant chains such as Walmart or McDonalds have been missing, unions have been quite successful in organizing workers employed in home care, auxiliary hospital services, university support staff, security guards, and a few retail outlets. Recent union membership growth has tended to be disproportionately among older women with education. Women's rate of unionization rose to 31.1 per cent in 2011, while men's stayed at 28.2 per cent (Uppal, 2011).

For unions, organizing the unorganized has meant growing diversity in their own ranks. Internal membership diversity has challenged union strategic capacity as unions struggle to reconcile the demands of aging, often male members who expect the union to protect their benefits versus new members who are more likely to be women and/or racialized minorities. As unions become more complex and diverse, union politics become more complex and diverse. In those unions in which diversity has greatly increased, such as the National Union of Provincial Government Employees, USWA, CAW, and the United Food and Commercial Workers (UFCW), political strategies have tended to highlight human rights and social issues.

Greater membership diversity has in many instances led unions to engage in more transformative collective action and progressive politics, usually in alliance with other social movements. There are several examples of this. The Migrant Workers Alliance for Change is a coalition of "advocacy and community groups, unions, workers and community members, [aimed] at improving working conditions and fighting for better protections for live-in caregivers, seasonal agricultural workers and other temporary foreign workers" (Migrant Workers Alliance, 2013). This group works closely with the Agricultural Workers Alliance, an organization supported in large part by the UFCW, that provides community and social services to agricultural workers across Canada, including workshops and assistance with filing tax returns, Canada Pension Plan applications, employment insurance and parental benefits claims, workers compensation claims, provincial health coverage, and translation services (Agricultural Workers Alliance, 2013). The Workers' Action Centre in Toronto is one of many community-based worker centres across North America (Fine, 2006) that bring together social justice and labour groups aimed at using community-based mobilization strategies to improve the wages and working and living conditions of vulnerable workers, most of whom are not union members. Childcare coalitions across Canada have mobilized also with the strong support of several unions, including the CAW, British Columbia Government Employees Union and CUPE, all of which ran their own campaigns in support of affordable and accessible child care (Coles and Yates, 2012). These types of broad-based coalitions that rely upon mass membership mobilization and community alliances open a new form of politics to unions that forces them to define issues along class rather than membership lines. These alliances also press unions to engage more seriously with questions of race, gender, citizenship, sexuality, and ability, opening the possibility for a broader coalition not only for progressive politics but also a radical redefinition of union politics.

Yet neoliberalism continues to threaten to undo any such progress. Neoliberalism has leveraged deep cleavages and resentment within the working class between those who hold "good" jobs and those who do not. These resentments are fed by weak labour markets characterized by high un- and under-employment, income insecurity, and employment insecurity. The emphasis on consumer credit further depoliticizes working-class politics as working people and their families are encouraged to adopt an identity defined by levels of consumption, where your right to buy supersedes your right to earn. The long-term effects of neoliberalism are to put unions, and the working class more broadly, on the defensive. Defensive politics have inhibited unions from advancing a clear of vision of an alternative future that would rely more on the redistribution of wealth and the extension of workplace and collective rights. This lack of vision, combined with the internal divisions and competition that riddle the Canadian labour movement, has reduced the possibility of future concerted labour political activism. Consequently, many individual unions are pursuing their own political goals using their own means, often resorting to a politics of pragmatism.

The old socialist and social democratic left offered a blueprint for labour politics in the postwar years that had a decisive effect on political economies around the world. This vision of politics has been eclipsed, and many of the underlying relationships that underpinned unions' involvement in party politics are being undone. This is, however, not to say that class politics is dead—this is merely to suggest that class politics are becoming increasingly more complex, demanding new grassroots responses to very old and powerful political economic structures. For a fleeting moment, it looked as though the Occupy Movement might offer a new alternative to left-wing coalition politics. Unfortunately, this movement burned bright but fast, failing to sustain a broader transformation in progressive politics. Yet, the driving narrative of the Occupy Movement may offer something more lasting for a transformative politics. "We are the 99 per cent" is at its core an expression of anti-capitalism and a biting critique of social, political, and economic inequality (see chapter 5, this volume). For much of the fall of 2011, it was this critique of global capitalism that captured the media's attention and, consequently, part of the broader public's social imagination (Kilibarda, 2012). This provides one example of a critique of the current economy and its inherent inequalities that offers hope for the mobilization of a set of alternative political solutions to those currently advocated by political parties in Canada.

Union renewal—both in the workplace and in politics—requires new organizing strategies, member outreach and engagement and perhaps most importantly, a return to grassroots mobilizing, not only within their memberships *but within their communities more broadly*. This is something for which many others have been calling. Defensive politics—what we have argued is a non-ideological politics of pragmatism—fails to achieve political change, reduces labour politics to particularistic issues and single union actions, and, most significantly, fails to harness the collective power of working people or address the growing diversity and difficulties experienced by workers across Canada. The working class needs, and deserves, better.

NOTES

1 Anderson, 1983, as referenced in Garton and McCallum, 1996.

2 Labour federations are umbrella groups that represent affiliated unions. In Canada, the CLC is the pan-Canadian labour federation while, as discussed in Chapter 11, there are several union federations in Quebec that have supported the nationalist movement. There are also other provincial labour federations across the country. A key function of labour federations is political advocacy.

3 The roots of the Canadian welfare state date back to the turn of the century. For example, British Columbia and Manitoba introduced minimum wage legislation in 1918 (Canada, HRSDC, 2012).

REFERENCES AND FURTHER READING

Agricultural Workers Alliance. 2013. http://www.ufcw.ca/index.php?option= com_content&view=article&id=2009&Itemid=198&lang=en (accessed February 27, 2013).

Avakumovic, Ivan. 1978. *Socialism in Canada: A Study of the CCF-NDP in Federal and Provincial Politics*. Toronto: McClelland and Stewart.

Anderson, Benedict. 1983. *Imagined Communities: Reflections on the Origins and Spread of Nationalism*. London: Verso.

Benzie, Robert. 2011. "Working Families to Launch Election Blitz on Oscar Telecast." *Thestar.com—Ontario* (February 26). http://www.thestar.com/news/ ontario/2011/02/26/working_families_to_launch_election_blitz_on_oscar_ telecast.html.

Briskin, Linda, and Patricia McDermott. 1993. *Women Challenging Unions: Feminism, Democracy, and Militancy*. Toronto: University of Toronto Press.

Burke, Mike, and John Shields. 2000. "Tracking Inequality in the New Canadian Labour Market." In *Restructuring and Resistance: Canadian Public Policy in an Age of Global Capitalism*, ed. Mike Burke, Colin Mooers, and John Shields, 98–123. Halifax: Fernwood.

Camfield, David. 2000. "Assessing Resistance in Harris's Ontario, 1995–1999." In *Restructuring and Resistance: Canadian Public Policy in an Age of Global Capitalism*, ed. Mike Burke, Colin Mooers, and John Shields, 306–317. Halifax: Fernwood.

Canada. Human Resources and Skills Development Canada (HRSDC). Labour Program. 2012. *Minimum Wage Database Introduction*. http://srv116.services. gc.ca/dimt-wid/sm-mw/intro.aspx?lang=eng (accessed September 16, 2013).

Coles, Amanda, and Yates, Charlotte, A.B. 2012. "Unions, Gender Equity and Neoconservative Politics." In *Revisiting the Politics of Labour in Canada*, ed. Larry Savage and Stephanie Ross, 102–15. Halifax: Fernwood.

Corman, June, Meg Luxton, D.W. Livingstone, and Wally Secombe. 1993. *Recasting Steel Labour: The Stelco Story*. Halifax: Fernwood.

Evans, Bryan. 2011. "The Politics of Public Sector Wages: Ontario's Social Dialogue for Austerity." *Socialist Studies/Études socialistes* 7 (1/2): 171–90.

Fairbrother, Peter, and Edward Webster. 2008. "Social Movement Unionism: Questions and Possibilities." *Employee Responsibilities and Rights Journal* 20 (4): 309–13.

Fine, Janice Ruth. 2006. *Worker Centers: Organizing Communities at the Edge of the Dream*. Ithaca, NY: Cornell University Press.

Garton, Stephen, and Margaret E. McCallum. 1996. "Workers' Welfare: Labour and the Welfare State in 20th-century Australia and Canada." *Labour/Le Travail* 38:116–41.

Goar, Carol. 2012. "Two-tiered Wage System Announced by Tories." *Toronto Star* (April 28). http://www.thestar.com/opinion/editorials/article/1168905-two-tiered-wage-system-announced-by-tories (accessed July 6, 2012).

Graefe, Peter. 2012. "Québec Labour: Days of Glory or the Same Old Story?" In *Revisiting the Politics of Labour in Canada*, ed. Larry Savage and Stephanie Ross, 62–74. Halifax: Fernwood.

Horowitz, Gad. 1968. *Canadian Labour in Politics*. Toronto: University of Toronto Press.

Jackson, Andrew, and Bob Baldwin. 2005. *Policy Analysis by the Labour Movement in a Hostile Environment*, Working Paper 41. Kingston: Queen's University School of Policy Studies.

Kilibarda, Konstantin. 2012. "Lessons from #Occupy in Canada: Contesting Space, Settler Consciousness and Erasures Within the 99%." *Journal of Critical Globalisation Studies* 5: 24–41.

Luxton, Meg. 2001. "Feminism as a Class Act: Working-class Feminism and the Women's Movement in Canada." *Labour/Le Travail* 48: 63–88.

McBride, Stephen. 2005. "'If You Don't Know Where You're Going You'll End Up Somewhere Else': Ideological and Policy Failure in the Ontario NDP." In *Challenges and Perils: Social Democracy in Neoliberal Times*, ed. William Carroll and R.S. Ratner, 25–45. Halifax: Fernwood.

McBride, Stephen, and Heather Whiteside. 2011. "Austerity for Whom?" *Socialist Studies/Études socialistes* 7(1/2): 42–64.

Migrant Workers Alliance. 2013. http://www.migrantworkersalliance.org/.

Palmer, Bryan. 1987. *Solidarity: The Rise and Fall of an Opposition in British Columbia*. Vancouver: New Star Books.

Panitch, Leo, and Donald Swartz. 2003. *From Consent to Coercion: The Assault on Trade Union Freedoms*. 3rd ed. Toronto: Garamond.

Public Service Alliance of Canada (PSAC). 2012. PSAC Criticism of Budget Implementation Act (June 6). http://www.psac-afpc.com/news/2012/issues/20120606-e.shtml.

Savage, Larry. 2012. "Organized Labour and the Politics of Strategic Voting." In *Revisiting the Politics of Labour in Canada*, ed. L. Savage and S. Ross, 75–87. Halifax: Fernwood.

Uppal, Sharanjit. 2010. Unionization 2010. Statistics Canada. http://www.statcan.gc.ca/pub/75–001-x/2010110/pdf/11358-eng.pdf.

Uppal, Sharanjit. 2011. Unionization 2011. Statistics Canada. http://www.statcan.gc.ca/pub/75–001-x/2011004/article/11579-eng.htm.

Versace, Vince. 2007. "Working Families Coalition Not a Front for Liberal Party: Dillon." *Daily Commercial News* (September 20). http://www.dailycommercialnews.com/article/id24437.

Whitehorn, Alan. 1993. *Canadian Socialism: Essays on the CCF-NDP*. Don Mills: Oxford University Press.

Yates, Charlotte A. B. 1990. "Labour and Lobbying: A Political Economy Approach." In *Policy Communities and Public Policy in Canada*, ed. W. Coleman and G. Skogstad, 266–90. Toronto: Copp and Pitman.

Yates, Charlotte A. B. 1993. *From Plant to Politics: The Autoworkers Union in Postwar Canada*. Philadelphia: Temple University Press.

THREE

Farm Groups in Canadian Politics

GRACE SKOGSTAD

Along with those who mobilized in support of labour rights, farm groups played a prominent role in the history of radical politics in Canada.[1] In the early decades of the twentieth century, farm organizations set out to transform the role of the Canadian state in agriculture and secured several victories in the process. These early policy successes were garnered during a period when farmers constituted a sizeable portion of the Canadian population. Even as the number of farmers and their voting clout in provincial and federal elections declined decade after decade, farm groups nonetheless continued to exert considerable influence on agricultural and food (agri-food) policy matters.

Although farm groups as a whole continue to exert decisive influence on agricultural and food policy issues, they face several significant challenges today. Major among these challenges are their diminished numbers and organizational fragmentation. Canadian farmers have become less numerous, more specialized, and more diverse. The producers who operate Canada's 200,000 farms comprise less than 3 per cent of the Canadian population. They are differentiated by the commodities they produce, the size of their farms, and, not least, their beliefs about the appropriate role of the state in agricultural markets. Farmers' multiple lines of cleavage are replicated in farm group politics; not one, but multiple organizations exist to represent farmers' interests in the political arena. This organizational fragmentation, especially visible in prairie Canada, hampers the formulation of *national* policies for Canada's agri-food sector.

The specialization and diversification of Canadian agriculture is only one of the challenges confronting contemporary Canadian farm groups. Farm groups must also deal with an expanded policy agenda that includes consumer concerns about food safety and increased public scrutiny of the environmental effects of contemporary agricultural practices. As liberalizing trade agreements remove border protection for agricultural products, an additional challenge for Canadian agriculture is the heightened imperative to be competitive in regionally and globally integrated markets. Both developments broaden the membership of the agri-food policy community beyond the groups representing commodity and food producers that have historically dominated discussions around the role of governments in Canadian agriculture.

Such shifts in the political economy of Canadian agriculture have significantly affected the pattern of farm group politics. If the sector was once organizationally united in pursuit of radical policy change, today it is a sector fragmented by groups divided in their values, goals, and strategies in the political arena. At odds with one another over fundamental policy issues, Canadian farm groups today are as likely to be a force for conservative politics—preserving past policies and upholding the status quo—as they are for radical politics that transform understandings of desirable public policies and farmer-state relations.

It is this transition in the pattern of farm group politics that is the focus of this chapter. It documents how Canadian farmers have organized in the political arena, the issues that have preoccupied them, the strategies they have used to promote these issues, and the factors that have affected the success of farm organizations. The chapter makes the following arguments. First, groups representing Canadian farmers have historically used, and continue today to employ, plural modes of political action to translate their policy preferences into government policy. Second, farm groups' recourse to plural modes of political action is an important factor in accounting for government attention to farm problems. Third, the influence and policy success of any individual farm group varies across issues—and success for one farm group on a specific issue may well mean failure for other farm groups. And fourth, farm group influence is increasingly dependent upon the alignment of a group's goals with non-farmer interests in the agri-food sector and the partisan interests of the incumbent government.

HISTORICAL OVERVIEW

Farmers mobilized from the early twentieth century onward in quest of changes that would improve their economic situation and the quality of life in rural Canada. Material interests were front and centre; farmers sought the assistance of their Canadian and provincial governments in providing them with the marketing institutions, regulations, financial assistance, and trade policies they believed they needed to lower their costs of production and receive higher prices for their products. Constituting hundreds of thousands of independent producers, they had limited individual leverage in the marketplace. They purchased the supplies they needed to produce food (capital to buy land, machinery, and later as agriculture became more mechanized, fuel and fertilizer) from a much smaller number of firms and sold their commodities—such as grain, livestock, and milk—to a limited number of buyers. Prairie farmers, for example, relied on a few grain traders and railway companies to buy and transport their grain to Canadian ports for shipment to overseas markets. In such a market economy, farmers acting individually could not demand a fair price for either their input supplies or the agricultural commodities they produced. They turned to collective action in the political arena and sought the support of governments to improve their terms of trade in the market economy.

In the 1920s and 1930s, the fact that farmers constituted a significant share of the provincial population made electoral politics their ally. Farm groups were the constituent base of political parties that formed the government in Ontario, Alberta, Manitoba, and Saskatchewan.[2] At the national level, farmers championed their causes through the Progressive Party and achieved some success when the Progressives formed the official opposition in the minority Liberal government of Mackenzie King elected in 1925.

Once the number of farmers peaked after 1940 as farm units became increasingly consolidated,[3] collective action through farm organizations became more and more important to farmers' ability to promote their economic interests, especially at the national level. An umbrella national organization of provincial farm groups, the Canadian Chamber of Agriculture, was created in 1935 and renamed the Canadian Federation of Agriculture (CFA) in 1940. Since then, the CFA, whose current members are listed in Table 3.1, has been the foremost nationwide organization advocating on behalf of Canadian farmers.

The organizational strength of the CFA derives from its federal character: it is a federation of general provincial farm organizations, as well as of commodity groups organized on an interprovincial or national basis. Collectively, the CFA's member organizations bring together farmers who produce different commodities, who operate different sized farms, who live in all provinces, and who comprise Canada's two official language groups. The CFA's credibility as an organization of Canadian farmers has depended significantly on the organizational resources of its farm federation and commodity group affiliates. Unlike some of its member organizations, the CFA has no legislative mandate to extract compulsory membership dues from Canadian farmers.

Although the CFA enjoys membership from provincial farm organizations in all Canadian provinces, it has benefited especially from strong provincial

TABLE 3.1   Canadian Farm Organizations: CFA Members

Canadian Federation of Agriculture (CFA)

National Farmers Union (NFU)

Dairy Farmers of Canada

Chicken Farmers of Canada

Canadian Egg Marketing Agency

Canadian Turkey Marketing Agency

Canadian Broiler Hatching Egg Marketing Agency

Canadian Cattlemen's Association

Canadian Pork Council

Canadian Soybean Growers

Canadian Horticultural Council

Grain Growers of Canada (grain and oilseed producers)

Canadian Young Farmers

*Canola Council of Canada

*Canadian Grains Council

*Canadian Agri-Food Trade Alliance (CAFTA)

* Associations represent not only producers but also processors and others involved in the industry.

federations in Ontario and Quebec. In these central Canadian provinces, home to 40 per cent of Canadian farms, general farm organizations have historically had a wide membership base among farmers, financial resources, administrative staff, and ultimately the capacity to provide informed policy advice. The organizational cohesion of Quebec farmers has long been re-markable. The Union catholique des cultivateurs, formed in 1924, became the Union des producteurs agricoles (UPA) in 1972. Legislation passed that year by the Quebec government allowed a single farm organization—which has been the UPA—to accredit itself as the monopoly voice and—especially important—to extract a compulsory membership fee from every Quebec farmer. In Ontario, the Ontario Federation of Agriculture (OFA) is the oldest and largest farm federation by members, but it has two general farm organizational rivals: the Christian Farmers Federation of Ontario and the National Farmers Union-Ontario. Since 1993, all three general farm organizations have been accredited by the Ontario government; that is, farmers are required to pay a membership fee to one of these organizations.

Given the significance of agriculture to the region—45 per cent of Canadian farms are located there—the struggles of general farm organizations in the three prairie provinces to attract members and maintain organizational cohesion since the 1980s has been especially problematic. Here, conflicts between growers of different commodities—most notably, between farmers who grow grain and want a high price for it and those who raise livestock and want cheap feed grain for their animals—have often challenged the capacity of general farm federations to broker competing interests. This conflict of economic interest came to a head in the early 1980s when the Trudeau Liberal government set out to end a 90-year-old statutory obligation on Canadian railway companies to ship prairie grain to export terminals at fixed and low costs to farmers. Grain farmers opposed the Liberal government's move, worried that the loss of the export subsidy would mean higher freight costs for them. Prairie livestock farmers, who would be able to purchase locally grown grain for their cattle more cheaply, supported the railway companies in their determination to end the Crow's Nest freight rates. Provincial farm federations in the three prairie provinces, and the CFA itself, found it impossible to represent both groups of farmers. The eventual policy solution—an increase in freight rates but one largely paid for by the Government of Canada—did not prevent the collapse of the provincial farm federations in Saskatchewan and Alberta (Skogstad, 1987: 139–141).

Since the early 1980s, groups representing specific commodity growers—wheat, barley, canola, and cattle, for example—have become better organized, spurred on in part by public funding from provincial and/or national governments. For example, the Canadian government financially supported the creation of the Canada Grains Council, as an organizational competitor to the prairie wheat pools that were members of the CFA. The Alberta government subsidized the creation of the Palliser Wheat Growers Association (later renamed the Western Canadian Wheat Growers Association) and the Western Barley Growers Association in the 1970s. While most commodity groups belong to the CFA, some large commodity groups have either been intermittent members or are not currently members (e.g., the organization representing Canadian cattlemen). These commodity organizations are philosophically committed to a greater role for market forces and a lesser role for state intervention in Canadian agriculture.

Besides specialist commodity organizations, the CFA also has a rival general farm federation in the form of the National Farmers Union (NFU). Organized first in the 1930s in the three prairie provinces, the current NFU dates from 1969 when farmers' unions in Saskatchewan, Manitoba, Ontario, and British Columbia merged. They were later joined by farmers' unions in Alberta and the Maritime provinces. In contrast to the CFA's federated structure, the NFU is a direct membership organization of farm families. With an estimated 10,000 members, the NFU represents far fewer Canadian farmers (4 per cent) than the CFA and, indeed, fewer farmers than do some commodity organizations. A major representational handicap is the NFU's lack of representation in Quebec, the home of 12 per cent of Canadian farmers and, as noted above, the best organized on a provincial level.[4] The NFU's chronic problem of inadequate financing and debt has been alleviated in part since Ontario implemented legislation in 1993 accrediting it as one of three farm organizations eligible for a due when farmers sell their commodities.

Although some Canadian farmers belong to both the CFA and NFU, the NFU has its base in small and medium-sized family farms whereas the CFA's member organizations also include operators of large farms. To preserve the family farm, the NFU, unlike the CFA, has opposed government policies geared toward rendering farmers more competitive through consolidation of farm units and adoption of technological advancements. These positions have limited the NFU's influence with both Liberal and Conservative governments. On selected positions on which the NFU and CFA agree—the importance of preserving orderly marketing in the export grain sector (via the Canadian Wheat Board's monopoly) and supply management in the dairy and poultry sectors—the two organizations worked in concert to influence national Liberal governments.

POLITICAL ISSUES, MODES OF POLITICAL ACTION, AND SUCCESS

The most enduring issues that have preoccupied Canadian farm groups are economic issues and, more specifically, the intertwined issues of farm commodity prices and farm income stability. In pursuit of higher and more stable farm incomes, farmers have sought to influence government policies that directly affect farmers' profitability, namely and most prominently, farm income support programs, marketing institutions that regulate markets for agricultural products, external trade policy, rural transportation infrastructure, and farm credit. In recent years, the issues on farm groups' agenda has had to expand to include matters that are of concern to the non-farm population such as food safety, environmental protection, and products of modern biotechnology (genetic modification, GM).[5]

In pursuit of their goals, farmers and farm groups have always used multiple modes of political action. As noted above, in the early twentieth century when they formed a significant part of the population, farmers not only organized into groups but also formed their own political parties rather than rely on the Conservative and Liberal parties to represent their interests. Today, like most interest groups, farm organizations are officially non-partisan even if their leaders have not always been.[6] Nonetheless, some organizations have closer links with a particular political party than with others; for example, commodity groups representing western oilseeds and grain farmers make little effort to conceal their partisan support for the Harper Conservative Party.

The CFA and the largest commodity groups have usually attempted to achieve their goals as members of the policy community, seeking to persuade officials and politicians with responsibility for agri-food policy to adopt policies that serve their (farmers') interests. However, farm groups have not relied exclusively on bargaining with government officials inside the policy community. Rather, they have used a full repertoire of tactics, including lobbying parliamentarians, mass demonstrations of their members on the grounds of legislatures, and litigation to challenge the authority of governments when they proceed with unwanted policies. Mass demonstrations have often been vital to securing coveted public policies. The creation of the national system of dairy supply management in the late 1960s (discussed below) followed repeated demonstrations on Parliament Hill by thousands of Quebec and Ontario farmers and their provincial farm union leaders. In more recent years, when farm incomes have suffered in the face of crop failures and/or low commodity prices, farm demonstrations, including tractor blockades of capital city roads, have been commonplace. Both the CFA and NFU use protest politics. Farm groups have also launched publicity campaigns to inform and sway urban public opinion. Who among us, who goes to the movies or watches television, has not been urged to "Drink Milk" (and save farms in rural Canada) and been reminded that "Farmers Feed Cities?"

Indeed, the success of Canadian farm groups in the political arena turns increasingly on their ability to form coalitions with other components of the agri-food sector. The need for coalitions is apparent in both the domestic and international arenas. For the CFA and commodity groups, coalition allies usually include groups representing other agribusinesses, that is, food processors, food manufacturers, input suppliers, and credit institutions. The NFU has partnered with the Council of Canadians[7] to oppose international trade agreements and with social action groups organized around such issues as local food security and environmental issues.[8] In the international arena, the NFU is a founding member of La Via Campesina, an international social movement of almost 70 organizations in over 30 countries opposed to free trade agreements. For its part, the CFA is a member of an international coalition of farm groups in Europe, Asia, and North Africa committed to fair and equitable world trade rules. These international networks are especially visible at sites of international trade negotiations. National capitals are targets of political action at other times; for example, the Cattlemen's Association has repeatedly lobbied politicians in Washington to open American markets to

Canadian beef, often in concert with American groups that are disadvantaged by restrictions on Canadian imports.

Canadian farm groups thus draw on plural modes of conventional and protest political action in an effort to secure their public policy goals and do so with varying degrees of success. It is not possible within the confines of this chapter to discuss all the political issues that have consumed the attention of farm groups (and governments) in recent decades. However, the following issues provide insight into the strategies used by farm groups to press their interests and the success farm groups individually and collectively have enjoyed. The survey demonstrates that the success of farm groups is importantly affected by, first, the degree of unanimity/discord across farm groups in their preferred public policies; second, the alignment of their goals with other interests in the agri-food policy community; and third, the congruence of farm groups' preferences with the political philosophy and goals of incumbent governments.

Farm Income Support Programs

It was not the first issue around which farm groups mobilized historically, but at least since the 1930s Depression when agricultural commodity prices—and farm incomes—plummeted dramatically, government measures to raise and stabilize farm incomes have been a chronic quest of most farm organizations. Farm incomes can decline because of a drop in a farmer's volume of production (when a drought or disease wipes out a crop or poultry flock, for example) and/or in market prices (because of producer supply exceeding consumer demand). Fluctuations in agricultural commodity prices are commonplace. When their members suffer significant income losses—as Canadian beef producers did when their export markets closed following the discovery of BSE in Alberta in May 2003—even commodity groups, such as the Canadian Cattlemen's Association, that are philosophically opposed to governments intervening in the marketplace, have lobbied hard for government payments to help farmers cover their losses.

Farmers first secured federal financial assistance to support commodity prices during World War II. In subsequent decades, their concerted lobbying led to stabilization programs for all major commodities being established by the 1970s. These programs, which required governments to make payments to farmers when prices of their commodities fell below a pre-determined amount (Skogstad, 1987: ch. 4), meant the state (governments) reduced farmers' income risks in the marketplace.[9] By the late 1980s, the Canadian government was intent on reforming income stabilization programs. Not only were the programs costly for deficit- and debt-riddled governments, domestic income support measures were widely criticized for distorting international trade markets and a target for reform during the Uruguay Round multilateral General Agreement on Tariffs and Trade (GATT) trade negotiations.

Over the next two decades, Canadian governments repeatedly redesigned farm income support programs in an effort to make them compatible with not only the provisions of the WTO Agreement on Agriculture but also their own fiscal capacity. Through to 2012, although farm groups often fell short in achieving the level of farm income support they sought and had to assume a bigger portion of the cost of insuring their individual income risks, they nonetheless prevailed in persuading Canadian governments of different political stripes that farmers alone should not shoulder the burden of ensuring they are sufficiently profitable to remain in business. How did they do so?

Among the most important factors that account for farm groups' influence on farm income support programs is the continuous involvement of the CFA and other farm organizations in the redesign of these programs. Inside a policy network constituted also by agribusiness representatives and government officials, farm groups have been at the table in designing income safety net programs and, later, business risk management programs—as they have been called.[10] Over time, these policy networks became more pluralist; while producer groups continued to enjoy strong representation, they were joined by representatives of input suppliers, food processors, the financial sector (banks), the retail sector, and academics. By no means are these policy networks conflict-free; CFA leaders have periodically complained that they are not treated by agricultural officials and ministers as full partners in the design of the income support programs that they co-finance. They have also sometimes broken down when farm groups have lost trust in government officials (Skogstad, 2008: 99–101).

Farm groups have certainly not relied exclusively on bargaining with government officials inside policy networks to get the financial assistance they believe they need. They have often had to mount publicly visible campaigns to get government action. In the late 1990s and early 2000s, as farm incomes plummeted across many commodity producers and existing income safety nets failed to compensate farmers sufficiently for their losses, farm groups united to build a broad coalition to press for more government financial assistance. The coalition included business and financial organizations whose fate is closely tied to the well-being of the farm community, political parties of all persuasion, and provincial governments. Two prairie premiers personally petitioned the prime minister, the opposition parties launched emergency debates on agriculture in the House of Commons, parliamentary agriculture committees held hearings and issued reports recommending more government assistance, and the rural caucus of the governing Liberal Party concurred. All these actions were augmented by public demonstrations drawing attention to farm income woes. The all-party support farmers garnered succeeded in securing ad hoc, income disaster assistance programs and caused government transfers to the farm community to rise quite dramatically (Skogstad, 2008: ch. 3). These ad hoc programs were followed subsequently by a new suite of income support programs. Although their configuration differed from one five-year lifespan to another, these programs transferred significant payments from Canadian governments to Canadian farmers through to April 2013.

The impressive past success of Canadian farm groups in securing income support payments from Canadian governments is no guarantee of future success. In late 2012, the Conservative agriculture minister and his officials warned Canadian farmers that a new farm program framework, one that encouraged greater farmer competitiveness and reduced government support, was on its way. For their part, farm leaders reported inadequate input into the design of new program options (Wilson, 2012a: 16–17).

Marketing Institutions and Market Regulation

Besides the high tariffs of the National Policy (discussed below), a major impetus to the political mobilization of Canadian farmers historically was their desire to obtain better terms of trade with those from whom they purchased their supplies and to whom they sold their commodities. They reasoned that by organizing collectively in the marketplace they could exert more influence than acting as individual buyers or sellers. Producer-owned and controlled marketing cooperatives, in the form of the wheat pools in the three prairie provinces, were one example. These voluntary marketing institutions fell short, however, of farmers' goal of establishing marketing institutions with real bargaining power. They succeeded when the Government of Canada created the Canadian Wheat Board and gave it a monopoly in 1943 to purchase prairie-grown wheat for export (and barley, in 1949).

The Canadian Wheat Board had no powers to set prices for prairie-grown wheat (or barley), but the national marketing boards established in the dairy, chicken, and egg sectors in the late 1960s and 1970s did. They came into existence during a period when net farm incomes for many farmers were declining and following concerted lobbying and mass demonstrations by farm groups, especially those based in Ontario and Quebec.[11] In these "supply managed" sectors, national marketing agencies limit the volume of production of the commodity (milk, chickens, eggs) to the estimated market demand and, further, either set or negotiate the price at which the commodity is purchased. Restrictions on imports (initially, quotas and today, tariffs) provide protection from lower-cost imports. These marketing boards increase the ability of producers to extract a much better price for their product than an unregulated market would yield (Skogstad, 1987: ch. 5). Alongside government income support measures, the supply management marketing boards signalled an important measure of government intervention in agricultural markets.

If there was once virtual unanimity among grain farmers on the desirability of institutions of collective marketing as a way to increase farmer bargaining power over commodity prices, it is not the case today. The tensions across Canadian farm groups over the trade policy implications of supply management marketing boards are discussed below. Here the discussion focuses on divisions across farm groups on the export monopoly of the Canadian Wheat Board. The battle that waged over more than two decades regarding the export monopoly of the Canadian Wheat Board highlights several features of contemporary farm group politics. It reveals, first, the deep cleavages within the farm community over the appropriate role of the state in agricultural marketing; second, the wide repertoire of modes of political action that farm groups have used to translate their policy preferences into government policy; and third, the contingency of the success of organized farm group politics on the congruence of their goals with the goals of governing parties.

From the late 1980s onward, commodity groups representing prairie wheat and barley producers, whose members resented having to sell their crops to the Wheat Board and believed they should have individual freedom to decide to whom to sell their grain, challenged the Canadian Wheat Board's monopoly over exports of prairie-grown wheat, durum, and barley crops. While these farmers and their organizations scored some early victories with the incumbent Mulroney Progressive Conservative government in limiting the Wheat Board's mandate, their victories were overturned by the courts. The election of the Liberal Party in 1993 stymied the success of opponents of the Wheat Board monopoly for almost two decades, and their recourse to the legal arena to challenge the constitutionality of the Wheat Board's monopoly also failed. In office as a minority government after 2006, the Harper Conservative government, which had long campaigned for an end to the Wheat Board's monopoly, was knocked back by the courts. The governments' executive order to rid the Wheat Board of its monopoly over export barley sales, ruled the Federal Court, was illegal; a change to the Wheat Board's mandate, said the Court, required a statute of Parliament. Having secured a parliamentary majority in the May 2011 election, the Harper Conservative government then exercised its constitutional authority to end the Wheat Board's monopoly on export sales. Although opponents of the government's action mounted a legal challenge, waged public demonstrations across the prairies, and secured the support of federal opposition parties, they were unsuccessful in their endeavour to preserve the Wheat Board's export monopoly.[12]

Trade Policy

One of the earliest issues that propelled farmers into political action in the early decades of the twentieth century was the Government of Canada's National Policy of high tariffs on imported manufactured goods. The tariffs that protected Canadian manufacturers in the domestic market by driving up the costs of imports also increased the prices farmers paid for imported machinery. This discriminatory trade policy was eventually eliminated in the post–World War II period, as international negotiations under the GATT substantially reduced tariffs on imported manufactured products across all industrialized countries.

The implementation of supply management in the dairy, egg, and poultry sectors in the late 1960s and 1970s has made external trade policy a source of division across producers. Commodity organizations representing dairy and poultry producers, as well as the two general farm organizations, have lobbied hard for retention of the restrictions on imports of dairy and poultry products and for continuing protection of Canadian supply managed sectors. While these groups seek a protectionist trade policy, groups representing farmers (producers of grains, oilseeds, cattle, and hogs) who depend for up to 50 per cent of their farm cash receipts on export markets support liberalized trade. Liberal trade agreements give these farmers access to additional markets and the possibility of higher prices for products competitive in foreign markets.

Given the conflict of economic interest between export-oriented and import-oriented farmers, the negotiation of international trade agreements is difficult for general farm organizations whose membership includes both types. The CFA has always attempted to bridge the differences by urging Canadian governments to "achieve the maximum possible access for agricultural exports, but also respect the domestic interests of Canadian farmers."[13] Other organizations have made clear choices between agricultural protectionism and trade liberalization. The NFU is highly critical of free trade agreements, believing that they invariably limit the powers of governments to protect domestic producers and benefit global corporations. Specialist commodity groups make no effort to bridge what they think is unbridgeable but rather engage in coalition politics to press their positions on governments. Grain commodity groups united as the Canadian Agricultural Policy Alliance, and, since 2001 in alliance with other export-oriented groups under the umbrella of the Canadian Agri-Food Trade Alliance (CAFTA), lobby strenuously for the Canadian government to adopt a policy of liberal trade across all commodities. Groups representing dairy, egg, and poultry farmers have likewise banded together to defend supply management.

Farm groups have used several modes of political action in an effort to shape the outcomes of the regional and global liberalizing trade agreements negotiated by Canadian governments since the mid-1980s. At the invitation of the Government of Canada, general farm groups such as the CFA and UPA, as well as commodity groups, participated in the Sectoral Advisory Groups on International Trade (SAGIT), first established by Mulroney's Progressive Conservative government (1984–93) to receive industry input during the negotiations of the CUFTA, NAFTA, and Uruguay Round of GATT negotiations (1986–93) and continued by successor Liberal governments (1993–2006). The SAGITs have not been able to resolve the obvious conflicts of interest between export- and domestic-oriented producers other than in terms of the "balanced position" of the CFA, that is, maintaining protection for supply managed commodities even while pursuing trade liberalization for other Canadian farm products.

Membership in the trade policy community has certainly not been the only mode of political action used by farm groups to press their trade policy preferences. To publicize their position, farm groups, especially those seeking to protect supply management from trade liberalization, have demonstrated publicly in provincial capitals, Ottawa, and at European sites of trade negotiations.[14] They have also successfully lobbied parliamentarians. In November 2005, the House of Commons unanimously endorsed a motion by Bloc Québécois member, André Bellavance, that stated the Government of Canada should mandate its negotiators to preserve the existing import restrictions on supply managed sectors during the Doha Round negotiations of the WTO.[15] A similar motion had been unanimously passed a week earlier by the Quebec National Assembly. Through to the end of 2012, the Harper Conservative government maintained the trade position of earlier Canadian governments, declaring its determination to preserve import protection for supply managed foodstuffs even while seeking trade liberalization for other commodities.

An Expanded Policy Agenda: Environmental and Social Issues

The above discussion captures key policy preoccupations of Canadian farm groups in recent decades. It does not include policy issues raised by civil society actors not historically part of the agri-food policy community but who are increasingly interested in how the food they consume is produced and the broader social and environmental impacts of existing modes of food production. Their concerns include biotechnology/genetically engineered crops and foods, the sustainability of the environment given current agricultural practices, and local food security. Although the NFU has often joined civil society organizations in pressing their positions on these issues to governments, they have not yet had much success to date in penetrating circles of agri-food policy-making (Abergel and McRae, 2012: 272).

The case of biotechnology is illustrative of the failure of civil society groups to dissuade governments away from agri-food policies that are seen to improve farmers' profitability. The Government of Canada's pro-biotechnology policy, intended to expedite farmers' access to GM seeds that pose no hazards to the environment or human health, has been a target of opposition by several organizations. Groups representing organic farmers, environmental groups,[16] the Council of Canadians, the Biotechnology Action Network, and the NFU—to name some of the most prominent—believe that genetically engineered (GE) plants pose serious environmental risks and potential health hazards. Accordingly, they have advocated for Canada to adopt a more precautionary approach to GE foods, including labelling them. The very real possibility that GE crops will contaminate non-GE crops (including organic crops) has also led to demands for changes to Canadian biotechnology regulations to make the licensing of GE products contingent upon consumer acceptance and farmer profitability. Canadian governments, Liberal and Conservative, have resisted all such reforms, coming down firmly on the side of the biotechnology companies, Canadian oilseeds commodity groups, and the CFA who oppose mandatory labelling and support the current promotional regulatory framework.

Notwithstanding its commitment to biotechnology, the Chrétien Liberal government did engage in a consultative exercise on biotechnology over the period 1999 to 2006. It created the Canadian Biotechnology Advisory Committee (CBAC) with a mandate to elicit advice from experts and repre-sentatives of the general public on policy issues related to the health, envi-ronmental, ethical, social, economic, and regulatory aspects of biotechnology. Although representatives of civil society groups critical of biotechnology were invited to participate, all but two boycotted CBAC's public consultation exercise. The process, they argued, was inherently flawed, with too many members with connections to or sympathetic with the biotechnology industry (Abergel, 2012: 111). The boycott, concludes Abergel (2012: 114), "failed" in-sofar as it failed to bring to the attention of Parliament or the wider Canadian public the issues and concerns of anti-GM organism activists.

The various policy fields discussed above confirm the considerable influ-ence of Canadian farm groups on agri-food issues. Yet, success for some farm groups can mean failure for other farm groups, given their often conflicting goals. Farm groups that are comparatively successful with one governing party—say, the CFA with Liberal governments—may lose influence when another governing party with other political priorities comes to office.

To the degree that a united voice is a more influential voice, the decline of the CFA as the representative of Canadian farmers is a development that bodes ill for the influence of Canadian famers as a whole. In the early 1980s, a veteran journalist of Canadian agricultural politics, Barry Wilson, described the CFA as "the most credible, respected, and listened-to farm organization in Ottawa" (Wilson, 1981: 245). A decade later, his appraisal was much more negative: the CFA was "lacking credibility or representation among more than half of Canada's farmers and struggling to control divisions even among those groups it counted as members" (Wilson, 1990: 142). Rather than being at the centre of important agricultural policy debates, the CFA was often relegated to the sidelines while its member organizations or non-member specialist commodity groups took centre stage. While the account of farm income safety nets sketched above would negate this view, Wilson's (2012b: 10) current appraisal of the CFA's role in policy development remains grim: "After more than 75 years of being Canada's primary 'house of agriculture' farm lobby, the CFA largely has been sidelined by this [the Conservatives led by Prime Minister Stephen Harper] government" and is "no longer the go-to farm lobby."

Is the decline of the CFA permanent, or will Canada's foremost national farm organization recapture its influence with a change in government in Ottawa? What should we expect by way of future collective action in Canada's farm community and farm groups' influence with governments? The final section probes answers to these questions by examining how the political economy of Canadian agriculture has affected the mobilization and influence of farm groups in the past and is likely to do so in the future.

THEORETICAL CONSIDERATIONS AND CONCLUSIONS

Past and current mobilization of Canadian farm groups, and their influence in the political arena, has been significantly shaped by the political economy of agriculture in Canada. By political economy, I mean the economic structures of agricultural production and marketing, as well as the political institutions that shape and interact with these same economic structures.

To recapitulate the discussion above, the economic structure of Canadian agriculture gives Canada's farmers strong incentives to engage in collective action in the political arena. Agricultural production is a sector of individual commodity producers; as noted in the introduction to the chapter, they now number 200,000. These farmers share a mutual identity as producers of food. They also share a mutual interest in that their contribution to the agri-food economy has declined over the years. Today, most of the one in seven Canadian jobs attributed to the agri-food sector are located off the farm, upstream in the farm input supply sector, or, more often, downstream in the food manufacturing, retail, and distribution sectors. Concentration in all these off-farm sectors impairs farmers' economic bargaining power and, historically and today, has given farmers the shared interest of seeking allies in the political arena to help them achieve the (economic) outcomes denied them in the marketplace. United under umbrella farm organizations such as the CFA or the NFU, their collective political influence is stronger than that exerted as individuals or members of specialist commodity groups.

At the same time, the structure of contemporary Canadian agriculture also gives farmers the incentive to conceive of their collective interests in fairly narrow terms. Farmers produce a range of commodities, high prices for some of which (grain) are high costs for other (livestock, poultry) farmers. Some—producers of grains, oilseeds, cattle, and hogs—rely importantly on export markets, while others—producers of milk, eggs, and poultry—are sold almost exclusively in the domestic market. As discussed above, this division between export- and domestic-oriented producers is a result of government policies, not dictated by economic or geographic factors of production. Further divisions occur between large commercial operators whose income is derived solely from agriculture and smaller, less viable farmers who often have to supplement their farm income with off-farm jobs. Such differences in how farmers earn their living often make it easier for Canadian farmers to conceive of their interests in fairly narrow terms (as cattlemen, for example) and, consistent with the logic of Mancur Olson (1965), give the advantage to groups that represent farmers' interests as producers of a shared commodity rather than as farmers who share a common fate with producers of different commodities.

Economic globalization—in the form of the integration of commodity markets, usually as a result of trade agreements such as the CUFTA, NAFTA, and WTO—has made it more difficult for general farm organizations to manage existing lines of division (between import and export sectors and small versus large farmers). The terms of international trade agreements, compounded with domestic agri-food policy changes, have resulted in some Canadian farmers (producers of grains and oilseeds) being more exposed to greater international competition in foreign and domestic markets than other producers (dairy, egg, and poultry farmers). Large commercial operators of export-dependent commodities—whose scale of operations arguably situates them favourably to be competitive on international markets—perceive their economic interests not only to be at odds with those of domestically protected farmers. They are also, as the emergence of CAFTA indicates, more likely to perceive their allies to be the agribusinesses that sell their products in export markets.

If economic globalization makes life harder for umbrella farm groups (as compared to specialist commodity organizations), it nonetheless gives farmers strong incentives to continue to mobilize collectively—and for governments to continue to invite farm organizations into the agri-food policy community. The integration of agri-food markets—by removing border restrictions to trade such as tariffs and import quotas—has not included the removal of a host of non-tariff and technical barriers to trade. The latter include domestic product standards with respect to food and environmental safety and quality assurance, for example, requirements in the European Union for GM foods to be labelled as such and prohibitions on the import of beef from animals injected with certain growth hormones. Canadian farmers, like those elsewhere, need collective action if they are to prevail in persuading governments to press their interests on such matters to other governments. For their part, governments also need the information provided by farm organizations to negotiate effectively for agri-food and agri-environmental policies that serve the economic interests of Canadian farmers.

The economic structure of agricultural production in Canada works in concert with Canada's political institutional framework to affect farmers' collective action opportunities, incentives, and influence. Under Canada's federal Constitution, agriculture is a concurrent jurisdiction; provincial and national governments share legislative authority and expenditure responsibility with regard to several agricultural matters, including research, price or income support, credit, and production incentives. On other matters—marketing of agricultural commodities, for example—authority is divided between the two orders of government. The provinces regulate marketing within their borders while the Government of Canada exercises exclusive authority over interprovincial and export marketing. This political-institutional framework gives incentives for farmers to organize on both provincial and national levels. National organization, either as a national commodity group or a general farm organization, is needed because the effective redress of many problems requires the cooperation of the (10) provincial and (one) national governments. Collective action on a provincial and commodity-specific basis is also encouraged by the exercise of legal authority of provincial governments on a host of agri-food and agri-environmental issues and by the concentration of certain commodities in particular provinces/regions.

How does Canada's federal system affect the influence of Canadian farm groups? On the one hand, there is some evidence that farm groups do suffer from the opportunity provided by shared jurisdiction for "buck passing" and "blame avoidance"—that is, for one order of government to shift responsibility for problems (such as financial responsibility for disaster assistance) to the other order of government. It is also the case, as Simeon (1972: 282) has suggested and the CFA has complained, that executive federalism—the Canadian practice of federal and provincial/territorial governments negotiating important policy matters behind closed doors—can undermine the influence of farm organizations. In these intergovernmental forums, the interests and goals of governments can often take precedence over those of the farm groups outside the room.

On the other hand, the weight of evidence suggests that Canada's federal system has historically increased the influence of farm groups, giving them two orders of government and up to 11 domestic venues (14 if the three territorial governments are included) in which to lobby. Farm groups have very often worked in alliance with provincial governments to improve their bargaining leverage with the Government of Canada. As the examples of farm income support programs and supply management show, this strategy works especially well on policy issues of shared federal-provincial jurisdiction. Even on matters of exclusive federal jurisdiction—such as the negotiation of international trade agreements and disputes surrounding them—farm groups have found provincial governments to be important allies in presenting their case to the Government of Canada.

The record of considerable success for farmers' collective action to date is not likely to disappear. What does seem clear, however, is that farm groups seeking to maintain government intervention—via either regulation of markets or fiscal transfers—are unlikely to secure their goals. The current Harper Conservative government, like governments in all Western industrialized countries, is committed to rolling back the state's presence in agriculture. The farm groups that will be successful are those whose goals are consistent with its deregulatory and market-oriented philosophy (i.e., livestock, oilseed, and cattle commodity groups). At the same time, unlike their beleaguered counterparts in Europe, Canadian farm groups are likely to continue to be successful in warding off challenges from public interest groups critical of current agricultural production practices. On matters of agricultural and food policy, Canadian farm groups, especially those that share the incumbent government's policy goals, will continue to enjoy privileged access to agri-food policy-makers.

NOTES

1   Insofar as agriculture is a shared jurisdiction by virtue of Canada's Constitution, a comprehensive account of Canadian farm groups would provide an account of farm group activities and influence not only at the Canada-wide level but also in Canada's 10 provinces and three territories. Consistent with the goal of this volume to provide insights into the activity of groups and social movements nationwide, this chapter focuses on farm groups that endeavour to influence the policies of Canadian governments for the agricultural and food sectors.

2   The United Farmers of Ontario formed the government in Ontario from 1919 to 1923 in coalition with the Independent Labour Party; the United Farmers of Alberta formed the government of Alberta from 1921 to 1935;

farm groups constituted themselves as the Progressive Party and were elected to office in Manitoba in 1922; and farm groups merged with labour groups to form the Co-operative Commonwealth Federation, which was elected to office in Saskatchewan in 1943.

3   Farm numbers peaked at 750,000 in 1941; they have since declined to 200,000 today.

4   Although the Quebec farm union adheres to much of the NFU's philosophy regarding state responsibility for agriculture, it was a member of the CFA before the NFU came into existence in 1969 as a national organization. By then, the UPA leaders had established a good working relationship with the CFA and saw little to gain by joining the upstart farm union

5   Issues of reform of domestic political institutions have not been central to the largest Canadian farm groups since the early twentieth century when farm organizations advocated forms of popular or direct democracy as a replacement to disciplined political parties.

6   For example, while the CFA and NFU are both officially non-partisan, Bob Friesen stepped down as CFA president to run as a Liberal Party candidate in the 2008 election, and Wayne Easter, a former president of the NFU (1982–1993), ran and was elected as a Liberal MP in 1993.

7   The Council of Canadians is a broad-based coalition that includes labour unions and generally opposes liberalizing trade agreements. It takes credit for helping to defeat the proposed Multilateral Agreement on Investment and stalling the launch of the Doha WTO Round.

8   See http://www.nfu.ca/links/networks-and-coalitions where the NFU lists its membership in networks devoted to food security (Food Secure Canada), small scale agriculture around the world (La Via Campesina), limiting the rights of biotechnology companies (Canadian Biotechnology Action Network), environmental issues (Canadian Environmental Network), and action on climate change (Climate Action Network).

9   The Agricultural Stabilization Act, passed in 1958 and amended in 1975, obliged government payments for nine commodities. The Western Grain Stabilization Act, implemented in 1976, made payments to contributing producers in order to stabilize the net profit of the six principal cereals grown in the prairie region.

10   The NFU refused to participate then and in subsequent similar efforts.

11   Skogstad (1987: 45) provides details of farmers' demonstrations in 1964, 1965, and 1967, the last of which involved 15,000 to 20,000 farmers, led by the Ontario Farmers Union, the OFA, and the Union catholique des cultivateurs de Quebec, marching on Parliament Hill to demand higher milk prices. Quebec farmers also used their voting strength in that province to elect 26 and 20 Social Credit members, respectively, in the 1962 and 1963 general elections. Their

support for the Social Credit Party undoubtedly played a role in the Liberal Party's failure to secure a minority government in the 1962 election and a majority in the 1963 election.

12   For a fuller account of developments through to the majority election of the Conservative government, see Skogstad, 2008, chapter 4.

13   CFA Standing Policy 2012 at http://www.cfa-fca.ca/sites/default/files/Policy%20Manual_E_2012_0.pdf.

14   Ontario's Federation of Agriculture and Quebec's UPA provided the leadership and numbers for street demonstrations in Montreal, Ottawa, and Brussels during ministerial meetings of the Uruguay Round of GATT negotiations. These negotiations were the most crucial to date for Canada's farm sector because until then agriculture had largely been excluded from the liberalizing impacts of the GATT trade regime.

15   André Bellavance, "Evidence," House of Commons Debates, 38th Parliament, 1st Session, No. 155, November 22, 2005: 1010 (recorded time).

16   The environmental groups include Greenpeace Canada, the Canadian Environmental Law Association, and the Environmental Law Centre.

REFERENCES AND FURTHER READING

Abergel, Elisabeth. 2012. "The Canadian Biotechnology Advisory Committee: Legitimacy, Participation, and Attempts to Improve GE Regulation in Canada." In *Health and Sustainability in the Canadian Food System: Advocacy and Opportunity for Civil Society*, ed. Rod McRae and Elisabeth Abergel, 97–126. Vancouver: University of British Columbia Press.

Abergel, Elisabeth, and Rod McRae. 2012. "Conclusion." In *Health and Sustainability in the Canadian Food System: Advocacy and Opportunity for Civil Society*, ed. Rod McRae and Elisabeth Abergel, 271–80. Vancouver: University of British Columbia Press.

Halpin, Darren, ed. 2005. *Surviving Global Change? Agricultural Interest Groups in Comparative Perspective*. Aldershot, UK: Ashgate.

McRae, Rod, Julia Langer, and Vijay Cuddeford. 2012. "Lessons from Twenty Years of CSO Advocacy to Advance Sustainable Pest Management in Canada." In *Health and Sustainability in the Canadian Food System: Advocacy and Opportunity for Civil Society*, ed. Rod McRae and Elisabeth Abergel, 127–52. Vancouver: University of British Columbia Press.

Olson, Mancur. 1965. *The Logic of Collective Action: Public Goods and the Theory of Groups*. Cambridge, MA: Harvard University Press.

Simeon, Richard. 1972. *Federal-Provincial Diplomacy: The Making of Recent Policy in Canada*. Toronto: University of Toronto Press.

Skogstad, Grace. 1987. *The Politics of Agricultural Policy-Making in Canada*. Toronto: University of Toronto Press.

Skogstad, Grace. 2005. "The Uphill Struggle to Prevail: National Farm Organizations in Canada." In *Surviving Global Change? Agricultural Interest Groups in Comparative Perspective*, ed. Darren Halpin, 189–212. Aldershot, UK: Ashgate.

Skogstad, Grace. 2008. *Internationalization and Canadian Agriculture*. Toronto: University of Toronto Press.

Wilson, Barry. 1981. *Beyond the Harvest: Canadian Grain at the Crossroads*. Saskatoon: Western Producer Prairie Books.

Wilson, Barry. 1990. *Farming the System: How Politicians and Producers Shape Canadian Agricultural Policy*. Saskatoon: Western Producer Prairie Books.

Wilson, Barry. 2012a. "Feds Deny Cost Cutting Behind Farm Program Change." *The Western Producer* (August 16): 16–17.

Wilson, Barry. 2012b. "Oldest Farm Organization Sidelined in Conservative Majority Era." *The Western Producer* (March 1): 10.

FOUR

Mobilizing on the Defensive: Anti-Poverty Advocacy and Activism in Times of Austerity[1]

JONATHAN GREENE

After a period of respite on the homeless front in Toronto, the shelter wars have heated up again. Sparked first by the decision of the city to close the Schoolhouse Shelter, followed by a crisis of overcrowding in emergency shelters and a notable rise in homeless deaths, activists and advocates mobilized urgently. Over the course of several months in the winter of 2012–13, the Ontario Coalition Against Poverty (OCAP)—the organization at the forefront of this activism—wrote letters, made deputations to council, organized demonstrations, and staged an "occupation" outside the mayor's office, leading up to a squat of Toronto's main civic centre. Demanding a stop to overcrowding in homeless shelters and homeless deaths, protesters at the squat invited homeless people to "take shelter at Metro Hall."

These recent actions on homelessness mark a change in the focus of anti-poverty activism and advocacy in Toronto in recent years. While never abandoning the issues of housing and homelessness altogether, through much of the past decade the mobilizing attention of anti-poverty activists, including OCAP, has been directed at other priorities: "raising the rates," reforming social assistance, and influencing the provincial government's poverty reduction strategy. Their tactics over this period have also been less visibly confrontational. The sense of urgency that has been generated in recent months—and the contentious activism that has ensued—is reminiscent of an earlier movement cycle that emerged in the province after 1995 but had its roots in a period of reform beginning much earlier, one that had as its central focus a visible crisis of homelessness. The pinnacle moment of this earlier mobilization of poor and homeless people and their supporters was a 1,500-person demonstration at Queen's Park in 2000—remembered as the "Queen's Park Riot." On that day, having been rebuffed on their request to have a delegation of six homeless people address the legislature, the demonstrators took a more militant stance; the police responded with action to clear the park. In the resulting melee, dozens of demonstrators, police, and horses were injured. Over the coming weeks, the police laid charges against dozens of protesters, including criminal charges against the organizers.

The "riot" and its aftermath were significant in that a group of citizens often considered quiescent and lacking mobilizing capacity had successfully staged one of the most militant demonstrations in contemporary Canadian history. Over the course of the next decade, the homeless issue receded as a priority among anti-poverty activists and advocates, but the local anti-poverty movement in Toronto did not go away, even as it altered course and developed in new organizational forms. It is this contemporary movement of poor people and their supporters that this chapter will examine.[2]

Describing and analyzing the anti-poverty movement in Canada within the confines of a single chapter is a daunting task. Not only is there a problem of scope but also of scale. In terms of scope, scholars studying the anti-poverty movement must define its parameters. Does the anti-poverty movement include groups agitating on behalf of, and in conjunction with, pensioners? Women's rights groups? Immigrants and refugees? At its broadest level, the answer must be yes. In their book on the national "poverty lobby" in Britain, Whiteley and Winyard (1987: 16) defined the lobby broadly as "those national voluntary organizations which regularly or sporadically attempt to influence the income maintenance policies of government in favour of the poor." The approach adopted in this chapter is both more specific and more extensive than that of Whiteley and Winyard. It is more specific insofar as the discussion is limited to those social movement organizations that have as one of their *central* organizing interests the amelioration of poverty. It is more extensive insofar as the analysis is not limited to the "poverty lobby" or what might be called advocacy groups; it also includes activist groups—those organizations that may engage in advocacy but also mobilize collective extra-institutional political action.

The second problem is one of scale. Although the most important legislation regarding poverty—both directly and indirectly—has emanated from federal and provincial governments, most anti-poverty organizing takes place at the local level (Wagner, 1993; Rosenthal, 1994; Wright, 1997; Cress and Snow, 2000; Gilbert, 2001). Poor people experience their poverty locally and therefore respond locally: "It is the daily experience of people that shapes their grievances, establishes the measure of their demands, and points out the targets of their anger" (Piven and Cloward, 1979: 20–21). Arguably, the potential to make gains is also greater at the local level.

In contrast to pluralist theory, which emphasizes the open nature of democratic institutions to competing interests, Canadian politics has historically been biased toward the interests of those with economic power. This has been the case for at least two reasons. First, poor people have generally lacked the resources—both of a tangible and intangible nature—to develop large national and provincial groups that have been able to effectively lobby government on their behalf. Second, the nature of liberal capitalism structurally and ideologically privileges the interests of economic elites over other interests in society (Panitch, 1995). As a result, poor people and their supporters have often found it necessary to organize outside of the traditional institutions of political power both to alter people's perceptions of poor people and to win concessions from the state. Analytically, it is therefore necessary to examine anti-poverty activism and advocacy at all three levels of governance, using a political economy and social movement framework. Specifically, I explain the changing dynamics of anti-poverty activism as a response to the combined influences of political opportunities, mobilizing resources, and social strain. The first part of the chapter briefly examines anti-poverty advocacy at the national level. The second part provides a more detailed overview of contemporary anti-poverty activism and advocacy in Toronto, a site of some of the most dynamic anti-poverty mobilization in Canada in the past two decades.

THE DEVELOPMENT OF CANADA'S WELFARE POLICY LANDSCAPE

The contours of contemporary Canadian policies targeted toward poor people were consolidated in the two decades following World War II. The culmination of expanded federal involvement in the area of social assistance was the establishment of the Canada Assistance Plan (CAP) in 1966, based on a proposal first put forward by the Canadian Welfare Council (CWC) (Dyck, 1976). The result of the CAP was to expand both the number of recipients eligible for assistance and the types of services provided, and to create for the first time national standards of eligibility. A second major postwar program targeting poor people was the creation of public, non-profit, and cooperative housing schemes commencing in the 1950s under the National Housing Act. These programs resulted in a dramatic increase in the rental stock available for low-income families, especially in Ontario, British Columbia, and Quebec, where provincial governments were most active.

It was during this period that the first contemporary poor people's social movement organizations and national advocacy groups emerged as a direct response to the "rediscovery of poverty" in the country. Local welfare rights groups proliferated between 1966 and 1971, demanding improved assistance benefits and services, humane treatment from welfare administrators, and better representation on agency boards (Felt, 1978; Buchbinder, 1979; Little, 2007). Many welfare recipients were organized with the mobilizing support of young activists employed in the federal government agency, the Company of Young Canadians, or through funds provided by the federal government directly (Walker, 1971: 9). In 1970, the federal government also restructured the advisory body, the National Council of Welfare (NCW), to be a more representative advocate for poor people within government. The NCW, in turn, laid the groundwork for the establishment of the National Anti-Poverty Organization (NAPO) the following year.[3] From its inception, NAPO's board comprised representatives of local poor people's organizations from all regions of the country. In recognition of new political realities, the CWC also entered a period of organizational adjustment and changed its name to the Canadian Council on Social Development (CCSD) (Haddow, 1993: 87; Splane, 1996: 39–41).

Despite the vibrancy and modernization of the anti-poverty movement in the late 1960s, anti-poverty activism and influence during this period was short-lived. Liberal cabinet and caucus members began to voice concerns about the "disquieting effect that low income groups were having on urban government, especially in the Toronto area" (Walker, 1971: 68). In response, the federal government withdrew funding from local anti-poverty groups. Lacking indigenous organizational resources, most local groups dissolved or became politically marginalized (Daly, 1970; Loney, 1977; Felt, 1978). National and provincial advocacy groups had an equally difficult time being heard (Splane, 1996: 145). The CCSD would never develop a close connection to poor people, being more inclined to cultivate relationships with professional community groups. The NCW was similarly unproductive as an advocate for poor people and influential policy innovator but became an important source of public information on welfare issues. By contrast, NAPO had a direct and positive relationship with poor people, but it was also ineffective as a policy advocate because it lacked both a strong presence in Ottawa and the strategic capacity to make detailed commentaries on evolving policy debate (Haddow, 1993: 179–83). NAPO was so weak that it almost collapsed in the early 1980s.

THE SHIFTING TERRAIN OF NATIONAL POVERTY POLITICS

By the middle of the 1970s, the political, economic, and social context was slowly shifting away from concerns about poverty and welfare state expansion to managing the effects of a changing global economic environment, specifically, Canada's unsatisfactory economic performance, growing deficit and debt, and supposedly uncontrollable program spending. When the Progressive Conservative Party was elected in 1984, welfare state reform became an important agenda item. Most of the important national social programs were affected (McBride, 1992; NCW, 1987, 1992; Rice and Prince, 1993). Within this context of institutional, economic, and social reform, the major national anti-poverty advocacy groups were forced to spend much of their time defending past gains, although the manner in which to do this was the subject of some debate within the poverty community. Despite attempts to better coordinate their work, and the positive reception received by the CCSD and NAPO within government circles, national anti-poverty groups were not powerful political actors and were ineffective at halting the Progressive Conservatives' reform agenda.

In 1993, a revitalized Liberal Party under the leadership of Jean Chrétien swept the federal Progressive Conservative government from office. Initially, the election of the new government aroused a sense of optimism within social policy circles. Optimism soon faded, however, when the Liberals launched their Social Security Review the following year. The proposals put forward by Human Resources Development Canada (HRDC) held out the prospect of a radical restructuring of existing programs that, if implemented, would undermine future federal involvement in social policy. Through the next two years, the Social Security Review dominated social activism at the national level. All of the major national advocacy groups focused their attention on lobbying the government against the existing proposals. Locally, the government committee tasked with consulting Canadians on the proposals was met with protests in cities across the country (Monsebraaten, 1994: A29). Most vociferous of all the critics were post-secondary students, who believed that the proposals concerning funding for post-secondary education would greatly affect accessibility.

Eventually, frustrated at the pace of the process and determined to make expenditure reductions, Finance Minister Paul Martin pre-empted the outcome of the Review and announced dramatic program changes in the 1995 federal budget (Greenspon and Wilson-Smith, 1996). The most dramatic social policy shift was the elimination of the CAP and Established Programs Financing (EPF) and their replacement by the Canada Health and Social Transfer (CHST). The CHST reduced transfers to the provinces by $7 billion dollars over two years for post-secondary education, health, social assistance and social services and eliminated most of the national standards imposed on the provinces with regard to social assistance. This opened the door for provinces to create more restrictive and onerous eligibility requirements, opportunities taken by many provincial governments.

National advocacy groups initially responded to the 1995 federal budget by publishing critical responses delineating the potentially harmful effects of the changes (CCSD, 1995; NCW, 1995). In conjunction with the Pro-Canada Network, NAPO also organized demonstrations against the CHST in cities across the country (NAPO, 1996a, 1996b). Recognizing the futility of the struggle, however, the CCSD altered its strategy and, on behalf of HRDC, convened a series of roundtable discussions to develop proposals to "minimize the pitfalls" of the new arrangement (CCSD, 1996). The resulting proposals, however, had little effect.

In the period since 1995, the landscape of national advocacy has weakened substantially. Having lost all its core government funding in 1992–93, the CCSD has become dependent on project grants and donations for most of its financing and has tried to retain some relevance in national social policy circles through the delivery of timely research reports and facilitation of discussions between government officials, stakeholder groups, and social policy experts. In recent years, however, the CCSD has been overshadowed by the Centre for Policy Alternatives, the Caledon Institute, and other think tanks and foundations as a source of independent progressive research and policy advocacy. NAPO shifted its attention to fighting "poor bashing" and the implementation of municipal anti-panhandling by-laws and took its concerns about poverty in Canada to the international level, most notably appearing before the United Nations Committee on Economic, Social and Cultural Rights (CCPI et al., 1995; NAPO, 1998). Despite this flurry of activity, NAPO had no success influencing national poverty policy; the organization became practically invisible as a national voice for poor people (*NAPO News;* Howlett, 2005a; Spendlove, 2005). Internal squabbling, weak and divided leadership, deteriorating provincial and local networks, and financial problems all took their toll on the organization. Despite financial assistance from the government to restructure the organization (Howlett, 2005a, 2005b), NAPO's influence never recovered. In 2008, NAPO adopted new mission, vision, and values statements and changed its name the following year to Canada Without Poverty (CWP). The focus of CWP is its national Dignity for All Campaign. Of all the national organizations, the NCW has suffered the worst fate. It was abolished in the 2012 federal budget.

In a context in which little opportunity has existed for effective advocacy at the national level, the most visible and sustained anti-poverty mobilization has taken place at the local and provincial levels of governance. The rest of this chapter will examine the contemporary anti-poverty movement in Toronto. Focusing on the period since 1995, I suggest that the mobilizing concerns of anti-poverty advocates and activists in Toronto, and indeed across Ontario, have shifted over time from an emphasis on homelessness and housing to poverty reduction and social assistance. This shift was, in part, a response to changing political opportunities, mobilizing resources, and the dynamics of social strain.

ANTI-POVERTY ORGANIZING IN TORONTO, 1985–1995

A year after the Progressive Conservatives came to office federally in 1984, a Liberal government was elected in Ontario. Forced to rely on the support of the NDP in their first two years in office, the Liberal government embarked on a public review of social assistance in July 1986. The Social Assistance Review Committee (SARC) heard from people in 14 cities and received over 1,500 submissions, an historically unprecedented response (Wharf, 1992: 72–77). Released in 1988, the SARC report recommended massive increases in social assistance. Already by this time, local anti-poverty groups and unemployed workers' unions, many established by welfare recipients directly, had emerged during the recession of the early 1980s as the numbers of people unemployed and forced on to social assistance spiked (Clarke, 1992: 216–18). Even as the economy improved after 1983, the numbers of people on social assistance did not recede, and, for the first time in contemporary history, homelessness became a visible problem in large urban centres. Both of these issues, but especially the housing crisis, attracted political and media attention and provided a political opportunity for collective mobilization (Clarke, 1992: 216–18; Layton, 2000: 3–5; Greene, 2006: 76–85). It was the initiation of SARC, however, that provided the most significant political opportunity for a more coordinated effort across the province to take shape, especially after the Liberal government hesitated to act on its progressive recommendations. Eventually, in the wake of a mass province-wide protest in 1989, the government responded with an increase in welfare rates of 9 per cent (Clarke, 1992: 216–18).

The following year, the NDP came to power for the first time in the province's history. Notwithstanding its early support for welfare reform, by 1992 the NDP had begun a process of welfare retrenchment that attracted criticism from anti-poverty advocates and activists (Scott, 1996; Lightman, 1997; Little, 1998: 160–63; Sheldrick, 1998). Having successfully established a coordinated response during the SARC reform process, anti-poverty groups in the province formalized their alliance, creating OCAP, initially bringing together anti-poverty groups from 27 communities in the province (Clarke, 2000). Very quickly, however, the coalition effort weakened, and OCAP's organizational base became largely restricted to Toronto, under the leadership of John Clarke, a former unemployed worker and long-time anti-poverty activist. After 1992, as it became apparent that the NDP was implementing regressive measures, OCAP began to attract organizational resources from allies, notably the labour movement. It was also during this period that OCAP's tactics became more visibly militant and the organization began to develop its program of "direct action casework" to help welfare recipients resolve legal and bureaucratic hurdles (Groves, 2003). Using a flexible, yet fairly standardized strategy of tactical escalation, OCAP has won more than 90 per cent of its welfare cases.

Recessionary budget-cutting measures at the local level also brought a new coalition of groups together in Toronto in an effort to halt dramatic program cuts, especially those targeted at poor people. This local effort, like the SARC process before it, provided the impetus for the establishment of a more formal organizational presence in the form of the Metro Network for Social Justice, which continued its work through the decade, focusing chiefly on influencing the metro budget process through institutional channels (Conway, 2004: 78–88, 143). For the most part, though, anti-poverty activism remained in its infancy. Neoliberalism had not entirely become entrenched either locally or provincially, and institutional channels of influence had not yet been entirely closed.

FIGHTING HOMELESSNESS IN NEOLIBERAL TIMES: 1995–2005

The election of a new Progressive Conservative government in Ontario in May 1995 severely altered the context for anti-poverty organizing in Ontario. Almost immediately upon taking office, Premier Mike Harris began to implement the party's neoliberal reform agenda. Poor people were particularly hard hit. Social assistance rates were cut by 21.6 per cent, a welfare fraud hotline was instituted, the "Spouse in the House" rule was reinstated, workfare was implemented, rent control was virtually eliminated, the development of new social housing was halted, and the budget for social agencies was slashed 7.5 per cent over two years (Ibbitson, 1997: ch. 6; NCW, 1997; Little, 1998; Peck, 2001: 236–60). The dramatic effects became clear quite quickly. Within six months of the Harris government taking office, 100,000 people had left the welfare rolls; by May 2001, this number had increased to 584,255 (Workfare Watch, 2001). A strengthened economy and falling unemployment were part of the reason; research also demonstrated that tightened eligibility requirements made it much more difficult for people to become, and remain, eligible for assistance (NCW, 1997; Little and Morrison, 1999; Workfare Watch, 2001). Food-bank use also increased (CAFB, 1998, 2004). Perhaps most significantly, homelessness became increasingly visible on the streets of Ontario cities. It also became more dangerous. Within the span of one month in early 1996, three homeless men froze to death on the streets of Toronto, an "incident" that would recur with increasing frequency (Layton, 2000; City of Toronto, 2006). In the face of these social problems, the government proved unwilling to meet with its critics, effectively silencing institutional advocates who feared the loss of government funding for services.

All these developments set in motion a series of mass protests by teachers, public and private sector trade unionists, students, and anti-poverty activists, among others. OCAP captured the opportunity provided by the enhanced desperation of poor people and the new cycle of activism to organize poor people and their supporters for independent political action against the provincial government. In doing so, OCAP continued to mobilize at the local level in efforts to defend poor and homeless people against the processes of neoliberal urbanism, especially the regulatory and legislative measures implemented to clear the streets of panhandlers and squeegee merchants, whose presence was considered a threat to the city's competitiveness (Safe Streets Act, 1999; Hermer and Mosher, 2002; Kipfer and Keil, 2002). More intensive gentrifying processes also took place, pitting homeowners, residents' and business associations, and some city councillors against poor and homeless people, service providers, and anti-poverty groups (notably OCAP). The result of these regulatory and policy shifts was to exacerbate the already existing problems of poverty, homelessness, and inequality, providing an opportunity for OCAP to attract broader tangible support and involvement for its mobilizing actions from poor people, activists, and conscious constituents (Greene, 2006: ch. 2).

In response to repressive government policies, humiliating remarks by government ministers, and discriminatory local practices, OCAP organized mass marches to Queen's Park and wealthy neighbourhoods, demonstrated against businesses considered complicit with government policies, and even took its demands directly to people's homes. More than any other issue, however, it was the crisis of homelessness that mobilized the most sustained and exciting movement activity in the city. OCAP mobilized to defend squatters' and hostel users' rights, demand affordable housing, fight gentrification, oppose the closure of emergency hostels, and defend the use of public space. On more than one occasion, OCAP took over city council meetings to force the city to keep open emergency hostels or to fight proposed by-laws outlawing second suites and rooming houses. They also squatted buildings with the intention of forcing governments to open more emergency shelters and to build more affordable housing (OCAP, 2001). The year 1999 was an especially noteworthy one, as OCAP was able to mount three mass actions: two large and vociferous demonstrations on Parliament Hill and an outdoor squat—"Safe Park"—in a downtown park in Toronto lasting four days (OCAP, 1999; Garrett and OCAP, 2001; Greene, 2006: 129–37). OCAP's capacity to carry out these actions successfully gave it the confidence to organize a large, province-wide demonstration at the Ontario legislature the following summer with the objective of having a delegation of homeless people address the members of the legislature directly—the "Queen's Park Riot."

In the struggle against homelessness, OCAP was not alone, even if it was the most tactically militant and most visible mobilizing force. One of the other more significant organizations was the Toronto Disaster Relief Committee (TDRC). The origins of the TDRC can be traced back to the 1980s, but the immediate impetus for its formation came from the events of January and February 1996 when three homeless men froze to death on the streets of Toronto. In the wake of these deaths, a coroner's inquest was convened and a new coalition—Toronto Coalition Against Homelessness (TCAH)—came together to advocate on behalf of homeless people at the inquest (Bragg, 1996: A24). After the inquest, the TCAH lobbied the provincial government to implement the coroner's recommendations but without success. It was at this time that Cathy Crowe, a street nurse and member of the TCAH, developed the idea that homelessness was a "national disaster" (Crowe, 2000). This would prove to be a useful mobilizing frame. With institutional channels closed at both the local and provincial levels of governance, Crowe and her colleagues recognized that it would be necessary to adopt the political approach of a professional social movement organization. Thus, the TDRC was born in 1998 with seed money from the labour movement and other supporters. The founding members of the steering committee brought together individuals from a cross-section of society, including business, academia, and social services. TDRC's principle demand was for all levels of government to increase the amount of money they spent on housing by 1 per cent of their total annual budget—the "1 per cent solution." More immediately, though, TDRC's objectives were to force the city to provide adequate and secure temporary shelter for homeless people and to create a groundswell of support for the cause. Homelessness was a "national disaster" demanding urgent political action.

The campaign to have homelessness declared a "national disaster" was officially launched on October 8, 1998, and the mayors of the 10 biggest cities, including Toronto, quickly adopted the resolution. The TDRC adopted a flexible tactical approach, combining sporadic demonstrative action with more traditional forms of political mobilization; they lobbied government and attracted attention through media events (including tours of homeless shelters), press releases, and reports on the homeless crisis. Drawing upon its members' experiences working with homeless people, their contacts in various agencies and hostels, and expert advice, the TDRC was an important source of information about homelessness in the city until the organization began to decline after 2003, leading to its ultimate demise in 2012.

As the two pre-eminent anti-poverty groups in Toronto, and arguably in the province as a whole, OCAP and TDRC at times worked closely together. However, OCAP's relationship with less militant groups in the province was quite hostile at times, largely because of its strict adherence to direct action, a strategy that in part led the CAW to withdraw its funding in 2001. Both OCAP and TDRC sought to build their own networks and, in doing so, were important forces broadening the anti-poverty movement beyond the borders of Toronto.

Almost from the moment Harris was elected, OCAP took the initiative to make greater linkages with anti-poverty groups outside Toronto. Since 1995, anti-poverty groups had been established in communities across the province, including Kingston, Kitchener-Waterloo, Peterborough, Sudbury, Ottawa, Belleville, Guelph, Northumberland, and Port Dover. Most of these groups adopted a similar tactical repertoire to that of OCAP, and many established a strong local presence fighting gentrification, police harassment, and homelessness (Freeman and Lamble, 2004; Lamble, 2005; TAG, 2005). Eventually these organizations formed an allied network—the Ontario Common Front—initially to campaign to defeat the Harris government and, since 2005, to campaign for an increase in social assistance rates in the province.

The TDRC also took part in allied efforts. Its central objective—the "1 per cent solution"—was by its very nature a multi-level policy goal. In this sense, perhaps the most notable achievement was the formation of the National Housing and Homelessness Network (NHHN) in March 1999 by Michael Shapcott, a long-time housing activist, founding member and research coordinator for the TDRC, and now the director of Affordable Housing and Social Innovation at the Wellesley Institute. Strategically, the NHHN publicized the issue of housing—and specifically promoted the "1 per cent solution"—through the dissemination of annual report cards on housing and homelessness in Canada and lobbying provincial and federal ministers to commit their governments to take remedial and positive action on the housing and homeless front. Following the example of the NHHN, housing advocacy groups from 14 communities in Ontario came together in 2002 to form a new partnership, the Housing and Homeless Network of Ontario.

Despite the strategic variability and ideological differences between the social movement organizations, the movement to fight homelessness achieved some tangible, if limited, victories at the local level: it defeated a proposed by-law to outlaw rooming houses, pressured the municipal government successfully to open emergency winter shelter spaces, was instrumental in the development of new "emergency" protocols such as the establishment of cold and warm weather advisories, and supported the residents of Tent City—a mass squat on polluted waterfront land—in negotiations with the city for a program of rent supplements to make possible their "relocation" into formal accommodation.

More broadly, the movement was instrumental in publicizing homelessness as a crisis and mobilizing conscientious constituents in Toronto and elsewhere to become vocal participants in the debate, playing a leading role in the diffusion of activism in local communities across the province. Although more difficult to assess, the movement did seem to have some impact on making homelessness a national concern, a concern that prompted the federal government to respond at least symbolically, first with the appointment of a minister responsible for homelessness in 1999 and then more substantively with proposed bilateral federal-provincial initiatives for the development of new affordable housing. By 2005, however, the movement cycle was clearly in decline as the priorities of anti-poverty activists began to shift to the issues of social assistance reform specifically and poverty reduction more generally.

Politically, the election of new governments at both provincial and municipal levels in 2003 held out the promise of some programmatic reforms on the homeless front and new opportunities for political engagement. During the provincial election, the Liberals promised substantial investments in affordable housing and increases to both social assistance rates and the minimum wage. More significant, perhaps, was that homelessness, especially street homelessness, attracted real programmatic attention from the municipal government, principally in the form of Streets to Homes (S2H), the City's Housing First initiative. While criticized by OCAP (2008a) and leading members of TDRC (German, 2008) as clearing exercises, the program has received support from experts in the province (Falvo, 2008; Gaetz, 2010) and buy-in from the executives of several voluntary sector agencies (personal interviews, 2011). And, according to the city, it is extremely effective. Since its inception in 2005, the program has housed over 3,300 homeless individuals (City of Toronto, 2012: 9). Between 2006 and 2009, the number of street homeless people in Toronto decreased by half (City of Toronto, 2009: 13), and, in combination with more aggressive policing (O'Grady et al., 2011), the visibility of homelessness—and thus its presence as a source of social strain in the community—has also declined substantially. Although homelessness has continued to spark sporadic outbursts of outrage and concern from OCAP, the years since 2003 have seen a shift both in the focus and the organizational dimensions of anti-poverty activism in Toronto and in the province as a whole. Perhaps there is no better indication of this shift than the decision, finally, to fold the TDRC in 2012.

FIGHTING POVERTY IN (NEO)LIBERAL TIMES: 2005–2012

Since 2005, anti-poverty activism in Toronto has focused on poverty reduction, with the specific goals of raising social assistance rates and reforming the social support system in the province. One path has been charted by OCAP and its Common Front allies and has taken the form of a province-wide movement to "Raise the Rates." Led by the 25in5 Network for Poverty Reduction

(25in5), the second path has focused more on "poverty reduction" and a restructuring of the system of social security in Ontario.

Initiated in 2004, the objective of the "Raise the Rates" movement has been to "restore the spending power" that recipients have lost since 1995. As part of this campaign—its most strategically successful component—OCAP and Common Front allies have taken it upon themselves to register thousands of Ontario Works (OW) and Ontario Disability Support Payment (ODSP) recipients for the Special Diet Allowance (SDA). The SDA provides up to an additional $250 per month to recipients to meet special dietary needs, if authorized by a health care professional. Although the SDA has existed since 1995, it was largely unknown and under-used until OCAP began to organize "hunger clinics," with support from allied health care professionals (Health Care Providers Against Poverty—HPAP), to register recipients. According to the members of HPAP, "income is a key determinant of health" and "social assistance rates in Ontario are grossly inadequate to maintain food security" (HPAP, 2010). Thus, according to over 100 health care practitioners and experts who signed a letter of support for the campaign, "everyone on OW and ODSP should be entitled to the full $250 supplement." (Medical Sign-on, n.d.).

Although the demand for the province to "Raise the Rates" to pre-Harris levels has not yet succeeded, the SDA campaign itself was immediately successful. Due to the campaign, issuances of the SDA in Toronto increased from 5,600 per month in January 2005 to over 12,000 in November 2005 (City of Toronto, 2005: 21). Political chaos ensued. Both the provincial and municipal governments implemented measures to try to limit access to the SDA; OCAP and the Common Front mobilized in response. In 2009, the Office of Auditor General (2009: 20) officially sounded the fiscal alarm and suggested many allowances were paid "under questionable circumstances." The following year, the Liberal government, citing the Auditor General's report, announced plans to eliminate the SDA entirely, prompting a political backlash from OCAP and its allies. The Liberals reversed course later in the year, reinstating the SDA, but the victory was not complete as the government nevertheless announced changes to both the SDA policy and its administration that have prompted continuing demands for a reinstatement of the allowance in its original form.

In the midst of OCAP's campaign to "Raise the Rates," a second cross-community mobilization began to take shape in the province in early 2007, resulting in the formation later that year of 25in5. Following precedents set in Quebec (in 2002) and Newfoundland and Labrador (in 2006), the specific objective of 25in5 has been to see the government implement a poverty reduction plan, backed up by a Poverty Reduction Act, with targets to reduce poverty by 25 per cent in five years and by 50 per cent before 2018 (25in5, n.d.). More generally, 25in5 has sought to promote a large-scale restructuring of the social support system in the province. Drawing on the individual strengths and connections of its members across the province, and with early tangible support from the City of Toronto and the Atkinson Foundation, the campaign has combined community-based consultation, coalition, and capacity building with "insider" tactics—lobbying of cabinet members and government advisers. This strategy was a source of both unity and division within 25in5. In the period between 2007 and 2009, important ideological and political fissures in the movement became apparent.

As explained in detail by Hudson and Graefe (2011), on one side was a group of modernizers—or what these authors call "social liberals"—who prioritized systemic restructuring with a focus on eliminating the "poverty trap," principally by rebuilding the relationship between the system of social security and work. On the other side was a group of "social democrats" who were more immediately concerned to restore the benefits lost during the Harris years. Of the two groups, the modernizers clearly were the more powerful and influential contingent within 25in5; largely based in Toronto, this group was able to use the connections they had with government members to push their modernizing agenda. As the "insider" strategy rolled forward in 2008, the tension between these two groups grew. Eventually, in March 2009, the Atkinson Foundation pulled its funding from the Social Planning Network of Ontario (SPNO), specifically its representative in 25in5, Peter Clutterbuck, who refused to back down on his insistence that 25in5 prioritize the demand to raise the rates by $100 a month—a demand that he argues came directly from the community consultation process that he was specifically funded by Atkinson to lead (Clutterbuck, 2013). Clutterbuck and the SPNO have since joined the cross-community collaboration Poverty Free Ontario, whose single most important demand is to raise the rates.

Despite the tensions, 25in5 did succeed in having the government produce a Poverty Reduction Strategy with specific targets and, within that strategy, commit to a government-sponsored review of the social assistance system. Several members of 25in5—most of them "modernizers"—advised the government on the terms of reference for the commission. Nevertheless, the successes have been limited. Instead of a poverty reduction strategy, the government has produced a *child* poverty reduction strategy, several of the programs in the strategy were not new, and the full implementation of even its modest programmatic objectives has not occurred (Campaign 2000 Ontario, 2012). On those issues considered most pressing by the SPNO and OCAP—notably social assistance rates—little progress has been made. From the outset, OCAP was skeptical of the consultation process, arguing that they didn't need to waste their time in "secret" consultations. What was needed instead, they argued, was government action: "We know what the problems are. Welfare and disability rates are too low, we need a livable minimum wage now, we need more affordable housing and we need the housing we do have to be in decent repair" (OCAP, 2008b). Most importantly, after achieving some progress in reducing child poverty between 2008 and 2010, in the context of the austerity budget presented by the government in 2012, it seems unlikely that the Liberal government will meet its 25 per cent target in 2013 as planned.

CONCLUSION

The last three decades have been trying times for poor people in Canada. Anti-poverty advocates have been consistently on the defensive and almost entirely ineffective at halting federal retrenchment initiatives. Although several important voices continue to promote anti-poverty initiatives nationally, there is no evidence of a national anti-poverty movement. If there is a national campaign to speak of, it is taking place at the provincial level of governance in the form of similar cross-community campaigns for poverty reduction strategies across the country. Following the precedent set in Quebec in 2002, since 2006, governments in seven provinces and two territories, including Ontario, have produced poverty reduction strategies, with several of them also passing poverty reduction acts.

These developments raise several important questions about the possibilities for anti-poverty organizing at a national level. First, is it possible to develop a truly national anti-poverty movement, or is anti-poverty activism forever fated to be rooted in the local, and perhaps, regional levels (Miliband, 1974; Bauman, 1998; Cloward and Piven, 1999)? Second, are the prospects for successful mobilization only available when favourable political opportunities present themselves, or can well-organized groups affect the political process even in unfavourable environments? What tactics might be most useful to achieve the sought-after goals? National anti-poverty groups in Canada have primarily adopted an institutionalized approach. Would a more dynamic and confrontational approach sometimes be more effective?

At the same time as national advocacy groups in Canada have proven weak and ineffective, anti-poverty organizing has grown at the municipal and provincial levels of governance to defend the rights, and promote the interests, of poor people. This chapter has briefly described the movement that has developed in Toronto and Ontario since the 1990s. These developments also raise several questions. Are there identifiable conditions and factors that are more likely to promote activism among a population that is widely considered quiescent and lacking in organizational capacity? What are the most effective tactics for local and provincial anti-poverty groups to utilize? Does the movement benefit from an ensemble of organizations using a variety of tactics, which may produce a "radical flank" effect, or would the movement be better served by organizations coming together to pursue their objectives as a coherent whole? Are the fissures that occurred in 25in5—the most heated of which pitted community-based advocates against more institutionalized advocates and experts—fated to occur in all cross-community coalitions? Are these fissures necessarily problematic? Can they be overcome? Finally, given the paucity of resources available to poor people, is it necessary for anti-poverty groups to cultivate ties with sympathetic allies such as the labour movement in the case of OCAP or the Atkinson Foundation in the case of 25in5? What effects do these ties have on the strategic and tactical forms mobilization might take?

OCAP has recently scored some small, if not total, victories in its battles to halt the closure of the School House Shelter, combat overcrowding in emergency shelters, and save the Community Start-Up and Maintenance Benefit (CSUMB), the latter program eliminated by the province in its austerity budget of 2012. Moving forward OCAP, 25in5, and members of Poverty Free Ontario are gearing up to influence the policies of the newly established provincial government headed by Kathleen Wynne. Wynne's victory in the competition to replace Dalton McGuinty as head of the Liberal Party and premier may open new opportunities for anti-poverty advocates and activists to score some gains. Not only does Wynne have roots in the progressive wing of the Liberal Party and connections to anti-poverty advocates, during her campaign she stated that, if elected as Liberal leader, social justice would be her top priority.

Having won only a temporary reprieve with regard to the CSUMB and still fighting the changes made to the SDA, OCAP continues its "Raise the Rates" campaign by demanding: (1) an increase of social assistance rates of 55 per cent, (2) an end to the three-year freeze on the minimum wage, (3) restoration of the CSUMB and SDA benefits, and (4) a halt to any plans to merge OW and ODSP.[4] The proposal to merge these two programs was made first by the Commission on the Reform of Public Services (in 2012), headed by economist Don Drummond, and then in *Brighter Prospects*, the final report of the Commission to Review Social Security released in October 2012. This latter report, promised in the province's Poverty Reduction Strategy, has received mixed reviews from the anti-poverty community, with anti-poverty advocates and activists especially critical of the commissioners' proposal to merge OW and ODSP into one program.

The mixed reviews that *Brighter Prospects* received from movement organizations in Ontario has been followed by varied responses to Wynne's first budget released in May 2013, indicating that there are significant strategic divisions within the movement that have not been bridged with the elevation of Wynne to the premiership. 25in5 (2013) welcomed the budget as a statement of "renewal" of the government's commitment to reduce poverty and has been encouraging Ontarians to become active in the government's consultation process to develop a new Poverty Reduction Strategy. OCAP (2013), by contrast, was critical of the budget; Clarke (2013) is convinced that the Liberals "are in the opening stages of a process of regressive welfare redesign" and has criticized 25in5, among other organizations, for cooperating in the Liberals' demobilizing strategy of "consultative engagement." It would seem one organization's political opportunity is another's source of social strain; social movement researchers have argued that both conditions are likely to induce collective action. It will be interesting to see what forms of collective action occur over the coming years and with what effects. This chapter has raised some key questions and provided some context for following the anti-poverty movement at what looks to be a critical juncture in the fight against poverty in Ontario.

NOTES

1 I would like to thank Abigail Sone for commenting on drafts of the paper.

2 A conceptual distinction must be made between "poor people's movements" and "anti-poverty movements." "Poor people's movements" denotes movements that involve poor people directly in some capacity. "Anti-poverty movements," by contrast, may or may not include poor people directly. In this paper the concept of "anti-poverty" activism is used most often, but it should be noted that some of the groups that will be discussed, such as OCAP, do include poor people directly.

3 Much of the information on NAPO comes from various issues of *NAPO News* and a personal interview with Rosemary Spendlove, resource coordinator and long-time staff-person at NAPO.

4 OCAP also opposes plans to download responsibility for a merged OW and ODSP to the municipalities—a plan Tim Hudak, leader of the Progressive Conservative Party, promises to implement were his party to win in the next election.

REFERENCES AND FURTHER READING

25in5 (25in5 Network for Poverty Reduction). n.d. 25in5 Founding Declaration. http://25in5.ca/publications/25-in-5-founding-declaration/ (accessed March 28, 2013).

25in5. 2013. "Press Release: Anti-Poverty Advocates: Budget Makes Progress Towards Poverty Reduction," May 3. http://25in5.ca/press-release-anti-poverty-advocates-budget-makes-progress-towards-poverty-reduction/ (accessed September 5, 2013).

Bauman, Zygmunt. 1998. *Work, Consumerism, and the New Poor*. Buckingham, UK: Open University Press.

Bragg, Rebecca. 1996. "Helpers for Homeless Seek Role at Inquest." *Toronto Star* (June 19).

Buchbinder, Howard. 1979. "The Just Society Movement." In *Community Work in Canada*, ed. Brian Wharf, 129–152. Toronto: McClelland and Stewart.

CAFB (Canadian Association of Food Banks). 1998. *Hunger Count 1998*. Ottawa: CAFB.

CAFB. 2004. *Hunger Count 2004*. Ottawa: CAFB.

Campaign 2000 Ontario. 2012. *Strengthening Families for Ontario's Future: 2012 Report Card on Child and Family Poverty in Ontario*. Toronto: Campaign 2000 Ontario.

CCSD (Canadian Council for Social Development). 1995. *Social Policy Beyond the Budget*. Ottawa: CCSD.

CCSD. 1996. *Position Statement: Maintaining a National Social Safety Net: Recommendations on the Canada Health and Social Transfer*. Ottawa: CCSD, March 5.

City of Toronto. 2005. "Advocating for Health Through Increases to Social Assistance," November 21.

City of Toronto. 2006. "Tracking Deaths in the Homeless Population," August 28.

City of Toronto. 2009. Shelter, Support, and Housing Administration. Street Needs Assessment Results. Toronto: City of Toronto.

City of Toronto. 2012. Shelter, Support, and Housing Administration. Operating Budget Analyst Notes. Toronto: City of Toronto.

Clarke, John. 1992. "Ontario's Social Movements—The Struggle Intensifies." In *Culture and Social Change: Social Movements in Québec and Ontario*, ed. Colin Leys and Marguerite Mendell, 213–24. Montreal: Black Rose Books.

Clarke, John. 2000. Personal Interview, February.

Clarke, John. 2013. "Austerity Agenda Targets the Disabled," *The Bullet* No. 821. http://www.socialistproject.ca/bullet/821.php (accessed September 5, 2013).

Cloward, Richard A., and Frances Fox Piven. 1999. "Disruptive Dissensus: People and Power in an Industrial Age." In *Reflections on Community Organization: Enduring Themes and Critical Issues*, ed. Jack Rothman, 165–93. Ithaca, NY: F.E. Peacock Publishers.

Clutterbuck, Peter. 2013. Personal Interview, January 18.

Commission on the Reform of Public Services. 2012. *Public Services for Ontarians: A Path to Sustainability and Excellence*. Toronto: Queen's Printer for Ontario.

Conway, Janet. 2004. *Identity, Place, Knowledge: Social Movements Contesting Globalization*. Halifax: Fernwood.

CCPI (Charter Committee on Poverty Issues), NAPO, and NAC. 1995. "Presentation to the Committee on Economic, Social, Cultural Rights by Non-Governmental Organizations from Canada." Ottawa: CCPI (May 1).

Cress, Daniel M., and David A. Snow. 2000. "The Outcomes of Homeless Mobilization: The Influence of Organization, Disruption, Political Mediation, and Framing." *American Journal of Sociology* 105 (4): 1063–104.

Crowe, Cathy. 2000. Personal Interview, February.

Daly, Margaret. 1970. *The Revolution Game: The Short, Unhappy Life of the Company of Young Canadians*. Toronto: New Press.

Dyck, Rand. 1976. "The Canada Assistance Plan: The Ultimate in Cooperative Federalism." *Canadian Public Administration* 19 (4): 587–602.

Falvo, Nick. 2008. "The 'Housing First' Model: Immediate Access to Permanent Housing." *Canadian Housing* Special Edition: 32–35.

Felt, Lawrence. 1978. "Militant Poor People and the Canadian State." In *Modernization and the Canadian State.*, ed. Daniel Glenday, Huibert Guindon, and Allan Turowetz, 417–41. Toronto: Macmillan.

Freeman, Lisa, and Sarah Lamble. 2004. "Squatting and the City." *Canadian Dimension* 38 (6): 44–46, 60.

Gaetz, Stephen. 2010. "The Struggle to End Homelessness in Canada: How We Created the Crisis, and How We Can End it." *Open Health Services and Policy Journal* 3 (2): 21–26.

Garrett, Rebecca, and OCAP (video). 2001. *Safe Park*. Toronto: OCAP.

German, Beric. 2000. Personal Interview, March.

German, Beric. 2008. "Toronto Adopts Bush Homeless Czar's Plan: Another View of 'Streets to Homes' Programs." *Cathy Crowe Newsletter* 48, Summer: 2–6. http://tdrc.net/index.php?page=48-summer-2008-newsletter.

Gilbert, Melissa R. 2001. "From the 'Walk for Adequate Welfare' to the 'March for Our Lives': Welfare Rights Organizing in the 1980s and 1990s." *Urban Geography* 22 (5): 440–56.

Greene, Jonathan. 2006. "Visibility, Urgency, and Protest: Anti-Poverty Activism in Neoliberal Times." Ph.D. dissertation. Queen's University.

Greenspon, Edward, and Anthony Wilson-Smith. 1996. *Double Vision: The Inside Story of the Liberals in Power*. Toronto: Doubleday.

Groves, Tim. 2003. *Direct Action Casework Manual*. Toronto: OCAP.

Haddow, Rodney. 1993. *Poverty Reform in Canada 1958–1978: State and Class Influences on Policy Making*. Montreal, Kingston: McGill-Queen's University Press.

Hermer, Joe, and Janet Mosher, eds. 2002. *Disorderly People: Law and the Politics of Exclusion in Ontario*. Halifax: Fernwood.

Howlett, Dennis. 2005a. Personal Interview, May 19.

Howlett, Dennis. 2005b. "The Call for a Living Wage—Cross Canada Campaigns." *Canadian Dimension* 39 (3): 25–28.

HPAP (Health Care Providers Against Poverty). 2010. Letter to Hon. Madeleine Meilleur, Minister of Community and Social Services, March 22. http://www. healthprovidersagainstpoverty.ca/current_campaigns/specialdiet.

Hudson, Carol-Anne, and Peter Graefe. 2011. "The Toronto Origins of Ontario's Poverty Reduction Strategy: Mobilizing Multiple Channels of Influence for Progressive Social Change." *Canadian Review of Social Policy* 65/66:1–15.

Ibbitson, John. 1997. *Promised Land: Inside the Mike Harris Revolution.* Scarborough: Prentice-Hall.

Kipfer, Stefan, and Roger Keil. 2002. "Toronto Inc? Planning the Competitive City in the New Toronto." *Antipode* 34 (2): 227–64.

Lamble, Sarah. 2005. Personal Interview, May.

Layton, Jack. 2000. *Homelessness: The Making and Unmaking of a Crisis.* Toronto: Penguin.

Lightman, Ernie. 1997. "It's Not a Walk in the Park: Workfare in Ontario." In *Workfare: Ideology for New Underclass*, ed. Eric Shragge, 85–107. Toronto: Garamond.

Little, Margaret. 1998. *"No Car, No Radio, No Liquor Permit": The Moral Regulation of Single Mothers in Ontario, 1920–1997.* Toronto: Oxford University Press.

Little, Margaret. 2007. "Militant Mothers Fight Poverty: The Just Society Movement, 1968–1971." *Labour/Le Travail* 59: 179–97.

Little, Margaret, and Ian Morrison. 1999. "'The Pecker Detectors are Back': Regulation of the Family Form in Ontario Welfare Policy." *Journal of Canadian Studies. Revue d'Etudes Canadiennes* 34 (2): 110–36.

Loney, Martin. 1977. "A Political Economy of Citizen Participation." In *The Canadian State: Political Economy and Political Power*, ed. Leo Panitch, 446–472. Toronto: University of Toronto Press.

McBride, Stephen. 1992. *Not Working: State, Unemployment, and Neoconservatism.* Toronto: University of Toronto Press.

Medical Sign-On. n.d. "Hunger: A Serious Medical issue for OW and ODSP Recipients." http://update.ocap.ca/node/348 (accessed March 28, 2013).

Miliband, Ralph. 1974. "Politics and Poverty." In *Poverty, Inequality and Class Structure*, ed. Dorothy Wedderburn, 186–96. Cambridge: Cambridge University Press.

Monsebraaten, Laurie. 1994. "Quiet Arguments Bolster Quest for Reform." *Toronto Star*, December 8.

NAPO (National Anti-Poverty Organization). 1996a. *Anti-Poverty News*, 51.

NAPO. 1996b. *Anti-Poverty News*, 52.

NAPO. 1998. "The 50th Anniversary of the UN Declaration: A Human Rights Meltdown in Canada" (November 16).

NAPO. *NAPO News* (various years).

NCW (National Council of Welfare). 1987. *The Tangled Safety Net*. Ottawa: Minister of Supply and Services Canada.

NCW. 1992. *Welfare Reform*. Ottawa: Minister of Supply and Services Canada.

NCW. 1995. *The 1995 Budget and Block Funding*. Ottawa: Minister of Supply and Services Canada, Spring.

NCW. 1997. *Another Look at Welfare Reform*. Ottawa: Minister of Public Works and Government Services Canada.

O'Grady, Bill, et al. 2011. *Can I See Your ID? The Policing of Youth Homelessness in Toronto*. Toronto: Justice for Children and Youth and Homeless Hub Press.

OCAP. (video). 1999. *Homeless on the Hill*. Toronto: Satan Macnuggit Popular Arts.

OCAP. (video). 2001. *OCAP Strikes Back*. Toronto: OCAP and Satan Macnuggit Popular Arts.

OCAP. 2008a. "OCAP Not Participating in Sham Consultations." http://update.ocap.ca/node/489 (accessed April 14, 2013).

OCAP. 2008b. "OCAP Challenges International Award Nomination." http://ocap.ca/node/1258 (accessed March 28, 2013).

OCAP. 2013. "Wynne's First Budget—More Austerity and Deeper Poverty," May 2. http://update.ocap.ca/node/1077 (accessed September 5, 2013).

Office of the Auditor General. 2009. *2009 Annual Report*. Toronto: Queen's Printer for Ontario.

Panitch, Leo V. 1995. "Elites, Classes, and Power in Canada." In *Canadian Politics in the 1990s*, 4th ed., eds. Michael Whittington and Glen Williams, 152–175. Scarborough: Nelson Canada.

Peck, Jamie. 2001. *Workfare States*. New York: The Guilford Press.

Piven, Frances Fox, and Richard A. Cloward. 1979. *Poor People's Movements: Why They Succeed, How They Fail*. New York: Vintage.

Rice, James J., and Michael J. Prince. 1993. "Lowering the Safety Net and Weakening the Bonds of Nationhood: Social Policy in the Mulroney Years." In *How Ottawa Spends 1993–94: A More Democratic Canada . . . ?*, ed. Susan D. Phillips, 381–416. Ottawa: Carleton University Press.

Rosenthal, Rob. 1994. *Homeless in Paradise: A Map of the Terrain*. Philadelphia: Temple University Press.

Safe Streets Act, 1999, S.O. 1999, c.8.

Scott, Katherine. 1996. "The Dilemma of Liberal Citizenship: Women and Social Assistance Reform in the 1990s." *Studies in Political Economy* 50:7–36.

Scott, MacDonald. 2000. Personal Interview, April.

Sheldrick, Byron. 1998. "Welfare Reform Under Ontario's NDP: Social Democracy and Social Group Representation." *Studies in Political Economy* 55:37–63.

Spendlove, Rosemary. 2005. Personal Interview, May.

Splane, Richard. 1996. *75 Years of Community Service to Canada: Canadian Council on Social Development*. Ottawa: CCSD.

TAG (Tenant Action Group). 2005. Focus Group, May.

UNCESCR (United Nations Committee on Economic, Social, and Cultural Rights). 1993. "Concluding Observations of the Committee on Economic, Social and Cultural Rights: Canada." June 10.

UNCESCR. 1998. "Concluding Observations of the Committee on Economic, Social and Cultural Rights: Canada." December 4.

Wagner, David. 1993. *Checkerboard Square: Culture and Resistance in a Homeless Community*. Boulder: Westview Press.

Walker, David Charles. 1971. "The Poor People's Conference: A Study of the Relationship Between the Federal Government and Low Income Interest Groups in Canada." M.A. thesis. Queen's University.

Wharf, Brian. 1992. *Communities and Social Policies in Canada*. Toronto: McClelland and Stewart.

Whiteley, Paul F., and Stephen J. Winyard. 1987. *Pressure for the Poor: The Poverty Lobby and Policy Making*. London: Methuen.

Workfare Watch. 2001. "After the Boom." *Workfare Bulletin*, No. 3.

Wright, Talmadge. 1997. *Out of Place: Homeless Mobilizations, Subcities, and Contested Landscapes*. Albany, NY: State University of New York Press.

FIVE

Occupy: History, Physicality, Virtuality

MATT JAMES

On October 15, 2011, people in 950 cities spanning 82 countries rallied, marched, and initiated encampments in support of the occupation of New York's Zuccotti Park, a plaza in New York's financial district chosen by activists for its proximity to Wall Street, the citadel of global capitalism ("Occupy protests").[1] By the time of the October actions, it had taken just one short month for an unknown group of youthful protestors to inspire millions: a significant departure from the prevailing neoliberal climate of apathetic consumerism and political repression. One immediate spark for Occupy was the amoral spectacle of public bailouts for the banks and financial services corporations whose control over government agendas had caused the 2008 world financial crisis in the first place. In the months after the October 2011 actions, "Occupy" became a rallying symbol for critics of rampant income inequality, corporate dominance, and closed-door decision-making.

Yet this schematic account fails to capture the spirit of a campaign marked by a profound ambivalence about staking out official demands and taking detailed political positions. For many Occupiers, engaging in such things would have meant tethering the movement's hopes to some possible future government response and thus doing exactly what they sought to avoid: approaching officialdom as the salve for rather than incorrigible cause of their indignation and critique. The idea of establishing some kind of quasi-definitive party line would also have contradicted the capaciously inclusive ethos of a campaign waged in the name of the "99 per cent." Perhaps it is better, then, to describe Occupy in terms of its sensibilities: critical of our era's harsh, neoliberal capitalism; jaded about electoral politics and the official political system; hostile to hierarchy and formal modes of organization; committed to consensus decision-making and grassroots direct democracy; devoted to experimentation; excited about the possibilities of nonviolent cooperation; and determined to respect the differences, aspirations, and talents of diverse individuals.

Despite the descriptive difficulties involved, this chapter explores the social change values and methods behind Occupy. It does so to explore a once-perennial concern of social movement scholars that, after having disappeared from research agendas in recent years, seems suddenly relevant again. This concern is with gauging how, why, and to what effect contemporary social change approaches differ from those of the past. In particular, I want to ask about the relation between Occupy and the earlier struggles of both the so-called "old left," and the "new" social movements associated popularly with the tumultuous 1960s.

THE MEANING OF OCCUPATION AS A POLITICAL TACTIC

While certainly offering dissent and criticism, Occupy is best remembered for its positive values. These values were embodied in the participatory protocols that helped make Occupy camps into sites of radical, bottom-up democracy: the "people's mic" repetition of a speaker's words for unamplified transmission in large groups; the "twinkling" upward hand movement for signalling approval of a point or claim; the "block" for individuals seeking to convey ultimate maximum disagreement in consensual discussion processes; and the always available opportunities to start working groups for people interested in new issues or directions (Blumenkranz and Gessen, 2011). Not only means for conducting political business, these innovations were forms of political experimentation born of a yearning for alternatives to the top-down, mediated processes of representative democracy.

To use a term associated with social movements that reject using the methods and means of the systems they are trying to change, the Occupiers were committed to prefiguration (Maeckelbergh, 2011). Linked famously to Gandhi's ideal of nonviolent civil disobedience, a commitment to prefiguration is a commitment to embodying and foreshadowing in one's actions and practices the values one wants to see embraced by others. At the level of groups, prefiguration is about nurturing new social models and forms in ways that are morally consistent with the hopes and visions inspiring the search for them. Thus, and in militant rejection of a cynically professional political class dealing in wedge issues, image consultancy, and robo-calls—real-world exemplars of the academy's "public choice" approach to political science—prefigurative social movements believe that the end never justifies the means.

As a way of defending group interests and pursuing social change, the notion of occupation is certainly not new. The 1871 Paris Commune, whose direct democratic modes of internal governance were praised by Karl Marx

(1978), was one of modernity's most celebrated cases of a movement organized around claiming and defending shared physical space. While the Paris Commune aimed at governing a city, even smaller acts of occupation or blockade involve drawing immediately physical yet symbolically potent distinctions between the group inside and the authorities outside or beyond, whose presumptions of routinized control the occupiers confront. Given this inside-outside/behind-beyond distinction, it should be unsurprising that the most politically vigorous occupations in Canada of recent decades—think Oka, Ipperwash, and Caledonia, for instance—have involved Indigenous peoples asserting their rights as self-governing communities. Indeed, one astute Canadian observer noted that while the 2011 Occupy encampments were taking place, there were already at least 39 ongoing Indigenous occupations in this country (Kilibarda, 2012: 36).

The debate about Occupy's relation to First Nations communities (e.g., Barker, 2012; Kilibarda, 2012; Walia, 2011) involved more than a claim about whose political struggles should take priority. More importantly, it was a question about the participation of Occupiers themselves in the Canadian settler society's occupation of Indigenous lands.[2] I will return to this question later in the chapter. The point I want to make here is that the centrality of occupation to Indigenous struggles—which involve real communities physically defending specific historic territories—casts in stark relief elements that are necessarily more partial, embryonic, and aspirational in non-Indigenous occupations.

Whether they are of factories, buildings, offices, roads, or public spaces, occupations stress radical opposition to outside forces while fostering internal senses of solidarity and common purpose. The very process of coming together to lay physical claim to space puts occupiers in confrontation with authorities and promotes intense experiences of community; people share risks, face a common opponent, and develop modes of practical cooperation that come to be valued as forms of democracy and togetherness in themselves (Aitchison, 2011; della Porta and Diani, 2006: 179; Hatherly, 2011). Non-Indigenous Canadian examples of these kinds of experiences include the occupation by unemployed protestors in the 1930s of the Vancouver post office, art gallery, and Hudson's Bay store (Barnholden, 2005: 59–74); the sit-down strikes of Windsor factory workers seeking union recognition in the same decade (Morton and Copp, 1984: 153–64); and the 1969 anti-racism protests at Sir George Williams University in Montreal (Palmer, 2009: 285–87).

THE RETURN OF OCCUPATION IN THE NON-INDIGENOUS TWENTY-FIRST-CENTURY GLOBAL NORTH

The immediate physicality of this focus on expressing radical contention and building oppositional identity establishes occupation as a political tactic outside the more or less formal systems of political participation, such as voting, lobbying, and interest-group support. It even places occupations somewhat beyond the standard liberal-democratic protest repertoire of boycotts, petitions, rallies, and marches (Meyer and Tarrow, 1998), which, among other things, does not differentiate between "inside" and "outside" with the same vigour and clarity. Instead, occupations tend to express the more far-reaching opposition of groups that are either excluded from official claims-making systems or that reject those systems themselves. The re-emergence of occupation as a non-Indigenous tactic of politico-economic protest in early twenty-first-century North America is for these reasons significant.

Consider the diminishing centrality of occupation in Canadian working-class struggles over the second half of the twentieth century. As unions became involved in an institutionalized and legally recognized system of collective bargaining, the ambitious social movement approaches of the 1930s and 1940s gave way to a more narrowly focused "business unionism" (Moody, 1988); in Canada, as in the United States, occupations became correspondingly less central as a result (Heron, 1996). Outside the collective bargaining arena, labour tended to press for socio-economic change via organic alliances with social-democratic political parties, by lobbying government, and through occasional protest marches and rallies. Occupy's spiritual kinship, by contrast, lies more with the Vancouver building takeovers that I mentioned earlier.

The return to grassroots radicalism in contemporary politico-economic struggles reflects in part the severe weakening of the institutionalized system of liberal democratic claims-making and civic participation that the postwar labour movement helped to build (Jenson, 1997). The collective bargaining rights and social safety net that emerged with this institutionalized participation system were civic goods, elements of social citizenship (Marshall, 1964) that, by giving people a modicum of stability in their lives and control over their conditions of work, helped to promote critical citizen engagement (e.g., Brodie, 1995). Today's neoliberal era is defined in part by the erosion of these goods and thus by the decline of the more participatory official citizenship associated with them (Jenson and Phillips, 2001; Smith, 2005). Coupled with deliberate government measures in interest-group funding designed to make state structures more resistant to progressive advocacy (James, 2013)—to say nothing of the Hobbesian culture of precarity and fearful individualism that neoliberalism strives endlessly to encourage—these developments have made dissenting voices more marginal in official politics than at any time since the red-baiting 1950s.

The renewed prominence of occupation reflects this context. For example, the "alter globalization" or global justice movement, seen widely as Occupy's most direct antecedent, started turning to confrontational militancy in the late

1990s to spark democratic deliberation—at global trade summits in Seattle, Quebec City, and Genoa, for instance—about issues that neoliberal dogma and international trade rules were removing from domestic political discussion (Dupuis-Déri, 2007). Facing similar problems on more local planes of struggle, North American homelessness activists began at around the same time to use occupation as a mode of radical democratic engagement; Vancouver's 2002 Woodsquat is an excellent example.[3] Harsh experiences of sudden immiseration also made occupation prominent in the more recent global wave of anti-austerity protests, starting with Argentina in 2002 and spreading to Western Europe after the 2008 financial crisis (Hughes, 2011). Yet it is too simplistic to depict the new collective action landscape as a straightforward reaction to intensified capitalist repression and injustice. A deeper consideration of the relationships between social protest and political and socio-economic conditions is necessary.

OCCUPY AND NEW SOCIAL MOVEMENT THEORY: VALUES

The dominant approaches to thinking about these relationships come from a body of scholarship known as new social movement theory. Despite important internal differences, this work rests on a foundational distinction between "new" and "old" social movements (Habermas, 1981; Melucci, 1996; Touraine, 1981). The most influential political science version of this distinction is Ronald Inglehart's (1990) New Politics theory. The theory begins by observing that movements stressing issues of class inequality and material deprivation were central in the pre-welfare state era, when large segments of the population lacked access to even the rudiments of economic security. New Politics theory goes on to use this historical backdrop as a foil for its basic understanding of "new" social movements, such as feminism, environmentalism, and queer liberation, as unique products of the transformed socio-economic circumstances of the postwar "long boom." As Inglehart's famous terminology puts it, people whose formative experiences involved unprecedented levels of assured access to shelter, social security, and education began to prioritize "postmaterialist" questions of meaning and identity instead of the "materialist" concerns pursued by their unluckier predecessors.

Although scholars, including the present author (2006), have criticized New Politics theory for misrepresenting the complexities of social movements (e.g., Calhoun, 1995: 174), it may still prove useful to consider Occupy's concerns in light of the materialism-versus-postmaterialism distinction. Does the rise of radical politico-economic contention among non-Indigenous youth in the global North reflect a harsh and increasingly anti-democratic neoliberal order that has forced a return to the economic issues and more confrontational methods of the pre-welfare state era, as New Politics theory might expect? Some analysts of the global justice movement and indeed more recently of Occupy have wondered whether this might indeed be the case (della Porta and Diani, 2006: 71; van Stekelenburg, 2012).

Non-academic observers with ties to the labour movement certainly embraced Occupy as a return to materialist themes spurred on by rising levels of economic inequality and injustice. For example, a writer affiliated with CUPE argued that "The youth have nothing to lose because they have no expectations of a standard of living even as good as their parents. That's why they started occupying cities" (Elliott-Buckley, 2011). A veteran of the Ontario labour movement claimed similarly that Occupy is about "something that the vast majority of . . . young people . . . know through experience: lousy and insecure jobs; unemployment; declining prospects for their future" (Rosenfeld, 2012). The president of Canada's National Union of Provincial Government Employees added that "The issues of economic and social equality [that] some of us have been highlighting . . . for a while [are] front and centre once again" (Clancy, 2011).

There can be no doubt that Occupy has focused public discussion on the same basic problems of social inequality, corporate power, and democratic exclusion that have concerned labour, social-democratic, and communist movements since the nineteenth century. But we must also attend to what might provisionally be called certain "new" social movement characteristics of Occupy. Consider the following findings from an analysis of the five most "liked" Occupy-related Canadian Facebook pages: Occupy Canada, Occupy Toronto Market Exchange, Occupy Montreal-Occupons Montréal, Occupy Ottawa, and Occupy Edmonton, respectively.[4] The analysis here centres on discussion threads initiated on September 30, October 31, and November 30, 2011, representing three days over the three key months of Occupying.

A total of 88 threads, some containing dozens of specific interjections and comments, addressed issues pertaining to banks and finance; 68 dwelled primarily on income inequality.[5] But other themes were also prominent. Most common were what we could call process-related threads, notably, organizational or publicity discussions related directly to Occupy (454), general exhortations to resistance and protest (144), and concerns related to civil liberties and policing (56). In terms of substantive themes, the following stood out: general non-economic discussion about Canadian government and politics (86), general non-economic discussion about American government and politics (44), and critiques of the idea of state authority (18). But also numerous were posts attempting to focus attention on a dizzying miscellany of less easily categorizable themes, including calls for the CIA to release Nikola Tesla's papers, exhortations to veganism, and denunciations of climate-change science (272).

Thus, while "materialist" themes relating to inequality and finance were predominant in the substantive discussions, they were far from the only concern; remarkably few participants even showed any sense that the miscellaneous would-be threads were beyond the scope of Occupy.

Moreover, parsing the specific message content of those posts that attempted to initiate discussions about income inequality or finance reveals that very few people expressed these concerns in quintessentially "materialist" ways, say, by demanding wealth redistribution or sharing concerns about their own economic situation. The meanings underlying these *prima facie* economic messages tended instead to involve moral denunciations of capitalism's cultural bankruptcy, anarchist-tinged critiques of the links between representative democracy and corporate power, and invocations to build sustainable local economies. These themes resonate strongly with the priorities that New Politics theory identifies as quintessentially postmaterialist: having more say in public decisions, developing healthier relationships to the environment, building less impersonal societies, and valuing ideas over money (Inglehart, 1990: 74–75).

The distinctive sensibility infusing these putatively economic discussions has implications for New Politics theory. While it suggests the possible continued salience of "postmaterialist" views, it also suggests that the New Politics expectation of a more or less linear relationship between formative socio-economic conditions and subsequent social movements may be unhelpful when it comes to understanding contemporary expressions of politico-economic radicalism such as Occupy. The youth generation at Occupy's core was certainly born into and came of age during a neoliberal era of decreasing economic security and increased state repression; indeed, Occupy targeted precisely these problems. Yet its underlying values often seemed closer to the quintessential "new" social movement ideas that New Politics theory associates with the markedly different conditions of prosperity and welfare-state expansion that characterized the baby-boom era. Thus, it would seem that we misunderstand Occupy by claiming it as a straightforward response to the demise of the welfare state amidst neoliberal hardship and repression.

Perhaps the values of Occupiers acting in the so-called offline world were different. Although my sense from visiting Occupy sites in Victoria, Vancouver, and Halifax is that they were not, answering such a complex investigative question is beyond this chapter's scope. Undoubtedly, each camp was distinctive, featuring different mixes of different people at different times with varying orientations and concerns. For example, Occupy Toronto drew particular strength from relationships with both trade unions and the more radical antipoverty groups analyzed in Jonathan Greene's chapter in this book.[6] In Victoria, where Indigenous concerns seemed to carry somewhat greater weight, activists voted to drop the "Occupy" moniker, given that label's connotations of unwitting blindness to settler positioning and privilege, in favour of the "People's Assembly of Victoria."[7]

OCCUPY AND NEW SOCIAL MOVEMENT THEORY: APPROACHES

Local variations aside, we can consider a further way in which we misunderstand Occupy as a simple return to radicalism occasioned by falling living standards and rising fears. This point has to do with differences between Occupy's overall vision of *how* to pursue social change as compared to its counterpart visions from the classic communist, labour, and social-democratic struggles of the pre-war era. To help think about these matters, I want briefly to discuss another variant of new social movement theory, one that focuses less *à la* New Politics on the relationship between economic conditions and values and more on the relationship between technological and sociological circumstances, on the one hand, and social change methods, on the other.

The Italian sociologist Alberto Melucci (1996) sees the "newness" of the so-called new movements as a reflection of postwar transformations in the worlds of communications, work, and social reproduction. He stresses in particular the partial replacement of "fordist" production of tactile goods in factories with activities revolving around the virtual manipulation of symbols requiring advanced expertise and high levels of education. How might these new forms of culture, knowledge, and workplace organization affect the methods of social movements? Melucci suggests that the dramatically heightened importance of symbols, mass communication, and specialist knowledge in complex societies tends to lead growing numbers of individuals toward more creative modes of political participation involving the development and diffusion of new social meanings and codes. On this view, what makes the "new" movements analytically revealing as symptoms of broader historical changes is, first, their preference for struggle at the levels of discourse and interpersonal relations and, second, their concomitant relative indifference to regularized participation oriented toward official routines and authorities. As will be seen below, Occupy's commitment to prefigurative methods suggests precisely this kind of "new" social movement orientation.

Although the earlier labour and socialist movements certainly envisioned a world of transformed social relations, they did so largely using the mass-production assumptions and organizational forms of the dominant capitalist society (Tilly, 1986). For example, trade unions wound up relying on divisions of labour and expertise similar to those used by employers (Moody, 1988). Social democratic parties used the same organizational, public persuasion, media relations, and voter mobilization strategies as mainstream parties (Brodie and Jenson, 1980). And in seeing the existing administrative machinery of the state as the basic instrument for their transformative visions, even communists tended to belong to what historian Doug Owram (1986) calls the "government generation."

At least in their more radical forms, "new" movements such as feminism, environmentalism, and queer liberation rejected these traditionalist approaches. Stressing that "the personal is the political," their grassroots activists were suspicious of formal organizations and hierarchies. They tended to view social change not as a matter of attaining or even of directly influencing state power, but rather as one of changing social attitudes and discourses. Indeed, the political scientist Claus Offe (1985) argues that this anti-statist commitment to transformative democratic practices is the essence of "new" social movements. Of course, the actual practices of "new" social movements in the real world were not always uncompromisingly prefigurative. Less radical wings of feminism and environmentalism developed fairly conventional organizational routines and forms (Scott, 1990); individuals with "new" social movement affiliations and values entered mainstream organizations striving to change them from within (Findlay, 1987).

Some Occupiers may travel these paths one day themselves. But whereas being, say, a "femocrat" working within a government department or social service agency is generally seen as at least one conceivable way of pursuing feminist commitments, prefiguration seems sufficiently central to the Occupy identity as to render such routes wholly incompatible with it. As the noted Canadian social movement veteran, Judy Rebick (2012: 20), remarks about the experimentalist and anti-hierarchical modes of operation at the several Occupy camps that she visited: "It's the deepest form of democracy I've ever seen. . . . People are invited to be leaders by doing whatever it is they choose to do."

Occupy's prefigurative commitment to grassroots democracy also drove the campaign's ambivalence about taking official positions—the theme with which this chapter began. In the various debates over whether to develop formal accounts of Occupy's values and aims, democracy was always the central issue. For example, Occupy Wall Street General Assembly (2011a) produced a "Declaration of the Occupation of New York City" early in its existence, but concerns about inclusivity and non-domination turned it into something only a sociopath or corporate titan would oppose. It stood for "better pay and safer working conditions," "health insurance," "privacy," "alternate forms of energy," and "generic forms of medicine"; it stood against "illegal foreclosure," "inequality and discrimination," "cruel treatment of . . . animals," "outsourcing," "colonialism," "torture and murder of innocent civilians," and "weapons of mass destruction." Just to be sure, the declaration added that

"These grievances are not all-inclusive." The only course of action it recom- mended was to "Exercise your right to peaceably assemble; occupy public space; create a process to address the problems we face, and generate solutions accessible to everyone."

Pressures for greater specificity ensued, particularly from mainstream me- dia outlets searching for "leaders" to explain Occupy's "demands." A group calling itself the International Occupy Assembly (2012) presented its Global May Manifesto of May 2012 as a kind of compromise response. While listing various concrete proposals for change, the authors stressed that these were not addressed to institutions, "which some of us see as illegitimate, unaccount- able, or corrupt." And while emphasizing that their manifesto had emerged from a process of electronic discussion, "consensus-based [and] open to all," the so-called International Assembly also disclaimed any attempt to "speak on behalf of everyone." Still, the May Manifesto was mocked as a "demand to be oppressed." Because it presumed to articulate the views of hundreds of thousands of diverse individuals via the "soundbite articulation of a con- crete agenda," for example, the manifesto was denounced by the UK-based Anticapitalist Initiative (2012) as a "betrayal" of Occupy's commitments to "autonomy and horizontalism": independent organizing without institutional affiliation (autonomism) and political action without leaders or hierarchy (horizontalism).[8]

Radical democratic commitments that saw definitive demands and detailed, official proposals as invitations to domination and exclusion also shaped Occupy in Canada. For example, a determination to remain open to a di- versity of ideas meant that the People's Assembly project in Victoria had to contend with 9/11 "truthers," Ron Paul devotees, and pamphleteers denouncing BC Hydro's wireless "smart" meters.[9] While some may have wished for a sharper focus on, say, questions of economic inequality, the whole business of declaring particular positions out of bounds was difficult for activ- ists who saw institutional lines and proscriptions as anti-democratic affronts.

OCCUPY AND PREFIGURATION

The basic Occupy project of searching for grassroots alternatives to the in- stitutionally mediated channels of contemporary liberal democracy reflects an activist emphasis that has been gaining depth and intensity since the early days of the global justice movement. This emphasis sees prefiguration as more than a moral stance, some simple commitment to non-hypocrisy redeemed by ensuring consistency between actions and values. Instead, it embraces prefiguration as a necessary way to develop practical road maps to better futures. According to the activist and social movement scholar, Marianne

Maeckelbergh (2011), for instance, it is false to say that movements face a choice between deciding "strategically" to use hierarchical, official system methods, on the one hand, or opting to stay "pure" by sticking with prefigurative commitments, on the other; the urgency of finding alternatives to ossified political systems congenitally enslaved to capital means that the strategically savvy thing to do is to develop more genuine kinds of democracy right now. Indeed, Occupy is itself an example of the cumulative democratic learning promoted by this kind of strategically oriented prefigurative searching. Many of Occupy's now famous hand gestures and discussion protocols were first developed in the global justice movement, picked up by European anti-austerity protestors in the actions of 2010–11 (Aitchison and Peters, 2011: 57), and then popularized via the attention-grabbing Zuccotti Park encampment.

Embracing this vision of prefiguration-as-necessity means being less interested in demanding particular things than in discovering methods of deliberation and action that honour diversity and choice, values trampled under neoliberalism's authoritarian enforcement of market imperatives. This vision shaped many of the protest actions taken against the International Monetary Fund and the World Bank during the first decade of this century. Cultivating ties of "affinity" rather than imposing bonds of unity, organizers found methods of collective action that showcased rather than submerged their political and tactical disagreements; they decided autonomously in small groups how to protest and what specific messages to bring, turning anti-globalization events into multifarious festivals of diverse positions and tactics. Mocking those critics who fretted about coherence, exponents even developed a playful new label for their approach: "social movement disorganisation" (Chesters and Welsh, 2004: 317).

While Chesters and Welsh argue that this radical pluralism of ideas and tactics reflected the organizational imperatives of bringing together multiple activist cultures on the new international terrain created by neoliberal globalization, a longer term view would also note the ideological similarities connecting the new focus back to the 1960s "postmaterialist" emphasis on creativity and free expression. Perhaps the central characteristic of what the sociologist and theorist Richard Day (2005) calls today's "new*est* social movements," Occupy manifested this emphasis with unprecedented clarity.

Although this account situates Occupy within the basic orbit of "new" (and "newer") social movement theory, there is also dissonance; Occupy's substantive focus on socio-economic inequality, which links it not only to its immediate global justice forebears but also to the traditional left, confounds the binary distinction between "old" and "new" movements. Indeed, there is a perhaps still more basic objection to consider: why continue to talk about "new" social movements when referring to claims and sensibilities that first started drawing widespread attention more than four decades ago?

"NEW" MOVEMENTS, OCCUPY, AND
RESPONSES TO CAPITALISM

By 1993, the sociologist Craig Calhoun had already published an important essay arguing that many "new" movement orientations and concerns were in fact as old as liberal democracy itself. Demonstrating a historical awareness ironically absent in many of the debates about "new" versus "old" movements, Calhoun noted that early nineteenth-century radicalism, in particular, was rife with groups—feminists and free thinkers, transcendentalist spirit-seekers and communitarian experimenters—practising alternative modes of life, stressing goals of freedom and autonomy, and seeking different ways of being in the world through unconventional collective action. He concluded that it was better to think of "new" social movements in metaphoric terms: not as unprecedented novelties with determinate beginnings that distinguish our world from some dichotomized predecessor, but rather as recurring long-run phenomena, waxing and waning at different times, and defined not temporally but rather by their anti-institutional and experimental character.

Thinking historically about the recent combination of prefigurative radical experimentalism with claims to socio-economic equality brings greater scrutiny to our paradigmatic understanding of "old" social movements as well. In fact, although he gives the point only a secondary emphasis, Calhoun (1993, 390–391) notes that anti-capitalists and economic equality-seekers have not always been uniformly defined by commitments to formal organization and a concern to gain state power. The more recent continuities between 1960s social movement landscapes and the politics of our present moment bring this observation into sharper focus. For example, young Canadian socialists in the 1960s and early 1970s shunned the sober political economy of Marxist orthodoxy in favour of moral critiques of capitalism as a perversion of human creativity; they confronted their nominal allies in the trade unions and NDP with a "deeply engrained opposition to all structures and hierarchies" (Palmer, 2009: 273). This stance garnered them precisely the same admonitions to discipline that today's left-wing critics have for Occupy.[10]

Broader historical context comes from the anthropologist and well-known Occupy supporter David Graeber (2009: 226), who stresses the prominent place of anarchism on the international left before the convulsive impact of the Russian Revolution. For Graeber, the dramatic re-emergence in Occupy of an emphasis on direct action unmediated by institutions heralds anarchism's revival after the long modernist detour through communism and social democracy. The political gloss of Graeber's assessment notwithstanding, his analysis poses an important question: is the link in new social movement theory between state-oriented approaches and aspirations for socio-economic equality really just a peculiar artifact of the twentieth century?

The role-reversing perspective offered by reading Graeber in conjunction with Calhoun is certainly interesting to consider. Their arguments tend to de-traditionalize the so-called traditional left, reframing it as the temporally specific project of a historical era defined by geopolitical conflict between ideologically defined superpowers and driven by modernist visions of progress via the Westphalian nation-state (cf. Magnusson and Walker, 1988). They also tend to de-exoticize Occupy and its prefigurative "new" movement forebears, whether these are of the 1960s, the early nineteenth century, or some other era or variety.

The historical persistence of radically democratic countercultural approaches across a wide range of movement themes and types indicates that these approaches are not the unique preserve of non-economic movements pursuing "postmaterialist" concerns in conditions of late-twentieth-century affluence. They resonated in the writings of the young Marx; they flourished as responses to capitalist pathologies among left-wing anarchists in the nineteenth century; they were rediscovered by anti-capitalists in the 1960s New Left; and they were taken in ambitious new directions by the global justice and urban antipoverty movements starting in the 1990s. They came most recently to the fore with Occupy.

OCCUPY AND OUR ERA: A MOBILIZATION TRIUMPH

The dramatic mobilization of thousands of youth over several months in dozens of cities under the Occupy banner broke with a predominantly apathetic North American political culture that had been prompting scholars to ask whether social movements were "past their apex" (Phillips, 1999; cf. Boggs, 2000). The mobilization is especially noteworthy for two, more specific reasons. First, the demands and risks of physically occupying space in direct confrontation with authorities raise significant barriers to participation, barriers that make large-scale, long-term occupations, in non-Indigenous North America at least, exceedingly rare.[11] Second, the risky, time-consuming physicality of the Occupy actions bucked the apparent tendency of dissent in the digital era to assume relatively effortless, virtual forms such as "clicktivism" (Earl and Kimport, 2011). These important departures from contemporary trends suggest limitations to this chapter's overarching emphasis on the continuities linking Occupy to its historical predecessors. In the face of such departures, we need to think about discontinuities—about the factors that helped Occupy to challenge neoliberalism's constraints on mobilization—as well.

As a possible spur to action, we have already considered the amoral harshness of neoliberal pseudo-democracy in conditions of recession and welfare state decline. But oppression is seldom enough on its own to prompt collective struggle; if it was, the world's most disadvantaged and exploited places would invariably be its most revolutionary (Moore, 1966). Some scholars have responded to Moore's point by emphasizing the importance of political opportunities (Tarrow, 1994): shifts in political alignments, regime crises, processes of rapid democratization, and similar conjunctural factors that open space for movements to act. Senses of possibility and agency are also required. For example, Sarah Kerton's (2012) account of Occupy stresses the aura of hope emanating from the 2011 Arab Spring, whose youth-led toppling of authoritarian regimes provided an emotionally resonant confirmation that collective action can bring change in adverse circumstances.[12]

For their part, resource mobilization theorists (Zald and McCarthy, 1987) remind us that organization is also crucial. Indeed, whether they draw explicitly on resource mobilization frameworks or not, analysts are virtually unanimous in stressing the important organizational role played by social media and wireless communication in both the Arab Spring and the Occupy actions (e.g., Castells, 2012; Glezos, 2013). New communications technologies and platforms, such as text messaging, Facebook, and Twitter, have made it easier to plan and spread the word about protests, to build senses of community among protestors, and to develop quick responses to sundry short-run changes and exigencies. Thus, while the advent of a virtual world may herald a coming "digital repertoire of contention" on the weightlessly liquid terrain of cyberspace (Earl and Kimport, 2011; cf. Tilly, 1986), the new information and communications technologies appear to help physical protest as well.

BEYOND RESOURCE MOBILIZATION: NEW TECHNOLOGIES AND THE DIGITAL HABITUS

But this resource mobilization view is on its own insufficient. Understanding social movements in the new information and communications landscape also requires paying attention to a classic theme of new social movement theory, which this chapter has already discussed in reference to the work of Alberto Melucci (1996): the ideational and cultural impact of new social and technological circumstances on dispositions toward collective action.

To help think about this impact, consider the following contrast between Occupy and another high-profile 2011 initiative. A Canada-wide "Vote Mob" campaign aimed at boosting youth turnout for the June 2001 federal election made extensive use of the Internet, coordinating flash mobs on college campuses; spreading the message via YouTube videos, Facebook groups, and Twitter hashtags; and getting considerable support, not only from the national web-based advocacy group leadnow.ca, for example, but from the mainstream media as well.[13] Yet from a mobilization standpoint the campaign was a failure; youth turnout in 2011 was a meagre 38.8 per cent of the age 18- to 24-year-old population, a scant 1.4 per cent improvement over the 37.4 per cent figure recorded in 2008 (Elections Canada, 2008, 2012). The result is particularly unimpressive in light of the overall 2011 voter turnout increase of 2.3 per cent (2012), which suggests that those youth who did vote may simply have been responding to whatever broader factors were prompting their older compatriots to do so as well. By contrast, Occupy mobilized Canadian youth in at least 11 different cities over several months to engage in activities immeasurably more demanding than voting.

Both the Vote Mob and the Occupy campaigns made extensive use of new communications platforms and technologies, and it seems implausible to suggest that Occupy's relative mobilization success somehow simply reflected its greater acumen in exploiting them. But this is not to say that the new platforms and technologies were irrelevant. Instead, we need to go beyond resource mobilization theory and think about them differently—not simply as tools for organizing protest but as cultural influences on dispositions toward collective action.

To get a better sense of the dispositions with which we are concerned, consider the following underlying technological and social developments stressed by the social theorist Manuel Castells (2010: 375–406): decentralized networked modes of spontaneous communication, instant information access, and free sharing of content. Arising in tandem have been various socially innovative ways of engaging the new technologies, such as the ubiquitous Facebook and Twitter, as well as the more diffusely visible "open source" mode of cooperation, which uses unplanned cumulative online collaboration to develop software (as in the famous Linux computer operating system) and knowledge (as in the still more famous website Wikipedia). The open-source model has also inspired "crowd-sourcing": using electronic communication to solicit everything from volunteers for community tasks, to financial contributors for arts projects, to protestors for quick-strike political actions.[14]

Clearly, these developments offer new ways to mobilize resources. But they are also cultural phenomena notable for the unprecedented expectations of spontaneity, diversity, and choice that they foster. Effortlessly and instantly, individuals can circulate and receive messages, ideas, or images across vast scales of physical and social distance. With similar ease, though over somewhat longer time scales, people can collaborate with hundreds or thousands of others with very little in the way of central coordination or direction. The impact of these transformations, particularly on those for whom the digital experience is not an epoch-defining novelty but rather a taken-for-granted fact, has been significant.

Important dimensions of this significance include distinctive expectations about speed, effortlessness, and choice in knowledge, communication, and social action that appear to be common to the so-called digital generation.[15] To use the social theorist Pierre Bourdieu's (1977) term for the unseen and unseeable human faculty by which individuals and groups derive dispositions and inclinations from their past patterns of experience, we can call this new constellation of expectations the "digital habitus."

Understanding Occupy's relative mobilization success requires noting the congruence between its radically prefigurative approach and the expectations of the digital habitus. Although they use different terms, this congruence has already been emphasized by analysts of Occupy. For example, Rebick (2012: 51) observes that Occupy's emphasis on individual choice and self-directed creativity in collective action appealed to the skills and desires of the first-ever generation to grow up in a broadband-connected, Web 2.0 world: "They're savvy at choosing the information they want from a dizzying supply. They know how to network online, make remarkably good video . . . They have the habit of citizen journalists to document and post events and information in real time." Like the student participants in the United Kingdom's earlier 2010 anti-austerity protests, they rejected the old "conventional and uninspiring . . . top-down model of [protest] organisation," with its "repeated marches from A to B to hear talks by the same old usual suspects" (Aitchison and Peters, 2011: 51–52). They wanted to create, to act, and indeed to make politics in their own voices and ways.

Noteworthy about this emphasis on choice, creativity, variety, and spontaneity is its individualistic flavour. This individualism shaped the particular character of Occupy's commitment to autonomism. As Jacquelien van Stekelenburg (2012: n.p.) explains, "Participants [were] welcome as individuals, [but] not as representatives of traditional organizations as trade unions or political parties."[16] While based specifically on the Occupy General Assembly in Amsterdam, van Stekelenburg's observation is broadly applicable to the many encampments that required either formally or informally that any individual acting as an adherent of a specific organization "disclose [their] affiliation at the outset" (Occupy Wall Street General Assembly, 2011b). A member of the Occupy Ottawa Facebook collective explained his group's distaste for institutional affiliation in the following terms: "We push people to search by themselves . . . to stop waiting for others to give them the answers all the time."[17]

By attending to Castells's characterization of the Internet and the web as tools of "mass self-communication" (2010: xxvii) we can better grasp the digital habitus as an important impetus for these positions and claims. The new information and communications technologies allow us each to choose to convey whatever we wish, on our own time, and in our own voice and way, to possible unknown millions; whatever the others in whom we might be interested wish to convey back to us takes place on precisely the same individuated terms. People accustomed to these modes of expression, learning, and interaction often appear to see the more structured, group-centred, and elite-directed methods of traditional protest as intolerable affronts to autonomy and self-expression.

This is not to say that individualistic dispositions hostile to leadership and structure are utterly new or have no sources beyond the digital habitus. The sociologist Ulrich Beck (1992: 92) suggests that the development of highly competitive labour markets in a culture of precarity has for the last few decades been forcing people to "make themselves the centre of their own life plans and conduct," a radical reorganization of human personality that he calls "individualization."[18] For their part, scholars of value change argue that increased access to higher education tends to promote increased resistance to elite-directed, follow-the-leader modes of participation (Nevitte, 1996). Indeed, this essay has already noted Melucci's (1996) claim that the preference in "new" social movements for symbolic and discursive struggle is a long-run trend reflecting the heightened importance of creativity and knowledge in complex societies. Thus, my point is simply that the digital habitus appears to interact with broader social developments and forces in ways that infuse contemporary commitments to grassroots prefigurative democracy with a radically individualistic character.

A KEY CHALLENGE: MOBILIZATION, COMMUNITY DIFFERENCE, AND THE DIGITAL HABITUS

Although I have suggested Occupy's appeal to it as a major factor in the campaign's mobilization success, it is useful to consider the digital habitus as a possible influence on certain pathologies of the campaign as well. Numerous commentators have noted the aversion of many Occupiers for critical discussions about differences of identity and power, both within the "99 per cent" in general and within Occupy in particular. In Canada, the sharpest concerns about this aversion came from anti-colonial perspectives. As we saw at the outset of the chapter, Indigenous and settler ally critics viewed the Occupy label as an unwitting emblem of the failure of self-professed radicals to consider their complicity in an ongoing colonial occupation. Now, rather than rejecting the campaign outright, these critics tried instead to seize what they saw as a teachable moment: an opportunity for educating people about the centrality of settler exploitation of Indigenous lands and resources to the very capitalist system the Occupiers professed to be confronting.

Although they contain encouraging reports of education and coalition-building success, the dominant mood conveyed by accounts of these anti-colonial efforts was frustration. Activists hoping to "foster critical education" and "facilitate a more nuanced discourse about inequality" found people reluctant to "open their heart to potentially uncomfortable truths" (Walia, 2011: 3–5). Occupiers resisted the challenge of "confront[ing] personal complicity in colonialism," showing an "unwillingness to engage with Indigenous concerns and settler colonial privilege" (Barker, 2012: 330, 333). Anti-colonial concerns were "only reluctantly internalised"; many participants "had problems taking leadership from Indigenous peoples" (Kilibarda, 2012: 30).

Of course debates over power and privilege are never easy. But these educative efforts may have faced a particularly distinctive obstacle in the apparent insistence of the digital habitus on maximum choice and freedom. Consider what the anti-colonial critics were asking: they wanted Occupiers to hear "uncomfortable truths," confront "personal complicity," and "tak[e] leadership" from others. In other words, Occupiers were being asked to reconsider their own immediate preferences and entertain unsolicited demands and unwelcome injunctions from others. These would seem to be precisely the sorts of impositions that the digital habitus resists.

Struggles within and between social movements are as important as a campaign's struggles with unjust forms of power and authority outside. Whether they are for trade union rights, women's equality, anti-racism, anti-capitalism, or sexual freedom, movements for social change always involve disputes over privilege and exclusion (Young, 1990): male domination and racism in traditional socialism, racism in second-wave feminism, class blindness and race privilege in sexual orientation struggles, colonial relations in alter-globalization and anti-capitalist struggles, and more besides. Battles over inequalities and exclusions among putative or potential allies are thus intrinsically indispensable parts of broader campaigns against injustice (Fraser, 1997), and Occupy was no exception.

But it may have been a distinctively important and difficult case. Perhaps Occupy's greatest strength, its congruence with the demands of the digital habitus, appears inextricably related to a grave weakness. Its free-wheeling, autonomist, and horizontal prefigurative approach enabled stunning mobilization achievements amid a pervasive climate of political apathy and detachment. But the individualistic inclinations of the digital habitus, to which the former kind of approach so successfully appealed, also seemed stubbornly resistant to a range of important concerns about privilege, obligation, and inter-group relationships. Successfully navigating the tension between appealing to the digital habitus while creatively confronting its limitations will be an important challenge for the coming generation of social movements.

NOTES

1 Thanks to Tyler Chartrand, Allison Howard, and Alison James-Lomax for research assistance.

2 For a running critique of Canadian colonialism informed by this point, see the Facebook page "Occupy(ed) Canada."

3 On Woodsquat, see http://woodsquat.wordpress.com/. On homelessness activism more generally, see Feldman (2004).

4 As of August 22, 2012, the "likes" tallied as follows: Occupy Canada (49,433), Occupy Toronto Market Exchange (16,880), Occupy Montréal-Occupons Montréal (13,478), Occupy Ottawa (8,935), and Occupy Edmonton (6,351).

5 My account of these discussions aims only to characterize them and identify some salient themes; it is therefore impressionistic and provisional and not a formal content analysis.

6 Personal communication with member of Occupy Toronto Facebook collective, August 8, 2012.

7 For an eloquent explanation of the critique, see Mark Pinkoski's (2011) speech to the Victoria People's Assembly.

8 For an expression of these principles that has been cited as an influence on Occupy, see The Invisible Committee (2005). These principles are often associated with the political philosophy of anarchism; indeed, Graeber (2011) argues that Occupy is fundamentally an anarchist movement. Yet support for horizontalism and autonomism in contemporary movements also extends to include people who embrace core elements of other traditions, including socialism and even liberalism. For a broader discussion, see Graeber (2009).

9 Many of these concerns were associated with the group We Are Change Victoria. See http://wearechangevictoria.org/2012/09/27/occupy-victoria-solutions-rally/.

10 Palmer's account of the 1960s New Left offers a gentle version of the admonition: "Strong on poetics, it was weaker on the politics of program; born with the aspirations of agency already formed on its young lips, it needed to learn the language of structure" (2009: 306).

11 Thanks for this point to my fellow panellist, Michael Heaney, on the roundtable, *Occupy This Room*, at the Canadian Political Science Association meetings, University of Alberta, June 15, 2012.

12 On hope more generally, see Castells (2012).

13 For a Victoria report, see Bell (2011).

14 On open-sourcing and social movements, see Aitchison and Peters (2011).

15 For an unabashedly utopian popular account, see http://www.edutopia.org/digital-generation. For measured criticism, see Glezos (2013).

16   My analysis here is indebted to van Stekelenburg's (2012: n.p.) view of Occupy as a product of "individualization processes amplified by ICTs [information and communications technologies]."

17   Email communication, August 9, 2012.

18   Also see Howard (2007).

REFERENCES AND FURTHER READING

Aitchison, Guy. 2011. "Reform, Rupture, or Re-Imagination: Understanding the Purpose of an Occupation." *Social Movement Studies* 10 (4): 431–9.

Aitchison, Guy, and Aaron Peters. 2011. "The Open Sourcing of Political Activism: How the Internet and Networks Help Build Resistance." In *Fight Back! A Reader on the Winter of Protest,* ed. Dan Hancox. http://www.open democracy.net/ourkingdom/ourkingdom/fight-back-reader-on-winter-of-protest.

Anticapitalist Initiative. 2012."The Global Occupy Manifesto: A Demand to be Oppressed." June 18. http://anticapitalists.org/2012/06/18/the-global-occupy-manifesto-a-demand-to-be-oppressed/.

Barker, Adam J. 2012. "Already Occupied: Indigenous Peoples, Settler Colonialism, and the Occupy Movements in North America." *Social Movement Studies* 11 (3–4): 327–34.

Barnholden, Michael. 2005. *Reading the Riot Act: A Brief History of Riots in Vancouver.* Vancouver: Anvil Press.

Beck, Ulrich. 1992. *Risk Society: Towards a New Modernity.* Trans. Mark Ritter. London: Sage.

Bell, Jeff. "UVic Flash Mob Part of Mobilizing the Youth Vote." *The Victoria Times-Colonist,* April 19, 2011. http://www2.canada.com/news/uvic+flash+part+mobilizing+youth+vote/4638693/story.html?id=4638693.

Blumenkranz, Carla, and Keith Gessen, eds. 2011. *Occupy! Scenes from Occupied America.* London: Verso.

Boggs, Carl. 2000. *The End of Politics: Corporate Power and the Decline of the Public Sphere.* New York: Guilford Press.

Bourdieu, Pierre. 1977. *Outline of a Theory of Practice.* Trans. Richard Nice. Cambridge: Cambridge University Press.

Brodie, Janine. 1995. *Politics on the Margins: Restructuring and the Canadian Women's Movement.* Halifax: Fernwood.

Brodie, Janine, and Jane Jenson. 1980. *Crisis, Challenge and Change: Party and Class in Canada.* Toronto: Methuen.

Calhoun, Craig. 1993. "'New Social Movements' of the Early Nineteenth Century." *Social Science History* 17 (3): 385–427.

Calhoun, Craig. 1995. *Critical Social Theory: Culture, History, and the Challenge of Difference*. Oxford: Blackwell.

Castells, Manuel. 2010. *The Rise of the Network Society*. 2nd ed. West Sussex, UK: Wiley-Blackwell.

Castells, Manuel. 2012. *Networks of Outrage and Hope: Social Movements in the Internet Age*. Cambridge: Polity Press.

Chesters, Graeme, and Ian Welsh. 2004. "Rebel Colours: 'Framing' in Global Social Movements." *Sociological Review* 52 (3): 314–35.

Clancy, Peter. "President's Commentary: Speaking Truth to Power—Occupy Has Already Won." November 15, 2011. http://www.nupge.ca/content/4632/presidents-commentary-speaking-truth-power-occupy-movement-has-already-won.

Day, Richard J.F. 2005. *Gramsci is Dead: Anarchist Currents in the Newest Social Movements*. Toronto: Between the Lines.

della Porta, Donatella, and Mario Diani. 2006. *Social Movements: An Introduction*. 2nd ed. Oxford: Blackwell.

Dupuis-Déri, Francis. 2007. "Global Protestors Versus Global Elites: Are Direct Action and Deliberative Politics Compatible?" *New Political Science* 29 (2): 167–86.

Earl, Jennifer, and Katrina Kimport. 2011. *Digitally Enabled Social Change*. Cambridge, MA: MIT Press.

Elections Canada. 2008. "Working Paper Series: Estimation of Voter Turnout by Age Group at the 2008 Federal General Election." http://www.elections.ca/res/rec/part/estim/estimation40_e.pdf.

Elections Canada. 2012. "Working Paper Series: Estimation of Voter Turnout by Age Group and Gender at the 2011 Federal General Election." http://www.elections.ca/res/rec/part/estim/estimation41_e.pdf.

Elliott-Buckley, Stephen. "Seeds of the Occupy Movement." *Our Times* 30 (5) (October/November 2011): 44.

Feldman, Leonard. 2004. *Citizens Without Shelter: Homelessness, Democracy, and Political Exclusion*. Ithaca, NY: Cornell University Press.

Findlay, Sue. 1987. "Facing the State: The Politics of the Women's Movement Reconsidered." In *Feminism and Political Economy: Women's Work, Women's Struggles*, ed. Heather Jon Mahoney and Meg Luxton, 31–50. Toronto: Methuen.

Fraser, Nancy. 1997. *Justice Interruptus: Reflections on the "Postsocialist" Condition*. New York: Routledge.

Glezos, Simon. 2013. "Of Fortuna and Facebook: Social Media and Social Networks in Global Politics." Unpublished paper presented at the International Studies Association, April 3-6, San Francisco.

Graeber, David. 2009. *Direct Action: An Ethnography*. Oakland, CA: AK Press.

Graeber, David. "Occupy Wall Street's Anarchist Roots." *Al Jazeera*, November 30, 2011. http://www.aljazeera.com/indepth/opinion/2011/11/201111287283590 4508.html.

Habermas, Jürgen. 1981. "New Social Movements." *Telos* (49): 33–37.

Hatherly, Dan. 2011. "The Occupation of Space." In *Fight Back! A Reader on the Winter of Protest*, ed. Dan Hancox. http://www.opendemocracy.net/ourkingdom/ ourkingdom/fight-back-reader-on-winter-of-protest.

Heron, Craig. 1996. *The Canadian Labour Movement: A Short History*. 2nd ed. Toronto: Lorimer.

Howard, Cosmo, ed. 2007. *Contested Individualization: Debates about Contemporary Personhood*. New York: Palgrave Macmillan.

Hughes, Neil. 2011. "'Young People Took to the Streets and All of a Sudden All of the Political Parties Got Old': The 15M Movement in Spain." *Social Movement Studies* 10 (4): 407–13.

Inglehart, Ronald. 1990. *Culture Shift in Advanced Industrial Society*. Princeton: Princeton University Press.

International Occupy Assembly. 2012. "Global May Manifesto of the International Occupy Assembly." (May 4, 2012.) *The Guardian*. May 11, 2012. http://www. guardian.co.uk/commentisfree/2012/may/11/occupy-globalmay-manifesto.

James, Matt. 2006. *Misrecognized Materialists: Social Movements in Canadian Constitutional Politics*. Vancouver: University of British Columbia Press.

James, Matt. 2013. "Neoliberal Heritage Redress." In *Reconciling Canada: Critical Perspectives on the Culture of Redress*, ed. Jennifer Henderson and Pauline Wakeham, 31–46. Toronto: University of Toronto Press.

Jenson, Jane. 1997. "Fated to Live in Interesting Times: Canada's Changing Citizenship Regimes." *Canadian Journal of Political Science* 30 (04): 627–44.

Jenson, Jane, and Susan D. Phillips. 2001. "Redesigning the Canadian Citizenship Regime: Remaking the Institutions of Representation." In *Citizenship, Markets, and the State*, ed. Colin Crouch, Klaus Eder, and Damian Tambini, 69–89. Oxford: Oxford University Press.

Kerton, Sarah. 2012. "Tahrir, Here? The Influence of the Arab Uprisings on the Emergence of Occupy." *Social Movement Studies* 11 (3–4): 302–8.

Kilibarda, Konstantin. 2012. "Lessons from #Occupy in Canada: Contesting Space, Settler Consciousness, and Erasures within the 99%." *Journal of Critical Globalisation Studies* 5:24–41.

Maeckelbergh, Marianne. 2011. "Doing is Believing: Prefiguration as Strategic Practice in the Alterglobalization Movement." *Social Movement Studies* 10 (1): 1–20.

Magnusson, Warren, and Rob Walker. 1988. "Decentring the State: Political Theory and Canadian Political Economy." *Studies in Political Economy* 26:37–71.

Marshall, T.H. 1964. *Class, Citizenship and Social Development*. Ed. Seymour Martin Lipset. Garden City, NY: Doubleday.

Marx, Karl. 1978. "The Civil War in France." In *The Marx-Engels Reader*, ed. Robert C. Tucker, 618–52. New York: W.W. Norton.

Melucci, Alberto. 1996. *Challenging Codes: Collective Action in the Information Age*. Cambridge: Cambridge University Press.

Meyer, David S., and Sidney Tarrow, eds. 1998. *The Social Movement Society*. Lanham, MD: Rowman and Littlefield.

Moody, Kim. 1988. *An Injury to All: The Decline of American Unionism*. London: Verso.

Moore, Barrington, Jr. 1966. *Social Origins of Dictatorship and Democracy*. Boston: Beacon Press.

Morton, Desmond, and Terry Copp. 1984. *Working People*. Rev. ed. Ottawa: Deneau.

Nevitte, Neil. 1996. *The Decline of Deference: Canadian Value Change in Cross-National Perspective*. Peterborough: Broadview Press.

"Occupy Protests Around the World: Full List Visualised." *The Guardian*. n.d. http://www.guardian.co.uk/news/datablog/2011/oct/17/occupy-protests-world-list-map.

Occupy Wall Street General Assembly. 2011a. "Declaration of the Occupation of New York City." September 29, 2011. http://occupywallst.org/forum/first-official-release-from-occupy-wall-street/.

Occupy Wall Street General Assembly. 2011b. "Statement of Autonomy." November 10, 2011. http://www.nycga.net/resources/documents/statement-of-autonomy/.

Offe, Claus. 1985. "New Social Movements: Changing Boundaries of the Political." *Social Research* 52:817–68.

Owram, Doug. 1986. *The Government Generation: Canadian Intellectuals and the State, 1900–1945*. Toronto: University of Toronto Press.

Palmer, Bryan D. 2009. *Canada's 1960s: The Ironies of Identity in a Rebellious Era*. Toronto: University of Toronto Press.

Phillips, Susan. 1999. "Social Movements in Canadian Politics: Past Their Apex?" In *Canadian Politics*, 3rd ed., ed. Alain-G. Gagnon and James Bickerton, 371–92. Peterborough: Broadview.

Pinkoski, Mark. "We Are Not One, We Are Many." Speech to People's Assembly of Victoria, October 15, 2011. http://www.smithpolitics.com/?p=105.

Rebick, Judy. 2012. *Occupy This! Roots and Wings of the Occupy Movement*. Toronto: Penguin.

Rosenfeld, Herman. 2012. "Occupy and Labour." *Canadian Dimension* 46 (1) (January/February): 8.

Scott, Alan. 1990. *Ideology and the New Social Movements*. London: Unwin Hyman.

Smith, Miriam. 2005. *A Civil Society? Collective Actors in Canadian Political Life*. Peterborough: Broadview.

Tarrow, Sidney. 1994. *Power in Movement: Social Movements, Collective Action, and Politics*. New York: Cambridge University Press.

The Invisible Committee. 2005. *The Coming Insurrection*. http://libcom.org/library/coming-insurrection-invisible-committee.

Tilly, Charles. 1986. *The Contentious French*. Cambridge, MA: Harvard University Press.

Touraine, Alain. 1981. *The Voice and the Eye: An Analysis of Social Movements*. Trans. Alan Duff. Cambridge: Cambridge University Press.

van Stekelenburg, Jacquelien. 2012. "The Occupy Movement: Product of this Time." *Development* 55 (2): 224–31.

Walia, Harsha. 2011. "Letter to the Occupy Together Movement." *Fuse Magazine* 35 (1): 3–5.

Young, Iris Marion. 1990. *Justice and the Politics of Difference*. Princeton: Princeton University Press.

Zald, Mayer N., and John D. McCarthy. 1987. *Social Movements in an Organizational Society: Collected Essays*. New Brunswick, NJ: Transaction Publishers.

PART TWO

Ethnicity, Gender, and Religion

SIX

Ethnocultural Political Mobilization, Multiculturalism, and Human Rights in Canada

AUDREY KOBAYASHI

Ethnocultural political mobilization became a significant feature of Canadian political life with the adoption of multiculturalism as both a public policy and a discourse on national identity during the latter decades of the twentieth century. There are isolated historical moments when ethnocultural or racialized groups have taken a stand against oppression, but these were relatively rare— and ineffectual—until the 1970s, when changes occurred both in official state policy and at the grassroots to propel such groups to fight for human rights.

Our national discourse over multiculturalism is based on these fundamental ideological questions: who is, and who has the right to be, Canadian? And how can those rights be achieved and protected in a plural society? I argue here that whereas the movement for full and equal citizenship has been the basis for ethnocultural mobilization, the terms of the discourse are overwhelmingly influenced by the structural conditions set by public policy, from the anglo-conformist conditions of the late nineteenth century to the neoliberal framework of the early twenty-first century. Whereas the Charter of Rights and Freedoms (the Charter) and other legal or constitutional devices have provided a very important enabling framework, the achievement of political rights also requires a high level of political openness and a will to action from government, the public in general, and ethnocultural groups themselves.

Since World War II, the concept of human rights has become a part of discourses over the fundamental characteristics of Canada, and Canadians as a whole now see themselves as representing the best of liberal democratic ideas of inclusion. The ability of ethnocultural and racialized minority groups to achieve full citizenship and to overcome human rights injustices, however, has been limited. Where achievements have occurred, as in the case of the Japanese–Canadian redress settlement described below, it is in that space created by both public policy and political will and given energy by the actions of the community itself. Within that space, four main factors— political will, coalition-building, community support, and public opinion—can create the most effective structures of "political opportunity" (as Miriam Smith has called them in the Introduction to this volume) for social movements. But such confluences are rare and unlikely to occur in the current neoliberal climate.

As Laura Pulido (2006) and others writing on social movements in the US have shown recently, social activism is very much a product of its times, and in my discussion here I try to show that the neoliberalism of the past two decades has had a dampening effect, much as the human rights fluorescence of the 1980s resulted in openings. In what follows I discuss three examples of so- cial activism in context: the Japanese–Canadian redress movement; Canadian participation in the World Conference on Racism, Racial Discrimination, Xenophobia, and Related Intolerance (WCAR); and the national lobby group, the Canadian Ethnocultural Council. Before going on to a discussion of some of the ways in which the political opportunity structure has opened up, and closed down, for ethnocultural and racialized minority groups in Canada, I discuss the background to Canada's particular form of multiculturalism.

GETTING TO THE TABLE: A BRIEF HISTORY

Although the concept of Canadian citizenship has been based on pluralism and built upon immigration since colonial times, most of the immigrants who made up what was to be known as the Canadian "mosaic"[1] were not origi- nally invited to partake at the table of citizenship, and many were deliberately shunned. The stories of those thousands of citizens who became the "others" in the mosaic are of struggling to make a place for themselves and their families in the face of exclusion, discrimination, and economic marginaliza- tion. The struggle has been to become full citizens not only in law but in the dominant political imaginary.

Black Canadians of African, Caribbean, and American origin were shunned and spatially marginalized from the time of the Loyalist movement (1780s) to the Underground Railway (mid-nineteenth century) and gained only a very tenuous presence, often as slaves or indentured servants (Winks, 1997; Mensah, 2002; Cooper, 2006). Asian immigrants were imported in large numbers as cheap and expendable labour for the railways, mines, and forest industries of western Canada from the time of Confederation until the first decade of the twentieth century (Li, 1998; Kobayashi and Ayukawa, 2002).

Settlers from eastern and southern European countries were largely discouraged, shunted into the lowest-paid jobs (e.g., Italian immigrants in the construction industry; see Zucchi, 1988) or used to support the agricultural settlement of the Prairies (Knowles, 1992).

From a public policy perspective, these are stories of government action both to preserve the dominance of British and French heritage and to use immigration policy instrumentally to serve a growing need for oppressed workers based on what Bonacich (1972) more than three decades ago called a "split labour market." Canadian history, like that of other settler societies, is based on a recursive relationship between the economic marginalization and social stigmatization of ethnocultural and racialized minorities and the ideological justification of the founding "nations" as dominant. While Others were imported as cheap labour, therefore, settlers of first French, then British origin were encouraged as the vanguard of colonial presence. Upon British ascendancy, Lord Durham envisioned immigration as a means of establishing the dominance of the British as an "effective barrier against the recurrence of many of the existing evils" (quoted in Knowles, 1992: 41; see Craig, 1963: 172)—who of course included the French Canadians. Federal and provincial governments went to extraordinary measures during the latter years of the twentieth century to keep Canada a "white man's country" (Ferguson, 1975; Ward, 1978) while still controlling the tap on cheap, particularly Asian, labour. The Chinese Immigration Act (1885), which imposed a "head tax" on new immigrants after their labour had been expended in building the national railroad, represents perhaps the most cynical of such measures.

Instrumentalism peaked during the Laurier administration (1896–1911) when Clifford Sifton, as Minister of the Interior, embarked upon his ambitious scheme to populate the prairie provinces with eastern Europeans, whom he described as a "stalwart peasant in a sheepskin coat . . . with a stout wife and a half dozen children" (quoted in Knowles, 1992: 64). Clifton engaged in secret negotiations with European governments to promote movement to Canada and augmented a plan to disperse them on agricultural land across vast swathes of the prairies. His successor, Frank Oliver, oversaw revisions to the Immigration Act that clearly set out the definition of "undesirable" Canadians (Knowles, 1992: 75–86). When Sifton returned to the portfolio during the 1920s, he responded to pressure from business for more immigrant labour by overseeing a startling agreement that turned immigrant recruitment over to the two national railways, opening the door to greater diversity in the highly selective selection process (Knowles, 1992: 107–08).

Thus, Sifton and others who controlled public policy actually set the conditions for ethnocultural mobilization decades later, albeit in a deeply ironic manner. It seems they had no intention of creating "equal" status for groups other than the dominant groups; on the contrary, their vision was deeply racist. Nonetheless, their actions, based on a deliberative attempt to diversify the Canadian population on the basis of putative racial characteristics linked to the capacity for labour, resulted in the creation of a significant number of minority ethnocultural groups, particularly in the farming regions of the prairie provinces, the very heartland from which ethnocultural political mobilization was to emerge decades later. I shall return to this point below.

Were we to speak of ethnocultural mobilization during those early years, however, it would be most accurate to describe it as mobilization of *white* Canadians of western European origins organizing in an attempt to keep Canada white. The "Vancouver Riot" of 1907, while it was a spontaneous event sparked by public speeches, skirmishes over a thrown rock, and fuelled by alcohol (Ward, 1978: 53–76), was also the result of organized demands from ethnoculturally defined (white) trade unionists to curb immigration levels. The subsequent Royal Commission Report—part of a string of similar documents—contains the vision of fledgling politician W.L. Mackenzie King for the restriction and regulation of the non-white population (Canada, 1908). To cite another example, several decades later the Christie Pitts anti-Semitic riot in Toronto, also spontaneous, occurred in a context of organized political mobilization to support one particular ethnocultural vision, that of Nazism (Levitt and Shaffir, 1985). To call these events the result of social movements may be overstating the case, but there is no question that they represented the active arm of ideologically formed social groups.

During the 1940s, in the most comprehensive program yet of racial exclusion, the Canadian government, now led by the same Mackenzie King, responded to organized public and political pressure after Canada's entry into the Pacific War (December 1941) with the uprooting, dispossession, and internment of Japanese Canadians (Adachi, 1976; Sunahara, 1981).

These events—and many others—were not completely without organized response. Following the Vancouver riots in October 1907, for example, Asian workers traumatized the city by going on strike and depriving wealthy white citizens of both laundry services and domestic labour. As early as 1938, the Japanese–Canadian community organized to send a delegation to Ottawa to lobby for the franchise, which was denied to most non-whites until passage of the Citizenship Act in 1947 (Goto and Shimizu, 1989 [1981]).[2] The Canadian Jewish Congress, formed in 1919 in the aftermath of World War I, began a serious human rights lobby in 1934, both to address anti-Semitism in Canada and to call attention to the escalating persecution of Jews in Europe. The Congress would grow to become a formidable political voice in the years following World War II (Tulchinsky, 1992).

Such early attempts at organizing for ethnocultural rights, however, were on the whole reactive, fragmentary, and unsustained. It took the widespread adoption by Canadians of the concept of human rights in the wake of World War II, and the promulgation by the UN of the International Declaration of Human Rights, to usher in a way of recognizing minority groups that would also lead over the next several decades to the rise of multiculturalism.

CANADA'S "THIRD FORCE"

Several events in Canada during the 1960s, beginning with the passage of the Human Rights Act in 1960, set the context for the rise of ethnocultural political mobilization that became one of the defining features of social movements and public debate during the 1970s and 1980s. Immigration policy was entirely revamped, resulting in an increase in both the numbers and the diversity of immigrants (Knowles, 2000). The student movement and, more specifically, the American civil rights movement sparked discussion over human rights issues. The arrival of war resisters from the US, then embroiled in the Vietnam War, prompted considerations of Canada's role in international peace and justice. These events occurred amid ongoing and often acrimonious debate over the relationship between the province of Quebec and the rest of Canada.

In 1963, Prime Minister Lester B. Pearson established the Royal Commission on Bilingualism and Biculturalism, which submitted a preliminary report in 1965 followed by three volumes comprising the main report in 1967. In 1969, the commission tabled a fourth volume entitled *The Cultural Contribution of the Other Ethnic Groups*, which resulted from discussions that took place across Canada during its investigations.

More important than the findings of the commission, however, is the fact that this era represented a period of unprecedented development of ethnocultural political awareness. In 1964, Paul Yuzyk, born in Saskatchewan in 1913 to Ukrainian-born parents, became the first individual of non-British, non-French background to be appointed to the Senate. He is credited with having introduced the term "multiculturalism" in his inaugural speech, in which he claimed that "Canada has become multicultural in fact" (Yuzyk, n.d.). Yuzyk went on to identify what he termed a "third force" in Canadian political life. Thus began his indefatigable Senate career as a champion of ethnocultural rights.

Pearson's successor, Pierre Elliott Trudeau, received the fourth volume of the commission and responded with a multiculturalism policy, introduced in Parliament on October 8, 1971, with the comment that "although there are two official languages, there is no official culture, nor does any ethnic group take precedence over any other" (Canada, 1971).[3] In the more than four decades since, the policy has undergone several reinventions, according to shifting political ideologies (Kobayashi, 1993; Abu-Laban and Gabriel, 2002: ch. 4; Fleras and Elliott, 2003: ch. 10), an issue that I take up again in the next section.

MOBILIZING ETHNOCULTURAL ACTIVISTS

Ethnocultural political mobilization took form in Canada as both a push for and a response to the introduction of multiculturalism. During the first decade of official multiculturalism, government documents show a decided sense of ethnicity as an add-on, a touch of flavour enriching but not fundamentally changing a society in which the concept of biculturalism (overlain with anglo-centrism) remained both dominant and normative. A strong partnership developed nonetheless between the federal government and multiculturalism stakeholders, although that partnership was contained and channelled through the Multiculturalism Secretariat.

To the extent that we can speak of a multicultural "movement," it occurred during the lead-up to the repatriation of the Constitution, when grassroots community groups came together to influence public policy on multiculturalism and human rights. Up until that time, multiculturalism had not been taken seriously by the federal government that created it. Politicians were more deeply concerned with appeasing francophones who might view multiculturalism as a threat to their historical status (Burnet, 1976: 206). Official statements played upon the growing and colourful idea that Canada was a "mosaic" in contrast to the American "melting pot."[4] But while the government promoted its program in simplistic terms as supporting so-called "red boots" multiculturalism—food and festivals—it also provided the resources for minority groups to begin to organize. The largesse intended by Prime Minister Trudeau to "assist all Canadian cultural groups . . . to continue to develop a capacity to grow and contribute to Canada" (Canada, 1971) supported a growing social movement.

The Canadian Ethnocultural Council (CEC) was formed in 1980 as a national umbrella organization for groups representing varied communities and has the following mission statement printed on the masthead of its newsletter, *Ethno Canada*:

> . . . to secure equality of opportunity, rights and dignity for ethnocultural communities in Canada. The CEC membership works by sharing information so as to develop a consensus on issues of concern to its membership and by advocating for changes on behalf of ethnic and visible minority groups.

Elsewhere, I have described the process through which the CEC became a significant lobby organization that influenced a range of public policy and legislative changes that took place during the heady days of the 1980s (Kobayashi, 2000). It was a very active organization with a significant educational role that not only empowered national ethnocultural groups to advance their human rights concerns but also reached out to "mainstream" society in an attempt to push that agenda.

As Canadians became more and more aware of the implications of the Charter proposed by the Trudeau government in 1980 (Kobayashi, 2000), group after group (many but not all organized under the umbrella of the CEC) appeared in the hearing held by the Special Joint Committee of the Senate and House of Commons. These groups emphasized three issues in particular: the entrenchment of multiculturalism, the preservation of non-official heritage languages, and support for ethnoculturally based religious education.

The result was only a partial victory. In the final version of the Charter passed in 1982, freedom from discrimination is specified under section 15 and gender equality is guaranteed under section 28, while "the multicultural heritage of Canadians" is recognized in an elusive clause in section 27. This point is important for two reasons. First, both clauses (section 28 on gender and section 27 on multiculturalism) were fought for strongly on the part of their relative constituents, especially because section 15 on equality rights can be overridden by federal or provincial governments using the notwithstanding clause (section 33), while sections 27 and 28 are not subject to the override. However, while section 28 clearly requires gender equality under the law, section 27 is a loose interpretative clause. The fact that one struggle resulted in a guarantee while the other did not speaks significantly of the effectiveness of the enthocultural lobby *vis-à-vis* the feminist lobby at the time: the latter was able to secure effective legal guarantees of gender equality while the former was unable to secure the same level of protection. Second, whereas section 15 guarantees *individual* freedom from discrimination, including discrimination based on race, ethnicity, religion, and national origin—all of which protect individuals who are members of minority ethnocultural groups—multiculturalism is a much more comprehensive notion, which would permit the adoption of policies and practices that address problems such as structural and systematic discrimination and racism in addition to the treatment of the individual and the group under the law.

It was not long after the adoption of the Charter before legal experts began to confirm what had been obvious to the many groups that had appeared before the committee: the legal basis for upholding the rights of ethnocultural groups was very ambiguous (Hudson, 1987). Furthermore, it had become clear that such rights were considerably down the list of political priorities for rights claims. Ethnocultural group organizers were told by politicians that their "issues" took a back seat to questions of the status of Quebec, land claims, and gender equity, creating the sense on all sides of a hierarchy of citizenship claims (Stasiulis and Abu-Laban, 1991; Stasiulis, 1994, 1997; Kobayashi, 2000).

In retrospect, the paradox of the multicultural rights movement of the 1980s was that its very success was its eventual undoing. The government opened the door through its multiculturalism policy, providing not only the resources but the forum in which to push for concerns that were quite different from those envisioned under the Trudeau administration. The multicultural movement stretched the concept of "culture" beyond the traditional definition of folkways to one that encompassed full citizenship; it was not the right to *culture* (at least as that term is commonly understood) that was most important, it was the right to equality in every sense. Equality entails not only the right to express one's own cultural identity but the right to full participation in all aspects of Canadian society, whether that means freedom from discrimination because of one's religion or equal access to employment opportunities. Once the naïve notion of folkways had been transcended, there was no turning back.

The 1980s represented a window of openness—indeed, something close to partnership—between parts of the federal government and ethnocultural communities. That openness allowed ethnocultural groups to strengthen a commitment to achieving equality rights and overcoming racism. There is probably no better example than the creation of another special committee, this time on the Participation of Visible Minorities in Canadian Society. Its report, released in 1984 (Canada, 1984), is based on evidence from more than 400 groups and individuals who argued passionately that, given the inadequacies of the Charter, there was a need for a broad range of public policy initiatives including social integration, employment, immigration, the justice system, media, and education. The 80 specific recommendations read as one of the most significant human rights documents ever written. And they envision human rights not simply as something that inheres in the freedom of the individual but, rather, as something fostered in an open and inclusive society. Furthermore, for perhaps the first time in Canadian history, this was a report compiled by a group of public servants drawn from racialized communities who were able to bring both their functionary and their activist roles to bear on the question of racism (see Canada, 1984: iv–v).

The next few years saw the implementation, both directly and indirectly, of some of the measures called for in the report in a range of legislative acts (employment equity, multiculturalism, broadcasting, immigration), in a proliferation of cases before the Canadian Human Rights Commission, and in a range of Charter cases before the Supreme Court (Kallen, 2003: ch. 9).[5] The

Department of Multiculturalism became a full department for the first time in 1988, although this status was short-lived as it was again downgraded to secretariat status after the Liberal government was elected in 1993. Organizations such as the CEC flourished under a reasonably high level of funding, community support, and both public and official recognition (Kobayashi, 2000). The signing of the Japanese–Canadian redress settlement in 1988 represents the culmination of this decade of multicultural fluorescence.

THE JAPANESE–CANADIAN REDRESS SETTLEMENT: A CASE STUDY

The Japanese–Canadian redress settlement is one of very few high points of successful ethnocultural anti-racist activism in Canadian history. The story is told elsewhere (Kobayashi, 1992; Miki and Kobayashi, 1991; Miki, 2005). Here, I am only concerned with the process of mobilizing activists to achieve the settlement. My analysis rests primarily on my observations as a member of the negotiating committee that represented the National Association of Japanese Canadians (NAJC).

Activism for full citizenship rights for racialized minorities had few precedents before World War II. For Japanese Canadians, as mentioned above, there had been limited activism for full citizenship on the part of a small group of second-generation individuals (Nisei) in the 1930s. Their concern to achieve the franchise, however, would pale in the context of the uprooting, dispossession, and denial of human rights and physical freedom that would occur from 1942 to 1949. The story of human rights activism begins during the latter part of this period, when up to 10,000 Japanese Canadians were slated for "repatriation"— which was actually deportation or exile, since most of them were born in Canada. During the wartime uprooting, there emerged in Toronto a small group of activists from mainstream (white) organizations, mainly churches, calling themselves the Cooperative Committee on Japanese Canadians (CCJC). They advocated against the human rights abuses toward Japanese Canadians and, in particular, were instrumental in lobbying to stop the deportations, albeit only after more than 4,000 had been sent to Japan in 1946.

The actions of the CCJC are ironic in two respects. First, they occurred at a time when Canada and other Allied nations were congratulating themselves for having won a just war in the name of human rights. Second, it took a group of white activists, not the Japanese–Canadian community or its own spokespersons, to achieve some political effect. As Ross Lambertson (2005: 141) notes, "Only a 'white'-dominated organization like the CCJC, with links to the Canadian establishment and support from several well-known respectable and largely middle-class citizens . . . could have exerted much pressure on Ottawa."

The attempts on the part of Japanese Canadians to organize at that time have been studied in some detail. Peter Nunoda (1991), while recognizing the reality that a racialized minority, especially one as socially reviled as the Japanese Canadians had been in the 1940s, could not (and indeed did not) achieve justice on their own behalf, also suggests that what the CCJC achieved was not necessarily what Japanese Canadians wanted. For, while the CCJC recognized the injustice of deportation, it also supported the concept of dispersal to eastern Canada rather than return to the communities and property that Japanese Canadians had held before 1942. This was an assimilationist perspective. The CCJC fixed on the justifiable concern over what many saw as the totalitarian power of government to deport its own citizens under the National Emergency Transitional Powers Act (see MacLennan, 2003: 37–38), but that concern in itself was not directed to overcoming racism.

Nunoda also chronicles in some detail the conflicts within a community divided over how hard to push for rights, that division a product of the experiences of racism that had left many community members afraid of further reprisals. He ties the reluctance to organize for rights to complicity on the part of a group of Nisei that came to dominate the community with the CCJC and their relatively conservative strategy. Roy Miki (2005: 128) goes beyond Nunoda's complicity argument, suggesting that, "The young Nisei who found themselves at the centre of a social and political cyclone were so bound up in the trauma of a displaced collective . . . that their own language quickly reached the limits of its grasp."

World War II and the period of febrile human rights activism that marked its aftermath may have created political opportunities for the mainstream to organize for a new vision of Canada, therefore, but those opportunities would be some time coming for Japanese Canadians and other racialized minorities. For years afterward, mobilization from within the community was limited. The close-knit communities on the Pacific Coast, particularly in Vancouver, had been physically dispersed. The physical dismantling also involved the destruction of most community infrastructure, although some of the churches re-established themselves during the 1950s. The community infrastructure they had lost was the very thing that would have supported a social movement, as many communities the world over have discovered. There were no initiatives to continue the fight for redress; indeed, those who tried to do so were deemed to be troublemakers. People were concerned with starting new lives, fulfilling new hopes, and maintaining a positive image in the eyes of both public and government officials.

The redress movement began to take hold during the 1970s, at a time when the international student movement, the civil rights movement in the US, and the rise of multiculturalism in Canada had created an escalated human rights discourse and a climate of social change. Japanese Canadians came together in 1977 to celebrate the centennial of the arrival of the first immigrant from Japan to Canada, and this occasion sparked discussion of a new push to obtain redress. The young people, mostly university students, who initiated those discussions were branded as "radicals" by many in the community for whom the thought of raising sensitive issues still brought forth painful memories. But the movement gained momentum, and the next decade saw a concerted effort, intensified from about 1986, to obtain a settlement.

Four elements are key to the settlement that was finally reached in September 1988. First, there was political will on the part of the federal government, which crafted redress as part of an emerging social justice agenda that was also politically popular. At a rally on Parliament Hill in April, the newly appointed Minister of Multiculturalism, Gerry Weiner (the first full minister in that portfolio), gave a speech that opened the way to negotiations that would see an agreement reached in the month of August, followed by a public announcement on September 22. During the final negotiation, which occurred in secret over several days, it became clear that key members of the government, including the prime minister, supported the process fully. When the settlement was announced in the House of Commons, it was greeted with unqualified support from all parties as expressed in a standing ovation by the entire House and emotional speeches from the opposition leaders.

Part of this political will may have come from the fact that the US had implemented a redress agreement with Japanese Americans a month before. That settlement had sparked considerable discussion in Canada, including calls in the media for the Canadian government to follow suit. But it would be far too simplistic to say that the settlement was only a matter of following the Americans. From the government perspective, there were several other factors. For one, it also came shortly after the retirement of parliamentary veteran and Minister of Veteran's Affairs, George Hees, who had been a strong opponent of a settlement and used every opportunity to link redress discussion with the plight of Canadian soldiers who had been captured by the Japanese at Hong Kong—a completely different issue, of course, involving a different national government, but one that nonetheless brought out reactionary views. For another, this was a key time in the build-up toward both a national election (October 1988) and what two years later would become a crisis of national unity (the Meech Lake Accord). Lucien Bouchard was still Secretary of State in 1988; indeed, it was he who, in person, initiated the redress negotiations with the NAJC before turning it over to Minister of Multiculturalism Weiner. This period, in which Bouchard and Prime Minister Mulroney were seen to be working together for unity and for a broader understanding of human rights, was perhaps the highest point of "red Tory"-ism in Canadian history

(Clément, Silver, and Trottier, 2012). During the stormy second Mulroney term that followed, however, marked by an economic recession as well as the failure of the Meech Lake Accord and Bouchard's break with the government to form the Bloc Québécois, the political opportunity for an achievement such as the Japanese–Canadian redress settlement would not have occurred.

Second, mobilization at the community level had been sufficient that most Japanese Canadians, originally reticent because of the fear of backlash, were now supportive of the negotiations. Broad community support was necessary to quell arguments from a succession of ministers who preceded Weiner that the NAJC could not represent all Japanese Canadians. That support was hard-won by community organizers who called meetings, staged fundraising and educational events, and encouraged people to talk about an issue that had been repressed for decades. The community discourse was part of a process of healing that had to occur before people could muster the will to fight for justice. Moreover, community mobilization occurred within a discourse of multiculturalism that had over the past decade become normalized. In another ironic twist, it is easier to achieve a social movement objective when the move occurs toward, rather than away from, perceived dominant values.

There is no more exhilarating feeling than the sense of common cause that occurs in the midst of a movement for social justice that is gaining ground. We could see a similar but much grander phenomenon on film in the pulsing crowds of South Africans before the downfall of apartheid or in the quiet, stubborn elation beneath the stoic crowds assembled to support the Polish Solidarity movement (both events that were developing at the same time as the redress settlement), expressions of collective optimism that belie the pain and suffering from which they emerged. More recently, the same sense of building national consensus for change was palpable in accounts of the 2011 "Arab Spring." To be part of the redress movement, frankly, was exciting. We felt so strong in our resolve. The sense of urgency was both compelling and contagious, especially with regard to the aged first generation (Issei) for whom a few months might make the difference of seeing a settlement in their lifetimes. And nothing mobilizes a community so much as the collective conviction that its cause is right and just and winnable. So, at the same time that the political conditions for redress advanced on Parliament Hill, the community readied itself for a victory, and, sensing a victory, those who may have been reticent in the past were eager to be part of this shared experience.

It is unlikely, nonetheless, that Japanese Canadians would have been so strong in their resolve were it not for a third factor: the swelling support of human rights groups, religious groups, labour unions, and other ethnocultural organizations who came together to make our battle theirs. A major difference between the late 1980s and the late 1940s is that Japanese Canadians were no longer bystanders for their own cause but leaders for a cause that was seen not only as providing justice for Japanese Canadians but as setting a precedent for other oppressed groups. There was widespread recognition among those groups (if not on the part of the government) that our common cause was against a history of racialization.

When the NAJC staged a rally on Parliament Hill in April 1988, representatives of many groups came out in force and spoke eloquently and passionately. The sound of Japanese–Canadian taiko drums and Aboriginal drums reverberating together through the halls of Parliament in a call for justice was symbolic of mutual support. So were the thousands of yellow postcards from Canadian citizens of many backgrounds signed and delivered to the minister's office. Key to the participation of a broad spectrum of human rights activists was not only their commitment to overcoming injustice but also their assertion that this settlement provided a model for addressing other injustices, including the Chinese head tax and the treatment of Aboriginal children in residential schools.

Finally, the approbation of the Canadian public in general brought together the perspectives of government and community. Popular opinion had swung drastically since the 1940s so that ordinary Japanese Canadians found that what had been a hidden and shameful topic could now be talked about in public. Their fellow citizens commonly expressed outrage at the injustices of the 1940s and were willing to support the redress movement vocally. The government clearly had a sense that the settlement would be a popular political move. It was seen as a good thing to do, especially in the lead-up to the federal election of October 1988.

Such moments as that in which the Japanese–Canadian redress settlement was negotiated occur rarely. Without taking away from the very high level of dedication to human rights that fuelled this initiative from the grassroots, I do not believe that it would have been successful had not the political conditions at the time been so accommodating. Political will, grassroots mobilization, coalition-building, and popular opinion came together at a time that, in retrospect, represented the high point of public policies designed to give minority ethnocultural groups a voice in national politics. Those who negotiated the settlement did so with a sense of optimism, therefore, because they saw it as the first of what could be several settlements to right wrongs of the past. But that course did not develop. Over the two decades and a half following the redress settlement, there has occurred instead a significant shift in public policy toward a neoliberal agenda against which mobilization of ethnocultural groups has become more and more difficult.

NEGOTIATING THE NEOLIBERAL PRESENT

While the neoliberal trajectory in which the Canadian state has been caught up has certainly gained strength for several decades, for ethnocultural organizations lobbying for human rights, the point of transition came during the second administration of the Progressive Conservative Party under Prime Minister Brian Mulroney (1988–93) and accelerated after the return in 1993 of the Liberal Party under Prime Minister Jean Chrétien. As Miriam Smith (2005) argues cogently, the neoliberal era has seen a fundamental restructuring of the relationship between the state and advocacy groups that has involved a general move from a collaborative relationship during the post-Charter era to an "accountability" relationship that was firmly in place by the end of the 1990s when the federal government formalized this shift with the adoption of the Volunteer Sector Initiative (Phillips and Graham, 2000; Brock, 2002). Abu-Laban and Gabriel (2002: 110–17) point out that even as commitment to the concepts of multiculturalism and anti-racism deepened during the 1980s, the Mulroney government was moving to a neoliberal model with a focus on ethnocultural entrepreneurialism, symbolized by a "Multiculturalism Means Business" conference held in Toronto in 1986.

Abu-Laban and Gabriel believe that the neoliberal shift has intensified. On the one hand, "selling diversity," as they put it, gives Canada a marketing edge in a global environment where multiculturalism can be packaged as a Canadian asset. On the other, there is a growing sense that "the state should not play a role in the area of culture—[which is] a 'private' matter to be dealt with in the home and family" (2002: 111). The "privacy" of culture is not, of course, a new concept. When Trudeau first introduced multiculturalism decades ago, he made it very clear that, for him, multiculturalism was about the freedom to make *individual* identity choices. Such a notion encourages the expression of multiculturalism as a set of choices around folk ways, such as "ethnic" food and other consumer items. The very different model of multiculturalism as human rights, anti-racism, and civic participation epitomized by the Japanese–Canadian redress settlement was probably not, therefore, what politicians and policy-makers had in mind back in the early 1980s.

What emerged from that decade, claims Howard-Hassmann (2003: 132–33) was the creation of a civil society based on "weak" cultural relativism (see also Donnelly, 1989) and an abiding notion of compassion based on the rights of the individual over those of the group. Howard-Hassmann's study of the opinions of leaders in the city of Hamilton shows that there are limits to the concept of multiculturalism and that those limits are met when people come up against what they see as hard cultural relativism that either sets group rights ahead of those of the individual or that creates an undemocratic ethnocentrism, social exclusion, or "tyranny of multiculturalism" (see Green, 1994: 116). Howard-Hassmann joins Kymlicka (1995, 2001) in endorsing this model of liberal democracy as a basis for balancing the rights of individuals and groups in ways that will advance multiculturalism as an expression of individual rights.

The liberal democratic model of citizenship and multiculturalism, and Kymlicka's vision in particular, has been debated extensively, and I make no attempt to cover it here (for a review, see Sunday, n.d.). Kymlicka has been widely criticized, however, for what Parekh (1997, 2000) and others have identified as a hierarchical notion of citizenship based on a distinction between national and cultural minorities in relation to dominant majorities (see also Young, 1997). The emphasis on the individual is usually seen as a way out of the dilemma of accommodating group rights, but the intractable conflict between liberalism and pluralism remains (see Burtonwood, 2003).

My much simpler point here, however, concerns the pragmatic results of this tension for ethnocultural and racialized minority groups for whom overcoming racism is not necessarily served by the terms of the debate over multiculturalism. Herein lies one of the paradoxes of the Japanese–Canadian redress settlement. Whereas the settlement represented for activists at the time an opening up of possibilities through which social movements could play a transformative role for both state and civil society, their hopes have not been realized. First, for all that it represented an important achievement of justice, the settlement was still based on individual rights as defined within a liberal democracy. And it was partly that emphasis that made the settlement so popular. Notwithstanding the creation of the Canadian Race Relations Foundation (CRRF) as part of the settlement, the rights of individual citizens always trump attempts to combat racism, especially when overcoming racism involves recognizing the extent to which Canada remains a colonial society based on ethnocultural hierarchies and a broad culture of whiteness.

Second, perhaps because the settlement was more about individual rights than about racism, the strength of that anti-racist message was lost as the neoliberal project gained momentum throughout the 1990s. In the process, minority ethnocultural groups—who had worked so hard to find a place at the table and who, it could be argued, were instrumental in rewriting the potential social and political role of minority groups in human rights advocacy—found that it became increasingly easier to sell diversity than to lobby for human rights. The two are not, of course, *intrinsically* opposed, but there are two significant difficulties. First, it is difficult to "sell" multiculturalism as an idyllic made-in-Canada social condition if questions of human rights, especially questions of racism, are raised. There is therefore a strong business incentive for keeping the lid on discussions of racism and other forms of oppression in the interests of marketing diversity. Second, ethnocultural groups, like others in the not-for-profit sector, are faced with the dilemma of having to choose between projects that will attract funding—especially those that follow a neoliberal model—and waging a human rights campaign in a climate where resources are increasingly scarce. Two further examples illustrate these two problems.

CANADA'S ROLE IN THE WORLD CONFERENCE AGAINST RACISM, RACIAL DISCRIMINATION, XENOPHOBIA AND RELATED INTOLERANCE (WCAR)

Canada was one of the more active nations in this international conference, which took place in Durban, South Africa, August 28 to September 7, 2001. The process began a year earlier when the federal government set up a consultation process with racialized minorities and Aboriginal groups. The WCAR secretariat organized regional meetings across the country designed both to mobilize non-governmental organization (NGO) participation and to hear concerns from grassroots organizations. The preparation/consultation process culminated in a national conference held in Ottawa on February 23–24.[6] The Canadian contingent that left for South Africa in August included a strong group of NGOs, who met in the days before the official government meetings.

The enthusiastic response from community groups might have resulted in another high point in the history of mobilizing for human rights in Canada, almost reminiscent of the events that took place during the 1980s. There was a sense among many of the participants of a partnership between officials and NGOs. The meetings were not, however, without tension. Some objected to the fact that the secretariat had created a separate national advisory committee for Aboriginal peoples but had "lumped" visible minorities together. Unity threatened to dissolve at the Toronto regional meeting when a group called for a separate advisory committee for those who experience anti-black racism and for whom issues such as slavery reparations were significant. Others were concerned that should the agenda be focused on the contemporary effects of the Atlantic slave trade, then issues such as present-day human trafficking, particularly of people from Asia, would be sidelined. Government officials and the majority of those who attended the meetings, however, remained firm in their commitment to a single visible minority advisory committee that would address all the issues on what turned out to be a rather contentious international agenda.

Unlike the US, which pulled out of the meetings as soon as the discussions began to hit areas where that administration had disagreements,[7] Canada stayed the course and played a prominent role in drafting the final declarations of the conference.[8] Internationally, the result was to place—or replace—on the agenda a range of significant issues of racism and xenophobia that have been the basis of oppression and its lingering effects for centuries. The UN and a significant number of international NGOs used the conference to continue to focus attention on injustices worldwide. One of the most significant concrete results was a draft international resolution on the Rights of Indigenous Peoples (Dialogue Between Nations, n.d.), which has since been developed, debated, and ratified.

As a basis for mobilizing racialized minorities in Canada, however, the WCAR has had few, if any, lasting effects. As my description above shows, the process discouraged coalition-building, especially in an environment where groups had to compete for coveted NGO designations and for government funding. The atmosphere of the regional preparation meetings was one more of getting individual issues on the agenda than of developing a concerted approach to addressing racism in Canada.

Indeed, while there was support for selling Canada as a nation in which racism does not occur, there was very little public support for using the WCAR as an opportunity to address the issue. During and immediately after the conference, my monitoring of the media coverage in Canadian newspapers revealed that there was far more coverage of the claim that racism doesn't exist in Canada than anything else, with virtually no attention paid to the issues put forward by "special interest groups" such as ethnocultural minorities. Margaret Wente (2001) dubbed the conference "an exercise in self-flagellation, a make-work project for our antiracism industry." Rex Murphy (2001) referred to it as "Babble from genocide's bystanders." In a more subtle message, Mark MacKinnon (2001), the main *Globe and Mail* correspondent at the conference, ended his description of the Canadian delegation with the comment, "And they're doing so with taxpayers' money. One government source said that a large chunk of the $2-million the federal government has spent on preparing for the conference was used to help the 60 NGOs take part in the civil-society anti-racism talks this week and the UN forum that begins today." And some time later, Christie Blatchford (2001), one of the most conservative of Canadian journalists, argued that, "It is only the federal Liberals, and those whose reputations (and occasionally livelihoods) are inextricably tied to the operating assumption that racism is a pervasive reality in this country, who continually see this bogeyman beneath the Canadian bed."

These comments are, of course, text-book examples of what anti-racist scholars term the "new racism": vociferous denial that racism exists, spoken by powerful white voices, with shades of (in this case not-so-subtle) innuendo that even to bring up the topic of racism is to give insult, to waste taxpayer money, or to somehow gain advantage. It is a discourse of denial and discreditation (see Henry and Tator, 2010: 10–12). Of course, the voices cited above are not the only ones that we might listen to, but it is not unimportant that these are the voices of *The Globe and Mail*, which may not represent all Canadians but is arguably the most public venue for the expression of opinions in this country, and they are the voices of white Canada. In the face of such overwhelming media oppression, the opportunities for the WCAR to become a forum for building coalitions among Canada's racialized groups were limited indeed.[9]

Attention to the conference ended abruptly, however, a few days later on September 11, 2001 with the attacks against the World Trade Center in New York and the Pentagon in Washington, DC. In the following days, among the millions of words and images that were devoted to 9/11, there was considerable attention paid to the need to guard against racism and intolerance toward minority groups, but whatever opportunity there may have been for groups to join together in light of the events in Durban simply never materialized. Events had followed too closely upon one another, and the international reaction was too raw to be able to make the obvious links between post-9/11 events and the issues raised at the WCAR.

Of course the timing of these events was unfortunate. Attention quickly shifted away from the WCAR with the result that opportunities for further mobilization and public dialogue were no doubt lost. An electronic search today for Canadian activities to follow up and maintain some of the momentum of the conference yields almost nothing. But there are two important ways in which the events in Durban and 9/11 came together. Racial profiling, including that by police departments as well as by a range of national security bodies, quickly became a major item of public discourse and public policy. As well, the discussions at the WCAR laid the basis for advancing discussions of redress and reparations for several Canadian groups, including First Nations, Chinese, German, Italian, Sikh, and Ukrainian Canadians, for whom the claims of injustice remain unresolved. All of those issues are ongoing, but aside from the efforts of the CRRF to make a case that they are related, there is little effective coalition-building among the affected groups to overcome human rights abuses. And research by Matt James (2006) supports my suggestion that issues that involve redress for racist acts are still relatively poorly understood in Canada.

Contrasting the pre- and post-WCAR world allows an interesting take on the question of how minority group concerns fit into a neoliberal agenda. Prior to the conference, the federal government spent a considerable sum to support a Canadian delegation whose mandate rested very significantly on the fact that Canada markets itself as a progressive place where multiculturalism makes good business. Notwithstanding the very sincere concern on the part of some politicians and policy-makers to overcome discrimination and inequality, it was nonetheless a giant marketing exercise with almost nothing to follow up the specific concerns of groups who continue to face racism and inequality. After 9/11, considerable efforts were turned to managing a radically transformed security environment in which occurred expressions of intolerance and hatred, including no few incidents of physical violence and vandalism against the property of brown-skinned people. But it has been business as usual on the multiculturalism front.

THE CANADIAN ETHNOCULTURAL COUNCIL TODAY

Business as usual for those mobilizing for equality means an increasing struggle both to maintain resources and to address a political and social context in which multiculturalism is viewed as a source of inequality rather than a principle of justice. On March 21, 2006, International Day for the Elimination of Racial Discrimination, *The Globe and Mail* ran an online poll asking, "Is it time for Canada to abandon its multiculturalism policy and insist that immigrants adopt Canadian cultural values?" The response was "Yes," 19,842 votes (66 per cent), "No," 10,153 votes (34 per cent), for a total of 29,995 votes. While this should not really be considered a poll, let alone either in-depth or unbiased, the sheer number of responses is telling. Even the most controversial issues debated in these daily "polls" seldom receive more than 20,000 votes (*The Globe and Mail INSIDER Edition*, 2006). Either the number of responses indicates a widespread public feeling about multiculturalism, or the anti-multiculturalism movement was especially successful on that day in encouraging its supporters to log on to the newspaper's website, or both.

Be that as it may, that "poll" is but one piece of evidence in a growing number of indications that since 9/11 the public attitude to multiculturalism has "hardened" because it is seen as promoting the difference of brown-skinned immigrant groups from countries considered to have cultural traditions less similar than others to Canadian traditions. A more scientific poll conducted by the Strategic Council in 2005, for example, showed that "Canadians are overwhelmingly in favour of abandoning the 'mosaic' approach to multiculturalism that has long been a defining feature of the nation's identity (Curry and Jimènez, 2005). This finding concurs with Howard-Hassmann's (2003) finding cited above that the civic leaders in her study accepted and supported multiculturalism, but within limits.[10]

Acknowledging what seems to be a continuing development, the CEC reports that the trend that makes mobilization for equality rights more difficult—trends that I noted in my in-depth fieldwork over a decade ago (Kobayashi, 2000)—has continued.[11] The CEC no longer acts as a direct lobbying organization, both because their efforts to influence federal politicians have been rebuffed and because the resources to bring members to Ottawa no longer exist. Funding from the Department of Canadian Heritage's multiculturalism program, long the mainstay of ethnocultural activism, dried up during the first part of the twenty-first century and shifted from sustaining to project-based funds, as they have for the entire third sector (Brock, 2002). In 2008, responsibility for administering the Multiculturalism Act shifted to Citizenship and Immigration Canada. The CEC now operates as an "outreach organization," providing information to groups on such things as health care, social services, and immigration. According to Executive Director Anna Chiappa, the sense of partnership with government that had been developing two decades ago has now dissolved, replaced with a message that "grassroots organizations [should] do things for themselves" (Chiappa, 2006).

Some CEC member organizations have had some success in doing things for themselves. The Canadian Armenian Federation opened an office in Ottawa for the specific purpose of encouraging the government to recognize the Armenian genocide, and they received an acknowledgment by Parliament of the genocide as a "crime against humanity."[12] The Chinese Canadian National Council has kept up a small but concerted mobilization around the Chinese head tax (Chinese Immigration Act) and the Chinese Exclusion Act (in force between 1885 and 1947) (CCNC, 2013) after achieving a much-contested but highly symbolic settlement in June 2006 (Harper, 2006). The Ukrainian Canadian Congress similarly maintains a struggle for redress for Ukrainian Canadians interned during World War I, linking that issue to present-day support for multiculturalism in Canada and democracy in the Ukraine (Ukrainian Canadian Congress, n.d.). The Canadian Arab Foundation was behind the creation of an Ottawa-based office to lobby for public information on Islam (Canadian Arab Federation, 2003) and maintains a very active and high-level lobbying profile toward both national and international issues. One of its position papers expresses the view that since 2001 Canada has displaced multiculturalism values with misplaced security concerns.

All of these organizations represent fraught issues with implications that go far beyond Canadian borders and involve complex webs of human rights issues. What characterizes all of them, however, is that they are targeting what they consider to be extreme examples of human rights abuses. The majority of the national groups (at least those that maintain websites where I can review current issues) are focused on institution building, and their agendas are driven by specific projects such as needs or capacity-building studies, youth forums, and cultural education projects, the sorts of projects that receive funding in the contemporary non-profit environment.

ETHNOCULTURAL MOBILIZATION IN A NEOLIBERAL REGIME

I do not mean to suggest that capacity-building projects, aimed at strengthening education, national linkages, and ethnocultural identity, are not important or worthwhile. What is troubling about the current situation, however, is the extent to which the national mobilization of human rights activists to support multiculturalism and anti-racism that seemed to be building across Canada following repatriation of the Constitution has been largely abandoned. The struggle to define multiculturalism as a program of equality rights and anti-racism, rather than (only) as a program to maintain cultural communities, has largely given way to the latter. And as the general perception of multiculturalism as something intended for a minority, especially new immigrants, has flourished, public opinion has inexorably begun to turn away from the concept. The majority of Canadians still support the idea of a cultural mosaic, but they also believe in an overriding "Canadian" culture, and that culture is a matter of private identity, not public policy. The sentiment is increasingly that multiculturalism has "gone too far," that there are limits to difference, and that ethnocultural groups should take care of themselves. Most of all, we have been unsuccessful in the attempt to make multiculturalism fundamentally about anti-discrimination. The limited success of the activities surrounding the WCAR and of the CEC point to the diminishing capacity for ethnocultural and racialized minority groups to muster the resources to extend the concept of multiculturalism as human rights to those who face the consequences of racism today, including African-origin groups enduring increasing relative poverty, Asians subject to human smuggling, and those of Islamic and Arab origin who experience racial profiling.

Researchers who have studied the course of multiculturalism and the role of ethnocultural groups in promoting human rights have remarked over and over that the 1970s and the 1980s saw a movement from multiculturalism as song, dance, and food festivals to human rights advocacy (e.g., Day, 2000; Abu-Laban and Gabriel, 2002; Fleras, 2002; Biles, Tolley, and Ibrahim, 2005). Over the past two decades we have come full circle. However, that does not mean that we have returned to the quaint festivals that marked ethnocultural groups' activities before the Charter era politicized them. Multiculturalism as a cultural commodity today is hip, not quaint.

Multiculturalism, and even putative racial equality, are increasingly commodities sold to "draw a link between diversity and business prosperity, international trade links, and Canada's global competitiveness" (Abu-Laban and Gabriel, 2002: 124). Ethnocultural groups must market themselves if they are to survive as institutions, and there is little room on the business agenda for human rights activism, much less for the kind of cross-cultural activism through which coalitions and social movements might be forged. Multiculturalism has become cosmopolitanism, more aptly epitomized by the diversity of ethnic restaurants in Canada's largest cities than by increasing access to human rights on the part of those most marginalized.

Meanwhile, I opened *The Globe and Mail* this morning to find an op-ed piece by Conservative Senator Leo Housakos (2013) dubbing multiculturalism an "outdated insult" used to buy "ethnic votes" and maintain inequality. How ironic that a policy once fought for to gain equality should now be used as an instrument in the politics of difference. There is little capacity in Canada today for the kinds of educational projects that might shift the current discourse over multiculturalism as something that is either a celebration of diverse folk ways, for some, or a means of keeping immigrants from joining the mainstream, for a growing group of others. Political mobilization will need to occur around a different discursive axis if an anti-racist, anti-oppression, equity-seeking social movement is to be revived. It is very much needed.

NOTES

1   The metaphor of the mosaic is widely used in public policy, by social scientists, and in public discourse to describe Canadian demographic pluralism and to distinguish it from the American "melting pot." The notion comes from John Murray Gibbon's *Canadian Mosaic: The Making of a Northern Nation* (1938), which, ironically, is based on a set of racialized categories of human difference and that leaves all non-white groups out of the picture. John Porter (1965) later coined the phrase "vertical mosaic" to address the issue of social class and power differences, although Porter, too, pays little attention to the process of racialization.

2   The 1947 *Citizenship Act* gave the federal franchise to all Canadians, except Japanese Canadians, who gained the right to vote in 1949, and status Indians (as defined under the Indian Act), who obtained it in 1960.

3   Popular critics of multiculturalism argue that Trudeau was less concerned with the status of minority ethnocultural groups than with using the policy to contrast Canada with the US and to weaken the notion of two founding groups by repositioning French and English Canada within a pluralist framework. See, for example, Coleman, 2006: 51.

4   See, for example, *The Canadian Family Tree* (Canada, 1967), a romantic depiction of Canada as a nation based on immigration where everyone gets along, with no issues of class or status, a remarkable piece of what even three decades ago Kostash (1977) called "whitewashing" (for a fuller discussion see Kobayashi, 1993: 214).

5 This period also saw the creation of the Court Challenges Program, established in 1978 to help individuals bring forward test cases that would clarify the Charter. In September 2006, the Harper government cancelled the program, citing as problematic the concept of government expending funds to challenge itself. This action perhaps more than any other signals an end to the reciprocal relationship between state and civil society that the period of multiculturalism building in the 1980s epitomized.

6 I attended both the regional meeting held in Toronto and the national meeting held in Ottawa as a participant. My comments are based in part on my notes from these meetings.

7 The two most contentious issues were slavery reparations and Israeli xenophobia against Palestinians, both issues on which the US took a minority opinion.

8 The WCAR website that was maintained by the Canadian government leading up to and following the Durban Conference is no longer active.

9 Of course, the agenda for the WCAR was much more complicated, devolving to a series of acrimonious debates over the issues of slavery reparations and—even more acrimonious—Arab-Israeli relations. These issues are not, however, the focus of my discussion here.

10 These indications notwithstanding, a comprehensive poll undertaken by Environics in 2001–02 showed that about 80 per cent of Canadians supported the concept of multiculturalism, but a decade later that number had dropped to 60 per cent (Jedwab, 2012). But those who tout the strength of Canadian support for multiculturalism often fail to acknowledge that supporting the concept and putting limits to the concept are two different things.

11 Interview with Anna Chiappa, Executive Director, Canadian Ethnocultural Council, May 10, 2006.

12 Bill M-380 passed by a vote of 153 to 68 on April 22, 2004. Members of the Liberal cabinet, however, were instructed to vote against the bill because of its implications for Canada-Turkish relations.

REFERENCES AND FURTHER READING

Abu-Laban, Yasmeen, and Christina Gabriel. 2002. *Selling Diversity: Immigration, Multiculturalism, Employment Equity, and Globalization.* Peterborough: Broadview Press.

Adachi, Ken. 1976. *A History of the Japanese Canadians: The Enemy that Never Was.* Toronto: McClelland and Stewart.

Biles, John, Erin Tolley, and Humera Ibrahim. 2005. "Does Canada Have a Multicultural Future?" *Canadian Diversity* 41:23–28.

Blatchford, Christie. 2001. "$2.4 Million to Preach to the Converted." *National Post* (October 20: A17).

Bonacich, Edna. 1972. "A Theory of Ethnic Antagonism: The Split Labor Market." *American Sociological Review* 37 (5): 547–59.

Brock, Kathy, ed. 2002. *Improving Connections Between Governments and Nonprofit and Voluntary Organizations: Public Policy and the Third Sector*. Montreal: School of Policy Studies and McGill-Queen's University Press.

Burnet, Jean. 1975. "Multiculturalism, Immigration, and Racism: A Comment on the Canadian Immigration and Population Study." *Canadian Ethnic Studies* 8 (1): 35–39.

Burnet, Jean. 1976. "Ethnicity: Canadian Experience and Policy." *Sociological Focus* 9 (2): 199–207.

Burtonwood, Neil. 2003. "Social Cohesion, Autonomy and the Liberal Defence of Faith Schools." *Journal of Philosophy of Education* 37 (3): 415–25.

CAIR-CAN (Council on American Islamic Relations of Canada). n.d. http://www.caircan.ca/aboutus.php (accessed April 7, 2013).

Canada. 1908. *Report of W.L. Mackenzie King, C.M.G., Commissioner Appointed to Enquire into the Methods by Which Oriental Labourers have been Induced to Come to Canada*. Ottawa: King's Printer.

Canada. 1967. *The Canadian Family Tree*. Secretary of State, Citizenship Branch. Ottawa: Queen's Printer.

Canada. 1971. *House of Commons Debates*. October 8.

Canada. 1984. *Equality Now! Report of the Special Committee on Participation of Visible Minorities in Canadian Society*. Bob Daudlin, Chair. Ottawa: Queen's Printer.

Canada. 2005. *Canada's Action Plan Against Racism*. Ottawa: Department of Canadian Heritage. http://publications.gc.ca/collections/Collection/CH34-7-2005E.pdf (accessed April 17, 2013).

Canadian Arab Federation. 2003. "Multiculturalism and Civil Rights." Position paper. http://www.caf.ca/2003/04/multiculturalism-and-civil-rights/ (accessed April 17, 2013).

Canadian Ethnocultural Council. n.d. "Projects and Activities" http://www.ethnocultural.ca/ (accessed April 17, 2013).

CCNC. 2013. "Acknowledging BC's Racist Past by Returning Head Tax Monies to the Families." March 1. http://www.ccnc.ca/content/pr.php?entry=258 (accessed April 17, 2013).

Chiappa, Anna. 2006. *Personal Interview with the Author*. May 10.

Clément, D.,W. Silver, and D. Trottier. 2012. *The Evolution of Human Rights in Canada*. Ottawa: The Canadian Human Rights Commission.

Coleman, Ronald. 2006. *Just Watch Me: Trudeau's Tragic Legacy*. Victoria: Trafford.

Cooper, Afua. 2006. *The Hanging of Angelique: Canada, Slavery, and the Burning of Montreal*. Toronto: HarperCollins.

Craig, Gerald M., ed. 1963. *Lord Durham's Report*. Carleton Library No. 1. Toronto: McClelland and Stewart.

CRRF (Canadian Race Relations Foundation). 2005. *A Background Paper on the CRRF's Policy on Redress and Reparations*. http://www.crr.ca/Load.do?section=28&subSection=46&type=2 (accessed April 17, 2013).

Curry, Bill, and Marina Jimènez. 2005. "Many Believe European Newcomers Make More Positive Contribution, Poll Shows." *The Globe and Mail* August 8: A6.

Day, Richard. 2000. *Multiculturalism and the History of Canadian Diversity*. Toronto: University of Toronto Press.

Dialogue Between Nations. n.d. http://www.dialoguebetweennations.com/db network/english/selfdetermination.htm (accessed April 17, 2013).

Donnelly, Jack. 1989. *Universal Human Rights in Theory and Practice*. Ithaca, NY: Cornell University Press.

Ferguson, Ted. 1975. *A White Man's Country*. Toronto: Doubleday.

Fleras, Augie. 2002. "Multiculturalism as Critical Discourse: Contesting Modernity." *Canadian Issues* (February): 9–11.

Fleras, Augie, and Jean Leonard Elliott. 2003. *Unequal Relations: An Introduction to Race and Ethnic Dynamics in Canada*. 4th ed. Toronto: Prentice Hall.

Gibbon, John Murray. 1938. *Canadian Mosaic: The Making of a Northern Nation*. Toronto: McClelland and Stewart.

Globe and Mail INSIDER Edition. 2006. "Is It Time for Canada to Abandon its Multiculturalism Policy and Insist That Immigrants Adopt Canadian Cultural Values?" (March 21).

Goto, Edy, and Ron Shimizu. 1989 [1981]. "On the N.A.J.C. Presentation to the Special Joint Committee on the Constitution: An Entrenched and Inviolate Charter of Rights." In *Asian Canadians: Regional Perspectives, Selection from the Proceedings, Asian Canadian Symposium V*, ed. Victor Ujimoto and Gordon Hirabayashi, 380–390. Guelph: Guelph University Press.

Green, Leslie. 1994. "Internal Minorities and Their Rights." In *Group Rights*, ed. Judith Baker, 101–17. Toronto: University of Toronto Press.

Harper, Stephen. 2006. "Address by the Prime Minister on the Chinese Head Tax Redress." http://www.pm.gc.ca/eng/media.asp?category=2&id=1220 (accessed April 17, 2013).

Henry, Frances, and Carol Tator. 2010. *The Colour of Democracy: Racism in Canadian Society*. 4th ed. Toronto: Thomson Nelson.

Housakos, Leo. 2013. "Multiculturalism's an Outdated Insult." *The Globe and Mail* (March 8).

Howard-Hassmann, Rhoda. 2003. *Compassionate Canadians: Civic Leaders Discuss Human Rights*. Toronto: University of Toronto Press.

Hudson, Michael. 1987. *Multiculturalism and the Charter: A Legal Perspective*. Toronto: Carswell.

James, Matt. 2006. "Do Campaigns for Historical Redress Erode the Canadian Welfare State?" In *Multiculturalism and the Welfare State: Recognition and Redistribution in Contemporary Democracies*, ed. Keith Banting and Will Kymlicka, 222–246. Oxford: Oxford University Press.

Jedwab, Jack. 2012. "Younger Canadians Believe Multiculturalism Works; Older Canadians, Not So Sure." http://www.acs-aec.ca/en/social-research/multiculturalism-diversity/ (accessed April 17, 2013).

Kallen, Evelyn. 2003. *Ethnicity and Human Rights in Canada*. 3rd ed. Toronto: Oxford University Press.

Knowles, Valerie. 1992. *Strangers at Our Gates: Canadian Immigration and Immigration Policy, 1540–1990*. Toronto: Dundurn Press.

Knowles, Valerie. 2000. *Forging Our Legacy: Canadian Citizenship and Immigration, 1900–1977*. Ottawa: Citizenship and Immigration Canada.

Kobayashi, Audrey. 1992. "The Japanese–Canadian Redress Settlement and its Implications for 'Race Relations.'" *Canadian Ethnic Studies* 24 (1): 1–19.

Kobayashi, Audrey. 1993. "Multiculturalism: Representing a Canadian Institution." In *Place/Culture/Representation*, ed. James Duncan and David Ley, 205–31. London: Routledge.

Kobayashi, Audrey. 2000. "Advocacy from the Margins: The Role of Minority Enthocultural Associations in Affecting Public Policy in Canada." In *The Nonprofit Sector in Canada: Roles and Relationships*, ed. Keith Banting, 229–66. Montreal: School of Policy Studies and McGill-Queen's University Press.

Kobayashi, Audrey, and Midge Ayukawa. 2002. "A Brief History of Japanese Canadians." In *Encyclopedia of Japanese Descendants in the Americas: An Illustrated History of the Nikkei*, ed. Akemi Kikumura Yano, 150–61. Walnut Creek, CA: Altamira Press.

Kostash, M. 1977. *All of Baba's Children*. Edmonton: Hurtig.

Kymlicka, Will. 1995. *Multicultural Citizenship: A Liberal Theory of Minority Rights*. Oxford: Oxford and Clarendon Press.

Kymlicka, Will. 2001. *Politics in the Vernacular: Nationalism, Multiculturalism, and Citizenship*. Oxford: Oxford University Press.

Lambertson, Ross. 2005. *Repression and Resistance: Canadian Human Rights Activists 1930–1960*. Toronto: University of Toronto Press.

Levitt, Cyril, and William Shaffir. 1985. "The Christie Pits Riot: A Case Study in the Dynamics of Ethnic Violence—Toronto, August 16, 1933." *Canadian Jewish History Society Journal* 9 (1): 2–30.

Li, Peter. 1998. *The Chinese in Canada*. 2nd ed. Toronto: Oxford University Press.

Li, Peter. 1999. *Race and Ethnic Relations in Canada*. 2nd ed. Toronto: Oxford University Press.

MacKinnon, Mark. 2001. "Canadian Delegates Blast Homeland: Intolerance Exists, Say Activists Sponsored by Ottawa, But Few Turn Up to Listen." *The Globe and Mail* (August 31).

MacLennan, Christopher. 2003. *Toward the Charter; Canadians and the Demand for a National Bill of Rights, 1929–1960*. Montreal: McGill-Queen's University Press.

Mensah, Joseph. 2002. *Black Canadians: History, Experiences, Social Conditions*. Halifax: Fernwood.

Miki, Roy. 2005. *Redress: Inside the Japanese Canadian Call for Justice*. Vancouver: Raincoast Books.

Miki, Roy, and Cassandra Kobayashi. 1991. *Justice in Our Time: The Japanese Canadian Redress Settlement*. Vancouver: Talonbooks and National Association of Japanese Canadians.

Murphy, Rex. 2001. "Babble from Genocide's Bystanders." *The Globe and Mail* (September 1).

Nunoda, Peter Takaji. 1991. "A Community in Transition and Conflict: The Japanese Canadians, 1935–1951." Ph.D. dissertation, University of Manitoba.

Parekh, Bhikhu. 1997. "Dilemmas of a Multicultural Theory of Citizenship." *Constellations (Oxford, England)* 4 (1): 54–62.

Parekh, Bhikhu. 2000. *Rethinking Multiculturalism: Cultural Diversity and Political Theory*. London: Macmillan.

Phillips, Susan D., and Katherine A. Graham. 2000. "Hand-in-Hand: When Accountability Meets Collaboration in the Voluntary Sector." In *The Nonprofit Sector in Canada: Roles and Relationships*, ed. Keith Banting, 149–90. Montreal: School of Policy Studies and McGill-Queen's University Press.

Porter, John. 1965. *The Vertical Mosaic: An Analysis of Social Class and Power in Canada*. Toronto: University of Toronto Press.

Pulido, Laura. 2006. *Black, Brown, Yellow, and Left: Radical Activism in Los Angeles*. Berkeley, CA: University of California Press.

Smith, Miriam. 2005. *A Civil Society? Collective Actors in Canadian Political Life*. Peterborough: Broadview Press.

Stasiulis, D.K. 1994. "'Deep Diversity': Race and Ethnicity in Canadian Politics." In *Canadian Politics in the 1990s*, ed. Michael S. Whittington and Glen Williams, 181–217. Toronto: Nelson.

Stasiulis, D.K. 1997. "Participation by Immigrants, Ethnocultural/Visible Minorities in the Canadian Political Process." Paper prepared for Heritage Canada, presented at the Research Domain Seminar on "Immigrants and Civic Participation: Contemporary Policy and Research Issues." Montreal, November 23.

Stasiulis, D.K., and Y. Abu-Laban. 1991. "The House the Parties Built: (Re)constructing Ethnic Representation in Canadian Politics." In *Ethno-cultural Groups and Visible Minorities in Canadian Politics: The Question of Access*. Vol. 7 of the Research Series, Royal Commission on Electoral Reform and Party Financing, ed. Kathy Megyery, 3–99. Toronto: Dundurn Press.

Sunahara, Ann Gomer. 1981. *The Politics of Racism: The Uprooting of Japanese Canadians During the Second World War*. Toronto: Lorimer.

Sunday, Julie. n.d. "Minority Rights." *Globalization and Autonomy Online Compendium*. Ottawa: SSHRC-MCRI. http://globalautonomy.ca/global1/glossary_entry.jsp?id=CO.0030 (accessed April 17, 2013).

Tulchinsky, Gerald. 1992. *Taking Root: The Origins of the Canadian Jewish Community*. Toronto: Lester Publishing.

Ukrainian Canadian Congress. n.d. "News." http://www.ucc.ca/category/news/ (accessed April 17, 2013).

Ward, Peter W. 1978. *White Canada Forever: Popular Attitudes and Public Policy Toward Orientals in British Columbia*. Montreal: McGill-Queen's University Press.

Wente, Margaret. 2001. "A Burning Cross to Bear." *The Globe and Mail* (September 1).

Winks, Robin W. 1997. *The Blacks in Canada: A History*. Ottawa: Carleton University Press.

Young, Iris Marion. 1997. "Polity and Group Difference: A Polity of Presence?" In *Contemporary Political Philosophy*, ed. R.E. Goodin and P. Pettit, 256–72. Oxford: Blackwell.

Yuzyk, Paul. n.d. http://www.yuzyk.com/biog-e.shtml (accessed April 17, 2013).

Zucchi, John E. 1988. *Italians in Toronto: Development of a National Identity, 1875–1935*. Montreal: McGill-Queen's University Press.

SEVEN

The Women's Movement in Flux: Feminism and Framing, Passion and Politics[1]

ALEXANDRA DOBROWOLSKY

The women's movement embraces multiple ideas, identities, and strategies. It articulates diverse views about feminism such as liberal, socialist, radical, and post-structuralist, as well as anti-racist, LGBTQ, and disability. In Canada, the women's movement is also diversified in terms of its position on nation (e.g., Canadian nationalism or Quebec and Aboriginal nationhood), its regional (e.g., the West differs from Atlantic Canada or the North) and provincial differentiation (Collier, 2009: Jenson, 2009), as well as its urban versus rural distinctiveness (e.g., agrarian feminism: Carbert, 1995; Wiebe, 1995).

These different visions are not only intellectually rooted but are often emotionally charged and experientially felt, validated, and vindicated. This stems from the fact that the women's movement is made up of an array of actors, organizations, and coalitions. The women involved have fluid, multiple, and intersecting identities in terms of race, ethnicity, class, sexual orientation, ability, age, location, and so on. Women's organizations take different shapes "ranging from informal women's collectives, to women's studies programs in universities, to more structured professional organizations" (Gelb and Hart, 1999: 177). Moreover, they have varied network structures, networking within the women's movement (intra-movement; see Phillips, 1991) and forming alliances with other social movements (inter-movement networking; see Dobrowolsky, 2000) and sometimes other representational forms (such as political parties or states). Such networks can be consciously crafted "and embedded in society and institutions" (Tarrow, 1994: 184) or can be "dispersed, fragmented and submerged" emerging only "sporadically in response to specific issues" (Melucci, 2000: 94).

This sweep of ideas and identities, along with such organizational complexity, translate into varied forms of activism. The women's movement can model itself on a pressure group or even a political party. It can also take the form of a service provider offering practical assistance directly to women (Michaud, 1997: 201). Alternatively, it can eschew institutionalization and hierarchies, push countercultural buttons, and resort to dramatic disruptions and even violent protests. It pioneered the idea that "the personal is political," drawing attention to the fact that if politics is truly about power relations, then political struggles can occur beyond formal political arenas in workplaces, communities, homes, and families, as well as in personal interactions (Rebick, 2009). All this gives rise to contested views and contentious choices about whether to work outside conventional political structures, or to engage with them (Adamson et al., 1988; Bashevkin, 1993; Briskin and Eliasson, 1999; Whitaker, 1999), or to do both, which is typically the case (Macpherson, 1994).

In spite of the heterogeneity of the women's movement and its forms of organizing, in different periods it has sought to achieve degrees of consensus and coordinate efforts to press for change. Certain perceived injustices served to focus the movement: suffrage as the defining feature of the so-called "first wave" of the women's movement; and abortion, violence against women, and diversity concerns in the "second" and "third waves."

This chapter highlights the complex strategies, identities, and ideas of Canada's women's movements. While identities and ideas clearly influence movement mobilization (see Dobrowolsky, 1998, 2000, 2002; Dobrowolsky and Hart, 2003), overall, more attention is paid to the women's movement's strategic interventions—and interruptions—which are analyzed by selectively drawing from and building on the "framing" approach (Snow and Benford, 1988, 1992; Benford and Snow, 2000). The aim is to show how this movement has demonstrated the capacity to engage across multiple levels from the state to the grassroots, locally and globally, and how it has shaped the broader "universe of political discourse" in Canada (Jenson, 1989).

The first part of the chapter provides a sampling of the forms mobilization has taken across space, in Canada, the UK, and the US. In the second section, I review social movement theories and situate the framing approach. Through examples from Canada across time, I then show how coordinating women's movement action across multiple levels can lead to challenges to existing political meanings and practices. I also critically evaluate the oft-proclaimed demise of the women's movement by drawing on a feminist-inspired framing analysis. This demonstrates not only how pan-Canadian women's groups whose "collective-action frames" tended to be more *pro-active* in the 1960s, 1970s, and early 1980s grew more *reactive* from the late-1980s to the detriment of women's movement passions and politics, but also how recent developments hold more promise.

WOMEN'S MOVEMENTS: PASSION AND POLITICS

Because it has always been concerned with ideological and cultural as well as legislative change, and given that it operates on many fronts, the women's movement engages in a passionate politics of the deepest and broadest kind. This can include small "p" politics, as when second-wave feminists wove political statements through quilts or chain link fences (e.g., the women's Greenham Common peace camp protest of nuclear missiles being housed at a UK air force base). In Canada, the group Equality Eve made it clear that constitutionalism was not the reserve of "high politics" by printing women's equality rights demands on kitchen table placemats (see Dobrowolsky, 2000). Third-wave Guerrilla Girl campaigns in the US (Henderson and Jeydel, 2010: 63) included spray painting "FEED ME" across billboards featuring stick-like female fashion models. This use of wit and ingenuity to spark changes in individual consciousness and spur broader collective action are often associated with mobilizing ideas and action from "without" and are considered typical of the grassroots women's movement.

Beyond providing a challenge from without, in civil society, in everyday speech and acts, and in the so-called "private" sphere, the women's movement has also mobilized from "within," contesting various public and mostly male-dominated institutions (Katzenstein and Mueller, 1987; Henderson and Jeydel, 2010), making it distinctive from other social movements. As Mary Katzenstein observes, "Most feminists of the second wave live their lives inside institutions—inside universities, churches, professions, unions, hospitals, social service agencies, schools, police forces, military corps, athletic teams. They have learned that the linkages connecting those on the inside to those on the outside are multi-layered" (1998: 41). While it is sometimes "unobtrusive," this mobilization has nonetheless had transformative effects (Katzenstein, 1990), even within male bastions such as the American military and the Catholic Church (Katzenstein, 1998).

Furthermore, the women's movement has been intent on infiltrating and influencing large "P" politics or traditional political forms (Bashevkin, 1993). Examples include professional organizations, such as Canada's Committee for 94, which sought to increase women's numbers in the House of Commons by 1994 (Young, 2000), and, more recently, Equal Voice's efforts aimed at increasing and easing women's entry into formal politics (Equal Voice, 2013). Groups such as Emily's List, in the US and the UK, work to raise funds to achieve these ends (Gelb and Hart, 1999: 153). Some, such as the British Women's Labour Network, are directly tied to political parties, but others work outside them, as does Britain's long-standing Fawcett Society (established 1866). These organizations study, scheme, and support various actions—from training workshops and fundraising to sustaining educational and media outreach—aimed at boosting women's traditional political participation and keeping women's concerns in the public eye.

The women's movement's influence is also apparent inside state structures. For instance, "Status-of-women" machinery was developed in the US Department of Labor in the 1920s and with the Women's Bureau established in Canada's Labour Department in 1950 (Rankin and Vickers, 2001: 7). Femocrat (feminist bureaucrats; Eisenstein, 1996) efforts intensified especially in the 1970s and early 1980s in Canada and in the late 1990s in the UK (Findlay, 1987; Chappell, 2002). There were also attempts to forge inside-outside connections with the establishment of bodies such as the Canadian Advisory Council on the Status of Women (CACSW, established 1973; see Burt, 1998).

If any categorical claims can be made about women's movements it is that their strategies epitomize multi-pronged activism. To illustrate, women's mobilization at both provincial and federal levels was necessary to achieve basic political reforms whereby many (most, but not all) Canadian women could vote by 1918. Even so, 11 years later, five prominent women resorted to launching a notorious legal battle to acknowledge that women in this country were indeed "persons" and thus could be appointed to the Senate. This fight went to what was then Canada's highest court of appeal, the Judicial Committee of the Privy Council in the UK. Over five decades later, in the 1970s, Aboriginal and non-Aboriginal women's groups resorted to sit-ins, marches, and legal battles that extended beyond Canadian courts to the UN Human Rights Committee to ensure that equality before the law applied to Aboriginal women.

In other places as well, acquiring basic political and legal rights for women involved more than lobbying and legal challenges. The tactics used to get women the vote in the US and the UK could be quite dramatic. American militant suffragettes declared: "We . . . believe in standing on street corners and fighting our way to recognition forcing the men to think about us . . . We glory that we are theatrical" (Dubois, 1990: 189). In the UK, suffragettes "stormed the House of Commons, heckled cabinet ministers, broke windows and went to prison," and while in jail, resorted to hunger strikes and endured force feeding to secure the female franchise (Rowbotham, 1997: 11).

Whereas some accounts distinguish more conventional or "institutionalized" women's movement efforts (Adamson et al., 1988) from grassroots campaigns, or categorize groups as reformist versus radical, such distinctions are problematic (Ryan, 1992). Reformist organizations can radicalize, just as grassroots groups can institutionalize. Similarly, inside/outside orientations can change over time and space. In the 1970s, Canada's National Action Committee on the Status of Women (NAC) was considered to be a mainstream interest group, but it certainly displayed a different face and focus in the 1980s and 1990s as its executive diversified and adopted confrontational social movement tactics that challenged fundamental state commitments from free trade to constitutional reform (Bashevkin, 1989; Vickers, Rankin, and Appelle, 1993; Macdonald, 1995).

The women's movement clearly draws upon a wide and diversified strategic repertoire. Certain activities may be manifestly obvious, but others may be imperceptible. Visible action can include the work of forming women's caucuses in political parties or women's centres on university campuses, as well as establishing feminist publishing houses, striking task forces, creating collectives, and organizing marches and demonstrations. Raising public awareness, forging alliances, creating and having new discourses take hold, and inspiring individual consciousness are not as easily observable. Gains at this level are especially difficult to assess. However, even discursive innovations—such terms coined by the women's movement as gender, sexual harassment, date or marital rape, maternity/paternity leave, and pay or employment equity—have not only changed "social discourse" (Fraser, 1992) but politico-legal practices as well.

Women's movements have been bold and confrontational, but they have also mobilized in less combative ways, using silence and non-violent means, playing on psyches, and counting on personal transformations to build support. They have challenged conventional and unconventional political spaces in very noticeable as well as less conspicuous manners by keeping gender at the forefront and often accommodating other identities as well. In sum, the women's movement has used *multi-level political coordination* to act as a *signifying agent*. In so doing, it has helped to transform the terms of what it means to be political, as well as the terrain of political struggle.

SOCIAL MOVEMENT THEORY AND THE WOMEN'S MOVEMENT

This complexity poses analytical challenges. In general, there have been three schools of thought in the study of social movements: (1) resource mobilization, (2) the political process model, and (3) new social movement theory (Smith, 2005: 38–39). Each approach contains strengths and weaknesses (Staggenborg, 2012). The first two, which are American-inspired orientations, focus more on tactics and political institutional factors, whereas the third, a European-influenced school, considers broader structures, ideas, and identities. However, all three have had difficulty reconciling that social movements negotiate both strategy and identity, that politics must be understood broadly in ways that encompass traditional political forms as well as a wider universe of political discourse, and that social movements are both affected by and can also affect politics. As we have seen, these are precisely the issues at stake for women's movements.

The framing approach attempts to bridge the divide between American and European scholarship on social movements (see Polletta and Jasper, 2001) as it includes a "sense of a dynamic evolving process" (Benford and Snow, 2000: 614) as well as an appreciation of agency, which have been lacking in both political process and European structuralist models. Framing is based on collective action frames: "action-oriented sets of beliefs and meanings that inspire and legitimate the activities and campaigns of a social movement organization" (Benford and Snow, 2000: 614). In others words, framing underscores the meaning construction of social movements. This is useful when it comes to evaluating the scope of the women's movement because it considers not only conventional mobilization patterns but also the politics of ideas and signification.

Nevertheless, framing tends to downplay powerful structural determinants and still grapples with the nature and impact of discursive processes. It has been criticized by some feminist scholars for essentially "cooling" the analysis of social movements in that it is ultimately more at home in the American camp that relies on "cool" tactical calculations and "cold" cognitive analyses (Masson, 1997: 64; Ferree and Merrill, 2000: 457). Less quantifiable variables such as emotion are not factored in sufficiently (Taylor, 1995; Aminzade and McAdam, 2001; Tarrow, 2001: 8). The framing approach, in effect if not intent, is therefore gendered as it succumbs to a reason versus emotion dichotomy that corresponds to male/female social constructions whereby men are considered rational and dispassionate and women irrational and emotional (Ferree and Merrill, 2000: 457). In contrast, feminist scholarship has not only exposed "the rationalist assumptions that disconnect reason and emotions" but also points to "the emotional dimension of rationality" (Aminzade and McAdam, 2001: 23).

The balance of this chapter will attempt to fill in the gaps of the framing approach by highlighting important strategic and discursive interventions on the part of the Canadian women's movement, drawing on the contributions of feminist scholars whose work often preceded the framing analysis (e.g., Jenson, 1985, 1989). It will keep "up the heat" by not losing sight of the passionate, emotional, and provocative side of women's movement organizing and how it feeds and fans its past and present mobilizational fires. And yet, it will also remain heedful of some of the excesses of new social movement theorists who contend that collective action is mostly cultural and that traditional political actors and institutions are waning in importance (Melucci, 1996). The women's movement illustrates that both passion and politics (in the broadest sense) are intertwined as its organizing has attempted to transform politics in bedrooms and kitchens and on the streets as well as throughout formal political institutions at home and abroad.

Structures, dominant ideologies, institutional discourses, and traditional political practices matter—and they can certainly influence women's movement organizational forms and affect strategic choices; nevertheless, the women's movement does not necessarily grow out of structural arrangements, conventional political institutions, or ideologies (the view taken in Vickers, Rankin, and Appelle, 1993). Rather, the claim being made here is that the women's movement has been, in and of itself, a *signifying agent* particularly when it engages in *multi-level political coordination*. When this occurs, the women's movement produces alternative words and deeds, challenging, and in some cases changing, institutions, ideas, and identities. As we shall see, this also can create a backlash; and so, repercussions and remedies also require exploration.

FROM PRO-ACTIVE TO REACTIVE FRAMES

Today, the general perception is that the women's movement is, if not dead, in chronic decline (Rebick, 2005: 254). However, framing analysis helps us to critically assess these claims. From the 1960s to the present, the Canadian women's movement, broadly speaking, has shifted the nature of its strategizing, with an overall change in orientation from *pro-active* to more *reactive* "collective action frames." Pro-active frames challenge ideas, identities, and institutions on a range of fronts, epitomizing multi-level political coordination. Here the blurring of small and big "P" politics is most apparent: the women's movement truly acts as a *signifying agent* promoting new discourses and actions, challenging and changing informal and formal political structures and spaces. In contrast, *reactive* frames draw on strategies that are less diversified. Compelled to respond to detrimental socio-economic and political developments, the women's movement is unable to achieve the same degree of political and cultural recognition and responsiveness. Consequently, its efforts at signification, re-signification, and transformation are slowed and/or stymied.

Very briefly, the women's movement in Canada grew and diversified from the 1960s onward. Women mobilized in the streets, in collectives, and in an array of institutions, and they also worked on achieving policy impact. Until roughly the mid-1980s, the movement took hold of, and helped to open, various "windows of reform" (Helfferich and Kolb, 2001: 145) at a time when the political climate was warmer. Inside/outside political interactions proliferated and helped to push the state to take action. The women's movement not only prodded the construction of state machinery noted above but also made strategic alliances with women on the inside (Findlay, 1987; O'Neil, 1993; Geller-Schwartz, 1995). Institutions such as the Status of Women Canada (SWC—1971) and the Secretary of State's Women's Program were established, the latter providing pivotal funding to women's organizations (Chappell, 2002: 87). The state's financial support of the women's movement grew and facilitated movement expansion. For example, the state allocated resources to support the projects of women's organizations large and small. It also set up initiatives such as the Court Challenges Program, which could assist women's litigation strategies and equality struggles, bolstering the efforts of groups such as the Women's Legal Education and Action Fund (LEAF, established 1985).

Up to the mid-1980s, the tail end of the welfare state meant there were funds available to support organizational activity and launch new structures and programs in and outside the state. This was legitimized by prevailing notions of a socially just, fair, and equitable society. The women's movement not only seized but also tried to shape these opportunities by, for instance, formulating new sexual equality provisions for the new Charter of Rights and Freedoms in the hope that this would prompt moves beyond formal to more substantive equality.

As the women's movement grew more multi-dimensional, it required more careful, and often more complicated, thought and action. Feminist fundamentals were unpacked and deconstructed. They not only had to accommodate liberal, socialist, and radical feminist ideas but anti-racist, critical disability, post-modernist, and post-structuralist feminism, causing some feminists to tie "themselves in theoretical knots" (Rebick and Roach, 1996: 189). Debates over the need for a multi-racial women's movement were difficult and often highly emotionally charged, but building such a movement proved even more challenging and impassioned.

This growing sophistication and hybridization took place as the socio-economic, political, and cultural environment grew less congenial (Brodie, 1995; Bashevkin, 1998, 2002) and the nature and meanings of citizenship began to change (Jenson and Phillips, 1996; Dobrowolsky and Jenson, 2004). The women's movement had helped to promote discourses of equality and social citizenship, but these no longer resonated with the embrace of a more individualistic, market-oriented culture epitomized by the adoption of neoliberal terminology and policy preferences (including state downsizing, downloading, deregulation) that disproportionately negatively affected women. (Bashevkin, 2002; Cossman and Fudge, 2002; Dobrowolsky, 2004, 2009b) Equality of opportunity and economic competitiveness eclipsed social justice concerns, and social spending diminished or was disguised by the term "social investment," all of which served to undercut a collectivist women's movement demanding equality of condition as an end result (Dobrowolsky 2009a; Jenson 2009).

To be sure, the women's movement's multi-pronged political coordination had left its mark on both formal and informal political terrains, influencing discourses and practices from the level of the state to people's identities, thinking, and ways of acting. Symbolically, there were now many more women "firsts" on legal and political fronts—from the first female Supreme Court justice (Bertha Wilson) to the first female prime minister (Kim Campbell)—but there had been other, more destabilizing political benchmarks. Women had put issues such as employment and pay equity, abortion, and pornography on the policy agenda. Societal transformations had taken place through the instigation of the women's movement, including unprecedented numbers of women with small children working outside the home, as well as a revolution in terms of sexual mores. To be sure, women still worked for less pay than men; they were typically employed in "pink collar ghettos"; and their sexuality was still not unconstrained by both social and political circumstances. Nevertheless, there was general acknowledgment that the women's movement had brought about positive changes for women.

These perceived gains also contributed to a backlash against the movement and feminism in Canada and elsewhere (Faludi, 1992). Given neoliberal priorities, the Canadian state's women's group funding diminished, but along with the cuts, the federal government stepped up its campaign of delegitimization. The women's movement and other social movements were now portrayed as irksome "special interests" (Dobrowolsky, 1998). State feminism contracted, as in 1995, when the CACSW and the Women's Program were collapsed into the SWC (Jenson and Phillips, 1996; Burt, 1998; Dobrowolsky, 2004), which, in turn, was progressively downsized and marginalized. As pressure from within and without weakened, women fell off the radar screen of governments and down the list of parties' policy priorities (Young, 2000).

Concomitantly, the women's movement was compelled both to diversify (in terms of identity) and specialize (with respect to strategy): it could not work on the assumption that all women were concerned about the same things, and this had an impact on how it organized. It found it increasingly difficult to speak with one voice and had to work more concertedly at its intra-movement (in the women's movement) networking. Inter-movement (between various social movements) networking and coalition building grew, also out of necessity. However, divisions over issues of race, ethnicity, sexual orientation, ability, and even nationalism could freeze movement activism. For example, when some women's organizations in the rest of Canada opposed the Meech Lake Accord, many Québécois feminist organizations were incensed as this deal was meant to bring Quebec back into the constitutional family (Roberts, 1988). Then, when it came to subsequent constitutional negotiations, the "Canada Round" of the early 1990s, which not only tried to accommodate two nations (Quebec and the rest of Canada) but Three Nations (adding First Nations), some national women's organizations refrained from taking a public stand on the multi-layered identities and issues involved (Dobrowolsky, 2000, 2003).

Moreover, counter-movements such as REAL (Real, Equal, and Active for Life) Women emerged in the 1980s to promote anti-feminist policies, rail against women's movement gains, and challenge women's movement funding provided by the Secretary of State Women's Program (MacIvor, 1996: 145–46). While the women's movement was no stranger to being questioned, caricatured, and even ridiculed, the intensity and pervasiveness of such critiques grew. High profile feminist organizations such as NAC and LEAF were specifically targeted in both the academic and popular press. By the early 1990s, buttons that read "NAC does not speak for me" appeared in response to NAC's high profile role in "No" forces around the Charlottetown Accord referendum.

Overall, the women's movement, as Sylvia Bashevkin (1998) recounts, was on "the defensive." Pauline Rankin and Jill Vickers also note that its relationship with the state grew "increasingly disengaged and conflictual" (Rankin and Vickers, 2001: 2). The women's movement appeared to retreat from the federal political scene. It had little alternative but to concentrate on providing services for women on the ground, given the fallout from state streamlining and privatization, but this had to be done with dwindling resources. Coalition work grew out of necessity as women aligned with other beleaguered, cash-strapped social movements. Given growing disillusionment with politics on the national scene, networking at the transnational level intensified. This was especially evident around and after the UN 1995 Fourth World Conference on Women held in Beijing, China (Rankin and Vickers, 2001: 53).

At the tail end of the 1990s and into the new millennium, the federal government took a new tack, no longer castigating "special interests" but promoting "partnerships." By this point, however, the women's movement was not the preferred partner (Dobrowolsky and Jenson, 2004; Jenson, 2009), and discourses had shifted to such a degree that women's movement claims appeared anachronistic. Novel Liberal government "social investments," such as its work toward a national child care scheme, were not grounded in a logic of equality but rather in a rationale of "employability," getting women into paid work, or calculations that suggested that investing in children (eventual workers) would provide good financial returns in the future. Then, even these ideas were nixed by the mid-2000s under a Conservative government that put in place a woefully inadequate $100 per month allocation billed as giving parents a "Choice in Childcare" (Newman and White, 2012: 232).

EXPLAINING THE CHANGING FRAMES

Like other movements, the women's movement needs to identify targets that cause injustice, propose solutions, and motivate people to action (Benford and Snow, 2000: 616–17; Staggenborg, 2012) And so, as Benford and Snow outline, a movement's collective action frames need to resonate (2000: 619). In the case of the women's movement, this resonance might have been affected by its own successes at multi-level political coordination and signification, as it adopted new discourses that had traction and worked to change socio-political realities. This caused the backlash recounted above, but also, for new generations of women, it made it appear as if the women's movement had already won the war when in many cases the battle has not even been decided. This came at a time when women's movement resources (financial, physical, and emotional) were depleted. Long-time feminist activists were burnt-out and worn out. New blood was needed, and yet the women's movement (with some exceptions) did not seem to be able to capture young women's imagination and inspire action as it used to. In short, this contributed to the diminution of the women's movement's passions and politics.

Consider just one example of how this played out. Across its waves, the women's movement has promoted equality, but now Canadians in general, and many young people in particular, assume equality exists between men and women. Recall that the women's movement not only ensured that women were considered "persons" but helped to entrench formal equality guarantees for women in the Charter in 1982 and fend off perceived incursions to these rights in the Meech Lake and Charlottetown Accord dramas (in 1987 and 1992). These formal victories did not, however, translate into substantive ones. Still, the assumption is that Canadian women have achieved equality, and thus it is difficult to stir young women's hearts or to spread awareness about how much more needs to be done so that substantive equality becomes a reality (Dobrowolsky, 2009a).

Granted, some feminists have been dubious about the equality focus altogether. From as far back as the first wave of the women's movement, there have been those who have sought to validate women's differences from men. In the second and third waves, equality has been further problematized as differences between women were highlighted and as the movement dealt with the fallout of its false universalism, that is, the women's movement tried to broaden its appeal in an effort to create a "universal sisterhood" and in so doing downplayed the multi-faceted nature of the movement and the identities involved. As Jacinthe Michaud explains, "the building of solidarity and consensus among several women's organizations set in motion a variety of ideological tendencies aimed at creating a convergence of interest or at least reaching solidarity at the level of organization forms" (1997: 201). Thus, Aboriginal women, women of colour, immigrant women, lesbians, women with disabilities, and others contested these portrayals (Lachappelle, 1982; Driedger, 1996; Agnew, 1996; Stone, 1997), resulting in more, and sometimes competing, issues being added to the Canadian women's movement agenda. This certainly helped make it more inclusive, but it meant that consensus became harder to reach, and it made framing less consistent. As Arun Mukherjee observed, this was when "plurality and difference" split "feminism" into "feminisms" and resulted in a "crisis of legitimation" (1992: 165–66). This had an impact on what Benford and Snow (2000) describe as frame consistency; that is, social movements require a measure of consistency in the messages they propagate. And yet, the women's movement, in particular, has had to negotiate such seemingly contradictory demands as equality, difference, and diversity (Harrison, 2003; Squires, 2003).

The issue of violence against women is instructive. For instance, the benefits of feminist-inspired sexual assault reforms were tempered when Aboriginal women and women of colour explained what was at stake for them. Women of colour criticized strategies that called for more police intervention, given their more contentious relations with police due to the intersecting dynamics of gender, race, and class. As Vijay Agnew explained, "It is unlikely that an abused black woman in Ontario would have much confidence in the police force, whose racism has so often been publicly examined and criticized" (1996: 202). To be clear, these were important interventions that showed how crucial it was for the women's movement to be more sensitive to diversity and divergent experiences. However, this also necessitated the disruption of frame consistency.

Finally, Benford and Snow (2000) point to the importance of the credibility of the frame articulators. The vilification of women's movement leaders has been present across the waves. A few examples include the caustic and even cruel cartoons drawn of suffragettes in the first wave (e.g., unattractive female caricatures with slogans such as "Women who've never been kissed"); second-wave women's movement icons portrayed, in the third wave, as misguided and even mentally unstable; and the third-wave championing of "former" feminists who retracted their commitments. This framing, however, grew consistently more negative. References to national women's groups in Canada were few and far between, and they were limited to stories recounting their divisiveness or unrepresentativeness. Women's movement leaders were blamed for the struggles of women's groups and their credibility was (highly inappropriately) especially questioned when women's organizations were no longer headed by white middle-class women. After Judy Rebick's tenure as president of NAC ended, several women of colour, in succession, went on to lead the organization. She recalls:

> [B]y the time I stepped down . . . women of colour and Aboriginal women held 40 per cent of the seats on the board and the next president, Sunera Thobani, was South Asian and an immigrant. The reaction to her election outside the organization was shocking. A Reform Party MP claimed—falsely—in the House of Commons that Thobani was an illegal immigrant. Lots of debate also surrounded the view that she couldn't represent Canadian women (2009: 107).

In a case of very bad timing, this more diverse leadership coincided with the period when NAC faced its most significant financial crisis, as the state would no longer provide operational but only project funding. While this is what primarily contributed to NAC's organizational decline, the media spread misinformation in describing how women of colour had taken over the organization. Racism and sexism clearly came into play with headlines such as this one in *The Globe and Mail:* "NAC has fallen into a 'skin trap,' critic says" (Sarick, 1996: A8). Negative framing by the media, combined with lack of federal support, helped to bring the organization to its knees.

Other women's groups focused on bringing about social and political change at the national level were also forced to operate in dramatically diminished circumstances or to close. As one recent study indicates, organizations prominent in the 1980s and 1990s "that had previously had large offices with several staff members were now reduced to a single individual working in temporary, borrowed spaces or from their homes." It is not at all surprising, then, that respondents in this same study "expressed their concern that the movement is losing human capital—research and writing skills, organizational memory, media savvy" (Rodgers and Knight, 2011: 575).

In short, both women's movement passion and politics have suffered over the last few decades. Certain recent developments suggest that the situation has moved from bad to worse. In the fall of 2006, the federal government proceeded to delete the goal of equality from the mandate of the SWC and removed $5 million from its $13 million budget. As a result, most SWC regional and provincial program offices had closed their doors by March 31, 2007. Moreover, SWC funding guidelines were revised so that women's groups that engaged in advocacy, lobbying, or research—core women's movement activities—could no longer apply for financial support. The Conservative government launched another round of cuts in May 2010, which ended project funding for "12 prominent, advocacy-oriented, national and provincial women's organizations" (Masson, 2012: 84). Other equality-seeking routes were also cut off when funding to the Court Challenges Program was eliminated. In so doing, the Harper government swiftly swept away the last vestiges of the status of women machinery in this country and did its best to wipe out any other avenues for equality seeking. Simply put, these "dramatic budgetary moves . . . served to cement the decades-long erosion and delegitimization of the women's movement" (Rodgers and Knight, 2011: 570).

The women's movement's multi-level action coordination and its capability to be a signifying agent have been seriously and negatively affected at a time when evidence of equality policy backsliding in Canada mounts (Dobrowolsky, 2009a). Recall the federal government's efforts to bury legislative changes to pay equity in its massive 2009 omnibus bill. The latter served to deflect scrutiny from the fact that pay equity complaints would now be heard by a federal labour relations tribunal instead of by the Canadian Human Rights Commission, and that unions could now face stiff fines for assisting complainants. In addition, despite claims that the Conservatives had no "hidden agenda" on abortion, and in spite of Prime Minister Harper's promise not to reopen the abortion issue, there have been several attempts to do just that since 2010 via Conservative backbenchers' private members bills.

Concomitantly, along with its constrained approach to child care, the Harper government's constricted maternal and child health initiatives, arising from the June 2010 G8 and G20 summits in Muskoka and Toronto (and that were reiterated in the Conservative Party platform of 2011), underscore the ironies involved. Not only is this maternal health policy exclusively directed toward the "poorest" countries around the world (i.e., not Canada, where equality, the government asserts, exists), but its circumscribed nature and ideological underpinnings were revealed when the government eventually disclosed that this plan would not include support for abortion services.

The current government is committed to neoliberal market solutions and fiscal austerity and neoconservative ideals and symbols. This helps to explain why it ignores (most notably with the plight of Aboriginal women) or dismisses equality seekers, why it demonizes certain movement campaigns (e.g., so-called "radical" environmental groups), and why the landscape for women's collective action appears more daunting than ever. Yet, precisely because these political, policy, and discursive shifts come at a time when various inequalities—from economic to environmental—are becoming all too apparent, as Rebick optimistically declares, "there are signs of hope for those who look" (2009: 9). In other words, this time of extreme socio-economic and political flux may be when such tensions and contradictions can be plumbed to once again open windows of reform and stir up winds of change.

THE WOMEN'S MOVEMENT REFRAMED:
LOCAL AND GLOBAL STIRRINGS

Given the mutability and perseverance of the women's movement across many waves, the challenges to its passion and politics recounted above do not represent a static, inevitable process. In other words, the foregoing is by no means a freeze frame—the potential exists to reframe the women's movement. The women's movement has been a political signifier and can again assume this role, but it needs to revive its multi-level political coordination in the context of contemporary local, national, and transnational configurations and through the adoption of novel strategies that draw in new and diverse supporters.

There are growing indications of these types of transitions taking place, suggesting that, just as feminism is always in the process of being reborn, so is the women's movement. As Rodgers and Knight's research reveals, "while some organizations have disappeared and others have declined, others have managed to survive by transforming the purpose of their organizations, reconnecting to their mass base and/or going online" (2011: 577). Their study indicates that feminist organizations are working to remake themselves via renewed alliances and through working within the broader social movement community (Rodgers and Knight, 2011). This is taking place at both local and global levels, and in ways that connect the two (on transnationalizing women's movements, see Dufour, Masson and Caouette, 2010).

To illustrate, Dominique Masson draws attention to mobilization taking place at the local level. She contends that "localized versions of restructuring coexist that have different implications in terms of the perspectives they open, preserve or foreclose for the pursuit of feminist politics" (1999–2000: 50). She writes:

> The now-classic feminist story about changing state forms and the funding of women's groups in Canada most often stops here: deprived of federal resources, groups were forced to reduce staff, change their mission, or simply put the key in the door. This certainly rings true for many national women-organizations—the eclipse of . . . [NAC] in 1998 is the best known example—but the effect these cuts had on grassroots groups is less clear (2012: 83–83).

And so, Masson makes a strong case "for fine-grained, institutional analyses of funding conditions that are attentive to context-specific and program specific variations, as well as to the potential impact of women's and community groups' mobilizations" (2012: 97–98). Otherwise, the marginalization of women's groups becomes an inevitable, unmovable process.

Consider local activism in 2012 around the thirtieth anniversary of women's constitutional recognition in Canada's Charter of Rights and Freedoms. The Harper government refused to acknowledge, let alone commemorate, this women's rights milestone and, instead, chose to pour over *$28 million* (Fitzpatrick, 2012) into events venerating the 200-year anniversary of the War of 1812! Undaunted, young feminist law students in Halifax launched an energetic campaign under the banner "Revisit. Renew. Rally." that included a book club, a film night, a panel of speakers—who appeared before a large, very full lecture hall—and a multi-media dance party, as well as a lobbying campaign in which birthday cards were signed, sealed, and sent to the prime minister to make the point that women were celebrating women's formal equality "birthday" but were no less concerned about ongoing substantive equality shortfalls.

Feminist mobilization requires the forging of strong links across experiences, cultures, and countries, but in ways that avoid occluding their differences. To do this, prevalent assumptions about frame consistency and legitimacy must be challenged. This does not mean reverting to a focus on universal ideals and single identities but, rather, harnessing fluid, multiple, reflexive feminist solidarities (Desai, 2002: 33) and reviving multi-level political coordination. In the contemporary context, this entails engaging local, national, and transnational networks around common concerns.

In the early 2000s, the Bread and Roses marches in Quebec provided an oft-cited example: what began as "la marche des femmes à travers le Québec" in 1995, when the Fédération des femmes du Québec (FFQ, 2013) worked with 20 different women's organizations across the province to focus on poverty and violence against women (Rebick and Roach, 1996: 183) transmuted into the pan-Canadian Bread and Roses March of 1996, which mobilized over 100,000 women in more than 100 communities across the county (CCA, 1999: 4). This then developed into the World March of 2000, and today the World March of Women is "a worldwide and new permanent mobilization of over 6,000 grassroots women's groups on every continent, unified by a common platform of demands and punctuated by periodic global mobilizations" (Conway, 2008: 208). To achieve this expression of transnational feminism (Dufour, 2005: Giraud and Dufour, 2010), women networked; built inter- and intra-movement alliances; and consolidated local, national, and global networks.

Worldwide protests instigated by Occupy Wall Street provide a glimpse of how individuals and groups can reframe causes, reforge alliances, and revive broader forms of mobilization. With a very clear and direct message, feminists made it known how and why Occupy matters for women:

> It boils down to one simple fact: Women suffer disproportion-
> ately in the current economic climate, which means that a protest
> for economic equality is a feminist protest—whether it admits it
> or not. A majority of the nation's poor unemployed are women,
> especially women of colour and single mothers. (Rogers, 2011)

At the same time, however, and quite notably, diversity was at the forefront of
this feminist Occupy campaign. As one blogger wrote:

> And while the rest of us, "the 99%," tend to [be] characterized
> by the media as a homogenous mass of ordinary, middle-class
> citizens (read: white and male), we are anything but. We are
> women, we are black, we are Latino/a, we are transgender, we
> are queer, we are disabled, we are homeless, we are indigenous,
> we are young, we are old . . . We have such an incredible op-
> portunity here. We've created an activist movement that is not
> only about examining the symptoms of inequality, but the very
> systems. (Kacere, 2011)

The women's movement must renegotiate local, national, and global spaces
with a combination of strategies that are more pro-active rather than reactive.
It needs to draw on destabilizing tactics that involve both the grassroots as
well as conventional political forms. This means reworking alliances between
outsiders and insiders. This also requires both personal and cultural change.
And, as Ryan suggests, "mobilization of people is not enough; social movements must also mobilize sustaining ideas" (1992: 156). For the women's
movement, these ideas need to resonate on many political and societal levels,
as well as for diverse women, young and old.

To do so, long-standing concerns may require addressing in new ways that
will reignite not only passions but also political controversies. To illustrate,
the confluence of gendered sexual stereotyping and violence against women
turned a local outrage into a contentious global campaign that not only
inspired and moved many but also fuelled heated debates around the choice
of discourses and strategies involved. A Toronto police officer's flippant comment that to remain safe "women should avoid dressing like sluts" spurred
thousands of women (and men) to take to the streets in a highly publicized
"SlutWalk" that took place in Toronto on April 3, 2011. Women donned a
range of attire from jeans and T-shirts to lingerie, fishnet stockings, and roller-
blades. The "revealing outfits" were intended "to bring attention to 'slut-
shaming' or shaming women for being sexual, and the treatment of sexual

assault victims" (CBC News, 2011). By May, a series of SlutWalk protests were staged nationally and internationally. Not only news but social media helped to publicize the protests. For instance, "organizers had planned for about 100 to attend the Boston event; by Thursday, more than 2,300 had responded to a Facebook shout-out. Another 2,000 have similarly committed to attend the SlutWalk Seattle on June 19" (CBC News, 2011).

Notably, the SlutWalk did not associate itself with feminism, and the choice of the term "slut," as well as the attention-grabbing attire featured in the marches, elicited criticisms from some feminists, especially women of colour and feminists in the Global South. Critics underscored how "capitalism mediates the feminist façade of choice by creating an entire industry that commodifies women's sexuality and links a woman's self-esteem and self-worth to fashion and beauty" (Walia, 2011). Others pointed out that "People need to realize that being 'scantily clad' is not the only patriarchal excuse that victimizes women. Sexual assaults against Muslim women are often minimized in our society because Muslim women are perceived as repressed, and therefore in need of sexual emancipation. I would much rather have attended a 'Do Not Rape' walk" (Nassim Elbardough, quoted in Walia, 2011). Moreover, some activists in the Global South failed to see the point in reclaiming a word, "slut," that was foreign to their vocabulary and therefore denounced this as just another example of Western feminist ideological imposition.

Nevertheless, SlutWalk marches and rallies were held in cities around the world from Austin and Bhopal to Jerusalem and Sao Paulo, where women flamboyantly drove home the message that they should be able to choose what they wear without being harassed and thereby laying bare the dangerous myth that feminists have sought to debunk for decades: that how women dress determines whether they will be raped. What is more, rallies typically ended with strong and clear feminist messages "with speakers and workshops on stopping sexual violence and calling on law enforcement agencies not to blame victims after sexual assaults" (CBC News, 2011). And even feminist critics have admitted to participating in SlutWalks to draw attention to the broader women's movement concerns at stake. As Harsha Walia, a "South Asian organizer and writer based in Vancouver" and active in a "range of anti-racist, anti-colonial, and feminist movements" explains:

> I attended for the simple reason that I am committed to ending victim blaming. The Slutwalks in Toronto and Vancouver came out of the specific contexts of comments by police officers . . . that were reinforcing to young women about how to avoid getting raped. In Manitoba, Judge Robert Dewar commented

that a young aboriginal rape survivor acted "inviting." Even though I did not march under the banner of "sluthood," I marched to mark the unceded territory of women's bodies. I marched because language is a weapon yielded against the powerless. I marched because rape and sexual assault can never be justified . . . to make visible the staggering reality of rape and violence against all women in so-called civilized countries like Canada. (Walia, 2011)

By the time the SlutWalk hit Vancouver on May 15, 2011, and despite the debates around it that had raged for weeks, this same commentator observed:

I was surprised at the actual diversity of the streets not captured by photographers seeking sensationalist images of bras and fish nets. There was no attempt to recruit everyone into one uniform vision of femininity, nor was there an overarching romanticizing of "sluttiness"; sexual autonomy was being self determined . . . Most heartening was the significant number of teenagers, who are perhaps most pressured . . . and most impacted by self-shame and victim-blaming and supporting their voices on the street was a critical gesture of solidarity. (Walia, 2011)

What is more, both the SlutWalk and Occupy phenomena also highlight the current mobilizational potential of social media. Indeed, new technologies and social media are being deployed in creative ways by both fledgling and deeply rooted women's organizations concerned with new and old feminist concerns. For instance, Hollaback! is a global network with a mandate to combat gender-based street harassment via Twitter and Facebook. Local websites are launched with the help of webinars. When an incident occurs, a text message or picture can be uploaded immediately, and mapping mechanisms record the location of the street harassment. As Rebecca Faria, who established Halifax's Hollaback! chapter in April 2012, explains, the site "gives a place for people to share stories of street harassment, whether it has happened to them or whether they have witnessed it . . . We want to ensure that everyone has access to public spaces, and that people realize what it can be like to be a woman or a queer person in public spaces" (d'Entremont, 2012: 1). Hollaback! sites contain a wealth of information, including models for how to support someone you witness being harassed. In some locales, as in New York, website managers have begun meeting with city officials to try to coordinate their efforts and create policies to combat street harassment.

In a new "Twitter guide for feminists," we find the announcement that one of Canada's oldest women's organizations, the YWCA, has developed the Safety Siren iPhone app (web-based application) to combat violence against women. Moreover, this same guide lists innovations such as "Up-to-the-minute tweets on racial justice issues" and advertises events such as the SPARK Summit that is "designed to engage girls in discussions about healthy sexuality vs. objectification in order to challenge the damage caused by the media's unhealthy sexualisation of girls." (YWCA, 2012). These are but a few recent examples intended to illustrate the potential to reframe women's movement causes and revamp multi-level coordination via innovative strategies and technologies that reach out to diverse women in the contemporary "glocal" environment.

In conclusion, more than any other social movement, the women's movement has helped to blur the distinctions between small "p" and big "P" politics. It has brought new issues to the fore, devised new discourses, and engaged in multi-level political coordination to elicit both societal and political action whereby countless diverse women "transformed themselves from passive observers of the world into active agents of change" (Rebick, 2005: xiv). This is precisely why the women's movement can be characterized as a dynamic, evolving process that is at once passionate and political and therefore has had and continues to have multi-dimensional impact. It is truly a signifying agent, albeit one marked by changes over space and time. In the words of one Occupy blogger:

> We feminists have been arguing all along the society needed to change. We've always wondered why those around us weren't angrier at the way women and other non-dominant and marginalized groups were being treated. Well here it is—the anger, the frustration, the passion and the energy to change the underlying values that govern society. We've long understood the interconnectedness of all forms of oppression, that one cannot dismantle one form of inequality without dismantling them all. The people are ready, the dismantling has begun. The time is now (Kacere, 2011).

NOTE

1   My sincere thanks to Mathieu Lapointe and Steve Lelievre for their research assistance, and to Marc Doucet for his comments on a much earlier draft of this chapter. Thanks also to Jennie Donovan for her efforts to track more recent research on this topic for this version.

REFERENCES AND FURTHER READING

Adamson, Nancy, Linda Briskin, and Margaret McPhail. 1988. *Feminist Organizing for Change: The Contemporary Women's Movement in Canada*. Toronto: Oxford University Press.

Agnew, Vijay. 1996. *Resisting Discrimination: Women From Asia, Africa, and the Caribbean and the Women's Movement in Canada*. Toronto: University of Toronto Press.

Aminzade, Ronald, and Doug McAdam. 2001. "Emotions and Contentious Politics." In *Silence and Voice in the Study of Contentious Politics*, ed. Ronald Aminzade, et al., 14–50. Cambridge: Cambridge University Press.

Bashevkin, Sylvia. 1989. "Free Trade and Canadian Feminism: The Case of the National Action Committee on the Status of Women." *Canadian Public Policy* 15 (4): 363–75.

Bashevkin, Sylvia. 1993. *Toeing the Lines: Women and Party Politics in English Canada*. 2nd ed. Toronto: Oxford University Press.

Bashevkin, Sylvia. 1998. *Women on the Defensive: Living Through Conservative Times*. Toronto: University of Toronto Press.

Bashevkin, Sylvia. 2002. *Welfare Hot Buttons: Women, Work, and Social Policy Reform*. Toronto: University of Toronto Press.

Benford, Robert D., and David Snow. 2000. "Framing Process and Social Movements: An Overview and Assessment." *Annual Review of Sociology* 26 (1): 611–39.

Briskin, Linda, and Mona Eliasson. 1999. *Women's Organizing and Public Policy in Canada and Sweden*. Montreal: McGill-Queen's University Press.

Brodie, Janine. 1995. *Politics on the Margins: Restructuring and the Canadian Women's Movement*. Halifax: Fernwood.

Burt, Sandra. 1998. "The Canadian Advisory Council on the Status of Women: Possibilities and Limitations." In *Women and Political Representation in Canada*, ed. Manon Tremblay and Caroline Andrew, 115–44. Ottawa: University of Ottawa Press.

Carbert, Louise. 1995. *Agrarian Feminism: The Politics of Ontario Farm Women*. Toronto: University of Toronto Press.

CBC News. 2011. http://www.cbc.ca/news/canada/story/2011/05/06/slut-walk.html (accessed April 4, 2013).

CCA (Comité canadien d'action sur le statut de la femme). 1999. La marche mondiale des femmes 2000." *A L'action!* 9: 1, 4.

Chappell, Louise. 2002. "The 'Femocrat' Strategy: Expanding the Repertoire of Feminist Activists." In *Women, Politics and Change*, ed. Karen Ross, 85–98. Oxford: Oxford University Press.

Collier, Cheryl. 2009. "Violence against Women or Violence against 'People'?: Neo-liberalism, 'Post-neo-liberalism', and Anti-violence Policy in Ontario and British Columbia." In *Women and Public Policy in Canada: Neo-liberalism and After?* ed. Alexandra Dobrowolsky, 166–86. Don Mills: Oxford University Press.

Conway, Janet. 2008. "Geographies of Transnational Feminisms: The Politics of Place and Scale in the World March of Women." *Social Politics* 15 (2) (Summer): 207–31.

Cossman, Brenda, and Judy Fudge. 2002. *Privatization, Law, and the Challenge to Feminism.* Toronto: University of Toronto Press.

d'Entremont, Yvette. 2012. "Taking harassment off the street." *Halifax Newsnet* (December 4) http://www.halifaxnewsnet.ca/News/2012-12-04/article-3133162/Taking-harassment-off-the-street (accessed January 3, 2013).

Desai, Manisha. 2002. "Transnational Solidarity: Women's Agency, Structural Adjustment, and Globalization." In *Women's Activism and Globalization: Linking Local Struggles and Transnational Politics*, ed. Nancy A. Naples and Manisha Desai, 15–33. New York: Routledge.

Dobrowolsky, Alexandra. 1998. "'Of Special Interest': Interest, Identity, and Feminist Constitutional Activism in Canada." *Canadian Journal of Political Science* 31 (04): 707–42.

Dobrowolsky, Alexandra. 2000. *The Politics of Pragmatism: Women, Representation, and Constitutional Activism in Canada.* Toronto: Oxford University Press.

Dobrowolsky, Alexandra. 2002. "Crossing Boundaries: Exploring and Mapping Women's Constitutional Interventions in England, Scotland, and Northern Ireland." *Social Politics* 9 (2) (Summer): 291–340.

Dobrowolsky, Alexandra. 2003. "Shifting States: Women's Constitutional Organizing Across Time and Space." In *Women's Movements Facing the Reconfigured State*, ed. Lee Ann Banaszak, Karen Beckwith, and Dieter Rucht, 114–40. Cambridge: Cambridge University Press.

Dobrowolsky, Alexandra. 2004. "The Chrétien Legacy and Women: Changing Policy Priorities With Little Cause for Celebration." *Review of Constitutional Studies* 9 (1/2): 171–98.

Dobrowolsky, Alexandra. 2009a. "Charter Champions? Equality Backsliding, the Charter and the Courts." In *Women and Public Policy in Canada: Neo-liberalism and After?* ed. Alexandra Dobrowolsky, 205–25. Don Mills: Oxford University Press.

Dobrowolsky, Alexandra. 2009b. *Women and Public Policy in Canada: Neo-liberalism and After?* Don Mills: Oxford University Press.

Dobrowolsky, Alexandra, and Vivien Hart, eds. 2003. *Women Making Constitutions: New Politics and Comparative Perspectives.* Houndmills, UK: Palgrave.

Dobrowolsky, Alexandra, and Jane Jenson. 2004. "Shifting Representations of Citizenship: Canadian Politics of 'Women' and 'Children.'" *Social Politics* 11 (2): 154–80.

Dobrowolsky, Alexandra, and Denis Saint-Martin. 2005. "Agency, Actors, and Change in a Child-Focused Future: Path Dependency Problematized." *Journal of Commonwealth & Comparative Politics* 4 (1): 1–33.

Driedger, Diane. 1996. "Emerging from the Shadows: Women with Disabilities Organize." In *Across Borders: Women with Disabilities Working Together*, ed. Diane Driedger, Irene Feika, and Eileen Giron Batres, 10–25. Charlottetown: Gynergy Books.

Dubois, Ellen Carol. 1990. "Working Women, Class Relations, and Suffrage Militancy: Harriot Stanton Blatch and the New York Woman Suffrage Movement." In *Unequal Sisters: A Multi-cultural Reader in US Women's History*, ed. Ellen Carol DuBois and Vicki L. Ruiz, 176–94. New York: Routledge.

Dufour, Pascale. 2005. "The World March of Women: First Quebec, Then the World?" *Claiming Citizenship in the Americas* (May 27).

Dufour, Pascale, Dominique Masson, and Dominique Caouette, eds. 2010. *Solidarities beyond Borders: Transnationalizing Women's Movements*. Vancouver: University of British Columbia Press.

Eisenstein, Hester. 1996. *Inside Agitators: Australian Femocrats and the Australian State*. Sydney: Allen and Unwin.

Equal Voice. 2013. *Mission Statement*. http://www.equalvoice.ca/mission.cfm (accessed April 4, 2013).

Faludi, Susan. 1992. *Backlash: The Undeclared War Against American Women*. New York: Anchor Books.

Ferree, Myra Marx, and David A. Merrill. 2000. "Hot Movements, Cold Cognition: Thinking about Social Movements in Gendered Frames." *Contemporary Sociology* 29 (3): 454–62.

FFQ (Fédération des femmes du Québec). 2013. http://www.ffq.qc.ca/ (accessed April 3, 2013).

Findlay, Sue. 1987. "Facing the State: The Politics of the Women's Movement Reconsidered." In Feminism and Political Economy, ed. Heather Jon Maroney and Meg Luxton, 31–50. Toronto: Methuen.

Fitzpatrick, Maureen. 2012. CBC News (June 15). http://www.cbc.ca/news/politics/story/2012/06/14/pol-war-of-1812-bicentennial-federal-events.html (accessed April 4, 2013).

Fraser, Nancy. 1992. "The Uses and Abuses of French Discourse Theories for Feminist Politics." In *Revaluing French Feminism: Critical Essays on Difference, Agency, and Culture*, ed. Nancy Fraser and Sandra Lee Bartky, 177–94. Bloomington: Indiana University Press.

Gelb, Joyce, and Vivien Hart. 1999. "Feminist Politics in a Hostile Environment." In *How Social Movements Matter*, ed. Marco Guigni, Doug McAdam, and Charles Tilly, 149–81. Minneapolis: University of Minnesota Press.

Geller-Schwartz, Linda. 1995. "Array of Agencies: Feminism and State Institutions in Canada." In *Comparative State Feminism*, ed. Dorothy McBride Stetson and Amy G. Mazur, 40–58. Thousand Oaks, CA: Sage.

Giraud, Isabelle et Pascale Dufour. 2010. *Dix ans de solidarité planétaire. Perspectives sociologiques sur la Marche mondiale des femmes*. Montreal: Les Éditions du remue-ménage.

Harrison, Cynthia.. 2003. "'Heightened Scrutiny': A Judicial Route to Constitutional Equality for US Women." In *Women Making Constitutions: New Politics and Comparative Perspectives*, ed. Alexandra Dobrowolsky and Vivien Hart, 155–172. Houndmills, UK: Palgrave.

Haussman, Melissa. 2000. "What Does Gender Have to Do with Abortion Law? Canadian Women's Movement-Parliament Interactions on Reform Attempts, 1969–1991." *International Journal of Canadian Studies* 21 (Spring): 127–54.

Helfferich, Barbara, and Felix Kolb. 2001. "Multilevel Action Coordination in European Contentious Politics." In *Contentious Europeans: Protest and Politics in an Emerging Polity*, ed. Doug Imig and Sidney Tarrow, 143–61. New York: Rowman and Littlefield.

Henderson, Sarah L., and Alana S. Jeydel. 2010. *Women and Politics in a Global World*. New York: Oxford University Press.

Jenson, Jane. 1985. "Struggling for Identity: The Women's Movement and the State." *West European Politics* 8 (4): 5–18.

Jenson, Jane. 1989. "Paradigms and Political Discourse: Protective Legislation in France and the United States." *Canadian Journal of Political Science* 22 (2): 235–58.

Jenson, Jane. 2000. "Canada's Shifting Citizenship Regime. Investing in Children." In *The Dynamics of Decentralization*, ed. T.C. Salmon and Michael Keating, 107–23. Montreal: McGill-Queen's University Press.

Jenson, Jane. 2001. "Rethinking Equality and Equity: Canadian Children and the Social Union." In *Democratic Equality: What Went Wrong?*, ed. Edward Broadbent, 111–29. Toronto: University of Toronto Press.

Jenson, Jane. 2009. "Writing Gender Out: The Continuing Effects of the Social Investment Perspective." In *Women and Public Policy in Canada: Neo-liberalism and After?* ed. Alexandra Dobrowolsky, 25–47. Don Mills: Oxford University Press.

Jenson, Jane, and Susan D. Phillips. 1996. "Regime Shift: New Citizenship Practices in Canada." *International Journal of Canadian Studies* 14 (Fall): 111–35.

Kacere, Laura. 2011. Feministcampus.org Blog (November 15). http://feminist campus.org/blog/index.php/2011/11/15/occupypatriarchy-why-feminists-should-care-about-the-occupy-movement/ (accessed December 13, 2013).

Katzenstein, Mary Fainsod. 1990. "Feminism Within American Institutions: Unobtrusive Mobilization in the 1980s." *Signs* 16 (11) (Autumn): 27–52.

Katzenstein, Mary Fainsod. 1998. *Faithful and Fearless: Moving Feminist Protest Inside the Church and Military*. Princeton: Princeton University Press.

Katzenstein, Mary Fainsod, and Carol McClurg Mueller. 1987. *The Women's Movements of the United States and Western Europe: Consciousness, Political Opportunity, and Public Policy*. Philadelphia: Temple University Press.

Lachappelle, Caroline. 1982. "Beyond Barriers: Native Women and the Women's Movement." In *Still Ain't Satisfied! Canadian Feminism Today*, ed. Maureen Fitzgerald, Connie Guberman, and Margie Wolfe, 257–64. Toronto: Women's Press.

Macdonald, Martha. 1995. "Economic Restructuring and Gender in Canada: Feminist Policy Initiatives." *World Development* 23 (11): 2005–17.

MacIvor, Heather. 1996. *Women and Politics in Canada*. Peterborough: Broadview Press.

Macpherson, Kay. 1994. *When in Doubt, Do Both: The Times of My Life*. Toronto: University of Toronto Press.

Masson, Dominique. 1997. "Language, Power, and Politics: Revisiting the Symbolic Challenges of Movements." In *Organizing Dissent: Contemporary Social Movements in Theory and Practice*, 2nd ed., ed. William K. Carroll, 57–75. Toronto: Garamond.

Masson, Dominique. 1999–2000. "Constituting 'Post-Welfare State' Welfare Arrangements: The Role of Women's Movement Service Groups in Quebec." *Resources for Feminist Research* 27 (3/4): 49–69.

Masson, Dominique. 2012. "Changing State Forms, Competing State Projects: Funding Women's Organizations in Quebec." *Studies in Political Economy* 89:70–103.

Melucci, Alberto. 1996. *Changing Codes: Collective Action in the Information Age*. Cambridge: Cambridge University Press.

Melucci, Alberto. 2000. "Social Movements in Complex Societies: A European Perspective." *Arena* 15:81–99.

Michaud, Jacinthe. 1997. "On Counterhegemonic Formation in the Women's Movement and the Difficult Integration of Collective Identities." In *Organizing Dissent: Contemporary Social Movements in Theory and Practice*, 2nd ed., ed. William K. Carroll, 197–212. Toronto: Garamond.

Mukherjee, Arun. 1992. "A House Divided: Women of Colour and American Feminist Theory." In *Challenging Times: The Women's Movement in Canada and the United States*, ed. Constance Backhouse and David H. Flaherty, 165–74. Montreal: McGill-Queen's University Press.

Newman, Jacquetta, and Linda A. White. 2012. *Women, Politics and Public Policy*. 2nd ed. Don Mills: Oxford University Press.

O'Neil, Maureen. 1993. "Citizenship and Social Change: Canadian Women's Struggle for Equality." In *Belonging: The Meaning and Future of Canadian Citizenship*, ed. William Kaplan, 314–32. Montreal: McGill-Queen's University Press.

Phillips, Susan D. 1991. "Meaning and Structure in Social Movements: Mapping the Network of National Canadian Women's Organizations." *Canadian Journal of Political Science* 24 (4): 755–82.

Polletta, Francesca, and James M. Jasper. 2001. "Collective Identity and Social Movements." *Annual Review of Sociology* 27 (1): 283–305.

Rankin, Pauline, and Jill Vickers. 2001. *Women's Movements and State Feminism: Integrating Diversity into Public Policy*. Study for the Status of Women Canada (May). Ottawa.

Rebick, Judy. 2005. *Ten Thousand Roses: The Making of a Feminist Revolution*. Toronto: Penguin.

Rebick, Judy. 2009. *Transforming Power: From the Personal to the Political*. Toronto: Penguin.

Rebick, Judy, and Kiké Roach. 1996. *Politically Speaking*. Vancouver: Douglas and McIntyre.

Roberts, Barbara. 1988. "Smooth Sailing or Storm Warnings? Canadian and Quebec Women's Groups on the Meech Lake Accord." A Report prepared for the Canadian Research Institute for the Advancement of Women. Ottawa: CRIAW.

Rodgers, Kathleen, and Melanie Knight. 2011. "'You Just Felt the Collective Wind Being Knocked Out of Us': The Deinstitutionalization of Feminism and the Survival of Women's Organizing in Canada." *Women's Studies International Forum* 34 (6): 570–81.

Rogers, Stephanie. 2011. "What Occupy Wall Street Owes to Feminist Consciousness Raising." (December 13). http://msmagazine.com/blog/2011/12/13/what-occupy-wall-street-owes-to-feminist-consciousness-raising/ (accessed December 12, 2012).

Rowbotham, Sheila. 1997. *A Century of Women: The History of Women in Britain and the United States*. London: Viking.

Ryan, Barbara. 1992. *Feminism and The Women's Movement: Dynamics of Change in Social Movement Ideology and Activism*. New York: Routledge.

Sarick, Lila. 1996. "NAC Has Fallen into 'Skin Trap,' Critic Says." *The Globe and Mail* (June 14): p. A8.

Smith, Miriam. 2005. *A Civil Society? Collective Actors in Canadian Political Life*. Peterborough: Broadview Press.

Snow, David, and Robert D. Benford. 1988. "Ideology, Frame Resonance, and Participant Mobilization." *International Social Movement Research* 1:197–218.

Snow, David, and Robert D. Benford. 1992. "Master Frames and Cycles of Protest." In *Frontiers in Social Movement Theory*, ed. Aldon D. Morris and Carol McClerg Mueller, 133–55. New Haven: Yale University Press.

Squires, Judith. 2003. "Reviewing the UK Equality Agenda in the Context of Constitutional Change." In *Women Making Constitutions: New Politics and Comparative Perspectives*, ed. Alexandra Dobrowolsky and Vivien Hart, 200–13. Houndmills, UK: Palgrave.

Staggenborg, Suzanne. 2012. *Social Movements*. 2nd ed. Don Mills: Oxford University Press.

Stone, Sharon Dale. 1997. "From Stereotypes to Visible Diversity: Lesbian Political Organizing." In *Organizing Dissent: Contemporary Social Movements in Theory and Practice*, 2nd ed., ed. William K. Carroll, 171–96. Toronto: Garamond.

Tarrow, Sidney. 1994. *Power in Movement: Social Movements, Collective Action, and Politics*. Cambridge: Cambridge University Press.

Tarrow, Sidney. 2001. "Silence and Voice in the Study of Contentious Politics: Introduction." In *Silence and Voice in the Study of Contentious Politics*, ed. Ronald Aminzade, et al., 1–13. Cambridge: Cambridge University Press.

Taylor, Verta. 1995. "Watching for Vibes: Bringing Emotions into the Study of Feminist Organizations." In *Feminist Organizations: Harvest of the New Women's Movement*, ed. Myra Marx Ferree and Patricia Yancey Martin, 223–33. Philadelphia: Temple University Press.

Vickers, Jill, Pauline Rankin, and Christine Appelle. 1993. *Politics As If Women Mattered: A Political Analysis of the National Action Committee on the Status of Women*. Toronto: University of Toronto Press.

Walia, Harsha. 2011. "Slutwalk: To march or not to march. In Her Own Words" (May 18). http://rabble.ca/news/2011/05/slutwalk-march-or-not-march (accessed April 4, 2013).

Whitaker, Lois Duke. 1999. *Women in Politics: Outsiders or Insiders?* 3rd ed. Englewood Cliffs, NJ: Prentice Hall.

Wiebe, Nettie. 1995. "Farm Women: Cultivating Hope and Sowing Change." In *Changing Methods: Feminists Transforming Practice*, ed. Sandra Burt and Lorraine Code, 137–62. Peterborough: Broadview Press.

Young, Lisa. 2000. *Women and Party Politics*. Vancouver: University of British Columbia Press.

YWCA. 2012. *New Twitter Guide for Feminists*. http://www.gender-focus.com/2012/09/14/new-twitter-guide-for-feminists/(accessed December 13, 2012).

EIGHT

Identity and Opportunity: The Lesbian, Gay, Bisexual, and Transgender Movement[1]

MIRIAM SMITH

Until the 1960s, lesbians and gay men led their personal lives in the shadows of Canadian society. Same-sex relationships were stigmatized and considered to be shameful and indicative of moral deviance or mental illness. The police routinely raided lesbian, gay, bisexual, and transgender (LGBT) gathering places such as bars, rounding up the clientele and sending them off to the police station to be charged with "gross indecency" or "buggery." The RCMP's "fruit machine" weeded out lesbians and gay men from government service, especially in the military and diplomatic services where their presence was thought to undermine moral and state security (Kinsman and Gentile, 2010). Many lesbians, gay men, and bisexuals socialized with each other in private networks, meeting only in each other's homes for fear of discovery; hiding their relationships and sexual lives from their families, co-workers, and communities; and living a veritable double life, in some cases, for all of their lives. Homosexuality was illegal, shameful, and hidden. Transgender (trans) people faced major barriers to transitioning, and stories of those who had successfully transitioned, such as Christine Jorgenson, were only beginning to be known to the public.

The status of LGBT people in Canadian law, society, and politics has changed fundamentally since the 1960s. In 2002–03, courts in Quebec, British Columbia, and Ontario ruled in favour of same-sex marriage, and, as these rulings were followed by courts in other provinces and territories, the federal Liberal government of Paul Martin legalized same-sex marriage in 2005. Discrimination on the basis of sexual orientation is prohibited in all Canadian jurisdictions, and discrimination on the basis of gender identity and expression are prohibited in Ontario and the Northwest Territories. Lively gay villages exist in Montreal, Toronto, and Vancouver. Huge Pride festivals in Canadian cities have brought queer life out into the open. Courts no longer routinely bar lesbian mothers from custody of their children, and, in most Canadian jurisdictions, same-sex couples have gained the right to adopt (including the right of second-parent adoption) and to enjoy a range of partner benefits. In Quebec and British Columbia, lesbian partners enjoy full filiation rights, meaning that same-sex parents can be listed together on the birth certificate, obviating the need for second-parent adoption. In an important tribunal decision, the Ontario Human Rights Tribunal ruled in 2012 that trans people do not have to have had surgery to register their gender identity of choice on their birth certificate, opening up the possibility of reform of passport regulations to permit the recognition of trans identities (*XY v. Ontario*, 2012; Houston, 2011). Queer student organizations exist on most Canadian university campuses, and professional associations have recognized lesbian and gay networks in their midst, such as the Sexual Orientation and Gender Identity Conference of the Canadian Bar Association.

Like the women's movement, the environmental movement, and other new social movements of the 1960s and 1970s, the LGBT movement challenges dominant social norms. As Alberto Melucci (1997) has pointed out, social movements do not always primarily dedicate themselves to changing public policies but also to changing the dominant "codes" of society. The LGBT movement challenges heteronormative norms or social codes. Heteronormativity means that social organization is structured around the assumption that heterosexual sexual preference and heterosexual coupling are the dominant modes of sexual, intimate, and family organization and that homosexuality is deviant. Even when dominant norms are not openly homophobic or hostile toward homosexuality, lesbian, gay, and bisexual people are outside of the "norm." So, for example, people are usually assumed to be heterosexual unless they state or are shown to be otherwise, an assumption that is an example of "heteronormativity." Some lesbian, gay, and bisexual people label themselves "queer"—traditionally a hostile epithet aimed at them—in part to call attention to the power of "naming" as a means of enforcing social expectations and defining "normalcy." Heteronormativity is not confined to social attitudes, norms, and values but is also enshrined in public policies. Until very recently, same-sex couples were not entitled to benefits provided to heterosexual couples, such as pensions or medical benefits provided by private or public sector employers. Such policies are "heteronormative" because they assume that heterosexual couples are the only form of couple or the only form of the couple that is worthy of the social and economic support they provide.

By the same token, emerging trans identities challenge the gender binary and the assumption that biological gender determines gender identity and expression. Trans people have pushed for the recognition of gender variance in Canadian social and political life (on trans issues in general, see Currah et al., 2006; on trans issues in Canada, see Trans Lobby Group, 2012).

This chapter will present the contemporary history of the LGBT rights movement(s) in terms of its origins in the gay liberation and feminist movements, and will survey the major issues that have been raised by queer activists in light of the theories of social movements outlined in the Introduction. Theories that highlight the role of the political process in creating obstacles and opportunities for social movement action as well as theories of legal mobilization are particularly relevant to the Canadian LGBT movement, which has successfully exploited the new political opportunities created by the empowerment of the judiciary under the Charter of Rights and Freedoms. While resource mobilization approaches stress the internal resources of the movement, the political process model stresses its external opportunities. The lesbian and gay movement has exploited external opportunities, despite the fact that it is not well-resourced in terms of formal organizations or large-scale funding. At the same time, new social movement theories call attention to the role of identity in the mobilization of collective actors. While the lesbian and gay movement engages the dynamics of recognition by the state and other societal actors as well as that of redistribution (e.g., through the material stakes in relationship recognition; see Fraser, 1995), the movement calls our attention to the ways in which collective identity is constructed through social and political processes. While same-sex behaviour has existed in many societies, it is only in the Western world since the 1960s that the identities of "gay" and "lesbian" have been formulated as identity options that are culturally available. The lesbian and gay movement could not exist unless LGBT people were willing to "come out" and embrace their identity. This "coming out" process constituted a direct and open challenge to heteronormative social codes. Therefore, theories that pay attention to culture and identity as well as to the political process of movement mobilization are the most useful in understanding the dynamics of this movement.

THE 1960S: HOMOPHILE ORGANIZING AND THE 1969 REFORMS

Several developments during the 1960s formed the essential backdrop for the emergence of the modern lesbian and gay rights movement as we know it in Canada today. In 1964, a homophile group called the Association for Social Knowledge (ASK) was founded in Vancouver to advocate for the legalization of homosexuality and for greater education and understanding of same-sex relationships. This group was similar to homophile groups in the US such as the Mattachine Society and the Daughters of Bilitis, which had been founded over the postwar period. The 1960s were dangerous times for lesbians and gay men, making political organizing difficult. These dangers were called to public attention by the case in the Northwest Territories of Everett George Klippert, who was convicted of "gross indecency" after admitting that he had engaged in consensual sex with other men. Klippert was then labelled a dangerous sex offender, meaning that he could be imprisoned indefinitely, and his sex offender status was upheld on appeal to the Supreme Court of Canada in 1967 (see *Klippert v. the Queen*). The Court's decision "raised the chilling prospect that any gay man could be imprisoned for life unless he could prove he was unlikely to recommit a same-sex act" (Warner, 2002: 46).

Partially in response to the public outcry over the Klippert case and to advocacy work by ASK and by the Canadian Bar Association, the federal government in 1967 followed the lead of the UK in tabling a bill to decriminalize homosexual acts between consenting adults 21 years of age or over. This bill, which was passed in 1969, meant that homosexual sex was "legal" in Canada, although the age of consent was higher for homosexual acts than for heterosexual acts. The 1969 reforms also provided for no-fault divorce and established a procedure by which women could obtain legal abortions. Therefore, the decriminalization of homosexuality was part of that package of legal reforms of the late 1960s that were epitomized by the famous quote from Liberal Prime Minister Pierre Trudeau "the state has no place in the bedrooms of the nation" (cited in English, 2006: 471). As for Klippert, he was released from prison in 1971, his only crime having been his relationships with other men.

Aside from the 1969 legal changes, the late 1960s and early 1970s also saw other developments that were important for the evolution of the lesbian and gay rights movement in Canada. The effervescent youth movement of this period and the rise of the women's movement were important precursors to the gay liberation movement. The women's movement politicized the questions of gender and sexuality as never before. It challenged traditional gender roles, the patriarchal nuclear family, and the regulation of women's bodies by men and by the state. Many lesbians were active in the women's movement, although the movement itself was not always friendly to lesbian politics. The youth movement of the late 1960s and the arrival of a large number of baby boomers in higher education helped fuel countercultural movements of the New Left. Many of the early activists in the gay liberation movement were drawn from university campuses. They led the transition from the homophile organizing of the previous generation, which had focused on the guarded strategies of education, and transformed themselves into gay liberation groups in 1970–71. As we shall see, unlike the early homophile activists of the 1950s and 1960s, gay liberation and lesbian feminist activists directly challenged the idea that homosexuality and lesbianism should be stigmatized or that they were in any way inferior to heterosexuality.

THE 1970S: GAY LIBERATION AND LESBIAN FEMINISM

The 1969 Stonewall riots in New York City marked the beginning of a new phase of radical gay politics in the US that almost immediately had repercussions in Canada. The police raid on a New York bar was similar to many other police raids on such establishments in both the US and in Canadian cities such as Montreal and Toronto. The difference in 1969 was that a group of lesbians, transsexuals, transvestites, and gay men at the Stonewall bar fought back against the police, defending their right to a public space—the bar—free from state repression (Duberman, 1993). By 1970 gay liberation groups, such as the Gay Liberation Front, had sprung up in New York.

An important aspect of the gay liberation movement was the way in which it was organized. While the homophile movement had been dominated by small groups of professionals who held educational evenings, the gay liberation movement held kiss-ins (or "zaps") and demonstrations. The more radical tactics were borrowed from strategies of the other countercultural movements of the 1960s. Further, the gay liberation movement was not centred in formal organizations but in a plethora of relatively small groups, which operated according to New Left principles of democratic and participatory decision-making rather than by conventional majoritarian decision-making. Its resources were located much more in informal organizing networks than in large-scale social movement organizations.

With regard to its interpretation of homosexuality and its demands on society and the state, gay liberation went much further than the homophile movement. Early gay liberationists claimed that everyone was inherently bisexual and aimed to free everyone from the rigid categories of gender and sexual preference (Altman, 1993 [1971]). At the same time, however, the gay liberation movement early on encountered a tension between the idea that categories of gender and sexuality should be erased and the need to construct lesbian and gay identities as a necessary prerequisite to the building of the movement. If everyone was inherently bisexual and "polymorphously perverse" (in the Freudian term used by early gay liberationists), then what was the distinctive basis for a gay liberation movement? Like other social movements, the gay liberation movement eventually sought to build a collective identity. Boundaries were drawn around the idea of "gay" as innate sexual orientation. The claim that people were born lesbian or gay was used to advance the cause of human rights. After all, it would be unfair to discriminate against people based on an innate characteristic they could neither change nor control (Epstein, 1987: 13–20). Therefore, in terms of the networked methods of organization of the movement, the emphasis on the personal as political, and the importance of culture and identity in the process of political identity, the lesbian and gay movement conformed to the model of new social movements and, with respect to these characteristics, was similar to and inspired by the second-wave feminists of the 1960s and 1970s.

The gay liberation movement took off in major Canadian cities over the course of the 1970s. Groups such as Toronto Gay Action, Gay Alliance Toward Equality in Toronto and Vancouver, the Association des gai(e)s du Québec in Montreal, the Coalition for Gay Rights in Ontario, and the Canadian Lesbian and Gay Rights Coalition worked on a common human rights agenda. Their demands were articulated in the document presented to Parliament by the protestors at the first gay liberation demonstration on Parliament Hill in August 1971. These included:

- removing "gross indecency" and "buggery" from the Criminal Code (and as a basis for declaration of dangerous offender status);
- equalizing penalties for sexual assault between heterosexual and homosexual acts;
- providing the same age of legal consent for heterosexual and homosexual sex;
- amending the Immigration Act to enable lesbians and gay men to immigrate to Canada;
- providing that lesbians and gay men may not be discriminated against in employment or promotion in public service;
- removing sodomy and homosexuality as grounds for divorce or for denial of child custody;
- permitting lesbians and gay men to serve in the Canadian Forces without discrimination;
- forcing the RCMP to publicly report on its witch hunt against lesbians and gay men in government service;
- providing equal status for homosexuals with respect to legal marriage, pensions, and income tax; and
- amending the Canadian Human Rights Act to include sexual orientation as a prohibited ground of discrimination (Waite and DeNovo, 1971).

Gay liberation groups throughout the 1970s used different strategies in pursuing this agenda, including demonstrating, lobbying, and litigating. Except in Quebec, where sexual orientation was included in the province's human rights legislation in 1977, these efforts at public policy change were not successful (for examples, see Higgins, 2000; Korinek, 2003).

Like other social movements, gay liberation was deeply structured by gendered relations between women and men. Many women felt that the movement's emphasis on sexuality and discrimination was not as relevant for lesbians as it was for gay men. They argued that, as women, they occupied a different position in society than men. Discrimination based on sex was probably more important for many lesbians than discrimination based on sexual orientation, even assuming that these could be meaningfully separated. A plethora of women's issues—such as male violence, gender inequality in the labour market, and child care—were also important issues. Similarly, sexual freedom was not prioritized by many lesbians, who viewed gay male activities such as public sex, bathhouses, and bars as activities that were not particularly worthy of political energies (Ross, 1995).

While some women participated in the gay liberation movement, others participated in the women's movement or in the autonomous lesbian movement. The women's movement was not particular friendly to lesbian issues during the 1970s and early 1980s; many lesbians worked mainly on "women's" rather than "lesbian" issues over this period. The autonomous lesbian movement focused on building social and political space to define the distinctive political interests of lesbians as separate from gay men or from straight women. Aside from the creation of social space and the building of collective identity, the autonomous lesbian movement spawned a range of groups such as the Lesbian Organization of Toronto and Lesbians against the Right in Vancouver (Ross, 1995). One of the most important groups to emerge from lesbian politics of this decade in Canada were lesbian mothers' groups, which took up the important political and legal issue of securing child custody for lesbian parents (Stone, 1991).

Yet, over the course of the 1970s, the subcultures of lesbian and gay life grew substantially in Canada's major cities. Whether at Church/Wellesley in Toronto, the famous gay village of Montreal, or the West End of Vancouver, lesbian and gay male life was increasingly lived out in the open. The cultures of queer life spawned social institutions ranging from Pride Day to the women's chorus. Community institutions such as the 519 Community Centre in Toronto and queer media such as *RG*, *Fugues*, and (later) *Être* in Montreal or *The Body Politic* and, later, the *Xtra* chain in Ottawa, Toronto, and Vancouver, all permitted the construction of a collective culture and identity for Canadian gay men and, to a lesser extent, lesbians.

THE 1980S: AIDS AND THE CHARTER

The AIDS epidemic had important effects on the evolution of LGBT politics in Canada as elsewhere. The epidemic resulted in the deaths of many of the pioneers of the gay communities of Canada's major cities while, at the same time, it reinforced the rise of the New Right by associating gay male sexuality with the spread of disease. The idea of open sexual expression became problematic as some argued that traditional gay spaces such as washrooms, parks, bars, and bathhouses should be regulated in the interests of public health. Others argued that what was needed was education about safe sex. Either way, the stigma of HIV/AIDS was very strong during the 1980s, and the liberatory potential of sex and sexual expression that had been so important in the gay liberation movement was undermined. The rise of the Moral Majority in the US, the election of the Progressive Conservative government of Brian Mulroney in 1984, and the establishment of the right-wing populist Reform Party in 1987, all indicated that the 1960s and 1970s had not been a one-way street to sexual openness and liberation but that traditional social conservative values, especially those associated with evangelical Protestantism, were still an important political force. The forces of moral regulation brought a new vulnerability to the LGBT communities, which expressed itself in part in new forms of politics that formed the roots of the contemporary Conservative Party and Conservative government of Stephen Harper (Herman, 1994; McDonald, 2010).

AIDS organizing shifted the balance in lesbian and gay organizing away from the human rights campaigns of the 1970s and toward political action centred on ending the epidemic. This does not mean that human rights issues went away. On the contrary, AIDS drew attention to the legal inequality of gay men, especially with regard to relationship recognition. When a gay man fell ill or died, his partner was often left with no legal rights and could be shut out by his partner's family of origin. A particularly important issue was that of medical decision-making. Same-sex partners were often prevented from participating in medical and health decisions.

The effects of AIDS were also felt in political organizing. The perceived lack of attention to HIV/AIDS in the medical community and the direction of resources for research and treatments sparked the revival of some of the earlier tactics of gay liberation as well as new forms of direct action. ACT UP (AIDS Coalition to Unleash Power), the radical American AIDS group, pioneered the use of direct action tactics to focus public action and attention on the AIDS crisis. With the slogan "Silence = Death," ACT UP used civil disobedience such as demonstrations and "die-ins" (a variation of a "sit-in") and directly targeted pharmaceutical corporations as well as the US Food and Drug Administration, which was responsible for certifying new drugs in the US (Sommella, 1997). In Canada, groups such as AIDS Action Now! in Toronto played an important role in putting AIDS on the agenda of the federal government (Rayside and Lindquist, 1992: 37–70). Further, over the course of the late 1980s, several groups were established to deal with the specific needs of racialized people with HIV/AIDS. Toronto's Black Coalition for AIDS Prevention and Vancouver's Black AIDS Network were formed to provide services and education in black communities. Gay Asians Toronto established the Gay Asians AIDS project, and similar organizations were established in the early 1990s by other groups (Warner, 2002: 325–26).

The radicalization and decentring of social movement politics over this period can also be seen in the rise of groups such as Lesbian Avengers and Queer Nation. These focused on direct action tactics to counter bashing and homophobic attacks on lesbians and gays in urban areas, as well as other issues (Visser, 1990: 1). The ideology and tactics of Queer Nation formed a striking contrast to mainstream political organizations. Instead of simply demanding that lesbians and gays be treated in the same way as straights through claims to equal rights, Queer Nation asserted a distinctive queer political identity while at the same time questioning the binary opposition of queer and straight. Instead of presenting briefs to government, Queer Nation engaged in direct action such as kiss-ins and street patrols. It represented a return to gay liberation ideology, especially in its assertion of a broader vision of social transformation. The tactic of kiss-in or "zap," for example, had been used in the early days of gay liberation in New York, Toronto, and elsewhere. While Queer Nation groups themselves were short-lived as political organizations in Canadian cities, they raised the flag on important issues that would animate lesbian and gay politics in the 1990s and after; in particular, groups such as Queer Nation and Lesbian Avengers called attention to the fact that lesbian and gay life constituted a distinctive culture or set of cultures of its own.

These forms of social movement politics highlighted the ways in which the movement over this period was not represented in a single movement or movement organization. Rather, lesbians and gay men organized in different locations, in AIDS organizing, in the women's movement, and in other locations. Often, as well, the targets of social movement activism were not only governments but also corporations, scientists, pharmaceutical companies, and the media. AIDS organizations such as ACT UP and urban groups such as Queer Nation and Lesbian Avengers often drew upon the radical template of the gay liberation and feminist movements, especially in their commitment to direct action (see Shepard and Hayduk, 2001). During this period, the resources of the movement were built up in AIDS organizations, yet much of the politics of the movement still occurred in decentred and decentralized social movement networks.

While the AIDS crisis and the radical politics of Queer Nation were emerging in the 1980s and early 1990s, another important development occurred that would shape lesbian and gay politics in Canada over the coming decades:

the entrenchment of the Charter of Rights and Freedoms in the Canadian Constitution. The Charter was proposed as part of Trudeau's "people's package" of constitutional reforms in 1980. It was intended to reinforce a sense of Canadian identity and to defuse regionalism and Quebec nationalism by reinforcing a sense of pan-Canadian political identity. The Charter became the object of a substantial political mobilization by First Nations, the disabled people's movement, the women's movement, and ethnocultural groups who were partially successful in shaping its equality rights guarantees in the debate over its enactment in 1980–81 (as discussed in chapters 7, 10, and 13). The lesbian and gay rights movement did not play a major role in these developments in part because it lacked a viable pan-Canadian organization at the moment of the Charter debates. In addition, the human rights agenda of the gay liberation groups of the 1970s had exhausted itself. As the pursuit of legislative and policy change had not been successful over the course of that decade, the fragmented gay rights groups were not very interested in the Charter, did not have the political and financial resources to mount a substantial mobilization, and were preoccupied with the first onset of the AIDS crisis. However, the issue was raised by MP Svend Robinson, who was unsuccessful in his efforts to have sexual orientation included in the proposed Charter. Despite this exclusion, it was understood that the open-ended wording of the equality rights section of the Charter (section 15) left the door open to the addition of sexual orientation in the future. The Liberal government was well aware that sexual orientation might be added to the Charter by the courts because of the wording of the clause (Smith, 1999).

Over the course of the mid-1980s and into the 1990s, political mobilizing in the lesbian and gay rights movement slowly began to focus on the political opening provided to the movement by the Charter. This realization was slow to take hold. In cities such as Toronto, Montreal, and Vancouver, this was the major period for AIDS activism. In Quebec, attention was not as focused on the Charter because of the impact of the Quebec nationalist movement, which perceived it as part of the politically illegitimate constitutional patriation of 1982. Lawyers were among the first to realize the potential impact of the Charter: lesbian and gay lawyers and law students began to organize both within law schools and bar associations, and lesbian and gay legal issues began to obtain coverage in law journals and legal scholarship (Duplé, 1984; Girard, 1986; Herman, 1989; Cossman, 1994). Moreover, lesbian and gay movement organizing at the pan-Canadian level was spurred in part by the political opportunity provided by the Charter. Therefore, rather than resources making the movement, as resource mobilization theory would contend, in this case it was the existence of political opportunities that galvanized resources and organization. The parliamentary sub-committee on section 15 equality rights, held in 1985, was a major fulcrum for legal and political debate. The equality rights hearings drew a large number of submissions from lesbian and gay groups and resulted in the creation in 1986 of Egale, a lesbian and gay rights group that would work on human rights issues at the federal level.

THE 1990S AND 2000S: THE CHARTER AND BEYOND

Over the course of the 1990s and 2000s, lesbian, gay, bisexual, transgender, and queer (LGBTQ) organizing occurred in many different institutions and organizations of Canadian society and across a broad range of issues ranging from the use of queer-positive reading materials in the education system to the issue of same-sex marriage. The Charter provided an important opening for lesbian and gay litigation. In keeping with the political process model, the movement was able to take advantage of this opportunity and to secure public policy change through the courts in areas ranging from discrimination in employment to same-sex marriage. The movement was able to achieve this despite the fact that its main organization in federal politics—Egale—was poorly resourced.[2]

One of the major areas of public policy change has been that of freedom from discrimination based on sexual orientation in areas such as employment and housing. With regard to government policies, this was the main goal of gay liberation groups of the 1970s, although in most cases this type of discrimination is covered by provincial and federal human rights legislation. The Charter itself does not directly regulate relationships between private citizens (such as the relationship between landlord and tenant), although it indirectly shapes human rights legislation at both federal and provincial levels. Human rights campaigns in the provinces focused on amending provincial human rights legislation to include sexual orientation as a prohibited ground of discrimination, while at the federal level lobbying and litigation focused on the addition or "reading in" of section 15 to include sexual orientation and the amendment of the federal Human Rights Act along the same lines. Citizen-to-citizen discrimination is governed by a patchwork of provincial and federal human rights legislation, including the Charter itself, which governs state-to-citizen relationships. While Quebec's human rights legislation was amended in 1977 and Ontario's in 1986, at the federal level, a Charter challenge by litigants Haig and Birch resulted in the *de facto* addition of sexual orientation to the federal human rights code in 1992. However, even then, the Liberal government of Jean Chrétien prevaricated on the formal amendment of the federal Human Rights Act to include sexual orientation by 1996. The Alberta government only included sexual orientation in its human rights legislation when forced to do so by the Supreme Court decision in *Vriend v. Alberta* in

1998. Most provinces had amended their human rights legislation to include a formal ban on sexual orientation discrimination in provincial/territorial jurisdiction by the early 1990s (Smith, 2008).

The recognition of same-sex relationship and parenting rights is another important area of social movement mobilization. After several early cases such as *Canada (A.G.) v. Mossop* and *Correctional Service of Canada v. Veysey,* the Supreme Court of Canada ruled that sexual orientation was included in section 15 in the 1995 *Egan & Nesbitt v. Canada (Egan)* case on same-sex spousal benefits under the Old Age Security program. However, the court ruled that the "reasonable limits" clause of the Charter provided grounds on which to deny benefits to same-sex couples. In the late 1990s, two important cases were decided, one on the right of same-sex couples to access spousal benefits in employer pensions under federal tax rules (*Rosenberg v. Canada*) and the other on the constitutionality of Ontario's Family Law Act, which denied spousal support to same-sex partners upon the break-up of their relationship (*M v. H*). In the latter case, the most important ruling on same-sex spousal rights to date, one of the former partners, "M," pursued "H" for support upon the break-up of their relationship, arguing that the family law of Ontario discriminated against same-sex couples in preventing former same-sex couples from making claims of spousal support. In ruling that Ontario's family law discriminated against same-sex couples and violated their equality rights under the Charter, the Supreme Court of Canada moved away from the logic of the *Egan* case and indicated that it would not accept anything less than full equality under the law for same-sex couples and, in so doing, set the stage for the next step, which was the move to same-sex marriage. At the same time, grassroots campaigns by same-sex parents in Ontario, British Columbia, and Quebec led to recognition of parenting rights for same-sex couples, ranging from second parent adoption in Ontario and British Columbia to filiation rights in Quebec (Rayside, 2008; Leckey, 2009). These reforms were achieved through litigation and, in the case of Quebec, through legislative change enacted by the government in 2002.

Therefore, litigation and lobbying in response to litigation have constituted important political strategies for the movement. In this context, once again we can see the impact of the structure of political opportunity in social movement politics. The movement was not particularly well-resourced during this period and did not have the means of bringing political pressure to bear on the Liberal government, except through the courts. It is highly unlikely that the Liberal government would have recognized lesbian and gay rights if it had not been for these court decisions. Provincial governments were reluctant to recognize parenting rights with the exception of the NDP government in British Columbia in 2000–01 and the Parti Québécois (PQ) government in Quebec in the early 2000s. An earlier effort by the NDP government of Bob Rae in Ontario to recognize same-sex couples went down to defeat in 1994 after Rae permitted a free vote in the legislature. In the mid-1990s, Parliament voted on several occasions against spousal recognition for same-sex couples, and it was only in response to the Supreme Court decision in *M v. H* (which recognized the constitutional necessity of equality in spousal support laws) that the federal government passed the Modernization of Benefits and Obligations Act of 2000, which extended most benefits (except immigration rights) to same-sex couples in federal jurisdiction, short of marriage (Smith, 2005b). Similarly, the move from relationship recognition in common law (or *union de fait*) relationships to the recognition of same-sex marriage was also sparked by a series of court decisions in the early 2000s and not by the pressure brought to bear by the movement on the Liberal government. Therefore, with few exceptions, the pressure of litigation has played a major role in policy change over the 1990s and the first half of the 2000s.

Same-sex marriage litigation took place across Canada. In 1998, a Quebec gay couple brought a legal challenge to the heterosexual definition of marriage in Quebec's civil law. In 2000, the first of what would eventually be two sets of couples began their litigation on same-sex marriage in British Columbia. In 2001, four couples were married in Metropolitan Community Church in Toronto after the publication of banns, in a challenge to Ontario's laws governing marriage. Evangelical Christians and their supporters have been forceful opponents of such measures, arguing that recognizing same-sex benefits will undermine the traditional family or that such recognition will "condone" a "lifestyle" that leads to AIDS and other diseases (Canada, 2000). A wide range of religious organizations and lesbian and gay organizations spoke to the courts through the litigation in British Columbia, Quebec, Ontario, and other provinces which led to the key set of court decisions in 2002–03. The first decision, in British Columbia, rejected the same-sex couples' claims for the right to access to legal marriage. The judge argued that marriage had always been heterosexual and that the Charter did not require marriage equality for same-sex couples. However, this decision was appealed to the provincial Court of Appeal, which ruled that barring same-sex couples from same-sex marriage was unconstitutional but that the legislature should have the right to devise a solution. At the same time, in Quebec, a long battle for parenting and partnership rights, led by a wide range of social movement organizations including the labour movement, resulted in the recognition of parenting rights and the creation of a new civil union regime in Quebec, one that included same-sex partners. Nova Scotia passed domestic partnership legislation in 2001. For a time, therefore, it looked as though civil unions might emerge as the dominant policy in this area. However, this was brought to an end by the Court of Appeal decision in Ontario in 2003 in the case of *Halpern et al. v. Ontario,* in which the Ontario Court of Appeal not only agreed with the British Columbia court that same-sex marriage was constitutional but ruled that marriage licences had to be issued immediately. Quebec followed with a decision in favour of same-sex marriage in 2004. Rather than appealing these decisions, the Chrétien government developed legislation to legalize same-sex civil marriage and then referred the question of its constitutionality to the Supreme Court. The Court (*Reference re Same-Sex Marriage* [2004]) indicated that the government's same-sex marriage was constitutional and that it did not infringe on religious freedom. Under the Liberal government of Paul Martin, the same-sex marriage legislation became law in June 2005. Although the Conservative government elected in January 2006 opposes same-sex marriage, it did not roll back the measure, despite holding a vote on the possibility of doing so in December 2006 (for overviews of these developments, see Rayside, 2008; Smith, 2008; and Hurley, 2010).

Several voices within the lesbian and gay communities questioned the extent to which same-sex marriage was a worthwhile expenditure of movement resources. Some opposed relationship recognition as a co-optation of the original goals of the gay liberation movement—sexual freedom—and as marking the conservatization of the movement ,while others were critical of relationship recognition because they shared the feminist critique of family as a patriarchal institution (on this debate, see Boyd and Young, 2003). Despite this, lesbian and gay rights-seeking organizations are caught up in a political dynamic that demands the articulation of a clear-cut, almost "ethnic" identity to make their rights claims legible to the Canadian public, the media, the courts, the governing caucus, and policy-makers (Smith, 2005a; see also Epstein, 1987). In this dynamic, it has been very difficult for the movement(s)—especially as decentred networks of activism and community—to counter the dynamic generated by the course of litigation. In this sense, then, opportunities have shaped not only the success of the movement but also its priorities, claims, and demands.

In the post-marriage period, the LGBT movement has moved on to other political issues, including the age of consent, the full recognition of transgender human rights, the fight against homophobia (especially in schools), and health care for LGBT people, specifically ensuring that health research and health care delivery reflect the health needs of their communities. Activism on behalf of trans people has become a major issue in the movement in the 2000s and 2010s. A campaign for inclusion of trans people in the Canadian Human Rights Act took place in the early 2010s with the support of the federal NDP. In March 2013, a bill passed the House of Commons providing for the inclusion of gender identity as a prohibited ground of discrimination under the Canadian Human Rights Act. While gender expression was not included in the legislation, this was an important milestone. Trends in litigation in the US and Canada suggest that the ways in which gender is expressed in outward appearance (e.g., clothing and hairstyles) will eventually receive explicit protection, along with gender identity. Campaigns continue to ensure that trans people are fully protected in all Canadian jurisdictions (Trans Lobby Group, 2012).

With regard to the age of consent, many groups of queer youth and others contested the Harper government's move to increase the age of consent to 16 in 2008 and its failure to equalize the age of consent for anal sex (Dauda, 2010; Wong, 2006). Sexual freedom is an issue that has the potential to openly challenge the line between "good sex" and "bad sex" and between sexual order and sexual chaos, in Gayle Rubin's terms (Rubin, 1984). While relationship recognition has the potential to (in part) fit lesbian and gay couples into an acceptable "family" model (precisely the point of the feminist and gay liberationist critiques of "family" in the lesbian and gay communities), the political issues surrounding sexuality and sexual expression such as pornography threaten this cozy picture of middle-class and monogamously coupled respectability by pushing at the line between "good" and "bad."

Another important arena of contestation by the lesbian and gay rights movement is the area of education and social policy. The legal advances of the movement at the level of public policy cannot obscure the fact that, at the local level, life is still very difficult for some LGBTQ people, especially youth. There are still tremendous social sanctions and dangers in coming out, especially in Canada's smaller communities. Queer youth face bullying and harassment in school, and the stresses caused by facing such harassment are surely one of the factors behind the higher suicide rate for queer teens than for straight youth (Taylor et al., 2008). In some parts of Canada, notably Toronto, Vancouver, and the lower mainland of British Columbia, LGBT activists, including youth activists in high schools, have challenged school board policies. A sustained and concerted effort by activists in the Toronto boards of education (merged into the Toronto District School Board) over the course of the 1990s resulted in the adoption of equity policies on sexual orientation and gender identity, although there are still important problems with the implementation of these policies, especially because of budget cuts (Frances, 2000). In the lower mainland of British Columbia, the province's lesbian and gay educators group, Gay and Lesbian Educators of British Columbia, has worked to create a social and support space for teachers and school administrators. From this effort came the campaign led by James Chamberlain and Murray Warren to introduce gay- and lesbian-positive reading materials into the elementary school grades in the Port Coquitlam and Surrey school districts. Chamberlain and Warren sought to use books that depicted families with same-sex parents for young children. This sparked a backlash from the evangelical movement, which had undertaken a concerted campaign to control school boards in the "Bible Belt" of the province. The Surrey School Board banned the gay- and lesbian-positive books from the elementary school classroom and was immediately challenged by parents, teachers (including Chamberlain and Warren), and others who undertook a successful Charter challenge to this censorship of reading materials (*Chamberlain v. Surrey School District*, 2002).

In the 2000s, Egale commissioned a study that provided evidence for LGBTQ claims about the need for queer-friendly education policies in Canadian schools. The study, which was carried out by researchers from the University of Winnipeg, surveyed 1,700 high school students online and through in-school focus groups. The researchers provided evidence of extensive exclusion and bullying of queer and trans students and also documented the lack of administrative response on this issue (Taylor et al., 2008: 7). This evidence was important to debates over the passage of anti-bullying legislation in Ontario in 2012, after Catholic school boards resisted the establishment of Gay-Straight Alliances (GSAs) in their schools. The Liberal legislation guarantees access to GSAs in all Ontario schools as well as establishing anti-bullying programs to ensure a welcoming environment for LGBTQ youth (Canadian Press, 2012). Similarly, in Quebec, there has been a major campaign against homophobia involving LGBTQ parent groups as well as researchers. As a result, a policy against homophobia in schools was instituted in 2010. These developments represent in part a turn to evidence-based policy and demonstrate the need for social movement organizations to produce and present different forms of evidence as a basis for policy claims (Grundy and Smith, 2007).

New forms of local and pan-Canadian organizing have arisen recently in the area of lesbian and gay health policy. The Canadian Rainbow Health Coalition, founded in Saskatoon, has been paralleled by local organizations across Canada, which centre on the health needs of lesbian and gay people with regard to issues including sexual health, breast cancer, domestic violence, mental health, sex reassignment surgery, and other health needs of trans people (Rainbow Health Coalition, 2006). In most major cities, queer youth projects have sprung up, in some cases funded by local government and public health agencies; these provide health and social services for queer youth, as well as facilitating organizing and community-building by them. To date, efforts to politicize social and economic policy to highlight the situation and needs of lesbian and gay youth communities have not succeeded. For example, queer and trans youth are at greater risk of homelessness than straight youth (for an overview of LGBTQ health issues, see Mulé et al., 2009). Yet, social services for youth and the homeless do not clearly recognize how sexuality is intertwined with other bases of social and economic inequality (Abrahamovitch, 2012).

CONCLUSIONS: LESBIAN AND GAY POLITICS AND SOCIAL MOVEMENT THEORIES

Social movement theories from sociology and political science provide a useful perspective on some aspects of lesbian and gay social movement challenges in Canadian politics. As discussed in the Introduction to this volume, resource mobilization theory stresses the idea that movements arise when they are able to obtain economic and political resources, the political process model stresses that movements must have political opportunities to achieve success, and new social movement theory stresses the cultural dimension of movement challenges that lead to the formation of collective identity (Della Porta and Diani, 1999).

All three of these dimensions may be seen at work in the evolution of lesbian and gay organizing described here. Without a sense of political identity and without a mass exit of lesbian and gay people from the closet, the modern LGBTQ movement in Canada would not exist. The first step in the formation of the movement was the process of establishing a collective identity. In the early years of gay liberation, the very act of holding a gay dance posed a radical challenge to the dominance and raw economic, social, and political power of heteronormativity. The construction of local LGBTQ cultures formed the basis of social movement networks. Formal organizations such as Egale are the tip of the iceberg of these broader networks of organizing. New social movement theories highlight the creation of new social and political identities that underpin collective action. Similarly, they highlight post-materialism and historical specificity in the context of the politics of the 1960s and after, at least in the context of developed countries such as Canada. The women's movement, the gay liberation movement, and the lesbian feminist movements were the product of this period of youth revolt and, initially at least, drew on the template of 1960s organizing.

Resources have played less of a role in the politics of the LGBTQ movement in Canada. The movement is not well-resourced at the pan-Canadian level, and even at the height of the same-sex marriage debate in the early 2000s, the movement's organizational resources consisted of two small lobbying groups with meagre budgets. While the movement enjoys some material support from allies in the labour movement and the legal community, LGBTQ organizations in the US are much better resourced than organizations in Canada. Nonetheless, despite these far greater resources, the US is far behind Canada in its recognition of the legal equality of lesbian and gay citizens or the recognition of same-sex relationships and parenting rights (see Cahill, 2004). Therefore, the success of the gay and lesbian movement cannot be attributed to internal social movement resources alone.

The political process model offers a more convincing account of the recent history of the LGBTQ movement. In particular, the political and legal opportunities afforded by the Charter have provided an opening for lesbian and gay organizations and individual litigants to use the courts to force public policy changes on reluctant governments. These Charter challenges have also disrupted the normative status of straight life by calling media and public attention to issues ranging from censorship and discrimination to same-sex marriage. In LGBTQ rights cases, the material consequences of changes to public policy, such as the right of same-sex couples to spousal benefits, are intertwined with the symbolic and cultural challenge to the traditional norms of Canadian (and other) societies. The Charter has proven to be a potent and effective weapon for lesbian and gay litigation and organizing, and has forced governments to act where, otherwise, they were clearly unwilling to touch the "gay rights" hot button. The result has been a dramatic period of change in Canadian politics and one of the few success stories for progressive social movements in the neoliberal era.

NOTES

1   This research was financed in part by grants from the Social Sciences and Research Council of Canada, and this support is gratefully acknowledged. Throughout the paper, I use the term LGBT to denote lesbian, gay, bisexual and transgender people. For the more recent period, I also use the terms "queer and trans" or LGBTQ (adding the term queer) in order to denote the complexities of identification around sexual orientation, gender identity, and gender expression. The terms "lesbian and gay" are seen as outdated in some quarters today. It is important to note that trans people are not necessarily involved in same-sex relationships nor are they necessarily gay, lesbian, or queer, depending on how those terms are defined or understood in a specific cultural context. I reject the use of the term "sexual minorities" as an overly broad category for my purposes.

2   Information on Egale's resources comes from a number of sources. For example, in several interviews with former executive director of Egale, John Fisher (in 1995 and 2001), he indicated to me that the Egale budget was very small—under $500,000. Egale's 2006 president, Gemma Schlamp-Hickey, estimated the budget at $350,000 in 2006 just before the Harper government held a free vote on rolling back same-sex marriage (see Barsotti, 2006).

CASES CITED

Canada (A.G.) v. Mossop [1993] 1 S.C.R. 554.

Chamberlain v. Surrey School District No. 36, [2002] 4 SCR 710.

Correctional Service of Canada v. Veysey [1990], 109 N.R. 300.

Egan & Nesbitt v. Canada [1995], 124 D.L.R. (4th) 609 SCC.

Halpern et al. v. Ontario [2003] O.A.C. 405.

Klippert v. the Queen [1967] S.C.R. 822.

M v. H [1999] S. C. J. No. 23.

Reference re Same-Sex Marriage [2004] SCC 79.

Rosenberg v. Canada (Attorney General) [1998] 38 O. R. (3d) 577.

Vriend v. Alberta [1998] 1 S. C. R. 493.

XY v. Ontario (Government and Consumer Services) 2012 HRTO 726.

REFERENCES AND FURTHER READING

Abrahamovitch, Ilona Alex. 2012. "No Safe Place to Go—LGBTQ Youth Homelessness in Canada: Reviewing the Literature." *Canadian Journal of Family and Youth* 4 (1). http://ejournals.library.ualberta.ca/index.php/cjfy/article/view/16579 (accessed December 22, 2012).

Adam, Barry D. 1995. *The Rise of a Gay and Lesbian Movement.* Rev. ed. New York: Twayne Publishers.

Altman, Dennis. 1993 [1971]. *Homosexual Oppression and Liberation.* New York: New York University Press.

Barsotti, Natasha. 2006. "More Resignations Rock Egale." *Xtra West* [Vancouver], December 6. http://www.xtra.ca/public/viewstory.aspx?AFF_TYPE=1&STORY_ID=2416&PUB_TEMPLATE_ID=2, (accessed December 10, 2006).

Black, W.W. 1979. "Gay Alliance Toward Equality v. Vancouver Sun." *Osgoode Hall Law Journal* 17: 649–75.

Body Politic [Toronto]. 1976 (August) and various issues 1971–87.

Boyd, Susan B., and Claire F. L. Young. 2003. "From Same-sex to No Sex?: Trends Towards Recognition of (Same-sex) Relationships in Canada." *Seattle Journal for Social Justice* 3: 757–93.

British Columbia Civil Liberties Association. 1998. "B.C. CLA Intervenes in Surrey Book Ban Case." June 29. Vancouver: Press Release.

Cahill, Sean. 2004. *Same-Sex Marriage in the United States: A Focus on the Facts.* Lanham, MD: Lexington Books.

Canada. 2000. *Minutes of Proceedings and Evidence.* Ottawa: House of Commons, Standing Committee on Justice and Human Rights (March 16).

Canadian Press. 2012. "Ontario Anti-bullying Law Passed." *CBC News Online* June 5. http://www.cbc.ca/news/canada/ottawa/story/2012/06/05/ontario-anti-bullying-bill-final-vote-controversy-over-gay-straight-alliance.html (accessed December 22, 2012).

Cossman, Brenda. 1994. "Family Inside/Out." *University of Toronto Law Journal* 44: 1–39.

Currah, Paisley, Richard M. Juang, and Shannon Price Minter, eds. 2006. *Transgender Rights*. Minneapolis: University Of Minnesota Press.

Dauda, Carol L. 2010. "Childhood, Age of Consent and Moral Regulation in Canada and the UK." *Contemporary Politics* 16 (3): 227–47.

Della Porta, Donatella, and Mario Diani. 1999. *Social Movements: An Introduction*. Oxford: Blackwell.

Demczuk, Irène, and Frank Remiggi. 1998. *Sortir de l'ombre: Histoires des communautés lesbienne et gaie de Montréal*. Montreal: VLB Éditeur.

Duberman, Martin. 1993. *Stonewall*. New York: E.P. Dutton.

Duplé, Nicole. 1984. "Homosexualité et droits à l'égalité dans les Chartes canadienne et québécoise." *Les cahiers de droit* 25 (4): 1–32.

English, John. 2006. *Citizen of the World: The Life of Pierre Elliott Trudeau, Vol. 1 1919–1969*. Toronto: Knopf.

Epstein, Steven. 1987. "Gay Politics, Ethnic Identity: The Limits of Social Constructionism." *Socialist Review* 17:9–54.

Frances, Margot. 2000. "Chalkboard Promises." *Xtra* (September 7).

Fraser, Nancy. 1995. "From Redistribution to Recognition? Dilemmas of Justice in a 'Post-Socialist' Age." *New Left Review* 212:68–93.

Fuller, Janine, and Stuart Blackley. 1995. *Restricted Entry: Censorship on Trial*. Vancouver: Press Gang.

Gallant, Paul. 2001. "Who Should Be Ashamed?" *Xtra* (November): 1.

Girard, Philip. 1986. "Sexual Orientation as a Human Rights Issue in Canada, 1969–1985." *Dalhousie Law Journal* 10 (2): 267–81.

Go, Avvy, and John Fisher. 1998. *Working Together Across our Differences: A Discussion Paper on Coalition-building, Participatory Litigation, and Strategic Litigation*. Ottawa: Court Challenges Program.

Grundy, John, and Miriam Smith. 2007. "Activist Knowledges in Queer Politics." *Economy and Society* 36 (2): 294–317.

Herman, Didi. 1989. "Are We Family? Lesbian Rights and Women's Liberation." *Osgoode Hall Law Journal* 28 (4): 789–824.

Herman, Didi. 1994. *Rights of Passage: Struggles for Lesbian and Gay Legal Equality*. Toronto: University of Toronto Press.

Higgins, Ross. 2000. *De la clandestinité à l'affirmation*. Montreal: Comeau/Nadeau.

Houston, Andrea. 2011. "Trans Canadians Fight for Recognition on Legal Documents." *Xtra*, April 16. http://www.xtra.ca/public/National/Trans_Canadians_fight_for_recognition_on_legal_documents-11256.aspx (accessed May 11, 2012).

Hunt, Gerald. 1999. "No Longer Outsiders: Labor's Response to Sexual Diversity in Canada." In *Laboring for Rights: Unions and Sexual Diversity Across Nations*, ed. Gerald Hunt, 10–36. Philadelphia: Temple University Press.

Hurley, Mary C. 2010. *Sexual Orientation and Legal Rights*. Ottawa: Parliamentary Information and Research Service Library of Parliament.

Kinsman, Gary. 1996. *The Regulation of Desire: Homo and Heterosexualities*. 2nd ed. Montreal: Black Rose.

Kinsman, Gary, and Patrizia Gentile. 2010. *The Canadian War on Queers: National Security as Sexual Regulation*. Vancouver: University of British Columbia Press.

Korinek, Valerie J. 2003. "'The Most Openly Gay Person for at Least a Thousand Miles': Doug Wilson and the Politicization of a Province, 1975–1983." *Canadian Historical Review* 84 (4) (December): 517–50.

Leckey, Robert. 2009. "'Where the Parents Are of the Same Sex': Quebec's Reforms to Filiation." *International Journal of Law, Policy and the Family* 23 (1): 62–82.

McDonald, Marci. 2010. *The Armageddon Factor: The Rise of Christian Nationalism in Canada*. 1st ed. Toronto: Random House Canada.

Melucci, Alberto. 1997. *Challenging Codes: Collective Action in the Information Age*. Cambridge: Cambridge University Press.

Mulé, N.J., L.E. Ross, B. Deeprose, B.E. Jackson, A. Daley, A. Travers, and D. Moore. 2009. "Promoting LGBT Health and Wellbeing through Inclusive Policy Development." *International Journal for Equity in Health* 8 (18). http://www.equityhealthj.com/content/8/1/18 (accessed April 22, 2012).

Namaste, Vivian K. 2000. *Invisible Lives, The Erasure of Transsexual and Transgendered People*. Chicago: University of Chicago Press.

Rainbow Health Coalition. 2006. *About Us*. http://www.rainbowhealthnetwork.ca/about (accessed March 31, 2013).

Rayside, David. 1988. "Gay Rights and Family Values: The Passage of Bill 7 in Ontario." *Studies in Political Economy* 26:109–47.

Rayside, David. 2008. *Queer Inclusions, Continental Divisions: Public Recognition of Sexual Diversity in Canada and the United States*. Toronto: University of Toronto Press.

Rayside, David, and Evert Lindquist. 1992. "AIDS Activism and the State in Canada." *Studies in Political Economy* 39: 37–76.

Ross, Becki. 1995. *The House That Jill Built: A Lesbian Nation in Formation*. Toronto: University of Toronto Press.

Rubin, Gayle. 1984. "Thinking Sex: Notes for a Radical Theory of the Politics of Sexuality." In *Pleasure and Danger: Exploring Female Sexuality*, ed. C.S. Vance, 267–319. Boston: Routledge and Kegan Paul.

Shepard, Benjamin, and Ronald Hayduk, eds. 2001. *From ACT UP To The WTO: Urban Protest and Community Building in the Era of Globalization*. London: Verso.

Smith, Miriam. 1999. *Lesbian and Gay Rights in Canada: Social Movements and Equality-Seeking, 1971–1995*. Toronto: University of Toronto Press.

Smith, Miriam. 2005a. "Resisting and Reinforcing Neoliberalism: Lesbian and Gay Organizing at the Federal and Local Levels in Canada." *Policy & Politics* 33 (1) (January): 75–93.

Smith, Miriam. 2005b. "Social Movements and Judicial Empowerment: Courts, Public Policy, and Lesbian and Gay Organizing in Canada." *Policy & Society* 33 (2): 327–53.

Smith, Miriam. 2008. *Political Institutions and Lesbian and Gay Rights in the United States and Canada*. New York: Routledge.

Sommella, Laraine. 1997. "This Is about People Dying: The Tactics of Early ACT UP and Lesbian Avengers in New York City." In *Queers in Space: Communities, Public Places, Sites of Resistance*, ed. G.B. Ingram, A.-M. Bouthillette, and Y. Retter, 407–37. Seattle: Bay Press.

Stone, Sharon Dale. 1991. "Lesbian Mothers Organize." In *Lesbians in Canada*, ed. S.D. Stone, 198–208. Toronto: Between the Lines.

Taylor, C., T. Peter, K. Schachter, S. Paquin, S. Beldom, Z. Gross, and T.L. McMinn. 2008. *Youth Speak Up about Homophobia and Transphobia: The First National Climate Survey on Homophobia in Canadian Schools. Phase One Report*. Toronto: Egale Canada Human Rights Trust.

Trans Lobby Group. 2012. *About Us*. http://www.translobbygroup.ca/?q=content/about-us (accessed May 11, 2012).

Visser, Andy. 1990. "Queer Notions." *Xtra* (September 14): 1.

Waite, Brian, and Cheri DeNovo. 1971. *We Demand*. Toronto: August 28th Gay Day Committee.

Warner, Tom. 2002. *Never Going Back: A History of Queer Activism in Canada*. Toronto: University of Toronto Press.

Wong, Josephine P. 2006. "Age of Consent to Sexual Activity in Canada: Background to Proposed New Legislation on 'Age of Protection'." *Canadian Journal of Human Sexuality* 15 (3/4): 163–69.

NINE

Populist and Conservative Christian Evangelical Movements: A Comparison of Canada and the United States[1]

TREVOR W. HARRISON

Recent decades have witnessed throughout much of the world political movements claiming to represent "the people." Side by side with this rebirth of "populism" in North America, especially in the US, has been a resurgence of conservative Christian, mainly Protestant, evangelicalism. This chapter is in two parts. The first briefly explores the wider phenomenon of "populism." The second details some conceptual links between populist and Christian evangelical movements and then goes on to compare evangelical movements in Canada and the US. Ultimately, it is argued the greater strength of the conservative Christian evangelical movement in the US results from several societal and organizational factors, including the greater fusion of religion and nationalism in the US, or what is often referred to as "civil religion."

POPULISM: DEFINITION

While the term "populism" is sometimes used to describe a personal leadership style, it is analytically more useful if we consider some of the elements common to populist movements (Sinclair, 1979; Conway, 1978; Harrison, 1995). First, populist movements and parties appeal to a mass audience, specifically a group defined as "the people." Second, this appeal is made urgent by the perception of a crisis threatening "the people." Third, the source of this threat is an identifiable group (a "power bloc"), sometimes geographically but often socio-culturally "external" to "the people," including various elites. In short, populism is defined as a mass political movement, mobilized around symbols and traditions congruent with the popular culture, that expresses a group's sense of threat arising from powerful "outsiders."

The term's use is relatively recent. It originated in Russia in the turbulent 1870s (Di Tella, 2001) when, following the emancipation of the serfs, many were seeking a third way between capitalist modernization and Marxist socialism. By the mid-twentieth century, the term was often used in Latin and South America in connection with the twin concepts of corporatism and clientelism (see Rea et al., 1992), populism being viewed as a political vehicle for nationalist mobilization. In between these two uses, populism first gained currency in North America in 1892 when American journalists adopted the term to describe supporters (mainly farmers and small business people) of the People's Party that was founded that year.

In Canada, the term is frequently associated with the various farmers' parties that arose in several provinces, especially Ontario and the Canadian west, in the early twentieth century, inspired by similar movements across the border. As in the US, Canadian farmers (already beset by natural perils) often found themselves victims of the monopoly practices of bankers, grain companies, and railways. The result was both the rise of "farmers' parties" in several provinces in the years immediately following World War I and, during the federal election of 1921, the sudden emergence of the newly founded Progressive Party, which took 65 seats, second only to the victorious Liberals (Morton, 1978). During the Great Depression of the 1930s, other populist parties followed, notably the socialist CCF in Saskatchewan (Lipset, 1968) and the more conservative Social Credit party in Alberta (Macpherson, 1953; Finkel, 1989; Bell, 1993).

After World War II, it appeared that populism as a mode of political mobilization was in retreat in both Canada and the US due to the shrinking of the agrarian class and the institutionalization of the party system. It seemed to survive only in particular locales, such as the American south and in rural Quebec (see Pinard, 1971), in both cases drawing upon suppressed nationalism and a sense of defeat. In retrospect, however, it is clear the spirit of populism remained alive. The sources of its later awakening are many, but disenchantment with the party system and with "big government" was a major contributor, leading to the re-emergence in the early 1980s of left and right populist expression in both the US and Canada. In Canada, the vehicle for this resurgence was the Reform Party, a brief history of which is instructive.

In 1987, Preston Manning, son of former Alberta Social Credit Premier Ernest Manning (Harrison, 1995; Flanagan, 2009), founded the Reform Party. The party resurrected several themes common to past western Canadian populist parties, such as demands for a more direct say in political matters (as opposed to representative democracy) and a belief in the "common sense of the common people" (in opposition to "elite" control). Within only a few years, the party became Canada's Official Opposition in the House of Commons. It soon stalled, however, and some supporters began complaining that it had become too "top down" (see Harrison, 1995), losing its grassroots, populist appeal. Three years after the 1997 Canadian federal election, and in time for the 2000 election, the party transformed itself into the Canadian Alliance Party and chose a new leader, Stockwell Day, in a bid to break out of its western political base. But the new party quickly disintegrated—a not uncommon trait of populist parties (see Harrison, 2002: 192–94)—resulting in its merger in early 2004 with the Progressive Conservative Party to form the "new" Conservative Party of Canada. The Conservative Party subsequently dropped many of the populist-inspired ideas carried over from Reform-Alliance, such as those suggesting the widespread use of referendums and initiatives to decide policy, though it continues to employ populist rhetoric as a mobilizing strategy (see Ramp and Harrison, 2012).[2] Nonetheless, the Reform Party played a major role in Canadian political history, breaking up the traditional two-party system; giving a greater voice to the regions, especially the west; and bringing to the fore numerous concerns, such as the need for balanced budgets and concern for debt repayment.

It is important to note that populism has no specific ideological content. Appeals to populism do not do away with the need to address questions such as the nature of society, the role of government, or the kind of economy preferred. In attempting to answer such questions, populist parties historically have varied a great deal.

TYPES OF POPULISM

Canovan (1981:8), based on American case studies, distinguishes two broad types of populism. Agrarian populism is defined as "a particular kind of socio-economic base (peasants or farmers), liable to arise in particular socio-economic circumstances (especially modernization of one sort or another), and perhaps sharing a particular socio-economic program." By contrast, political populism is defined as a "particular kind of political phenomenon where the tensions between the elite and the grassroots loom large."

By contrast, Richards's (1981) typology, based on Canadian experiences, situates populist movements along a traditional right-left continuum. Specifically, Richards argues that, historically, left populist movements in Canada have tended toward class (farm-labour) alliances that present a general critique of corporate capitalism, demand a greater role for the government and state in countering the power of the corporate sector, and spring from rural cooperative organizations. By contrast, right populist movements have tended to mobilize along regional rather than class lines; to restrict their critique to the power of banks, the money supply, and credit; to view big government as the primary enemy; and to downplay participatory democracy in favour of plebiscites.

Laycock's (1990) typology expands upon Richards's work and lists four categories of populism common to western Canada. Social democratic populism (e.g., the Saskatchewan CCF) opposed capitalism in general and emphasized national ownership and control of key industries. Radical democratic populism (e.g., the Ginger group within Alberta's United Farmers) opposed the party system, sometimes arguing in favour of group government. Plebiscitarian populism (e.g., Alberta Social Credit) favoured (in particular) "direct democracy" mechanisms, such as plebiscites, initiatives, and referendums to give voice to the people. Finally, crypto-Liberal populism (e.g., Manitoba in the 1940s) emphasized individual, market-based solutions to problems to offset "elite" control.

TABLE 9.1   A Comparison of Left-Wing vs. Right-Wing Populist Movements, Past and Present, in Canada

		Left	Right
	Characteristic		
Old	**"The People"**	Workers and farmers	Small-scale producers
	"The Power Bloc"	Militarists/imperialists and capitalists	Bankers and "big interests"
	Organizational Basis	Co-operatives, community groups, and educational institutions	Direct democracy initiatives and strong leaders
New	**"The People"**	Citizens	Taxpayers and consumers
	"The Power Bloc"	Corporations	Special interests, government, and technocratic elites
	Organizational Basis	NGOs, unions	Corporate think tanks and media

Source: Adapted with modifications from Richards (1981), Laycock (1990), and Harrison (2000).

More recently, Harrison (2000) introduced a temporal aspect to populist typologies, examining differences in populism in Alberta old and new. Table 9.1 attempts a provisional mapping of the core elements of populist movements in Canada during the past hundred years, borrowing from, and elaborating upon, the work of Richards (1981) and Harrison (2000).

It is one thing to classify movements. If different types of populist movements exist, how might these differences be explained? What factors underlie the rise of populist movements?

EXPLANATIONS OF POPULISM

There are six prominent explanations of populist movements. Economic explanations (both of the neo-Marxian and more liberal approach of scholars such as Harold Innis) typically argue populist movements arise out of the cyclical problems and uncertainties of hinterland or regional economies tied, in the larger sense, to the world capitalist economy. The structure of unequal exchanges between the hinterland and a more prosperous centre is viewed as the catalyst for local anger directed at the power of outside economic interests, such as bankers, financiers, and industrialists. Economic explanations argue that populist unrest is more likely to occur in volatile than in stable economies. The creation of the CCF in 1933 in Saskatchewan and the coming to power of Social Credit in Alberta in 1935, in the midst of the Great Depression, are events supportive of this theory.

Political explanations likewise contend that populist movements are most likely to arise in hinterland regions. While recognizing that economic issues play an important role in populist discontent, political explanations nonetheless emphasize the role of powerlessness and alienation and the subsequent capacity of local elements to mobilize this discontent. In this sense, economic disparity is viewed as secondary to structural-institutional inequities in the political realm. Political explanations view populist unrest as resulting from people feeling left out of political decision-making.

Class explanations take their cue initially from Marx and Engels' (1977 [1848]) theory of class conflict and later elaborated on by Lenin (1960, 1970). Populist movements are explained as products of a particular class—the petite bourgeoisie—facing destruction at the hands of larger capitalists, yet reactionary and nostalgic in defending the ideal of capitalism itself. Class explanations point to the impact of economic and political changes upon specific classes. The clearest application of this theory to a Canadian situation is Macpherson's (1953) study of the rise of Social Credit in Alberta, though he also combines it with a political/hinterland explanation (see also Bell, 1993).

Cultural explanations argue that populist movements stem either from a disturbance of "the peoples'" cultural or symbolic order or around whose construction identities can themselves be manufactured and mobilized (see Laclau, 2005). Accordingly, populist movements might be predicted to arise during periods of rapid demographic and economic change. Likewise, cultural threats to deeply held values and beliefs might result in populist movements, such as occurred among southern Whites during the reconstruction period in the American south after the US Civil War.

Resource mobilization theory explains populist movements as arising not out of discontent—discontent is always present in every society—but rather from organizational factors (see Zald and McCarthy, 1987). Specifically, populist alternatives are a product of a leadership's capacity to mobilize such resources as people, money, and materials. To give one example, when the Rev. William Aberhart began promoting the ideas of Social Credit, his already well-established weekly religious radio broadcasts provided a means not only of disseminating a political platform but also of obtaining funding and of mobilizing supporters (Finkel, 1989).

Hegemonic crisis explanations adopt the ideas of Italian political theorist Antonio Gramsci (1988) to argue that populist movements emerge in the context of "organic crises"—all-inclusive political, economic, and social crises—that (at least temporarily) disrupt the ability of the dominant class to shape the world view of subordinate classes (Harrison, 1995). In the midst of such crises, existing political alliances unravel, "freeing" some previously incorporated or suppressed elements. Under specific socio-historical circumstances, these elements may then coalesce in a counter-hegemonic movement that can also develop populist characteristics.

None of these explanations are necessarily exclusive of each other; each provides a possible answer to why populist movements arise. The next section of this chapter provides a comparative case study of a particular variety of populism, those mobilized specifically around a religious sense of mission.

CHRISTIAN EVANGELICAL MOVEMENTS IN THE UNITED STATES AND CANADA: A COMPARISON

What is a conservative Christian evangelical?[3] Following Hadden and Shupe (1988: 79–82) and Marsden (1991: 4–6), I use the term here to refer to persons belonging to a trans-denominational grouping of conservative Protestants whose belief system revolves around the following essential elements:

- A belief in the inerrancy and final authority of the Bible, including acceptance of a creationist explanation for the origins of the universe, earth, and humanity;

- A belief in the historical reality of Christ's crucifixion, atonement, and resurrection and the message of salvation;
- A belief in a holy mandate to promote the redeeming message of Christ to all the peoples of the world; and
- A belief in the spiritually transformed life (i.e., the capacity to be "born again").

Christian evangelicalism, in general, was a powerful force in both British North America and the US following the American Revolution. Citing Hatch (1989), Carroll (2005) argues Protestant evangelicals (notably Methodists and Baptists) in the American south especially adopted elements of the revolution—opposition to hierarchy, acceptance of emotional impulses, the concept of personal salvation (i.e., individualism), and belief in creating a better world—into religious precepts. Likewise, Rawlyk (1996: 10) argues that Radical Evangelicalism "set the religious tone" in the Maritimes and Upper Canada into the early nineteenth century. The War of 1812 blunted evangelicalism's rise in Canada, however. Its embrace of "American" (republican) ideas was curtailed by the rise in English-speaking Canada of British Toryism, advanced by the growing middle class and the Anglican Church, while, in French-speaking Quebec, the Catholic Church reigned supreme. Similarly, defeat of the south in the American Civil War (1861–65) drove evangelicalism underground or, rather, to the outskirts of mainstream American thought as determined by the victorious north and the more established churches of that region.

Despite these setbacks, Protestant evangelicalism grew on both sides of the border during the remainder of the century. "Especially during the Victorian era, broadly evangelical Protestants . . . were *the* establishment" (Smith, 1998: 2) in the US. Likewise, in the early days of the twentieth century, most Protestants in the US—and a goodly number in Canada—thought themselves to be evangelical Christians (Hadden and Shupe, 1988: 79). In both countries, however, there existed two versions of Protestant evangelicalism (see Smith, 1998; also Reimer, 2003: 28). The "right" version was primarily concerned with personal salvation and the hereafter. In contrast, the "left" version—reflected in the Social Gospel movements of the 1880s and after—was concerned with social salvation and the here and now.

As traditional rural society gave way to industrial and urban society in the late nineteenth and early twentieth centuries, many Christian evangelicals on both sides of the border came to support the new populist movements that dotted the political landscape (see Smith, 1998: 2–6). Prominent among American populist religious figures were William Jennings Bryan,[4] Father Coughlin,[5] and the Rev. Martin Luther King, Jr. In Canada, the list includes the Rev. William Aberhart (Alberta's Social Credit premier, 1935–43)

and his successor, Rev. Ernest Manning (premier, 1943–68), whose move-
ments/parties appear on the right of the political spectrum. On the left,
coming directly out of a Social Gospel tradition, the list includes the Rev.
J.S. Woodsworth (first leader of the CCF) and the Rev. Tommy Douglas
(CCF premier of Saskatchewan and later federal leader of the NDP).

There are several analytic links between the concept of populism and
evangelicalism. First, the notion of "a people" is often religiously constituted, for example, the notion of a religious group as a "chosen" people.
Second, evangelical movements and religious movements, like populist
movements, often arise at moments of crisis when "the people" are threatened. Indeed, the history of both populist and evangelical movements shows
they have often risen simultaneously amid circumstances of perceived economic, political, and cultural threat with a "mission" to deal with the threat.

Third, like populist movements, evangelical followers are often suspicious
of elites. As a result, just as populists often eschew the intermediating influence of intellectuals/experts or institutions in favour of a direct relationship
with a leader, so also evangelicals often seek a personal relationship with God
unmediated by a formal church establishment. In turn, this relationship is
often channelled through individual leaders viewed as "charismatic."

Though today often applied indiscriminately to telegenic political
leaders, the term "charisma" was coined originally by sociologist Max
Weber to refer to individuals perceived as having a "gift of grace" (Gerth
and Mills, 1946: 52), of being filled with "the spirit." Weber argued that
charismatic authority arises during periods of crisis when traditional lead-
erships and authority structures have been "de-legitimated." Charismatic
leaders are viewed (at least by their followers) as divinely gifted with extraordinary insights that allow them to show the people "the way" out of
the current crisis. The Rev. William Aberhart was considered a charismatic
political leader.

Like populism, the role and strength of religion generally was often
viewed after World War II as in decline, especially in those parts of the world
experiencing "modernization" but also including North America. Recent
years, however, have seen a resurgence of religious faith throughout much
of the world—Christian, Islamic, and otherwise. In Western countries, this
resurgence is particularly obvious among Christian fundamentalists and evangelicals. In Latin America, for example, the Catholic Church has found itself
competing with evangelical and charismatic Christian movements for followers, especially among the poor. Nowhere, however, has the resurgence of
evangelical religion been more apparent, or exerted greater social and political
consequences, than in the US.

CONSERVATIVE CHRISTIAN EVANGELICALS IN THE US

No American president in recent memory declared so strongly his Christian values or used religious imagery so openly as did George W. Bush. A reformed alcoholic and born-again Christian, Bush came to office in 2000 on a platform supportive of "family values" and promising to bring in "faith-based" initiatives that (along with tax cuts) would downsize "big government." In the immediate aftermath of 9/11, he initially proclaimed he would lead a crusade against terrorism—until warned by some that the word "crusade" was viewed poorly in the Muslim world.[6] But his language thereafter continued to emphasize a religious world view in which people of Christian faith were engaged in a conflict with "evildoers."[7] Indeed, there were repeated allegations during his presidency that Bush claimed divine inspiration for his actions, including invading Afghanistan and Iraq (Landau, 2005).

George Bush's rise to the presidency reflected the growing power of conservative Christian evangelicals in the US, beginning in the 1970s. Full appreciation of this accomplishment can only be gained if one considers that, before this time, the US was widely viewed as a "liberal" democracy gradually converging on social and political matters with other Western industrialized countries (Kerr et al., 1964). The Christian evangelical movement has played a significant role in transforming the US today into a conservative and deeply Christian nation (see Micklethwait and Wooldridge, 2004). How has this come about?

As we have seen, Christian—especially Protestant—evangelical beliefs have deep roots in American soil, especially the southern states, but these roots shrank throughout the early twentieth century in the context of what is often referred to as the Fundamentalist-Modernist struggle (Smith, 1998; Reimer, 2003). The already wide array of Protestant denominations in the US splintered, the fundamentalist wing pursuing a separatist strategy in regards to the "profane" world. While Christian evangelicals sustained their fight (and their faith) against "godless Communism," the other great champion of modernization—liberalism—remained largely impervious to the assaults of far right evangelical leaders.

Things began to change in the 1960s, however. Social and political unrest, including the assassinations of John F. Kennedy, Martin Luther King, Jr., and Robert F. Kennedy, combined with a declining economy and military defeat in Viet Nam, highlighted a period of intensified conflict over the US's identity and role in the world. The period also coincided with intense social changes, for example, sexual liberation, the emergence of new family forms, and the rise of feminism. Out of these events arose the New Left, a loose amalgam that included students, intellectuals, feminists, civil rights advocates, and environmentalists. But the New Left also created the conditions for its own counter-movement, the New Right, an umbrella movement that included among its adherents many Christian evangelicals (Harrison, 1995).

Before this time, many conservative Christian evangelicals had remained apolitical. But concerns that the US was on a path to economic, political, and *moral* ruin stimulated disparate elements of the community to action. A key moment was the founding in 1979 of the Moral Majority coalition by the Rev. Jerry Falwell and Paul Weyrich (also founder of the right-wing Heritage Foundation) (Micklethwait and Wooldridge, 2004: 16–17). The New Right brought together traditional conservatives and neoconservatives, right-wing populists, and evangelicals who—despite differences—held in common especially strong beliefs in free enterprise capitalism, the value of individualism, and a need to shrink government that, since Franklin D. Roosevelt, they believed had become too big. Each of these broad beliefs, in turn, was given specific interpretation and embellishment by conservative Christian evangelicals. Hill and Owen (1982: 17) describe the issues that mobilized the New Religious Political Right (NRPR) at that time:

(a) an opposition to governmental support for and general social tolerance of abortion;

(b) a determination to restore the right of public schools to hold concerted moments of prayer on a voluntary basis;

(c) a lament over the weakened military position of the United States over against the Soviet Union and a pledge to make this nation's military defense strongest;

(d) hostility to pornography—actually, to any [and] all flagrant exhibitions of sex;

(e) a commitment to defeat the Equal Rights Amendment and all forces that threaten to undermine the traditional roles of women in society.

With the exception of the specific threat of the Soviet Union, now past, conservative Christian evangelicals in the US are impelled by the same things today: strong families (nuclear, father-headed, and heterosexual), Christian values, and a powerful nation (see Diamond, 1998).

Conservative Christian evangelicals gained what they believed to be their first victory in 1980, electing Ronald Reagan as Republican president. Their hopes were often dashed in practice, however. Though a hawk on international matters, and a staunch supporter of free enterprise, Reagan proved a disappointment to many conservative Christian evangelicals in his efforts to turn back the tide of liberal, secular humanism (Micklethwait and Wooldridge, 2004: 92–93).

Undaunted in his efforts to save the US, the Rev. Jerry Falwell in 1988 made a bid for the presidency. Though defeated, his run sent a warning shot across the Republican bow; henceforth, conservative Christian evangelicals gained a major foothold within that party (Diamond, 1998), a foothold that the movement expanded over the next decade through its organizational efforts.

George W. Bush's election as president of the United States in 2000 and again in 2004 resulted from several factors, not the least of which in the latter case was fear following 9/11. But at least some of Bush's success can also be attributed to the significant support he received from conservative Christian evangelicals in both elections for, as noted above, his populist rhetoric was also bathed in religious imagery and the promise of rewards to that constituency. As one commentator described the result, the US election of 2004 was fought between two nations—"Worldly America and Godly America" (Schama, 2004)—and Godly America won.

Ultimately, Bush Jr. disappointed many conservative Christian evangelicals, as did his father and Reagan before him. At least rhetorically and through some direct policies, he supported the movement.[8] But he did not go far enough in the eyes of many Christian evangelicals and other social conservatives, and to the extent that his presidency became embroiled in a series of disastrous and costly wars and finally also was in charge at the onset of the Great Recession beginning in 2007, he also lost conservative support in general.

Yet, for Christian evangelicals, the Bush presidency created a real dilemma. If they did not support the Republicans, to whom could they turn? Surely not the "liberal" and "secular" Democrats!

In the aftermath of the 2008 election that saw the election of the first Black president in the US, conservative forces once again rallied, this time under the banner of the Tea Party movement. As Williamson et al. (2011) have detailed, the movement was not particularly a vehicle for the Christian right; indeed, many of its arguments were libertarian. Still, the rise of the Tea Party movement, at a time when Republican spirits were at a low ebb, provided space within which issues of abortion and same-sex marriage could once again be asserted leading up to the 2012 presidential election.

THE CONSERVATIVE CHRISTIAN EVANGELICAL MOVEMENT IN CANADA

We have already briefly examined the rise of the populist Reform Party, but it is worthwhile revisiting the party within the context of evangelical influence upon politics in Canada. The fall of 1987 is often remembered today as the date when the Reform Party was founded. Less remembered, however, is that the Christian Heritage Party (CHP) was founded at the same time. In the federal election held a year later, both of these new religiously inspired parties received a degree of popular electoral support, the CHP primarily in Ontario and the Reform Party in the west, mainly Alberta (Harrison, 1995). Thereafter, while the CHP faded, the more broadly based Reform Party continued to gain in popularity and influence, but its religious core remained extant through the leadership of both Preston Manning and Stockwell Day when (in 2000) the populist party morphed into the Canadian Reform Conservative Alliance Party.

Many evangelical Christians were outspoken in their support of both the Reform and Alliance parties. But their support arguably came at a price to the future success of these parties. In Reform's early days, Manning's own religious background and the strident positions sometimes taken by party supporters on matters of family, abortion, and gay rights raised concerns for many voters, concerns heightened when Day, a devout and even more outspoken evangelical Christian, took the Alliance Party's helm (see Harrison, 2002).

As already noted, however, the Alliance Party soon disintegrated as a functioning political vehicle, resulting in the forming of the new Conservative Party in 2004 out of a merger of the Alliance and old Progressive Conservative parties. The new party was similar in many ways to the American Republican party, bringing together free enterprisers, libertarians, western reformers, and social conservatives, including many Christian evangelicals; indeed, its leader, Stephen Harper, is a member of the Christian and Missionary Alliance denomination.

In the 2006 election, the party gained power in a minority Parliament and—two elections later (2011)—won a majority. Harper's evangelical beliefs, combined with those of other influential cabinet members, have led to some accusations that the party is in the vanguard of religious-based efforts to reshape Canada (see Macdonald, 2010). Some have argued, for example, that the government's beliefs in free markets and skepticism toward global warming are grounded in religious doctrine (Nikiforuk, 2012; Martin, 2012). In contrast to the American experience, however, many of the concerns of conservative Christian evangelicals in Canada remain largely outside the mainstream. While some backbench members of the federal Conservative Party have recently advanced such socially conservative policies as, for example, the rights of the fetus, most Canadians are not supportive of instituting policies based on conservative values, whether related to abortion, same-sex marriage, or other concerns of the evangelical right (see Bibby, 2006; Rayside, 2011; Farney, 2012). Why the differences between the two countries?

WHY IS THE CONSERVATIVE CHRISTIAN EVANGELICAL MOVEMENT STRONGER IN THE US THAN IN CANADA?

There are several possible explanations for why the conservative Christian evangelical movement in Canada has had less overtly political success than its American counterpart. First, there are important institutional religious differences between the two countries. Table 9.2 shows that the percentage of Catholics within the Canadian population is much larger than in the US (44 vs. 25). In part, this is because of Quebec's inclusion in the data. (Quebec is roughly 80 per cent Catholic.) But even if Quebec is excluded from the analysis, the percentage of Catholics remains almost 10 per cent higher in Canada than in the US. And while many practising Catholics are favourable to some concerns expressed by Christian evangelicals (e.g., gay rights, abortion), their support for the entire conservative platform (e.g., law and order) is less certain.

This demographic comparison does not tell the entire story, however. As van Die (2001: 7) notes, the US historically has experienced far greater denominationalism than Canada. Whereas two large, established "state churches"—the Catholic and Anglican—were historically dominant in Canada, and further consolidation occurred in the 1920s with the founding of the United Church, the US has a far greater smorgasbord of Protestant faiths (Reimer, 2003: 26). It is this plethora of smaller, non-bureaucratically organized faiths—many of them Christian evangelical—that have seen the largest growth in recent years. Altogether, roughly 26 per cent of Americans are Christian evangelicals compared with about one in 10 of Canadians (PEW Forum, 2007; Bibby, 2011: 197). In fact, 40 per cent of Americans (including

TABLE 9.2 Comparison of Religious Identification, Canada (2001) and the US (2008) (in 000s)

	Canada		United States	
	Total	%	Total	%
Catholic	12,936	44	57,199	25
Other Christian	9,915	33	116,203	51
Other/None	6,788	23	54,780	24
Total	29,639	100	228,182*	100

*Adult population only for the US.

Source: Statistics Canada (2005) and the US Census Bureau (2012).

former President George Bush Jr.) describe themselves as born-again Christians (Saad, 2009).

In addition, evangelicalism in Canada has been historically more often of the left variety than its counterpart in the US (see Allen, 2008). Until the emergence of the Reform Party in the 1980s, the leftist Social Gospel evangelicalism was more influential in shaping Canada than the right evangelical expressions of the Social Credit Party. In short, there are important denominational differences between the two countries, including the form of evangelicalism that has predominated in the past.

Second, surveys also reveal important value and ideological differences between Canadians and Americans at large (Adams, 2003; Grabb and Curtis, 2005). While most people on both sides of the border attend church (at least occasionally) and continue to hold religious beliefs, religion plays a more significant role in the lives of Americans than of Canadians—or, indeed, many other peoples. In a study by the Pew Research Center (2002), 59 per cent of Americans said religion played a very important role in their lives. By contrast, only 30 per cent of Canadians said the same, even less in most Western European countries. In fact, American responses to the question were closer to those found in developing countries.

Interpretation of this data comes with a caveat, however. As a subsequent Pew Research Center (2004) report points out, there is a significant regional effect. That is, religious beliefs in the US are strongest in the American south—the historic area of the evangelical right (see also Hunter, 1983: 52). When compared with Canada, the values of people living in states along the northern border are only marginally more "religious" or "conservative" than the values of people in Canada—a finding broadly supported by Adams (2003) and Grabb and Curtis (2005). In short, religious differences between regions of North America may disguise themselves as national differences between the two countries (Reimer, 2003).

That said, it is also true that a sizeable number of both Canadians and Americans—46 per cent vs. 56 per cent in a 1996 poll—support Christian values playing a role in politics (Lyon, 2000: 6). What seems different, however, is that Canadians are far less likely to believe that such values should translate into support or justification for the state's intrusion into individual rights. A poll by the Dominion Institute and Innovative Research Group, for example, found that even those Canadians who believed "gay sex is immoral" and that "a woman's place is in the home" were generally unwilling to support having their views enforced by law (reported in Cowan, 2005: A 12).

These value differences in turn appear to translate into ideological and political support. Roughly 34 per cent of Americans identify with the Christian right compared with only 18 per cent of Canadians. Even in the heyday of the Reform Party, more evangelicals voted Liberal than for Preston Manning's populist alternative (Lyon, 2000: 6–7; also, Reimer, 2003: 130). As Reimer (2003: 28) notes, there is not the same "alignment" of evangelicalism and conservatism in Canada as found in the US.

A third explanation for differences in evangelical support is rooted in historical experience. It is not entirely correct that the framers of the American Constitution sought unambiguously to separate Church and State, as often thought. It is correct, however, that the American state did not historically welcome religious institutions into the service of the state in the same way as occurred in Canada (Lipset, 1990: 16) where, for example, the Catholic and Anglican churches, as well as the smaller Methodist and Presbyterian churches, operated residential schools for the assimilation of Aboriginal children. One consequence of this, in the long term, was that these mainstream—and *not advertently evangelical*—churches became "tainted" by their involvement in state policies; indeed, they still face legal actions. By contrast, the relative isolation of religious organizations in the US from formal political power has protected them (until recently, at least) from the stigma of policies gone wrong; in this sense, evangelical churches in the US—like populist parties—have held the position of outsiders able to denounce the godless "establishment" for failing to create the New Jerusalem.

A fourth explanation for differences between the two countries can be drawn from resource mobilization theory (above). Simply put, the American movement consists of a wide swath of organizations, prominent religious leaders and political organizers (e.g., Ralph Reed), and a large membership. (The National Association of Evangelicals alone consists of 45,000 churches and 30 million adherents [Sharlet, 2005: 42].) Though relying upon "modest donations from hundreds of thousands of people" (Diamond, 1998: 12), it is also well-funded. Finally, the conservative Christian evangelical movement in the US obtains considerable publicity through various media, including several television programs and radio broadcasts throughout that country, as well as magazines and newsletters. One practical result of these assets is that the American movement is able "to get out the vote" during election time: 80 per cent of which chose George Bush Jr. in 2004 (Freedland, 2004: 5). Conservative Christian evangelicals in Canada do not have comparable resources in terms of organization, leadership, money, or media exposure.

Finally, in the very broadest political sense, the US is not like Canada or, frankly, any other Western industrialized (post-industrialized) country. The US is an "exceptional" country, though not in the self-congratulatory and excusatory way some American politicians have used the term. O'Brien (1994: 151) has said, "The United States is the heart and soul of the Enlightenment tradition." Though often repeated, this statement is less than accurate.

Between its east and west coasts, the heartland of liberalism and cosmopolitanism, there exists another US, one Richard Hofstadter (1964)—perhaps too harshly—described years ago as given to anti-intellectualism, paranoia, and irrationalism; a locale where American populism and much of the conservative Christian evangelical movement today meet; a place where evangelism's rejection of science, whether related to evolutionary biology or global warming (McKie, 2005), mirrors also rejection of the Enlightenment project.

Yet, there is at least one Enlightenment belief that resonates even in these quarters: the idea that the US is the last, best hope of humankind, that it has a mission to civilize the world and—in the eyes of many conservative Christian evangelicals—even to save it. No other Western country, including Canada, is motivated by such a political and religious imperative, wedded to national purpose; no other current country possesses a similar "civil religion."

CIVIL RELIGION: EVANGELICAL POLITICS AND THE NATION-STATE

> I went down on my knees and prayed to Almighty God for light and guidance more than one night. And one night late it came to me: 1) That we could not give them [the Philippines] back to Spain—that would be cowardly and dishonorable; 2) that we could not turn them over to France and Germany—our commercial rivals in the Orient—that would be bad business and discreditable; 3) that we could not leave them to themselves—they were unfit for self-government—and they would soon have anarchy and misrule over there worse than Spain's was; and 4) that there was nothing left for us to do but to take them all, and to educate the Filipinos, and uplift and civilize and Christianize them, and by God's grace do the very best we could by them, as our fellow-men for whom Christ also died. And then I went to bed, and went to sleep, and slept soundly, and the next morning I sent for the . . . war department map-maker, and told him to put the Philippines on the map of the United States . . . (quoted in Landau, 2005: 16).

Thus spoke President William McKinley, explaining in 1899 how he made his decision to incorporate the Philippines into the then nascent American empire. It provides a perfect example of what Bellah (1967) has termed "civil religion." The term describes the nature of belief in societies that mix religious and patriotic symbols and invoke divine support for state actions and policies. It is a particularly useful term for examining differences in the nature of power held by Christian evangelicals in the US and their counterparts in Canada.

This is not to say that Canada in the past has not displayed similar elements of civil religion. Lyon (2000: 8) notes that,

> For well over a century religion and politics in Canada were deeply intertwined. In anglophone Canada nationality itself was interpreted using evangelical referents, and political life was shot through with religious colouring. An alliance between Protestantism and British civilization was expressed in the hope of some that Canada would be God's Dominion.

However, the decline of Toryism and the British Empire, combined with "weak" Canadian nationalism—weak due to a combination of social forces (Quebec nationalists, labour unions, and organized farmers[9])—worked against the development of civil religion in Canada (see Reimer, 2003: 26). To be blunt, no imperial ambitions equals no civil religion.

As in Canada, the relationship of politics and religion in the US is old, complex, and often contradictory. For example, the Declaration of Independence invokes God; by contrast, the Constitution does not mention God at all. Side by side with their often stated desire to separate Church and State (for fear of what religious wars had done in Europe), the American founders also made clear through their speeches their belief that God had "chosen" their new country for a unique historical role. This latter belief, already well-established in the early nineteenth century, subsequently underpinned the twin notions of Manifest Destiny and the Monroe Doctrine that justified American expansion and intervention in the affairs of other countries in the hemisphere and that still resonate within US foreign policy today.

Later that century, the American novelist Herman Melville wrote in eulogistic terms of a messianic populism, "We Americans are the peculiar chosen people—the Israel of our time. We bear the ark of the liberties of the world." President Woodrow Wilson spoke of the US being led by the hand of God and of Americans being "the mortal instruments of His will" (both quotes from Resnick, 2005: 65).

In the nuclear afterglow of Hiroshima and Nagasaki in 1945, numerous American politicians and religious leaders were outspoken in contending God had given the US the bomb to defeat its enemies, chiefly communism (Ungar, 1991). In later years, American presidents often described the US as engaged in a quasi-religious battle against the Soviet Union (the "Evil Empire" in President Ronald Reagan's phrase) and the "Axis of Evil" (President George W. Bush's term to describe Iraq, Iran, and North Korea). No American president or presidential hopeful, Republican or Democrat, dare speak of the US in terms other than exceptional. Leading up to the 2012 election, President

Barack Obama—albeit subtly—championed the unique form of pluralist democracy in the US while his Republican opponent Mitt Romney declared the US "the greatest force for good the world has ever known" (see Raphael-Nakos, 2012).

American political culture is marked by a fusion of religious beliefs with nationalism, militarism, and consumer capitalism. Imperial expansion goes hand in hand with proselytizing mission-hood (Reimer, 2003: 123–24). Taken together, this complex of beliefs is a depthless pool into which the conservative Christian evangelical movement can repeatedly dip. As proof, a poll of 2,501 adults conducted in August 2012 found that 62 per cent of Americans believe God has granted the US "a special role in human history," this belief being highest among white evangelicals (85 per cent) followed closely by black Protestants (82 per cent) (Raphael-Nakos, 2012).

And so it is. There is no similar idea of Canada held by Canadians at large upon which conservative Christian evangelicals can build their political movement. Recent efforts by the Harper administration to militarize Canadian identity aside, there seems no immediate likelihood of triangulating nationalism, militarism, and God in Canada.

CONCLUSION

In a curious way, this paper has come full circle. It began by defining populism as a movement defending "the people" against powerful interests; it ends by explaining the increasing power of the conservative Christian evangelical movement in the US as resulting from its incorporation into and defence of the American nation-state. Yet, this should not surprise us. Populist movements, no less than other political efforts, exist within a given historical time and space and employ the cultural symbols and images at hand.

The explanations given for populist and other movements are not exclusive of each other. In studying the specific case of conservative Christian evangelical movements, however, some appear to have more explanatory power than others. Thus, strictly economic and class explanations appear to be a poor fit; by contrast, this case study seems congruent with cultural explanations that emphasize value and identity conflict. The case study also reinforces, as argued by resource mobilization theorists, the importance of organizational resources (including leadership) in the success of political movements and, from a political perspective, the importance of the political-institutional context in which differential resources are put to use. Finally, the case of evangelical movements illuminates the importance of historically constructed identifications among movement followers.

What is the political future of conservative Christian evangelicalism? As noted, the strength of the movement in the US, as opposed to Canada, stems in part from the fact that organized religion in the former has not historically been directly involved in political affairs. One possible consequence, therefore, of the conservative Christian evangelical movement taking a seat so close to the American power centre is that it may find itself held responsible for policies that fail or face a political backlash from those concerned about a blurring of Church and State and the movement's growing power.

But we should also keep in mind that, like populism, Christian evangelicalism (in general) is not wedded to any particular political program. Could the current strength of conservative evangelicalism be merely a passing phase, to be replaced by a more socially progressive, left alternative? Only time will tell.

NOTES

1   The author wishes to thank Reginald Bibby, William Ramp, and Miriam Smith for their very helpful comments on earlier drafts of this paper.

2   Referendums and initiatives are similar, the major difference being that governments institute referendums, while citizens launch initiatives.

3   There are a number of competing terms describing politically active Christians. The most common competitor to evangelicalism is fundamentalism. Technically, fundamentalism arose in the late nineteenth century as a revolt against modernism, including secularism. Unlike evangelicals, who wanted to change the world and convert non-believers, fundamentalists were then more interested in separating from the world. The lines have become more blurred since, but most scholars view fundamentalism as a subset of evangelicalism that includes Pentecostals, charismatics, and even neo-charismatics (Hadden and Shupe, 1988: 79). Marsden (1991: 1) says of fundamentalists, they are "not just religious conservatives, they are conservatives who are willing to take a stand and fight."

4   Bryan contested the presidential election for the People's Party in 1896 and 1900 but today is best remembered as the prosecutor in the 1925 Scopes Monkey trial.

5   Coughlin was a Roman Catholic priest whose radio broadcasts in the 1930s steadily veered toward pro-Fascism and anti-Semitism.

6   The Crusades were a series of military campaigns launched in the name of Christendom between the eleventh and thirteenth centuries in attempts to recapture Jerusalem and the Holy Land from the Muslims.

7   President George W. Bush's former speechwriter, David Frum, has stated the term "evildoers," used by the president after 9/11 to describe the enemy, is

taken from one of the president's favourite psalms, Psalm 27 ("When evildoers came upon me to devour my flesh") (Stolberg, 2006).

8   Bush invited faith communities to take over government social functions; cut off funding to agencies, such as Planned Parenthood, that provided information on procuring an abortion and otherwise supported the Right to Life Movement, through such actions as opposing stem cell research; and publicly endorsed the notion of "intelligent design," giving hope to those who wanted Creationism taught in public schools on an equal footing with the theory of evolution.

9   I owe particular thanks to Bill Ramp for emphasizing this point.

REFERENCES AND FURTHER READING

Adams, Michael. 2003. *Fire and Ice: The Myth of Value Convergence in Canada and the United States*. Toronto: Penguin.

Allen, A. Richard 2008. *The View from Murney Tower: Salem Bland, the Late-Victorian Controversies, and the Search for a New Christianity*. Toronto: University of Toronto Press.

Allen, A. Richard 2013. "Social Gospel." *The Canadian Encyclopedia*. http://www.thecanadianencyclopedia.com/articles/social-gospel (accessed September 7, 2013).

Bell, Edward. 1993. *Social Classes and Social Credit in Alberta*. Montreal: McGill-Queen's University Press.

Bellah, Robert N. 1967. "Civil Religion in America." *Daedalus* 96: 1–18.

Bibby, Reginald. 2006. *The Boomer Factor: What Canada's Most Famous Generation is Leaving Behind*. Toronto: Bastian Books.

Bibby, Reginald. 2011. *Beyond the Gods and Back*. Lethbridge: Project Canada Books.

Canovan, Margaret. 1981. *Populism*. New York: Harcourt Brace Jovanovich.

Carroll, Michael P. 2005. "Who Owns Democracy? Explaining the Long-running Debate Over Canadian/American Value Differences." *Canadian Review of Sociology and Anthropology. La Revue Canadienne de Sociologie et d'Anthropologie* 42 (3): 267–82.

Conway, John. 1978. "Populism in the United States, Russia, and Canada: Explaining the Roots of Canada's Third Parties." *Canadian Journal of Political Science* 11 (1): 99–124.

Cowan, James. 2005. "Morality Legislation Opposed." *National Post*, September 26: A12.

Di Tella, Torcuato S. 2001. "Populism." In *Political Philosophy: Theories, Thinkers, Concepts*, ed. Seymour Martin Lipset. Washington, DC: C.Q. Press.

Diamond, Sara. 1998. *Not By Politics Alone: The Enduring Influence of the Christian Right*. New York: The Guilford Press.

Farney, James. 2012. *Social Conservatives and Party Politics in Canada and the United States*. Toronto: University of Toronto Press.

Finkel, Alvin. 1989. *The Social Credit Phenomenon in Alberta*. Toronto: University of Toronto Press.

Flanagan, Tom. 2009. *Waiting for the Wave: The Reform Party and Preston Manning*. Toronto: Stoddart.

Freedland, Jonathan. 2004. "Democrats Need Rebirth." *Guardian Weekly*, November 12–18: 5.

Gerth, Hans H., and C. Wright Mills, eds. 1946. *From Max Weber: Essays in Sociology*. New York: Oxford University Press.

Grabb, Edward, and James Curtis. 2005. *Regions Apart: The Four Societies of Canada and the United States*. Oxford: Oxford University Press.

Gramsci, Antonio. 1988. *An Antonio Gramsci Reader: Selected Writings, 1916–1935*, ed. D. Forgacs. New York: Schocken Books.

Hadden, Jeffrey K., and Anson Shupe. 1988. *Televangelism: Power and Politics on God's Frontier*. New York: Henry Holt and Company.

Harrison, Trevor. 1995. *Of Passionate Intensity: Right-Wing Populism and the Reform Party of Canada*. Toronto: University of Toronto Press.

Harrison, Trevor. 2000. "The Changing Face of Prairie Politics: Populism in Alberta." In *Changing Prairie Landscapes*, ed. T.A. Radenbaugh and P. Douaud, 95–108. Regina: Canadian Plains Research Centre, University of Regina Press.

Harrison, Trevor. 2002. *Requiem for a Lightweight: Stockwell Day and Image Politics*. Montreal: Black Rose.

Hatch, N.O. 1989. *The Democratization of American Christianity*. New Haven: Yale University Press.

Hill, Samuel S., and Dennis E. Owen. 1982. *The New Religious Political Right in America*. Nashville: Abingdon.

Hofstadter, Richard. 1964. *The Paranoid Style in American Politics and Other Essays*. New York: Alfred A. Knopf.

Hunter, James Davison. 1983. *American Evangelicalism: Conservative Religion and the Quandary of Modernity*. New Brunswick, NJ: Rutgers University Press.

Kerr, Clark, J.T. Dunlop, Frederick Harbison, and C.A. Myers. 1964. *Industrialism and Industrial Man*. London: Oxford University Press.

Laclau, Ernesto. 2005. *On Populist Reason*. London: Verso.

Landau, Saul. 2005. "Conversations with God About Invading Other Countries." *Canadian Dimension* 39 (1) (January-February): 16–17.

Laycock, David. 1990. *Populism and Democratic Thought in the Canadian Prairies, 1910 to 1945*. Toronto: University of Toronto Press.

Lenin, Vladimir. 1960. "The Economic Content of Narodism and the Criticism of it in Mr. Struve's Book." In *Collected Works*. Moscow: Foreign Languages Publishing House.

Lenin, Vladimir. 1970. "The Heritage We Renounce." In *Selected Works*. Moscow: Progress Publishers.

Lipset, Seymour Martin. 1968. *Agrarian Socialism: The Cooperative Commonwealth Federation in Saskatchewan*. Garden City, NY: Doubleday.

Lipset, Seymour Martin. 1990. *Continental Divide: The Values and Institutions of the United States and Canada*. New York: Routledge.

Lyon, David. 2000. "Introduction." In *Rethinking Church, State, and Modernity. Canada Between Europe and America*, ed. D. Lyon and M. van Die, 3–19. Toronto: University of Toronto Press.

McDonald, Marci. 2010. *The Armageddon Factor: The Rise of Christian Nationalism in Canada*. Toronto: Random House.

Macpherson, C.B. 1953. *Democracy in Alberta: Social Credit and the Party System*. Toronto: University of Toronto Press.

Marsden, George M. 1991. *Understanding Fundamentalism and Evangelicalism*. Grand Rapids, MI: George Eerdmans Publishing.

Martin, Lawrence. 2012. "Religion's Fair Game If It Motivates Politics." *The Globe and Mail* (July 31: A11).

Marx, Karl, and Friedrich Engels. 1977 [1848]. "The Communist Manifesto." In *Karl Marx: Selected Writings*, ed. D. McLellan. Oxford: Oxford University Press.

McKie, Robin. 2005. "No Science, Please, We're Fanatics." *Guardian Weekly*, April 1–7: 22.

Micklethwait, John, and Adrian Wooldridge. 2004. *The Right Nation: Conservative Power in America*. Toronto: Penguin.

Morton, William L. 1978. *The Progressive Party in Canada*. Toronto: University of Toronto Press.

Nikiforuk, Andrew. 2012. "Understanding Harper's Evangelical Mission." *The Tyee*, March 26. http://thetyee.ca/Opinion/2012/03/26/Harper-Evangelical-Mission/ (accessed on September 4, 2013).

O'Brien, Conor C. 1994. *On the Eve of the Millennium*. Concord: House of Anansi.

Pew Forum on Religion and Public Life. 2007. "U.S. Religious Landscape Survey." http://religions.pewforum.org/reports (accessed on September 4, 2013).

Pew Research Center for the People and the Press. 2002. "Among Wealthy Nations . . . U.S. Stands Alone in its Embrace of Religion." Press release, December 9.

Pew Research Center for the People and the Press. 2004. "Americans and Canadians: The North American Not-so-odd Couple." Press release, January 14.

Pinard, Maurice. 1971. *The Rise of a Third Party: A Study in Crisis Politics*. Montreal: McGill-Queen's University Press.

Radenbaugh, T.A., and P. Douaud, eds. 2000. *Changing Prairie Landscapes*. Regina, Saskatchewan: Canadian Plains Research Centre, University of Regina Press.

Ramp, William, and Trevor W. Harrison. 2012. "Libertarian Populism, Neo-liberal Rationality, and the Mandatory Long Form Census: Implications for Sociology." *Canadian Journal of Sociology* 37 (3): 273–94.

Raphael-Nakos, Thomas. 2012. "Reflections on American 'Exceptionalism'." *Bettendorf.com*, October 16. http://www.bettendorf.com/node/1429 (accessed September 4, 2013).

Rawlyk, George A. 1996. *Is Jesus Your Personal Saviour?: In Search of Canadian Evangelicalism in the 1990s*. Montreal: McGill-Queen's University Press.

Rayside, David. 2011. "The Conservative Party of Canada and Its Religious Constituencies." In *Faith Politics and Sexual Diversity*, ed. D. Rayside and C. Wilcox, 279–99. Vancouver: University of British Columbia Press.

Rea, Julian Castro, Graciela Ducatenzeiler, and Philippe Faucher. 1992. "Back to Populism: Latin America's Alternative to Democracy." In *Latin America to the Year 2000*, ed. A.R.M. Ritter, M.A. Cameron, and D.H. Pollock, 125–46. New York: Praeger.

Reimer, Sam. 2003. *Evangelicals and the Continental Divide*. Montreal: McGill-Queen's University Press.

Resnick, Philip. 2005. *The European Roots of Canadian Identity*. Peterborough: Broadview Press.

Richards, John. 1981. "Populism: A Qualified Defence." *Studies in Political Economy* 5: 5–27.

Saad, Lydia. 2009. "Special Report: Ideologically, Where is the U.S. Moving?" http://www.gallup.com/poll/121403/special-report-ideologically-moving.aspx (accessed September 4, 2013).

Schama, Simon. 2004. "Onward Christian Soldiers." *Guardian Weekly* November 12–18: 19–20.

Sharlet, Jeff. 2005. "Inside the Nation's Most Powerful Megachurch." *Harper's Magazine* May: 41–54.

Sinclair, Peter. 1979. "Class Structure and Populist Protest: The Case of Western Canada." In *Society and Politics in Alberta: Research Papers*, ed. C. Caldarola, 73–86. Toronto: Methuen.

Smith, Christian. 1998. *American Evangelicalism: Embattled and Thriving*. Chicago: University of Chicago Press.

Statistics Canada. 2005. "Population by religion, by provinces and territories." *2001 Census*. Data modified January 25, 2005. Ottawa: Statistics Canada. http://www.statcan.gc.ca/tables-tableaux/sum-som/l01/cst01/demo30a-eng.htm (accessed September 7, 2013).

Stolberg, Sheryl Gay. 2006. "'Islamo-Fascism' Had Its Moment." *New York Times* (September 24).

Ungar, Sheldon. 1991. "Civil Religion and the Arms Race." *Canadian Review of Sociology and Anthropology/La Revue Canadienne de Sociologie et d'Anthropologie* 28 (4): 503–25.

United States Census Bureau. 2012. "Self-described Religious Identification of Adult Population 1990, 2001, and 2008." *Statistical Abstract of the United States: 2012*, p. 61. http://www.census.gov/compendia/statab/cats/population/religion.html (accessed September 4, 2013).

van Die, Marguerite. 2001. "Introduction." In *Religion and Public Life in Canada: Historical and Comparative Perspectives*, ed. M. van Die, 3–19. Toronto: University of Toronto Press.

Williamson, Vanessa, Theda Skocpol, and John Coggin. 2011. "The Tea Party and the Remaking of Republican Conservatism." *Perspectives on Politics* 9 (1): 25–43.

Zald, Mayer N., and John D. McCarthy, eds. 1987. *Social Movements in an Organizational Society: Collected Essays*. New Brunswick, NJ: Transaction Books.

PART THREE

Nations and Nationalism

TEN

Aysaka'paykinit: Contesting the Rope Around the Nations' Neck[1]

KIERA L. LADNER

The politics of contestation among Indigenous peoples in Canada has a history that predates colonialism. Since political and social dissidents seem to exist in every polity, it could be argued that this history goes back thousands of years. The dissidents and the movements they led spawned much transformation and change within their nations and internationally between and among nations. For instance, about 1,000 years ago, in a time characterized by crime, injustice, international war, and political chaos, the Peacemaker and his assistant, Hiawatha, travelled among the Mohawk, Cayuga, Onondaga, Oneida, and Seneca Nations bringing a message of peace, a good mind (sometimes translated as power), and righteousness. This sparked a peaceful revolution within and among the nations that resulted in the creation of a new Haudenosaunee confederacy and a new constitutional order called the Kayanerenkowa, or the Great Law of Peace. This message of peace and the new constitutional order inspired other revolutionaries and influenced the Constitution designed by the American Founding Fathers (Johansen, 1998: 19–39). While not all dissident efforts resulted in such radical change, there are many other pre-colonial examples where people mobilized and succeeded in achieving social and political change or in completely transforming the political and social structures of a nation or grouping of nations.

Acknowledging this historical foundation and continuity, this chapter will explore Indigenous politics of contestation in an historically grounded manner while focusing primarily on the mobilization of First Nations peoples (not Métis or Inuit). It weaves together a narrative of mobilization that focuses on the historical foundations of, and continuity among, several seemingly unrelated episodes of contestation. Rather than drawing on social movement theory or providing a comparative analysis of Indigenous movements *vis-à-vis* other movements, the chapter proceeds descriptively in a manner grounded in Indigenist theory and methodology that use storytelling or narration to create an awareness of the movement and an understanding of the issues, goals, aspirations, and tensions that define it. In so doing, it will draw attention to the idea that the goals and the mechanisms used to articulate and pursue the resolution of the goals, as well as the factions that exist within the movement, are predicated upon considerations of nationhood and (de)colonization. In this way, this chapter contributes to the theoretical literature on social movements. Indigenous movements contest the very foundation of the Canadian state as a colonial construction while most theories of group politics and social movements take the state for granted.

I will begin by examining the Indigenous politics of contestation historically by telling the story of several defining moments. Then I will describe the goals that have defined (and continue to define) the Indigenous politics of contestation, goals that have remained constant since issues of sovereignty, land, and economic rights have yet to be resolved in a mutually agreeable and mutually beneficial manner. Finally, having explored the history of the movement and explained why it exists, I will conclude by offering a more theoretical assessment of its underpinnings and explain how the deep belief in Indigenous nationhood and (de)colonization has defined the movement and its development.

FRAMING THE CONFLICT

With colonization, the Indigenous politics of contestation changed from a focus on national and sub-national issues and organizations to activities and movements that were typically external to the nation, between nations, or between individuals or groups and colonial nations. Discontent and episodes of mobilization focused on the primary concerns of each nation, such as territorial intrusions, territory-sharing arrangements, maintaining relationships with a nation's occupied territory, religious and spiritual freedom, sovereignty, self-determination, economic independence, economic assistance (such as farming), health care, treaties, trade networks, and international relations (with both Indigenous and colonial nations). The prominence of these issues and of the emerging international politics of contestation in the initial stages of discontent is apparent in many of the "early" struggles between Indigenous peoples and the colonizers. Among these were the 1763–66 rebellion against the British led by Obwandiyag (Pontiac) and involving a considerable number of nations including Odawa, Potawatomis, Huron, Shawnee, Delaware, Wendat, Kickapoo, and Anishnaabe; the 1869–70 and 1885 Métis resistance movements led by Louis Riel; and the mobilization between 1870 and 1885 of the Nehiyaw (Plains Cree) led by Mistahimaskwa (Big Bear). Though it should not be construed as being representative of these early struggles, the story of Mistahimaskwa's resistance does serve as a template for these events.

On July 15, 1870, the Government of Canada assumed sovereignty over the Northwest Territories, or so it was (and is) claimed. This assertion and the preceding purchase of the territory from the Hudson's Bay Company (HBC) were not met with enthusiasm by the Nehiyaw. According to them (and to their neighbouring nations) this was their territory, and the Queen had no claim to it, no right to rule it, and no right to assert any authority over them. This discontent was coupled with a growing array of issues and problems resulting from colonization—American incursions into Nehiyaw territory, a declining buffalo population, the growing influence of whisky traders, the catastrophic effects of disease and death—and led the Nehiyaw to lobby the Queen and her government for a treaty and a means for addressing their grievances. Employing the assistance of traders, policemen, missionaries, and government employees, Nehiyaw leaders such as Weekuskokisayin (Sweet Grass) effectively lobbied the Canadian government (Taylor, 1985: 2). Though he and other chiefs argued that their land was not for sale and that no one had the right or the ability to sell it (Christie, 1871), they were willing to share it and some of its resources with (a few) settlers and to build a "brotherly" relationship with the Queen and her people. Further, Weekuskokisayin argued that a treaty was needed because:

> Our Land is getting ruined of fur bearing animals, hitherto our soul support, and we are now poor and want help—we want you to pity us. We want cattle, tools, agriculture implements, and assistance in everything when we come to settle—our country is no longer able to support us.
>
> Make provisions for us against years of starvation. We have had a great starvation this past winter, and smallpox took away many of our people, the old, young and children.
>
> We want you to stop the Americans from coming to trade on our lands, and giving firewater, ammunition and arms to our enemies the Blackfeet. . . . (Christie, 1871; also see Morris, 1880: 186–71)

Six years after the Nehiyaw began lobbying, the government finally acted. However, they did not do so in good faith. Their negotiators failed to invite many Nehiyaw leaders to the table, especially those who were most vocal in their discontent with the Queen, and, worse, they proved unwilling to negotiate (or even discuss) key issues and problems. As a result, while Treaty Six was said to respond to the demands put forth by such leaders as Weekuskokisayin, many dissident leaders and their followers did not sign. Foremost among these was Mistahimaskwa who refused to sign because he refused to "live with a rope around his neck" (*aysaka'paykinit*): he would not give up his freedom, nor the freedom and sovereignty of his nation, to be led around like a domesticated animal in a *skunkun* (reserve or roped-off piece of land) (Dempsey, 1984: 241). Following the negotiations of 1876, Mistahimaskwa continued his efforts to engage the Queen's representatives in a discussion about the terms of the treaty, to foster a nation-to-nation relationship, and to attempt to mobilize the Nehiyaw to take a collective stance. With his people starving, and the government promising rations for all signatories to Treaty Six, he finally gave up his fight in 1882.

Nonetheless, Mistahimaskwa continued to advocate a message of unity and sovereignty and a peaceful resolution of problems with Canada. Further, despite the starvation and destitute conditions among the Nehiyaw and neighbouring nations, people continued to mobilize and gather at events such as the Thirst Dance that Mistahimaskwa hosted on Pitikahanapiwiyin's (Poundmaker's) reserve in June 1884. Despite the vision, dedication, and leadership of these two leaders, efforts to mobilize the Nehiyaw in peaceful union and to engage the Crown's representatives in discussion failed. Disillusioned by the lack of results of peaceful resistance, militant leaders such as Imasees (Wild Child) and Kapapamahchakwew (Wandering Spirit) used the opportunities provided by the nearby Métis uprising to take over the leadership of their nation and to pursue a more activist and militant strategy that involved the looting of government and HBC supply warehouses in Frog Lake and engaging in an armed conflict (the Northwest Rebellion) with Canada. This strategy did not secure resolution or action on any Nehiyaw grievances. In the end, though Mistahimaskwa did not participate, he was found guilty of treason and sentenced to three years in prison, his followers lost their reserve, the Nehiyaw lost their battle over the treaty with the government and were forcefully confined to the destitute conditions of reserves, and those who participated in the armed insurrection were either hung or escaped prosecution and found refuge in a garbage dump on the outskirts of Helena, Montana.

The subjugation of the Nehiyaw sent a message to other Indigenous peoples and their leaders throughout Canada—and it still serves witness to what can happen when Indigenous peoples engage in politics of contestation, no matter what the strategy or in which domain/arena. This incident, and others, served notice that change would be hard fought. Nonetheless, it remains a necessary battle in pursuit of a worthy vision of a life as individuals and nations defined not by rope but by self-determination, equality, and a standard of living comparable to those who occupy and claim sovereignty over their territories.

A BATTLE REKINDLED

This battle was rekindled after World War I by a Mohawk veteran, Frederick Loft. As a Pine Tree Chief (special appointee to the Haudenosaunee Confederacy Council defined in the Great Law), Loft was active in the immediate postwar period in lobbying the British Crown over issues of concern to the Confederacy Chiefs and Six Nations reserve. However, Loft had a much larger vision than defending the rights of the Haudenosaunee, particularly its sovereignty and self-determination, as the federal government was attempting to overthrow the traditional government and replace it with their own "puppet government" or Indian Act band council. Loft envisioned a national organization that would mobilize and unify Indigenous peoples and that would lobby the federal government to improve living standards on reserve, particularly with respect to education (Smith, 2002: 2). In 1918, he succeeded in establishing the League of Indians of Canada. Originally comprised primarily of band leadership from Ontario and Quebec, the League gradually expanded outward until its collapse in the mid-1930s. Though the collapse is typically attributed to Loft's declining health, one cannot forget the role that the federal government played in impeding the development and in contributing to the demise of this movement simply by enforcing the Indian Act and its restrictions on Indian mobilization, organization, and travel: Indians could not legally leave their reserves, gather for "unsanctioned" purposes, raise monies for "unsanctioned" use, or hire lawyers. Further, Loft's success was also confined in part by "Indian politics": nationalism, traditional alliances, treaty sentimentalities, internal and international divisions resulting from colonization, and the multiplicity of traditional Indigenous political traditions.

Though short-lived, Loft's initiatives can be credited with the creation of several provincial leagues and the growing sense that international cooperation and pan-Indian activism had great potential as a strategy for achieving real change. These efforts were thwarted by the Department of Indian Affairs and the RCMP, whose mere presence at gatherings of the movement posed the threat of arrests. Not only was it illegal for Indigenous peoples to gather, but their ceremonies—dancing, prayers, and the smoking of a pipe—were also proscribed. Loft's trip to Thunderchild's reserve in Saskatchewan in 1921 saw the threat of federal interference become reality as Nehiyaw leaders were arrested. Though these arrests were for dancing (not treason, as was the case for

Mistahimaskwa), they sent a strong message to the Nehiyaw and their leadership. It was a message that, when combined with the experiences of 1885 and the predominant Nehiyaw nationalism, stalled the development of a formal provincial organization in Saskatchewan until the late 1950s.

THE MOVEMENT TAKES HOLD

Neither these arrests nor the predominant Indigenous nationalist outlook halted efforts to organize. After a successful gathering in Hobemma (Alberta) in 1922, Loft's vision of international mobilization really took hold among the Nehiyaw in Alberta. Established in 1933, the League of Indians of Alberta was essentially an organization of Nehiyaw from Treaty Six in central Alberta that borrowed its leadership from band councils and organizations such as the "Half-Breed Association of Alberta" (later, the Métis National Association of Alberta) led by Joe Dion, a teacher from Kehiwin and nephew of Mistahimaskwa. In an attempt to expand its constituency to include non-Cree, the League joined with political organizations emerging among the Siiksikaawa (Blackfoot Confederacy) to become the Indian Association of Alberta (IAA).

When windows of opportunities presented themselves, the IAA proved itself to be a "mighty power." It was the IAA, under the leadership of Harold Cardinal, that formally responded to the federal government's 1969 White Paper (see discussion below) by releasing the Red Paper (Indian Chiefs of Alberta, 1970) and that was in the forefront of the charge to establish the National Indian Brotherhood (NIB). Similarly, the IAA was very active in the constitutional debates of the early 1980s when the opportunity arose to pressure governments to acknowledge and entrench Aboriginal and treaty rights into the Constitution Act, an opportunity to which the IAA and other groups responded by actively lobbying Canadian governments, the UN, the Canadian public, the British Crown, and the British Courts (the Judicial Committee of the Privy Council), among other venues (Sanders, 1992: 151–67). Interestingly enough, the IAA was recently resurrected in late November 2012 after years of stagnation, just as the Idle No More movement took off. Cardinal's daughter Tanya Kappo held a teach-in at Louis Bull First Nation on December 2, 2012, and in so doing launched her hashtag and the social media blitz that came to dominate Idle No More or what is increasingly becoming referred to as the Indigenous Nations/Nationhood Movement (Stolte, 2012).

Like other provincial Indigenous organizations, the IAA was a civil rights movement intent on forcing the federal government to assist the people in achieving equality and a standard of living comparable to Canadian citizens by addressing health care, housing, education, social assistance, and justice issues. Similarly, it also focused on matters pertinent to the nations that comprised its membership, including sovereignty, territory, Aboriginal rights, the nation-to-nation relationship, and self-determination (McFarlane, 1993: 42). Unlike those organizations based on non-treaty nations (such as the Union of British Columbia Indian Chiefs), however, the primary focus of "treaty organizations"—the IAA, the Federation of Saskatchewan Indian Nations (FSIN), and the Union of Nova Scotia Indians—is the implementation of the treaties and the treaty order, for the treaties were to have protected the nations from colonial intrusions and provided for economic and social assistance. It should also be noted that this focus on treaties not only served to separate treaty-based pan-Indian organizations from those focused on obtaining treaties (those without treaties), but also acts as a point of division and clash within organizations comprised of two or more treaty areas as different treaties afforded the signatories different rights and protections—a situation that further exacerbated national tensions within these organizations.

A "NATIONAL" INTERNATIONAL BROTHERHOOD

Changes to the Indian Act in 1951 lifted the restrictions on political activities, enabling status Indians both to gather for political purposes and to raise money to prove land claims and to hire lawyers. Though there had been several federal-sponsored initiatives to create an organization at the pan-Canadian level, it was not until 1968 that a new movement began to take shape. The NIB was created by uniting provincial organizations under a "federal" umbrella organization for reasons of political expediency and the need for organizational capacity and a knowledgeable leadership. A product of the times, the NIB began to take shape as a movement comprised of at least two distinct factions: (1) an organization of political elites intent on lobbying the government for better living conditions and self-determination; and (2) an activist network comprised of grassroots activists who were intent on creating change by rebuilding their cultures, languages, communities, and economies. These two groups converged when the federal government released its White Paper on Indian Policy in 1969. Threatened by the government's attempt to unilaterally disband reserves and eliminate their rights (their status as "citizens plus"), the First Nations mobilized and took to the streets and "war rooms" of their national, provincial, and federal political organizations and movements. For once, the movement was unified. Treaty divisions and nationalist sentiments mattered not when everyone's basic rights as Indigenous people and nations were in jeopardy. Finally, the movement saw success as the government shelved the White Paper.

The White Paper was a classical political opportunity: it provided a rallying point to the Indigenous movement, encouraged mobilization, demanded the development of organizational capacities, and provided access to the policy network. With the politicization of households, an increasingly unified movement, an increasingly educated Indigenous public[2]—a public with rising political, social, and economic expectations—and increased organizational capacity (both federally and provincially), the "new" Indigenous rights movement was firmly entrenched into the Canadian political landscape. But this unity did not last long, as it continued to be plagued by national and treaty differences and by the differences created by colonial authorities and colonial legislation (such as the Indian Act). The Indigenous rights movement was forced to grapple with the divisive legacies of the treaty period, which failed to include all Indigenous people in a treaty area and thus divided nations and families among treaty or status Indians, non-status Indians, and Métis. The Indian Act also divided the Indigenous community (and thus Nations) into status and non-status Indians or between federally recognized Indians and those Indigenous peoples recognized only as "Canadians."[3] All this served to divide the movement and in 1971 led to the creation of another national organization, the Native Council of Canada (NCC), which was to represent the interests of those who had never formally been represented by the NIB—off-reserve, non-status Indians and Métis people. The movement then also fractured along gender lines, as non-status women (who had lost status by marrying non-status men) and many Métis women and status women living both on and off reserve felt that their interests were not being fairly represented by the NIB. They forged their own movement in the late 1960s—the Native Women's Association of Canada (NWAC)—and created provincial and national organizations in the early 1970s to fight for women's rights under the Indian Act and to improve the social, political, and economic situation of Indigenous women.

Still, the NIB stayed at the helm of the movement and forged ahead with an aggressive rights-based strategy, which was very different from Loft's focus on education and social improvements. Though intent on improving the social and economic conditions of Indigenous peoples, the NIB approached this from a "new" vantage defined by national interests and began to frame a pan-Indian discourse of Aboriginal and treaty rights. To this end, it argued that, although the federal government had a responsibility to provide assistance and to address the catastrophic social and economic conditions on reserves, it had no right to interfere politically, as it was time for First Nations to exercise their rights of self-determination. The philosophy of self-determination was, in the words of George Manuel, "just give us the gas, we'll do the driving" (McFarlane, 1993:72).

The NIB's philosophy of self-determination and rights served to unify Indigenous peoples and created a true pan-Indian vision and movement involving all Indigenous peoples of all nations, treaty or non-treaty. Nonetheless, it was widely criticized by many treaty nations because they had already had their rights affirmed and a nation-to-nation relationship established in the treaties. Thus, despite greater unity, the movement continued to be plagued by the nationalist and treaty divisions of the past (as will be discussed in the final section of this chapter).

THE DAWNING OF A NEW ERA

Viewing the constitutional discussions as an opportunity to put Aboriginal and treaty rights on the centre stage of the political arena and seeing the possibility of gaining constitutional recognition and protection of Aboriginal and treaty rights, the Aboriginal rights movement and organizations such as the NIB, FSIN, NCC, and IAA jumped on every opportunity to pressure Canadian governments into accepting its vision. They were, by all accounts, "the least expected, and most exotic" (Sanders, 1992: 151) part of the patriation process, for they not only lobbied Canadian governments and parliamentarians, the Governor General, the Vatican, the British Parliament, and the Queen, they sought legal action in the UK (Venne, 1998: 105–06) and held mass demonstrations throughout Canada. Though they were never included as participants in the process (several organizations were provided with observer status when warranted), and while many of the issues that they sought to have addressed (such as treaty implementation and the sovereignty of First Nations) were not brought forward, they succeeded in putting their issues front and centre and in achieving some semblance of constitutional protection of their rights.

Pressured by national governments such as the Mi'kmaw Grand Council, treaty activists, and participating federal and provincial Indigenous organizations (such as the NIB and NCC), Aboriginal and treaty rights gained constitutional recognition in 1982. But the process strained the leadership and organizational capacities of the movement. The NIB struggled with its relationship with, and its perceived accountability to, First Nations' leadership (Indian Act chiefs) and the demands of treaty nations, which, in 1982, took over and restructured the organization, renaming it the Assembly of First Nations (AFN). Meanwhile, in 1983, the Métis (primarily the western Métis and the descendants of the historical Métis Nation) pulled out of the NCC and created the Métis National Council (MNC), leaving the NCC to represent the issues of off-reserve and non-status Indians and those Métis who did not fall within the mandate of the MNC. While these other groups were enduring a makeover, NWAC gained momentum. Following patriation of the Constitution, the major Indigenous organizations gathered with First Ministers on several occasions between 1983 and 1987 to discuss the meaning of "Aboriginal and treaty rights" and issues such as gender equality.

As a result of mega constitutionalism, this once-grassroots movement faced momentous transformative change as the rights-based orientation was enhanced by the new language of constitutional rights and the Constitution began to demand increased organizational capacity and to structure Indigenous people's relationship with Canada. Neither the movement nor any of the organizations had ever perceived themselves as interest groups, although they had used every opportunity available to force the government into dealing with their rights-based agenda and engaging in discussions of self-determination. Almost immediately, it appeared as though this struggle to frame the discussion of colonialism, past injustices, and the relationship between themselves and the state had been won with sections 25 and 35 of the Charter of Rights and Freedoms[4] and as the governments of Canada began preparing for a series of First Ministers' Conferences on Aboriginal and treaty rights. The conferences ended with no agreed-upon interpretation of the meaning of these rights. Constitutional inclusion had failed to result in any meaningful change in the relationship between Indigenous peoples and the Canadian state. This was made particularly clear by the Meech Lake Accord. Though negotiated shortly after the last First Ministers' Conference on Aboriginal Issues, the Accord not only failed to address the relationship between Indigenous peoples and the state or to address Indigenous issues of concern, but also Indigenous people were excluded from both the negotiations and the agreement itself.

The defiant "No" of MLA Elijah Harper "killed" the Accord on the floor of the Manitoba Legislature. Whether the result of Harper's activist gesture, the 1991 standoff between Mohawk warriors and the Canadian army over the Oka golf course, or the lobby efforts of groups such as the AFN, this is clear: when the constitutional debate was reopened during the "Canada Round" of constitutional talks (the Charlottetown Accord), Indigenous peoples were invited to the table where they succeeded at dominating much of the debate and securing further recognition of their constitutional rights—including the rights of Métis and the inherent right to self-government. It was an enormous victory, albeit a victory that was short-lived, for while it was an overwhelming victory for organizations such as the MNC, much of the AFN's constituency questioned the deal. In the end, internal differences (such as status), nationalisms, and treaty sentimentalities divided the movement, as most treaty nations denounced the Accord as an affront to treaty rights and status Indians questioned the soundness of the agreement. But it was not just treaty nations and dissident status

Indians who opposed the deal and voted against it in the referendum—the majority of Canadians also opposed the Accord, and it was defeated.

FINDING NEW MEANING IN THE POST-CONSTITUTION WORLD

Much of the substance of the Charlottetown Accord found life in non-constitutional agreements and policies such as the federal government's 1995 Inherent Right Policy, which affirmed self-government as a constitutionally recognized Aboriginal right. Nonetheless, the defeat of the Accord represented a catastrophic problem for the Indigenous rights movement and its organizations, for they had been so focused on achieving constitutional change that they had become little more than single-issue organizations with little mandate or capacity for anything else and thus had become fragmented and disengaged. As in the post-constitutional period of the 1980s, these organizations underwent a tremendous overhaul as they adapted to a new policy environment, created new capacities, and looked for new opportunities to engage the government and new ways to use (and fund) the tremendous infrastructure that had been developed (with government assistance).

Indigenous rights organizations have become increasingly bureaucratized, involved in policy networks, and integrated into the federal government's machinery to such an extent that many commonly "share" staff with federal departments (using secondment agreements) and are involved in all aspects of the policy process, including policy formulation and implementation. For example, in 2001 the Department of Indian Affairs and Northern Development contracted out to the NCC the responsibility for the consultations (the Communities First: First Nations Governance Initiative) that preceded the controversial First Nations Governance Act, 2002. Meanwhile, the AFN has entered into partnerships, service agreements, and contracting relationships with an assortment of departments including Finance, Health, and Indian Affairs to aid in program administration and to engage in policy discussions (agenda setting, development, and implementation) in areas of taxation, membership registries, and land management. Even NWAC managed to get into the game with both its Sisters in Spirit initiative (in 2005) which served as a de facto research commission (and in some ways an inquiry) on missing and murdered women, and its work on matrimonial real property rights (in 2006–08), which provided government with an apparatus for consultation and policy development in this area. While such arrangements offer creative ways of financing the organizations and provide opportunities to engage governments, to advance an Aboriginal rights agenda, and to improve economic and social conditions, these arrangements are not viewed favourably by the grassroots.

Amid the constant criticisms of these organizations for "sleeping with the enemy" and "being in bed with the government," the AFN was dealt a further blow when the federal government announced its plans in 2001 to use the NCC to consult with Indigenous peoples and revise the Indian Act with its First Nations Governance Act initiative. The AFN had been sidestepped and made to appear an ineffective (non)participant in the policy process. Despite attempts to demonstrate otherwise, the AFN was unable to shake this label, as it had proven itself unable to shape the policy initiative before consultations or to influence the First Nations Governance Act before it was tabled in the House of Commons in 2002. Worse yet, despite framing the issue as a threat similar to the White Paper of 1969, the AFN seemed unable to mobilize the grassroots or to get the government to listen—that is, until it called in its "heavy hitters" to address a Joint Ministerial Advisory Committee.

Though it was able to "save face," and the legislation died on the government's agenda when Paul Martin became prime minister, the AFN set out to alter its relationship or at least the perception of its relationship with the federal government. In fact, all of the national organizations underwent some sort of organizational renewal during this time, the real change occurring in their relationship with the federal government. Ushered in by both a change in government when Paul Martin became prime minister in December 2003 as well as by changes within all of the key organizations, this relationship was radically transformed in 2004 with the convening of the Canada-Aboriginal Peoples Roundtable process (Canada, 2004). The Roundtable was promoted as an opportunity to establish a new relationship between all Indigenous peoples and the federal government and to make actual progress on a new agenda. With its transparent, sectorally defined tables, its frank and open discussions, and real commitment to both process and product by all parties, the Roundtable was very successful. It resulted in a Political Accord on the Recognition and Implementation of First Nations Governments (the Kelowna Accord), the convening of a First Ministers' Meeting with Indigenous leaders from all major organizations on November 25, 2005, substantial progress in the negotiation of several other agreements, and an implementation strategy addressing a wide range of issues including health care (Canada, 2005). It should be noted that this transformation in the relationship between Indigenous peoples and government and the progressive changes in social policies, as negotiated in the Accord, were short-lived. Negotiated in the final days of Martin's minority Liberal government, the Kelowna Accord was immediately repudiated by Stephen Harper's minority Conservative government. This signalled not only the end of the Accord but the end of the new and improved relationship that was developing under Martin's leadership. It also signalled a return to, and a worsening of, the chilly climate that characterized Indigenous politics and Indigenous-state relations in the past.

DANCING AROUND THE TABLE: RETRENCHMENT, ABROGATION, AND DEROGATION

The death of the Kelowna Accord—and its promise of progressive change and increased financial resources for basic services in cash-strapped communities (a 2 per cent cap on federal transfers to reserves had been in place since 1996 despite the ongoing population explosion)—took the wind out of the sails of the major political organizations and Indigenous leaders. Instead of the positive change promised only months before, the change in government resulted in government retrenchment, deep cuts for both organizations and communities, and sweeping legislative change.

Indigenous rights organizations have had fewer and fewer opportunities to engage with the federal government to advance their agenda or secure any meaningful change. Though Harper has spoken of the need to create a new relationship with Indigenous peoples (a 2006 election promise), a First Nations Summit was not held until 2012 (precipitated by the declaration of a state of emergency in Attawapiskat in December 2011). The Summit was a failure for Indigenous people, and this failure has contributed to increased dissent within the movement and thus a questioning of the existing Indigenous rights organizations by both the grassroots and Indian Act chiefs (the constituents of the AFN). This crisis of legitimacy and functionality has defined elections in several of these organizations (including the AFN and NWAC) and has resulted in the establishment of (or calls for) new organizations (or movements) such as a national treaty coalition and Idle No More. Further, it is a crisis that is seemingly exacerbated by the actions (and inaction) of the Conservative government.

It should be noted that, even under Harper, these organizations and the movements they represent both domestically and internationally have achieved some measure of success. Following years of lobbying by the AFN, and mandated by a class action settlement agreement, the Truth and Reconciliation Commission (a compensation scheme) and Harper's Statement of Apology were offered to survivors of Indian residential schools in 2008. Further, although Canada refused to sign the UN Declaration on the Rights of Indigenous Peoples in 2007, following extensive lobbying and a changing international climate, the government officially endorsed the Declaration in 2010. Still, despite these major achievements, the chilly climate that characterizes the relationship between Indigenous peoples and the state has only worsened. Budget cuts (to core funding, programs, and services) have crippled

Indigenous organizations at all levels. At the same time, the government has all but refused to engage Indigenous peoples and their (representative) organizations in consultations and to address Indigenous concerns and/or their constitutionally recognized Aboriginal and treaty rights in its legislative agenda. This has forced communities and rights-based organizations into the courts, onto blockades, into the malls, or onto the streets.

The Conservative government's running roughshod over Indigenous peoples, their rights, and the Indigenous rights movement has brought new life to the movement. In late October 2012, four women from Saskatchewan (Sylvia McAdam, Jess Gordon, Nina Wilson, and Sheelah McLean) decided that they could be "idle no more" and organized a teach-in as a response to the environmental provisions of Bill C-45, Harper's omnibus budget bill, for its breach of treaty and its assault on Indigenous/shared territories and waters (Kappo, 2012). Tanya Kappo and others followed suit, holding teach-ins, using social media, hosting local events, and planning the December 10, 2012, National Day of Action. Thanks largely to Twitter and Facebook, Idle No More went viral and the National Day of Action went global. Within days, protests were planned across the nation; on December 18, these protests began to take a new form and to gain even more momentum when a round dance flash mob was organized in Regina—bringing the movement in from the cold and into the malls (and all in time for last minute Christmas shoppers).

As 2012 wound down, the movement exploded with round dances, teach-ins, hunger strikes, and demonstrations across Canada and beyond. Despite the frigid temperatures and the extraordinarily long winter that was experienced in much of Canada during 2013, the movement continued to grow online, in the streets, in the classrooms/teach-ins, and in the malls. Hundreds of youth marched on Ottawa in March to mark the end of a 1,600-kilometre walk for the Nishiyuu Walkers, which began when seven youth from James Bay decided to walk to Ottawa in support of Attawapiskat Chief Theresa Spence's hunger strike and Idle No More. While this movement has brought a unity to Indigenous politics, it has also exacerbated fractures between those who support imposed colonial institutions and their officials (Indian Act band councils) and those who do not; those who favour keeping protests peaceful (Idle No More) and those who see the need for blockades and more abrasive forms of action; those who are treaty and those who are non-treaty people; those who have been idle, or who are less educated, and those who have been engaged for years; and those who restrict the agenda to Harper's legislative suite, those who see the issue as one of sovereignty and nationhood (Indigenous Nation(hood) Movement), and those who do not. As this movement is still in its infancy—having survived the test of winter—only time will tell how effective it will be in maintaining grassroots mobilization with its multi-issue orientation and its youthful tone (though one very much different than the Occupy Movement).

Idle No More looks to have grown weary of a situation where Indigenous peoples are invited as observers to political conversations (both constitutional and legislative) where they can do little more than dance around the table as non-Indigenous politicians make the decisions for them. In dividing themselves from the Indian Act and its institutional processes, and by focusing on drawing out and educating the grassroots through both teach-ins and events such as marches and round dances, Idle No More is establishing itself as something more than what Peter Russell refers to as a flashpoint event (Russell, 2010). More than just a flashpoint to catch the attention of governments and Canadians, Idle No More seems to have captured the hearts and minds of a new generation of Indigenous leaders and a new generation of Indigenous scholars who are spreading a message of nationhood, decolonization, language, peace and righteousness, the rebuilding of Indigenous legal traditions, responsibility for land/territory, political systems and constitutional orders, resistance, and resurgence (Simpson, 2011; Alfred, 2005; Borrows, 2010; Simpson, 2013; Alfred, 2013; Belleau, 2013). Perhaps this movement is the lighting of the Eighth Fire, the igniting of a generation and the rebuilding of nations that has been talked about for generations and noted in the prophecies of countless Indigenous nations (Simpson, 2008).

SEEING BEYOND THE AFN

Despite the naming of Idle No More, Indigenous peoples have not been sitting idly by—there have always been other actors within the movement and other domains of mobilization since the onset of colonialism. These actors and domains are not limited to the "other" political organizations discussed in this chapter but involve a plethora of international and national organizations (including provincial, territorial, federal, band councils, treaty organizations, tribal councils, warrior societies, and grassroots) and "everyday Jo(e)s" such as those who show up at Idle No More round dances and teach-ins across the country. Though no extensive or formalized network connects all of these individuals and organizations, they are linked informally through the "moccasin telegraph" (or its modern equivalent, Facebook and Twitter) and seem able to develop more formal spontaneous linkages when opportunities or needs arise. This has been demonstrated continuously over the past few months with the Idle No More movement (and all variants thereof). In 2012, for example, several Indigenous peoples and organizations forged alliances and became involved with the Occupy Movement—an alliance and relationship that tended to be vicarious at best (see chapter 5 in this book).

The reason the movement is, and has always been, so extensive is quite simple: Indigenous peoples typically perceive themselves as being in a constant battle with the government over their rights to live as Indigenous peoples in their homelands; to govern themselves; to exercise those rights and responsibilities accorded to them as nations (such as the right to fish in their territory); and to better their economic, social, and political conditions.

This is especially the case when one considers that a simple everyday activity can be a political act for Indigenous peoples, whether it is perceived as such or not. Take, for instance, the crossing of the Canada-US border. While most Canadians see this as a simple non-political activity, many Indigenous people engage in political activism when they cross. By declaring their nationality or country of origin, they engage in the nationalist and self-determination struggles that have defined the movement by stating their true nation of origin and refusing to engage in the colonial rhetoric of citizenship (King, 1993). The border poses further sources of contestation for peoples through whose territories it runs and for those whose treaties suggest that they should have free movement for themselves and their goods across it. In short, the mere existence of the border has made activists out of Indigenous peoples.

Indigenous peoples engage in politics of contestation every day. Yet, aside from the major organizations (band, tribal, provincial, and federal), it is only when opportunities arise (or are created) that the masses mobilize, "kitchen table" networks such as that which led to the creation of Idle No More are engaged, wider networks are rekindled, and the movement becomes organized. Episodes of mobilization have varied and will continue to vary in orientation, issue, the level of mobilization (elite or popular), and the ability (and desire) to organize and create organizational capacity. This is quite evident when one considers the different ways in which the Nehiyaw attempted to engage the Crown's representatives over the course of some 15 years. It is even more evident when one considers that the Nehiyaw under the leadership of Weekuskokisayin, Mistahimaskwa, and Imasees were all "fighting" the government's Indian policy to achieve the same things as Harold Cardinal was demanding nearly 100 years later when he contested the federal government's Indian policy: assistance (gas) and sovereignty/self-determination (the ability to drive the car). And now, more than 40 years after he took a stand against the White Paper, his daughter Tanya Kappo joined the Idle No More movement started by other Nehiyaw (and an ally) in Saskatchewan and used the #IdleNoMore hashtag on Twitter in an attempt to engage Indigenous peoples, Canadians, the Crown and the government to fight the government's legislative and policy agenda and to take up the issue of treaty (both sovereignty and assistance). To take this one step further, though using different methods, these are the same issues that are being contested when Indigenous people passively question matters of citizenship, territoriality, and Canadian sovereignty when passing over the imagined line we call the border.

ONLY ACTORS AND ARENAS CHANGE WITH TIME

Recognizing this diversity, and the inherent flux within Indigenous politics of contestation and the Indigenous rights movement, it is fascinating that, by and large, the goals and the issues have remained constant among the various actors, nations, and organizations involved. Having explored several of the episodes of mobilization that have characterized Indigenous politics since the outset of colonization, I will now explore several of the goals that have defined the movement over space and time. Acknowledging that the movement has been divided and many of the goals contested, following this discussion I will turn our attention to explaining these disjunctures and divisions.

One of the primary goals of Indigenous activism, both before and following the onset of colonization, has been good governance. This was the vision and the mission of the Peacemaker: to bring peace, order, and good governance to the Haudenosaunee through the creation of a new constitutional order based on the Great Law of Peace. This was the vision and mission of Mistahimaskwa when he addressed the issue of the rope at the treaty talks, and it was behind his attempt to mobilize the Nehiyaw and engage in peaceful negotiations with the representatives of the Crown and the Canadian government. For Mistahimaskwa, the rope symbolized a future in which Canada would attempt to lead the Nehiyaw around like an animal—an animal that had lost the ability to govern itself. Given that they already had a system of good governance, and given that they saw the treaty as a means of protecting their sovereignty, neither Mistahimaskwa nor any other Nehiyaw leader agreed to be subject to this rope. But Mistahimaskwa did not trust the government, and, as a result, he attempted to mobilize the Nehiyaw and to engage the nation in a peaceful resistance against it. Similarly, the constitutional battles of the late twentieth century were as much about good governance as self-determination—if not more so. This is quite evident in the literature of this period, which presented self-government as an opportunity to overthrow the colonial system of oppressive government under the Indian Act and to (re) create a system of good governance (Mercredi and Turpel, 1993; Little Bear et al., 1984). This is also evident in the position advanced by treaty organizations that the Constitution simply offered the opportunity to affirm treaty rights (such as self-government) as constitutional rights (Henderson, 1995).

The vision and mission of good governance have also been at the forefront of much contemporary activism. Increasingly, Idle No More is being rebranded as the Indigenous Nation(hood) Movement, or simply INM, with strong messages being lauded by grassroots leaders such as Kappo as well as by scholars such as Leanne Simpson, Taiaiake Alfred, and Glen Coulthard, who advocate for good governance through a rebuilding of nation using each nation's legal, political, social, and economic systems and corresponding responsibilities (Belleau, 2013; Alfred, 2013; Simpson, 2013; Coulthard, 2012).

Sovereignty and self-determination have long been primary goals of Indigenous activism, both before and following the onset of colonization, as is evident in episodes of mobilization such as the treaties, the "last stands" of traditional governments, international activism, claims processes, and self-government negotiations as well as in the reaction to the First Nations Governance Act and the creation of Idle No More. The central role of the goals of sovereignty and self-determination is especially evident in the mobilization of the Haudensaunee government—the Council of Chiefs—in the Grand River Territory (Six Nations reserve) during the 1920s. From the outset, Canada's Indian policy had advocated regime change or "replacing" Indigenous political systems and constitutional orders with the Indian Act system of band government. Despite such policies and previous attempts to depose the Haudenosaunee government, the Council of Chiefs remained in place. But by the 1920s, it was becoming increasingly clear that the federal government would not stop until it had institutionalized the Indian Act and put in place a "puppet" government at Six Nations. In an attempt to gain support for their government and to assert their sovereignty as a nation (and thus their right of self-determination), the Haudenosaunee government sent delegates including Loft and Deskahe to discuss these matters with the Canadian government and the British Crown and to demand both representation at, and the support of, the newly established League of Nations (Staats, 1986).

Sovereignty and self-determination continue as a primary foundation of contemporary Indigenous politics and mobilization. This, as we saw above, was evident in the era of constitutional renewal and again today with Idle No More. But even when these foundations are not so evident, they ground the movement; for example, in reaction to the First Nations Governance Act, people mobilized not to support the status quo but to assert their right to govern themselves (Ladner and Orsini, 2005). This was particularly clear in the reaction of treaty nations; they advanced the position that the government had no right to be designing structures of governance nor asserting jurisdiction over Indigenous peoples for these matters had already been resolved when the treaties were negotiated.

Economic and resource rights have also been primary goals of Indigenous political mobilization and activism, both historically and currently. One need only look back to the words of Weekuskokisayin quoted earlier in this chapter and to the Nehiyaw's reasons for lobbying for a treaty before 1876 to understand that economic and resource issues have been part of Indigenous politics. Such is the case for the Mi'kmaw nation whose negotiations with the British in 1752 led to the recognition of their rights to their resources throughout their traditional territory as well as their rights to trade resources—the products of resource extraction or harvesting (Wicken, 2000). Disregarding such rights and its own treaty responsibilities, the Canadian government has failed to protect the Mi'kmaw economy and has denied them access to their resources through the legislated exclusion of Mi'kmaw from the salmon fishery (Ladner, 2005). As a result, Mi'kmaw have engaged in the politics of contestation as individuals, organizations, communities, and a nation. For example, in Listuguj, salmon fishers became activists simply by fishing (exercising their resource and economic rights); in doing so, they have faced harassment from Canadian officials, continuous legal battles, and, on two occasions, the "invasion" of their reserve by Quebec and Canadian officials to halt the "illegal fishery."

Indigenous peoples have also mobilized around issues such as education, social assistance, housing, and water quality in an effort to attain assistance and improve their standard and quality of life. This vision of a better future has driven treaty lobbyists, those active in the League of Indians of Canada and other political organizations, and community activists. Community leadership and grassroots activists have been mobilized against the state since the establishment of reserves and the forced confinement of Indigenous peoples to small plots of mainly economically useless land and deplorable conditions. Though constantly engaged in the lobbying of government officials, the grassroots have typically used issues such as residential school abuse, the lack of non-contaminated housing, schools, and sanitation in communities such as Attawapiskat, and the contamination of water in communities such as Kashechewan as opportunities to define and bring attention to "Canada's Indian problem" and to press governments into action. Though not the intent of the four founders of the Idle No More movement, when Chief Theresa Spence of Attawapiskat took up her hunger strike, it quickly became associated with improving conditions on reserves.

Territorial rights and a peoples' relationship to the land has also been central to the Indigenous movement. Recognition of territory and territorial rights has been one of the key issues that Indigenous people have been trying to advance since Europeans first arrived and were welcomed as visitors, intruders, and occupiers in their homelands. It has even been a major concern for the Métis—the national product of colonialism—as evidenced by the struggles of Riel to define and defend a provincial homeland for the Métis within Canada and the lobby effort by Malcolm Norris and Joe Dion to force the government of Alberta to establish Métis settlements (reserves) in the 1930s. These same struggles continue today for most Indigenous nations.

This is particularly the case for those nations without so-called "land-cession treaties" (and for those whose treaties were not respected), for their relationship with their territory and rights to use that territory have been ignored by the governments of Canada and they have never been compensated for their lands. These nations have been contesting the unlawful seizure and occupation of their lands since the beginning, using a variety of mechanisms, which today include lobbying governments to have their rights recognized, negotiating land claims and pursuing Aboriginal and treaty rights court cases, hosting teach-ins and organizing flash-mob round dances, and "occupying" their land to protect it from development (Simpson, 2008).

Irrespective of treaty issues, both nations and groups of citizens have contested the taking of territory, the use/development of their territory, and their inability to use/have a relationship with their traditional territories. Such episodes of contestation have often resulted in dramatic standoffs. For instance, during the summer of 1990, in an attempt to halt the development of a golf course on sacred land (a forest and graveyard that were already the subject of a land claim) by the town of Oka, citizens of Kanesatake engaged in a peaceful protest and blockade, a protest that escalated into a 78-day armed siege at Kanesatake and Kahnewake between Mohawk warriors, the Quebec police, and the Canadian army (York and Pindera, 1991; Simpson and Ladner, 2010). Meanwhile, in 1991, in their attempt to halt the development of the Oldman Dam (and the flooding of sensitive ecological areas in their homeland), the Lone Fighters Society of the Peigan Nation engaged in an armed standoff with the RCMP. While not marked with the same media coverage nor police presence, communities such as the Six Nations of the Grand River Territory (Caledonia) have continued to use standoffs, protests, and blockades to bring attention to their issues, to halt development of their lands, and to enable the use and occupation of their own territories (see Edwards, 2001). Though not supported by the founders of Idle No More, the use of rail and highway slowdowns and blockades over the winter of 2012–13 clearly demonstrates that the use of such modes of mobilization will continue.

UNDERSTANDING THE MOVEMENT: MECHANISMS AND FRACTURES

For most movements, mechanisms of redress and venues of mobilization are typically defined by opportunity structures and, to a lesser extent, by the nature of the movement and its goals. As has been demonstrated throughout this chapter, the Indigenous movement and its episodes of mobilization have been influenced, shaped, confined, and defined by the state—just as Tarrow (1998) and other social movement theorists who endorse the political process model suggest. That said, however, Indigenous politics of contestation do not fully fit these theories of social movements. Though influenced by the state and opportunity structures, Indigenous movements are fundamentally grounded in and defined by issues of nationhood and (de)colonization or, as scholars such as Simpson and Alfred have explained, Indigenous politics; thus, Indigenous movements are fundamentally grounded and (increasingly) defined by considerations of resistance and resurgence.

Though not exactly the same, nationhood and (de)colonization have defined and continue to define Indigenous movements, whereas resistance and resurgence reflect a more contemporary and nuanced understanding (Simpson, 2011). While Indigenous scholarship has been focused on these issues since Vine Deloria first published *Custer Died for Your Sins* in 1969, they have been largely overlooked in the social movement literature (Simpson, 2012). Considerations of nationhood and (de)colonization have defined and confined the movement and its issues, goals, values, and the mechanisms it has used. More importantly, they account for the divisions within and the fractious nature of the movement.

By and large, venues and points of mobilization have been defined and constrained by the intentions of the actors and by their underlying philosophical orientation of nationhood and (de)colonization. Such considerations contribute to the preference for nation-to-nation relationships and the use of international domains to resolve domestic issues, as was the case when Deskahe approached the League of Nations to force the Canadian government to cease and desist in its efforts to overthrow the Haudenosaunee government. They also contribute to the increasingly predominant view that domestic courts are not an appropriate venue for addressing Indigenous issues. Many Indigenous leaders and academics argue that their issues are not "domestic" issues; that Indigenous nations should not be subject to the courts of another nation; and that the courts should not be used because they have been quite ineffective in advancing the Indigenous agenda, providing for decolonization, and dealing with questions of nationhood (Monture-Angus, 1999: 135–52). Still, as a matter of necessity, and for the potential that they offer in addressing the Indigenous agenda, courts continue to be used, just as they are by other movements. That said, while party politics and voter mobilization are common strategies in the politics of contestation, they are seldom used by Indigenous activists because such activities are typically viewed as contrary to both the goals of Indigenous peoples and to the foundations of the movement—Indigenous nationhood.

Nationhood and (de)colonization, by and large, account for the mobilization strategies and opportunity choices of the Indigenous movement, although intentions, opportunity structures, and the nature of organizations also hold explanatory value. Not only do nationhood and (de)colonization assist in explaining the distinctiveness of the movement and its choices and strategies, but they also explain points of disjuncture and division within it.

These are, for the most part, the result of colonization. At issue are the artificial divisions, created by colonial administrators, that define and structure relationships among Indigenous nations and individuals and between Indigenous peoples and the state. These artificial divisions or points of inequality include those between treaty and non-treaty nations and/or individuals, status and non-status people, First Nations and "other" Indigenous nations such as the Métis, and men and women (rights and government policies are often gendered, as is the case of status and matrimonial property). These divisions are points of fraction and contestation that have continuously served to divide rather than unify the movement. In fact, this has been one of the strongest criticisms of Idle No More by Indigenous peoples, Canadians, and their respective governments since it has offered no singular unified message or simplified branding; moreover, it has experienced massive internal divisions and disagreements. Simply put, the movement is fractured and that fracture involves more than a simple schism between grassroots and the Indigenous establishment (be that Indian Act governments or organizations such as the AFN).

While all facets of the Indigenous movement agree on the goals of good governance, sovereignty, resource/economic rights, social well-being (education, child welfare, and living conditions), and self-determination, their framing of these goals is predicated on and defined by considerations of nationhood and (de)colonization. Treaty nations most often frame these goals in terms of their treaties, which afforded protection to Indigenous political systems, affirmed the existence (and continuance) of Indigenous constitutional orders, and created a nation-to-nation relationship between Indigenous nations and the Crown. Meanwhile, non-treaty nations see the need to engage Canadian governments in policy discussions and negotiations with the intent of defining and implementing self-determination and good governance while dealing with (ceding) claims of sovereignty and territoriality. Whereas treaty nations see these issues as having been dealt with in the past, non-treaty nations have not yet dealt with them. Therefore, while one feels the need to dust off the treaty and rebuild a relationship between equal and mutually dependent nations, the other sees the need to create public policy and legal (or constitutional) frameworks for the negotiation, development, and implementation of self-government. The distinction between these two groups is huge, and it often results in catastrophic fractures within the Indigenous movement as treaty nations view the goals and activities of non-treaty nations as jeopardizing their agenda and view self-government as diluting, abrogating, and derogating the treaties and their relationship with the Crown. Thus, while the shared goals serve to unify the movement, they also serve as complex and multifaceted points of internal fracture and contestation that likely impede progress on both fronts. This fracture is increasingly apparent within the AFN as treaty nations have recently threatened to sever their ties with this long-standing rights organization and develop a treaty alliance.

FINAL THOUGHTS: ACCOUNTING FOR THE LACK OF MOVEMENT

To understand the Indigenous politics of contestation in Canada, it is important to explore and understand its historical roots. By grounding the understanding of Indigenous contestation in a historical approach and by giving due place to Indigenist methodologies such as narrative and storytelling, it is possible to gain an understanding of the movement, its development, and its goals. The contestation of Indigenous people in contemporary Canada reflects a continuity with the past histories of the relationship between Indigenous nations and settler societies (in the case of the Nehiyaw, this was comparatively late). It is important for settler cultures to approach Indigenous contestation from the perspective of Indigenous peoples themselves, seeking to understand Indigenous perspectives and traditions on their own terms rather than strictly in terms of the dominant Euro-Canadian legal and political categories.

Why has there been so little movement for Indigenous peoples in Canada? Over the past 100 years, the government has made many advances in positively addressing its "Indian problem" and in responding to the demands and aspirations of Indigenous people. Indigenous people have achieved constitutional recognition of their Aboriginal and treaty rights and great victories in court as they have attempted to have these rights recognized and respected by governments. The Indian Act has been revised (to a very limited extent) to afford Indigenous peoples greater political rights and equality rights, and social and economic conditions have improved somewhat.

Yet, Indigenous people are still making the same demands today that were advanced by the Nehiyaw in the 1870s. This is because there has been little effort to address the underlying issues that form the foundation of the discontent—nationhood and (de)colonization. These not only account for the choice of venues or domains of mobilization and the fractures and divisions within the Indigenous rights movement, they also account for the differences and distinctiveness of the Indigenous movement *vis-à-vis* other social movements and for the staying power of both the movement and its demands. Indigenous peoples are still mobilizing in defence of their nations, seeking to have their rights (political, economic, and territorial) as nations recognized and respected, and establishing a relationship between nations based upon mutual respect and mutual benefit. At the end of the day, the dog with the rope around its neck will still want to deal with the issue of the rope, no matter how many cookies it is thrown.

NOTES

1   I wish to acknowledge the financial support of the Canada Research Chairs program. I also wish to thank Leanne Simpson, Miriam Smith, Myra Tait, Tanya Kappo, Chad Cowie and the reviewers for their comments, inspiration and assistance in the writing and updating of this chapter.

2   In 1951, federal policy had changed to allow Indians to go to university without loss of status, and reforms to federal education programs meant that high school graduates were increasing both in number and in quality.

3   Until 1985, status or the legal recognition of an Indian under the *Indian Act* with membership and rights in a community could be lost by women who married non-status (Indian or otherwise) men, while status could be gained by non-status (Indian or otherwise) women marrying status men.

4   The relevant sections of the Constitution are these:

> 25. The guarantee in this Charter of certain rights and freedoms shall not be construed so as to abrogate or derogate from any aboriginal, treaty or other rights or freedoms that pertain to the Aboriginal peoples of Canada including:
>
> 35. (1) The existing aboriginal and treaty rights of aboriginal peoples are hereby recognized and affirmed. (Canada,1989)

Treaty rights refer to the obligations incurred as a result of the signing of peace, friendship, and land treaties throughout this country between the Crown and Indigenous nations. Meanwhile, Aboriginal rights are best explained by Michael Asch as "encompassing a broad range of economic, social, cultural and political rights . . . These rights flow, first of all, from the fact that the aboriginal peoples were in sovereign occupation of Canada at the time of contact, and secondly from the assertion that their legitimacy and continued existence has not been extinguished by the subsequent occupation of Canada by immigrants" (Asch, 1984: 30).

REFERENCES AND FURTHER READING

Alfred, Taiaiake. 1999. *Peace Power and Righteousness: An Indigenous Manifesto.* Don Mills: Oxford University Press.

Alfred, Taiaiake. 2005. *Wasase: Indigenous Pathways of Action and Freedom.* Peterborough: Broadview Press.

Alfred, Taiaiake. 2013. "Idle No More and Indigenous Nationhood." January 27. http://taiaiake.net/ (accessed September 5, 2013).

Asch, Michael. 1984. *Home and Native Land: Aboriginal Rights and the Canadian Constitution*. Toronto: Methuen.

Belleau, Lesley. 2013. "Pauwauwaein: Idle No More to Indigenous Nation Movement." March 4. http://decolonization.wordpress.com/2013/03/04/pauwauwaein-idle-no-more-to-indigenous-nationhood-movement/ (accessed September 5, 2013).

Borrows, John. 2010. *Canada's Indigenous Constitution*. Toronto: University of Toronto Press.

Canada. 1989. *The Constitution Acts 1867 to 1982*. Ottawa: Department of Justice Canada.

Canada. 2004. *Strengthening the Relationship Report on the Canada-Aboriginal Peoples Roundtable*. April 19. http://www.aboriginalroundtable.ca/rtbl/strenght_rpt_e.pdf (accessed September 1, 2004).

Canada. 2005. A First Nations Implementation Plan. November 28. http://www.ainc-inac.gc.ca/nr/prs/s-d2005/2-02749_e.html (accessed September 1, 2004).

Christie, W.J. 1871. "To A.G. Archibald, April 13." Sessional Papers Canada 22. Ottawa: Queen's Printer, 1872.

Coulthard, Glen. 2012. "#IdleNoMore in Historical Context." December 24. http://decolonization.wordpress.com/2012/12/24/idlenomore-in-historical-context/ (accessed September 5 2013).

Deloria, Vine. 1969. *Custer Died for Your Sins: An Indian Manifesto*. Toronto: Macmillan.

Dempsey, Hugh A. 1984. *Big Bear: The End of Freedom*. Vancouver: Douglas and McIntyre.

Edwards, Peter. 2001. *One Dead Indian: The Premier, the Police, and the Ipperwash Crisis*. Toronto: Stoddart.

Henderson, James (Sákej) Youngblood. 1995. "First Nations Legal Inheritances in Canada: The Mikmaq Model." *Manitoba Law Journal* 23 (January): 1–31.

Howe, R. Brian. 2006. "What's Behind Stephen Harper's Anti-Aboriginal Agenda?" *Canadian Dimension* 40 (5): 16.

Indian Chiefs of Alberta. 1970. *Citizens Plus*. Edmonton: Indian Association of Alberta.

Johansen, Bruce E. 1998. *Debating Democracy: Native American Legacy of Freedom*. Santa Fe: Clear Light Publishers.

Kappo, Tanya. 2012. "Idle No More: Backgrounder." http://www.youtube.com/watch?v=YZaQBypqKyw (accessed April 7, 2013).

King, Thomas. 1993. *One Good Story, That One: Stories*. Toronto: Harper Perennial.

Ladner, Kiera L. 2005. "Up the Creek: Fishing for a New Constitutional Order." *Canadian Journal of Political Science* 38 (4): 923–53.

Ladner, Kiera L., and Michael Orsini. 2005. "The Persistence of Paradigm Paralysis: The *First Nations Governance Act* as the Continuation of Colonial Policy." In *Canada: State of the Federation*, ed. Mike Murphy, 185–203. Kingston: Queen's University, Institute of Intergovernmental Relations.

Little Bear, Leroy, Menno Boldt, J., and Anthony Long, eds. 1984. *Pathways to Self-Determination: Canadian Indians and the Canadian State*. Toronto: University of Toronto Press.

McFarlane, Peter. 1993. *Brotherhood to Nationhood: George Manuel and the Making of the Modern Indian Movement*. Toronto: Between the Lines.

Mercredi, Ovide, and Mary Ellen Turpel. 1993. *In the Rapids: Navigating the Future of First Nations*. Toronto: Penguin.

Monture-Angus, Patricia. 1999. *Journeying Forward: Dreaming First Nations' Independence*. Halifax: Fernwood.

Morris, Alexander. 1880. *The Treaties of Canada with the Indians of Manitoba, the Northwest Territories, and Kee-wa-tin*. Toronto: Willing and Williamson.

Rollo, Tobold. 2013. "How Idle No More Could Help Save Canadian Democracy." *Huffington Post* (January 29). http://www.huffingtonpost.ca/tobold-rollo/idle-no-more-democracy_b_2592410.html (accessed September 15, 2013).

Russell, Peter. 2010. "Oka to Ipperwash: The Necessity of Flashpoint Events." In *This is an Honour Song*, ed. Leanne Simpson and Kiera L. Ladner, 29–46. Winnipeg: Arbeiter Ring Press.

Sanders, Douglas E. 1992. "The Indian Lobby and the Canadian Constitution, 1978–1982." In *Indigenous Peoples and the Nation State: Fourth World Politics In Canada, Australia and Norway*, ed. Noel Dyck 151–89. St. John's: Memorial University of Newfoundland.

Simpson, Leanne, ed. 2008. *Lighting the Eighth Fire*. Winnipeg: Arbeiter Ring Press.

Simpson, Leanne. 2011. *Dancing On Our Turtle's Back*. Winnipeg: Arbeiter Ring Press.

Simpson, Leanne. 2012. "Aambe! Maajaadaa! What Idle No More Means to Me." December 21. http://leannesimpson.ca/2012/12/21/aambe-maajaadaa-what-idle-no-more-means-to-me/ (accessed September 5, 2013).

Simpson, Leanne. 2013. "Fish Broth & Fasting." January 16. http://dividedno more.ca/2013/01/16/fish-broth-fasting/ (accessed September 23, 2013).

Simpson, Leanne, and Kiera L. Ladner, eds. 2010. *This is an Honour Song*. Winnipeg: Arbeiter Ring Press.

Smith, Donald B. 2003. "Loft, Frederick Ogilvie." In *Dictionary of Canadian Biography*, vol. 16. University of Toronto/Université Laval. http://www.

biographi.ca/en/bio/loft_frederick_ogilvie_16E.html (accessed September 23, 2013).

Staats, Sheila. 1986. *Warriors: A Resource Guide*. Brantford: Woodland Indian Cultural Educational Centre.

Stolte, Elise. 2012. "Local Aboriginal Groups Black Highways, Plan a Week of Protests." British Columbia First Nations News (December 19). http://www.bcafn.ca/files/breaking-news-2012-12-19.php (accessed September 23, 2013.

Tarrow, Sidney. 1998. *Power in Movement: Social Movements, Collective Action, and Politics*. 2nd ed. Cambridge: Cambridge University Press.

Taylor, John Leonard. 1985. *Treaty Research Reports: Treaty Six (1876)*. Ottawa: Treaties and Historical Research Centre, Indian Affairs Canada.

Venne, Sharon Helen. 1998. *Our Elders Understand Our Rights: Evolving International Law Regarding Indigenous Peoples*. Penticton: Theytus Books.

Wicken, William C. 2000. *Mi'kmaq Treaties on Trial*. Toronto: University of Toronto Press.

Yarrow, David. 1987. *The Great Law of Peace: New World Roots of American Democracy*. http://www.kahonwes.com/iroquois/document1.html (accessed September 5, 2013).

York, Geoffrey, and Loreen Pindera. 1991. *People of the Pines: The Warriors and the Legacy of Oka*. Toronto: Little Brown Press.

ELEVEN

Nationalism and Protest: The Sovereignty Movement in Quebec

PASCALE DUFOUR AND CHRISTOPHE TRAISNEL

The rise of new social movements in Canada in the 1960s saw the upsurge of new forms of nationalism. In English-speaking Canada, youth of the late 1960s and 1970s contested American domination of Canada and argued for an independent Canadian approach in politics and culture. At the same time, in Quebec, the Quiet Revolution saw the birth of new forms of nationalist politics, a development that led to two referendums on sovereignty, the first held by the PQ government of René Lévesque in 1980 and the second held in October 1995 by the PQ government led by Jacques Parizeau. Although these referendums did not result in a victory for the sovereignist side, the political independence of Quebec from Canada remains a valid option for around 40 per cent of the population as of spring 2012 (CROP, 2012a, 2012b). Further, on September 4, 2012, Pauline Marois, leader of the main sovereignist party, the PQ, became the first woman prime minister elected in the province. She is governing with a minority government (54 seats won by the PQ and 50 by the Parti libéral du Québec [the Liberal Party of Quebec, the PLQ]). Nevertheless, some analysts have noted that the younger generation, traditionally more in favour of Quebec sovereignty, is less and less supportive of the idea (Yale and Durand, 2011). Behind this apparent continuity, could we say that the sovereignty movement in Quebec is actually in trouble or that it is currently mutating?

On the day of the provincial election that took the PQ back to power in Quebec after spending more than eight years in opposition, on September 4, 2012, the French daily *Le Monde* asked: "Are Quebeckers still sovereignist?" (our translation). The question deserves to be asked, since, as Gélineau recognizes, if "the question of Quebec sovereignty remains a latent issue [it does not seem that] the popularity of the PQ is linked to a desire for independence and sovereignty, but rather a desire for change. The debate [on sovereignty] is absent from the public sphere" (*Le Monde*, 2012, our translation). In this chapter, we will focus on the political mobilization of the sovereignty movement in Quebec, especially over the past 10 years of its development.

We argue that, contrary to the situation that prevailed for years, the political mobilization of the sovereignty movement today is radically different because of two main changes: 1) the increasing dominance of the right/left cleavage in the public space, and 2) the resurgence of a conservative nationalism that has re-enforced the division among sovereignist activists. These two trends have had dramatic effects on the dynamics among social and political actors and have profoundly challenged the direction of the sovereignist movement as well as its political content. Somehow, the "alliance of convenience" that existed between the left and the Quebec nationalists, which was crystallized through the creation of a sovereignty movement that was both nationalist and social democratic, seems to erode year after year, opening some space for a complete redefinition of what the sovereignist movement is today, 50 years after its creation.

Nationalism in Quebec or in Canada has very often been treated as an ideology (Couture, Nielsen, and Seymour, 1996; Monière, 1981) rather than as a social movement with its own political dynamics (Coleman, 1984; Fraser, 1984; Keating, 1997; Rumilly, 1975). In this chapter, we build on those who study the processes by which differences of language and culture are transformed into a distinct sense of belonging, which is represented and claimed in the political arena. As Benedict Anderson (1991) explained in his important book on nationalism, the "nation" is an "imagined community." This does not mean that the identities in question are artificial but that their existence implies the implementation of their representation by political actors.

From this perspective, collective identity and the concept of the nation are the product of collective political work, sometimes led by a specific group that believes in the existence of the nation and wants to carry this vision into the heart of the political game (Thiesse, 1999: 11). Political actors such as elites and political parties are the main focus of the analysis of nationalism, as it is their collective political work that aims to convince citizens of the existence of a distinct nation. Drawing on social movement literature, we take up a more inclusive view of the Quebec sovereignist movement, defining it as organizations and individuals sharing common frames of reference (practices, values, beliefs, and a common identity) united around the advocacy of a particular political option—Quebec sovereignty, meaning, the political independence of Quebec from the rest of Canada. This definition does not reduce analysis of sovereignty to merely an examination of the PQ, but neither does it exclude political parties from the analysis. In other words, unlike some of the other studies of social movements in this volume, this chapter explicitly includes the politics of political parties as a key component of social movement politics, an appropriate approach given that sovereignty in Quebec has been championed in the province by the PQ since its founding and by the Bloc québécois (BQ) at the federal level since the 1993 federal election. Indeed, analysis of the relationships between sovereignist social actors and the PQ in the same social movement is central to understanding the dynamic of the movement as a whole. Some authors, such as Jane Jenson (1995: 107–26, 1998: 235–62, 1999: A9), have already paved the way by analyzing the citizenship regime that applies to Quebec and the role the nationalist movement has played in its construction.

It is important to distinguish between nationalism and sovereignty. Nationalism in Quebec is not solely defined by the sovereignty movement. As Rocher and Lecours (2003: 112) argue, there are two major competing nationalisms in Quebec. The first, the nationalism espoused primarily by the Canadian state (but also by some pan-Canadian social movements), aims to convince Canadians (and Quebeckers) that a Canadian nation exists "from coast to coast (our translation)" The second challenges the nationalism of the Canadian state by claiming the existence of a distinct Quebec nation and the necessity for sovereignty for Quebec. Between these two positions, the PLQ advocates a Quebec nationalism that is nonetheless federalist (Ryan, 2002).

In the rest of the chapter, we briefly recall some key moments in the historical trajectory of the sovereignty movement since the 1960s. We then turn to the structure of the movement and its current dynamics, focusing on the important transformations that have occurred since 2003. The sovereignty movement is based on two types of protest (social protest and nationalist protest) which, while originally distinct, quickly found common ground and common cause: taking control of the Quebec state and sharing a vision—an independent Quebec (Traisnel, 2004). The last part of the chapter assesses the concrete achievements of the sovereignty movement and the impact of the movement on Quebec society and politics.

THE HISTORICAL TRAJECTORY OF THE SOVEREIGNIST MOVEMENT IN QUEBEC

As a result of growing industrialization, Quebec, like most modern Western societies, experienced profound social and economic change in the early twentieth century. The growth of an industrial and agricultural working class, mainly French-Canadian and immigrant, and of an overwhelmingly English-speaking industrial and financial bourgeoisie only served to widen the gap in prosperity between the two communities (Bourque and Legaré, 1979: 113). Slowly, however, the French-speaking middle class grew stronger, establishing itself not only in literature and the arts but also in economics and politics, thereby gradually opening up Quebec society to the modern world. French-speaking elites became much more receptive to liberal ideas. The death of long-serving Quebec Premier Maurice Duplessis in 1959 and the election of the Liberals led by Jean Lesage ushered in the Quiet Revolution, a period of unprecedented modernization of Quebec institutions and strong government intervention in social policy and economic and cultural development. The Quiet Revolution was not only a social and institutional revolution but a political revolution as well (for the whole period, see Laurendeau, Smart, and Howard, 1991). The contemporary sovereignty movement originates, in part, in this new French-Canadian nationalism, which rejects the traditional view of the French-Canadian elite that saw building Canada as the opportunity for French-Canadian identity, born on the banks of the St. Lawrence, to blossom (Martel, 1997).

By the end of the 1960s, part of the leadership of the PLQ believed that the reforms they had undertaken were on the right track but that they had now fulfilled their role. It was time to slow the pace. For others, including René Lévesque, the opposite was true: the time was right to further transform Quebec through continued reform of government and other institutions. The difference in opinion over the pace of reform soon became divisive, as confirmed by the departure from the PLQ of Lévesque and many other advocates of more rapid reform, especially those in the trade union movement. The growing role of the Quebec state profoundly influenced supporters of French-Canadian nationalism, who expressed themselves more actively through several organizations.

BOX 11.1   The Period from the Quiet Revolution to 1975

1957: Founding of the Alliance laurentienne.

1960: Founding of the Rassemblement pour l'indépendance nationale (RIN).

1966: Founding of the Ralliement national (RN).

1967: Creation of the sovereignty-association movement around René Lévesque.

1968: Creation of the Parti québécois (merging and rallying of the RIN, the MSA, and the RN).

1970, April: The PQ obtains 24 per cent of the vote in the provincial elections and seven seats in the National Assembly.

1970, October Crisis: Kidnapping of a British diplomat, James Richard Cross, and the kidnapping and murder of a provincial cabinet minister, Pierre Laporte; the War Measures Act is adopted.

1973: The PQ obtains 33 per cent of the vote in the provincial elections and forms the official opposition.

Between 1967 and 1970, Quebec's political landscape changed. The Mouvement souveraineté-association (MSA, the Sovereignty-association Movement), which had formed around the dissident René Lévesque, appeared on the political scene, and in 1968 the PQ was born (Fraser, 1984). The latter represented a coalition of the main nationalist organizations and a constellation of activists from the militant left and unions (Levine, 1990). After rapid growth, the PQ experienced a very difficult period related to the "October Crisis," (see Box 11.1) and lost two-third of its membership (Fraser, 1984). In 1973, the PQ received 33 per cent of the vote but only six seats in the National Assembly. For the first time, it had become the Official Opposition and the alternative to the PLQ.

Until 1976, the PQ, with help from other sovereignist organizations, sought to reassure its electors by proposing a gradual approach to the achievement of sovereignty. In other words, an eventual sovereignist victory would not lead to the immediate independence of Quebec. Unions such as the Fédération des travailleurs du Québec (FTQ, the Workers' Federation of Quebec) now officially supported the PQ, and the social base of the sovereignty movement gradually broadened. In the 1976 elections, the PQ won 41 per cent of the vote and was called upon to form a majority government.

Two years after its victory, the PQ, in keeping with its plan, delineated its preference for Quebec sovereignty within the framework of an association with Canada. Although a united front of sovereignists had formed around the party, the referendum failed to pass, receiving only 40 per cent of the vote. In 1984, the PQ lost the elections and became the opposition after eight years in power.

BOX 11. 2 The PQ in Power (1976–1985)

1976: The PQ wins the election with 41 per cent of the vote and forms the government.

1979: The VII Convention of the PQ outlines its plan for sovereignty association with Canada.

1980: The referendum on sovereignty association loses, taking only 40 per cent of the vote.

1981: The PQ wins the elections (49.2 per cent of the vote) and remains in power.

1982: The prime minister of Canada, Pierre Elliott Trudeau, repatriates the Canadian Constitution without the agreement of Quebec.

1985: June: René Lévesque resigns; leadership race results in Pierre Marc Johnson being elected leader of the PQ.
December: The PQ loses the elections, and the PLQ forms the new government.

The years it spent in opposition provided sovereignists with an opportunity to take stock and make choices. The PQ established itself as the main focal point for discussing sovereignty in Quebec and the vehicle for attaining this sovereignty. Its internal divisions demonstrated the extent to which the party was capable not only of rallying and of surviving the departure of its founder but also of delineating an everyday government agenda while planning national independence. With Jacques Parizeau at the helm, the PQ gradually started to win back the electorate, opening up multi-faceted opportunities for reflection on the leading constitutional, social, economic, and linguistic issues of the day. From 1987 to 1991, the PQ headed up a broad protest movement whose ranks would soon include more than just sovereignists; this movement opposed the Meech Lake Accord, which was negotiated by the Progressive Conservative Mulroney government with the Liberal government of Quebec, which was led by Robert Bourassa. The Meech Lake Accord made provision for constitutional change, offering full participation for Quebec in Canada's constitutional evolution. By 1990, several ministers and MPs from the governing Progressive Conservative Party, including Lucien Bouchard, departed the government to create the Bloc québécois (BQ), a sovereignist party at the federal level. Disaffection with the Accord also led to the formation of a new political party in Quebec, the Action démocratique du Québec (ADQ, Quebec Democratic Action), which was receptive to the sovereignist option. At this point, the pro-sovereignty vote was ahead in the polls. In the federal elections of 1993, the BQ captured 54 seats in Quebec and became the Official Opposition in Ottawa. The following year, the PQ won the election and Jacques Parizeau became premier. The time seemed ripe for another referendum.

Following virtually on the heels of the election, the PQ started to organize the promised referendum mobilization, and a coalition of political parties, unions, movements, or representatives of various social or professional groups formed a coalition of Partners for Sovereignty. Coalition members participated in the major public debates that the government organized across the province on the question of the political future of Quebec. There was a record voter turnout of 94 per cent for the referendum of October 30, 1995. Yet, it was another setback for the sovereignists. In spite of the victory for the "No" side, the "Yes" side managed to obtain 49.42 per cent of the vote. Parizeau resigned following his statement, on the evening of the referendum, that it was "money and the ethnic vote" that caused the defeat of the "Yes" side (Cantin, 1995: A4). The leader of the BQ, Lucien Bouchard, succeeded Parizeau and in 1996 became leader of the PQ and premier.

During this period, the pro-sovereignty government of Quebec, like the other provincial governments, had to contend with the budgetary cuts adopted by the federal government. A period of tension arose between the PQ and some of the Partners for Sovereignty, who felt extremely uncomfortable with its neo-liberal policies. The united front was over. Unions slowly left the coalition, dissociating themselves from a government with which they were increasingly in conflict over social issues. Similarly, community-based actors in the coalition gradually distanced themselves as well. The new referendum demanded by sovereignists was postponed. It seemed that the national question was no longer a priority. The Mouvement national des québécois (MNQ, The National Movement of Quebeckers), which was responsible for the coalition of the Partners for Sovereignty, found it difficult to keep together its coalition, which soon lost most of its members. The years from 1995 to 2003 constituted a period of uncertainty for the sovereignty movement.

However, little by little, and under pressure from its activists, the sovereignty movement modified the terms of its social vision. Globalization, the environment, sustainable development, and renewable energy emerged as topics in *péquiste* and *bloquiste* programs. Within the PQ, and especially at party conventions, the tension was palpable. On one side was the leadership, playing the game of economic pragmatism via a series of substantive reforms while sidelining the national and linguistic questions. On the other side was the activist rank and file, promoting social-democratic values, increasingly receptive to issues raised by the Global Justice Movement around the world concerning the need to invent another form of globalization and capitalism, and anxious to see if sovereignty and protection of the French language were still current concerns of the PQ. The texts, declarations, and political programs adopted by the main sovereignty movement organizations during that period reflected these tensions. While sovereignty remained on the agenda, the terms of accession, like "le projet de société" (societal project), were increasingly questioned, especially during PQ and BQ congresses.

BOX 11.3 Build-up to the Second Referendum (1986–1995)

1988: Jacques Parizeau is elected leader of the PQ.
1990: Failure of the Meech Lake Accord.
1990: The Bloc québécois (BQ) is formed at the federal level.
1992: Rejection of the Charlottetown Accord.
1993: The BQ obtains 54 seats in the federal election and forms the Official
 ·Opposition.
1994: Founding of a new party, the Action démocratique du Québec (ADQ), in
 the provincial arena; the PQ wins the election.
1995: Referendum campaign and creation of a coalition, Partners for
 Sovereignty (unions, intellectuals, students, community groups).
1995: The second referendum is held; with only 49.42 per cent of the vote, the
 "Yes" side loses.

The beginning of the new century was marked by an improvement in the financial situation of Quebec and especially of the federal government. Consequently, the sovereignist government, led by Bernard Landry, increasingly critiqued the fiscal imbalance that, it claimed, hampered their manoeuvrability. The notion of fiscal imbalance is contested in Canada. For the Quebec government, "fiscal imbalance" is used to describe the situation that Quebec and other provinces experience with regard to public finances: "given the current occupation of taxation fields, they do not have enough revenue to finance their program responsibilities whereas, conversely, the federal government has at its disposal more revenue than it needs to finance its own areas of jurisdiction" (Commission on Fiscal Imbalance, 2001: 9).

The Landry government also attacked the federal spending power that, in the PQ's view, threatened provincial jurisdiction and prevented the Quebec government from reinvesting in certain social programs such as health and education. Meanwhile, the Supreme Court ruled on the question of the legitimacy of the referendum process. Based on the Court's opinion, the federal government passed the Clarity Act to set out the criteria for recognizing the validity of a "Yes" vote. Among other conditions, the act stated that the federal government's recognition of the result would be contingent upon the clarity of the proposed referendum question and of the result (e.g., whether or not the result obtained was a clear expression of the will of the majority of voters).

Now on the defensive, the sovereignty movement was not able to mobilize around what seemed to be a challenge not only to Quebec's jurisdiction in social policy but also to the process for holding referendums on sovereignty. In 2003, after eight years in power, the PQ lost the elections to the Liberals, led by Jean Charest.

Between 2003 and 2012, the sovereignist movement has faced several challenges: its federal branch has been almost entirely cut, with the dramatic loss of the BQ in the 2011 federal election (from 49 seats in 2008 to four seats in 2011); its former partners on the protest side of the movement are increasingly distant from the PQ, with some clearly pushing for the emergence of a New Left party, Québec solidaire (QS, established in 2006), which clearly favours a social-democratic path to sovereignty; and, finally, a conservative current has re-emerged in the sovereignist movement, calling for a return to the defence of the heritage of an "authentic" Quebec identity rooted in the singular historical path of the French-speaking majority (Beauchemin, 2002; Bock-Côté, 2007).

While defending a highly Quebec nationalist approach, the ADQ also developed a political program very similar to the federal Conservatives. Riding the conservative wave that brought Stephen Harper to power, the ADQ even

BOX 11.4 The Evolution of the Sovereignist Movement (1995–2012)

1996: Lucien Bouchard becomes leader of the Parti québécois and prime minister of Quebec.

1998: PQ victory at the general elections (76 seats, 42.82 per cent of the votes).

2000: The BQ obtains 38 seats in the federal election.

2001: Bernard Landry becomes leader of the PQ and Quebec's prime minister.

2003: PQ is defeated (45 seats, 33.24 per cent of the vote). Landry is leader of the Official Opposition.

2004: Foundation of SPQ libre, a social-democrat club within the PQ; the BQ obtains 54 seats in the federal election.

2005: Landry resigns. André Boisclair becomes leader of the PQ.

2006: Creation of a new provincial sovereignist party, Québec solidaire (QS); the BQ obtains 51 seats of 75 possible seats in the federal election.

2007: PQ is defeated at the general elections (36 seats, 28.35 per cent of the votes). Mario Dumont (ADQ) is leader of the Official Opposition. André Boisclair resigns. Pauline Marois becomes leader of the PQ.

2008: PQ is defeated at the general elections (51 seats, 35.17 per cent of the votes,); first QS member is elected to the legislative assembly; BQ obtains 49 seats in the federal election.

2011: Creation of a new provincial soveignist party, Option national; BQ obtains only four seats and 6 per cent of the vote in the federal election. Its leader, Gilles Duceppe, resigns.

2012: Creation of a new party, the Coalition Avenir Québec, lead by François Legault.

2012: PQ victory in the general election in the province with 31.95 per cent of the votes and 55 seats. Pauline Marois is prime minister of a minority government.

managed to become the Official Opposition in Quebec in March 2007 against a Liberal minority government, clearly putting into question the survival of the PQ. This context changed the balance of forces in the sovereignist movement and opened the door to some realignment.

For sovereignist conservative forces, multiculturalism policies are increasingly perceived as obstacles to the full development of a threatened Quebec identity. For them, multiculturalism is not simply an openness to diversity but leads to a renunciation of what constitutes the distinctiveness of the francophone majority (its language, its culture). Yet these elements are seen as the basis of Quebec's quest for independence. By adopting multiculturalism, Quebec society is at risk of eroding its specific identity and thus the reason why sovereignty is needed (Belkhodja and Traisnel, 2012). For example, echoing the Quiet Revolution period, one of the most spirited representatives of this current, intellectual and polemist Mathieu Bock-Côté, does not hesitate to talk about "quiet denationalization" (Bock-Côté, 2007). For Bock-Côté, the Quebec elite is guilty of perverting the national identity and promoting a "Trudeauized souverainism," based on a disembodied conception of Quebec society and thus less and less authentic (Bock-Côté, 2007, 2012). In other words, Quebec nationalism has been contaminated by liberal critics: by responding to the critics of diversity and the need to take into account more seriously the multicultural character of Quebec society, Quebec nationalism has transformed in a way that renders it detached from the nationalist conception of Quebec as a nation (rooted in culture, identity, and linguistic characteristics) and much closer to the Pierre Trudeau vision of a civic political community detached from culture, identity, and language.

In the next section we present these changes and the consequences they have had for the sovereignty movement.

ONGOING DEBATES: THE CURRENT STATE OF THE SOVEREIGNTY MOVEMENT

The history of the sovereignist movement reveals that, over the years, it has formed a solid support system based on joint political action and shared values. Through these actions and values, it has been able to maintain links among campaigners and among organizations, thereby creating a coherent network. The period from the second referendum to the present has been much more turbulent: several political actions and values are today strongly challenged.

Structure of the Movement

In its current form, the sovereignty movement consists of constellations of organizations (see Figure 11.1).

Since 2011, in the first circle of the sovereignty movement, two sovereignist parties, which reinforce each other, were in place. Usually, the PQ has been in the lead in establishing the referendum agenda, the strategies for achieving sovereignty, and the government's sovereignty-oriented political program. This hegemony has been altered by the existence of the BQ, which, as the sovereignist force at the federal level, has played an increasingly important role in the sovereignty movement, in particular, by furnishing leaders for the movement such as Lucien Bouchard and Gilles Duceppe. Since the 2011 federal election, the federal scale of the sovereignist movement has clearly diminished, but it has not vanished. It could be reactivated at the next federal election if the BQ gains more seats. Indeed, in many polls, it appears that the 2011 "orange wave" (overwhelming support for the NDP in Quebec) seems to have fizzled: 31 per cent of the Quebec respondents gave their support to the BQ in a survey distributed between February 28 and March 5, 2012 (Léger Marketing, 2012).

FIGURE 11.1 The Sovereignist Sphere of Influence in Québec Politics

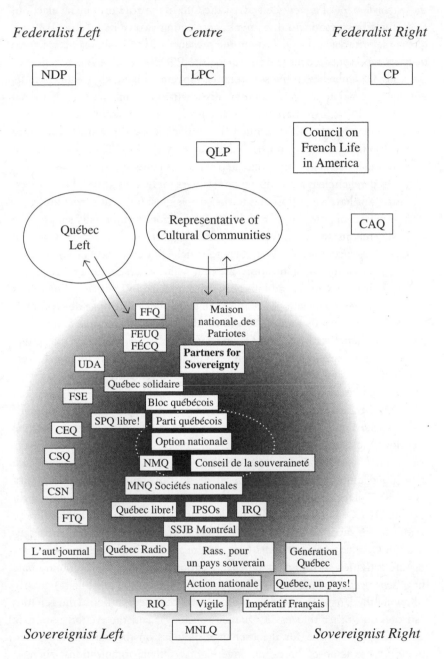

At the provincial level, several important changes have occurred including the establishment of a New Left party, the QS. In the 2012 provincial election, QS doubled its support to 6. 03 per cent, electing two of its leaders. Because of the majoritarian political system, the presence of QS in almost all electoral districts represents a concrete threat for the PQ. Because of this division of the vote, QS influence in the sovereignist movement is much greater than its voting share would suggest. In 2011, dissident PQ member of the National Assembly (MNA) Jean-Marc Aussant founded another new sovereignist party, the Option nationale, which argued for immediate steps toward sovereignty rather than the gradualist approach advocated by the PQ. Therefore, the first circle of the movement—the political parties—is increasingly diverse.

The second circle is made up of the Partners for Sovereignty. The partners' organizations have very close ties to the sovereignist political parties and provide them with ongoing support. These organizations traditionally support the PQ's sovereignist strategy, whether or not the party has been in power. The dozens of organizations involved form the nuclei of dense and specialized networks. Some of these organizations are old, while others are of a more recent vintage. They vary in size and in their stance toward PQ policies. The oldest and most active organizations are the Société Saint-Jean Baptiste de Montréal, the MNQ, the various regional Sociétés nationales and Sociétés Saint-Jean-Baptiste affiliated with the MNQ, and even the *Action nationale* magazine. Others emerged around the 1995 referendum, either in preparation for the referendum or afterwards. These include Génération Québec, Intellectuels pour la souveraineté (Intellectuals for Sovereignty), Vigile (an Internet site), the RIN, Québec, un pays! (Quebec, a Country), Opération Québec, Impératif français (the French Imperative), Souveraineté la solution (Sovereignty, the Solution), Le Québécois (the Quebecker), the Rassemblement pour un pays souverain (the Movement for a Sovereign Country), SPQ libre (very active in PQ and union circles), the Conseil de la souveraineté (the Sovereignty Council), Québec Radio, and the Institut de recherche sur l'économie du Québec (IREQ, the Research Institute on Quebec's Economy). Each of these organizations supports sovereignty in different ways: the MNQ by encouraging pride in Quebec's achievements (the organization is in charge of coordinating the activities surrounding Quebec's national holiday, the Fête nationale du Québec); the Société Saint-Jean-Baptiste by (among other things) closely following the language question and patriotic commemorations (the fête des Patriotes and other themes in Quebec's history); and the Action nationale by serving as a forum for the exchange of ideas on the national question, including the issue of hard-line sovereignty. Other organizations, such as Génération Québec, Intellectuels pour la souveraineté, and even SPQ libre build momentum for support in specific circles (among intellectuals, "young entrepreneurs" and other business circles, and unions). In the near future, it is possible that some of these actors will support the Option nationale or even the QS instead of the PQ.

Alongside the second circle, there are radical movements, which have a political plan for Quebec independence, one based on a clean break with the approach considered moderate by the PQ. For example, the Mouvement de libération nationale du Québec, led by Raymond Villeneuve, a former member of the Front de libération du Québec (FLQ), sees violence as an acceptable means of achieving its objective (the national liberation of Quebec). Several associations of young separatists, such as the Jeunes patriotes du Québec (the "Young Quebec Patriots") belong to this group. Relatively marginal, these movements and activist networks are continuing a radical tradition of separatist militancy; however, they seem on the fringes of the social movement working for sovereignty.

The third circle is less *in* the movement than *on* its front step. If most organizations that belong to it may be categorized as in the sovereignist "sphere of influence," their support for the cause is sporadic and their allegiance to the PQ even more so. They are pro-sovereignty rather than actively working toward sovereignty. Their primary mission is not to defend the sovereignty option, nor have they been given a mandate to do so, even if most of them have formally supported the PQ, were clearly committed to the "Yes" side in the referendum campaigns (in particular, by contributing to the Partners for Sovereignty coalition), and from time to time still display their sympathy for the sovereignist cause. Very often, these organizations' sympathies for the sovereignist cause stems from the large number of sovereignists within their ranks. This is especially true of unions and community groups in which much of the present or former leadership is openly sovereignist, even if they are not actually *péquistes*.

Who makes up the third circle? Most of Quebec's labour confederations, including the FTQ, the Confédération des syndicats nationaux (CSN), the Centrale des syndicats du Québec (CSQ, Quebec central labour body), and unions that are more sector-based, such as the Centrale de l'enseignement du Québec (CEQ, Quebec Teachers' Union), federations of student associations, the Union des artistes (UDA, Artists' Union) and the Fédération des femmes du Québec (FFQ, Quebec Women's Federation, the province's main coalition of women's movements). More recent networks, such as certain networks for global social justice, recognize in a more general way the right of all peoples to political self-determination; consequently, they recognize Quebeckers as a people that have this right. However, they do not give an opinion on the validity of the Quebec sovereignty movement per se. Lastly, there is a newspaper (*l'Aut'journal*—the Alternative Journal), a research institute (the Institut du

Nouveau Monde—Institute of the New World), and a museum (Maison nationale des patriotes—National Patriots House).

The unions, the student movement, and the women's movement (through
the FFQ) were traditionally in favour of sovereignty. For example, in the 2003
provincial elections, some of them lent explicit or implicit support to the PQ
(Collombat and Gagnon, 2003:1–14), but in the 2008 and 2012 elections, none
of them chose to support the PQ officially. Furthermore, there are strong links
between the PQ and some of these organizations, which are an important
source of militant *péquistes* and even *péquiste* leaders. Thus, one of the main
leaders of the 2012 student movement, Leo Bureau-Blouin, president of the
Fédération étudiante collégiale du Québec (FÉCQ) between 2010 and 2012,
was elected in the September 2012 election under the PQ banner. Even though
there were no formal links between the PQ and the 2012 student movement,
the party supported student demands in opposition and agreed to stop the
tuition hike when they returned to power in the fall 2012 election.

As we can see, the structure of the sovereignist movement has become
more complex. In the following two sections, we explore the changes on the
left of the movement as well as the resurgence of the identity question.

Post-Referendum Turbulence: The Normalization of Quebec Political Life

Although the PQ lost the 1995 referendum and lacked the power to negotiate
a constitution for a sovereign country, it remained in power and continued to
manage government business. Between 1996 and 2000, Lucien Bouchard was
premier, pursuing a politics of "zero deficit." Increasingly, the third circle of
social forces dissociated itself from the PQ organization and chose to struggle
against poverty (Dufour, 2005: 159–82).

Further political cleavage heightened this tense political atmosphere. The
Third Summit of the Americas, held in Quebec City in 2001, brought together
the continent's 34 elected heads of state; its primary objective was to negotiate
economic and trade issues as part of the Free Trade Area of the Americas
(FTAA) agreement. It was greeted by huge demonstrations by protestors who
supported alternative forms to globalization. As social protest against free
trade became better organized, it prompted Quebec's social forces to rethink
their allegiance to the PQ, in favour of free trade, and to build new networks
of partners at the pan-Canadian and transcontinental level. With increasing
clarity, Quebec's unions and leading social movements came to agree with
the movement for global social justice, rejecting the neo-liberal form of the
treaties being negotiated, and gave priority to the need for solidarity over
that of Quebec's political status. The Occupy movement in 2012 in Quebec
City and Montreal was another expression of this recent change, showing that

the young generation is highly focused on question of inequality (in Quebec, Canada, and at the global scale) and crisis of representative democracy (see chapter 5 in this volume). The framework for sovereignty has profoundly changed and an important part of new generations of activists do not seem to put the political status of Quebec at the heart of their engagement.

This focus on inequality was also shaped by the protest movements that emerged to oppose the Charest government, in power from 2003 to 2012. The 2012 student movement provides a useful case study. In March 2010, the Liberal government of Jean Charest announced an increase in university tuition fees to meet the fiscal needs of universities. He also convened a meeting of partners in education, held in Quebec City in December 2010. Representatives of university administrations, business, unions, and student associations participated (except one student association that boycotted the meeting). Quickly, the students and the government reached an impasse. On March 17, 2011, the government of Quebec announced a tuition fee increase of 75 per cent over five years ($1,625 per student). This decision launched a massive, long, and intense protest in Quebec society, beginning with a joint demonstration organized by the four principal student federations in November 2011. Considered as a success, it gave birth to a new temporary coalition—CLASSE (Coalition large de l'ASSÉ), which represented almost half the students on strike. On February 13, 2012, the first four associations voted for an unlimited general strike and hundreds more followed. On March 22, 200,000 people demonstrated in Montreal while 300,000 students declared themselves on strike for this day. This huge mobilization remained extremely steadfast till June 2012. From mid-April, the conflict escalated into a general protest focused on health, the environment, and education. In the hope of breaking the movement, the government adopted a bill (known as Bill 78), which temporarily restrained protest in the street and the possibility for student associations to block access to classes. In the face of this offence, the movement expanded into new tactics, including nightly demonstrations and banging of pots and pans. The government called an election in August. On the evening of September 4, the Liberal government was defeated and replaced by a PQ minority government.

What this huge movement showed is that the dominant political frame on the left of the political spectrum had shifted. First, the universe of public discourse had radicalized. In the course of the conflict, the issue became not only about tuition fees but also about free university education for all and a general fight against the marketization of education. Second, there was an absence or quasi-absence of links between education and the political status of Quebec, although education can be viewed as a question at the heart of political identity. In this issue, the political cleavage was clearly built on the basis of a left/right division, just as it is elsewhere in the world. The pre-eminence of this cleavage since 2003 is a big change in Quebec political life. It has, of course, something to do with the Liberal governing style in Quebec, which has provoked a resurgence of social protest since 2003. It has also something to do with the broader political context outside Quebec (the Conservative government in Ottawa that favours neo-liberal policies, as well as the global economic recession that renders economic issues more salient). But it has also something to do with changes internal to the sovereignist movement itself, especially the main focus of social groups situated at its periphery, which have shifted their main struggles more toward questions of social justice and less toward the question of sovereignty.

All in all, between 1995 and 2012, the political life in Quebec changed substantially. The political boundary along the federalist-sovereignist divide is now blurred and intersects other political splits, especially left-right splits, which previously played only a secondary role. That said, the very content of nationalism that is supposed to sustain the common belonging to a nation (or country) has also been challenged by recent changes. Let us now turn to this second destabilizing factor for the sovereignist movement.

Variations on a Sovereignist Theme: Renewal of Questions of Citizenship and Identity

If there is one common value among all sovereignists, it is that of challenging the federal state in a fundamental way. This "shared challenge" of opposing the federal government involves both the public policies and the authority of the Canadian state. It is based on the sovereignist idea that the Canadian state is not the state of Quebeckers and that the claims of Canadian "unity" that the federal government makes in Quebec about nationhood are nothing more than a myth masking a different reality. In the sovereignist view, only the Quebec government truly speaks for Quebeckers. The holding of power by the PQ ensures that this anti-establishment doctrine is communicated effectively and on a regular basis to provincial institutions. The doctrine is intended specifically for institutions under local control—such as the seat of government in Quebec, the Fête nationale du Québec (the holiday on June 24, also known as Saint-Jean-Baptiste Day), and the *fleur de lys* flag, all of which have become "national" institutions. In many respects, opposition to the Canadian state continues to be important to all of the movement's partners, including elements that are critical to its leadership. For example, they view the fiscal imbalance between the federal government and Quebec as undermining Quebeckers' freedom of action. Despite the bracketing of the separatist agenda, it appears that within the movement the contestation of the federal state role is still the subject of a broad consensus.

Aside from the challenge to the state, sovereignists are supposed to be united behind a political option and project: the sovereignty of Quebec. It is a project built simultaneously on the assertion of national identity (preparing for sovereignty) and Quebec's independence (whose form and content they are trying to envision). This, too, involves an imperative: regardless of their activist niche, sovereignists believe above all in national independence and in the idea that Quebec constitutes a nation. They also believe that Quebeckers are a people, whose fulfillment can take only one path: the independence of Quebec and the creation of "un pays pour le monde" (one country for the people), one title of the PQ program (Parti québécois, 2001: 40). From the sovereignist standpoint, this people's presence within Canada is more of an accident of history (the Conquest) than the product of a collective and voluntary choice. The myth of Canada as consisting of a pan-Canadian citizenship is well and truly dead among Quebec sovereignists. Rather, it is the dream of "le Grand Soir," expressed by René Lévesque during the 1980 referendum—the very moment when Quebec will become a country. There are many different views on the method by which independence can be achieved—implementation by stages to a unilateral declaration of independence to a referendum election to a constituent process. There are also different views on the form that the future state would take, for example, republic versus monarchy, secularism, cultural diversity, the status of the French language, armed forces, international policy, environmental issues, and so on. Certain activists tend to pay greater attention to this second aspect of sovereignist identity, focusing less on its legitimacy than on its effectiveness. For certain left activists especially, achieving sovereignty has for too long hindered the development of a social vision for Quebec. These activists do not view a social vision as a topic for future discussion, as something that will follow later or by default once national independence has been achieved. They maintain, rather, that the movement as a whole must support a social vision as an immediate political objective in the "here and now." Finally, it must be recognized that the indeterminacy of the "transition to sovereignty" makes the definition of such a "projet de société" all the more problematic. Without a well-defined transition plan, what can be the role of the sovereignist parties? What is their mission? What should be their position within Canadian federalism, and under what government program?

The third main line in sovereignist political identity is shared values. This includes affirming the role of the Quebec state as a key actor in Quebec society and advocating the values of social democracy by promoting a specific type of "Quebec model." Today, this aspect is more problematic for the sovereignist movement because the old alliance between social protest and nationalist protest tends to crumble or to be less automatic. Although the program of the two main sovereignist parties contains clear references to social democracy, and this bond is regularly asserted in the PQ, there is no consensus on the concrete content of this project. For example, would it be along the lines of Tony Blair's "Third Way," or a project of the radical left, or a broadening of the specific features of the Quebec "model" of governance?

The sovereignist movement is experiencing changes that in many ways are similar to those experienced by other social movements in Canada and, indeed, throughout the world. Like the women's movement or the workers' movement, it must deal with changes in the nature of activism (actions taken for one cause are often coupled with militant actions for other causes; allegiance to an organization is no longer taken for granted, but is in constant renegotiation) and in the role of the nation-state (Quebec or Canadian). In the past 10 years, part of the sovereignist movement became much more open to the new problems of globalization, economic equity (sustainable development, fair trade), reinvestment in the health and education sectors, and environmental issues. In other words, some actors of the movement adapt and learn from this new context and develop language policies taking into account the recognition of "all the constituent elements of the Quebec culture, including its historical, English-speaking community, First Nations and Inuit nations" (Commission des États généraux sur la situation et l'avenir de la langue française au Québec, 2001: 21). Nonetheless, this new openness has not been without its difficulties and has met resistance.

There is within the sovereignist movement an obvious tension between this desire for openness to Quebec's diversity in all its forms, which is found especially in the main sovereignist political program, and the sometimes virulent criticism of the Canadian model of multiculturalism. This model is not seen as consistent with the assertion of a Quebec distinctiveness that defines itself at the same time around the idea of the singular course of a historical, linguistic, and territorial national community but also a "projet de société" that aims to include linguistic minorities and newcomers (Labelle et al., 2012). In this problematic arrangement between national particularism and cultural diversity, the sovereignist movement is divided between several and sometimes contradictory options (from neoconservative proposals to feminist sovereignist ones). Since 2007 and the national debate about "reasonable compromises" put forward by the right-of-centre ADQ during the election campaign, the identity question has surfaced again in the movement (Bélanger and Nadeau, 2009; Tessier, 2008). We now find two main options. On one side are those who promote a discourse of openness and a conception of a national Quebec identity that includes "diverse diversity" within it (Bouchard, 2000). On the other hand, a network of neoconservatives and intellectuals worry about a national community described as besieged, or lacking memory, and prefer to turn back to history and ideology to reaffirm Quebec identity (Piotte and Couture, 2012: 152; Bock-Côté, 2007). This identity crisis currently characterizes the national question within the sovereignty movement and reflects also Quebec society debates. Let's turn to two concrete examples of this trend.

In 2007, Pauline Marois introduced a bill on Quebec identity that proposed to create a Quebec citizenship that would be conditional on an appropriate knowledge of French and an appropriate knowledge of Quebec and of responsibilities and advantages conferred by citizenship (National Assembly of Quebec, 2007). Those rules would be applied to new immigrants. The acquisition of Quebec citizenship would be a necessary condition to be eligible to stand as a candidate in school, municipal, or general elections. This bill was very controversial and was opposed by many leading politicians as well as union leaders and others. Even if the idea of formalizing Quebec identity was not new in PQ history (Lisée, 2007), the Marois initiative was interpreted as an attack against immigrants and the sign of an identity turn inside the PQ. On the left of the political spectrum, the QS declared that "we refused to say that the identity crises of what seems to be the francophone majority of Quebeckers should be solved by seeking scapegoats who are the 9 per cent of immigrants. It is not this way that we speak of an inclusive Quebec" (Dion-Viens, 2007, our translation).

More recently, in the 2012 electoral campaign, the PQ proposed a "Charter of Secularism" ("laïcité" in French) (Parti québécois, 2012). This charter would recognize the secular form of the Quebec state and its neutrality toward religious beliefs (or non-beliefs). Freedom of religion would not be allowed to infringe gender equality or the smooth functioning of public and para public institutions. Civil servants would not be allowed to wear religious insignia at work. And finally, the charter would constitute an interpretative tool for Quebec courts.

In a virulent critique, Jean Dorion, former BQ deputy and former president of the Société Saint-Jean-Baptiste of Montreal, argued that the proposed charter was too divisive for Quebec society and saw a high risk of breaking the relationships with the most important francophone immigrant community that Quebec has known (people coming from Maghreb countries) (Dorion, 2012). As we can see, the questions of who is a Quebecker and what does it mean to be from Quebec are particularly thorny inside the sovereignist movement.

The reactivation of this cleavage is not superimposed on the left-right divide. Some leftists prefer a conservative nationalism and some rightists support a pluralist one. These developments are similar to those in many European countries in which questions of immigration, secularism, and national identity have come to the fore (Kriesi et al., 2006) not to mention Ontario's debate over the funding of religious schools. As for the transformation of left parties, the sovereignist movement has to confront the question of globalization and the migrant mobility that comes with it. All in all, and considering seriously these transformations, it is reasonable to think that the sovereignist movement in Quebec will continue to be a diverse network of political and social activists. Nevertheless, it has been and will continue to be a motor for social and political change in the province.

ACHIEVEMENTS OF THE SOVEREIGNIST MOVEMENT

Although the sovereignist movement has not yet succeeded in its main goal of establishing Quebec as an independent nation-state, it has had important effects on public policy and on Quebec society. What makes the sovereignty movement unique is that it has been able to draw on a wide range of actions. As a force within the government, the movement has been able to implement linguistic and social policies through the PQ. As a social protest movement within Canada, it established a power relationship with the central government that yielded tangible results.

When the PQ came to power in 1976, it passed a range of important and progressive legislation, much of which incorporated the party's program. This legislation included the Charter of the French Language (Bill 101), which established the pre-eminent status of the French language for Quebec's businesses, workers, educational institutions, and public areas and in so doing transformed the linguistic character of the province and especially the City of Montreal. In addition, the government passed laws on abortion, the financing of political parties, and automobile insurance. Later, the area of health and social services, too, would experience strong growth, especially with the introduction of local community service centres. In the 1990s and 2000s, three sectors of public policy were particularly important for the PQ government: child care policy for young children and primary school children, economic development policy, and recognition and support for community-based actors. In these three fields, Quebec set itself apart from the other Canadian provinces through stronger government intervention in economic regulation and in its relationships with civil society.

As a force for social protest, the sovereignty movement's constant presence in the Quebec political sphere has allowed the provincial government (even when the latter was led by the PLQ) to establish a power relationship with the federal government and obtain specific legislative and financial benefits for Quebec. For example, if Quebec is not "a province like other provinces" in the Canadian confederation, then this is largely because the sovereignty movement and its sympathizers have for over 40 years threatened to separate Quebec from the rest of the country. Consequently, Quebec exercises broader jurisdiction than the other provinces in the areas of immigration and linguistic policy and has greater latitude in the areas of foreign policy and diplomatic representation abroad.

In addition, the existence of the sovereignty movement partially explains Quebec's distinctive form of governance. Compared to other Canadian provinces, Quebec gives social actors a greater role in the public decision-making process (this is entirely aside from the role of the so-called "Quebec model"). Thus, Quebec has adopted a policy of recognition and financing of the community sector in September 2001 that has no equivalent in the rest of Canada. This policy, which is the result of years of mobilization, provides basic financing even for those groups that struggle with the government and facilitates the representation of their voices in public debates. The connections we have described between the core of the sovereignty movement (especially the PQ) and the third circle of sovereignty supporters have played a role in establishing this particular model of governance; the fact remains that whenever the PQ was in power, it was more receptive to the demands of its social partners than were the other political parties.

On the other hand, when the PQ behaved as a monopolistic force, it forced the militant left to voice its demands more through community-based circles than through the political party. In the name of sovereignty and the need to build a consensus among progressive forces, any dissent expressed by these actors regarding the PQ's social vision was put on the back burner during elections and referendum campaigns. Since 1995, the exchange of ideas, concerns, and identities between these social forces and the PQ has slackened to the point where some observers believe that there will eventually be a split in the sovereignty movement between the PQ and its social partners. The question is whether the PQ, the government party since the 1970s, will accept the idea that it is not the sole representative of the sovereignist option in Quebec. This is what seems to have appeared at a rally organized by the Nouveau Mouvement pour le Québec held November 25, 2012, and entitled "Place publique sur l'indépendance et la réconciliation: se retrouver, se constituer, s'émanciper." The aim was clearly to draw out all the consequences of political fragmentation for the sovereignty movement and see if behind this new constraint there was no possibility of coalition, not in the form of a new political party but as an electoral alliance between the sovereignist forces. From this point of view, the recent November 2012 elections in Catalonia were of course discussed, notably by Bernard Landry, who called for the formation of such a coalition in the upcoming election (Zabihiyan, 2012).

CONCLUSION

In political analysis, we often focus on the failure of the sovereignist move-ment and its inability to convince most Quebeckers of the need for indepen-dence. But we perhaps do not stress enough its undeniable success: putting the national question on the political agenda for over 50 years and thus contributing so decisively to the invention of a new nation: the Quebec nation. When the PQ—the core of the movement—was the government party, it helped improve Quebeckers' access to rights (social rights and representation rights as a distinct community in Canada) while strengthening political participation mechanisms for Quebec citizens. Stated differently, over the past 30 years, Quebec's "citizenship regime" (Jenson, 1998: 235–62), which is different from the Canadian citizenship regime, has derived largely from the presence and political activities of the sovereignty movement.

From this point of view, the sovereignist movement is still carrying a desire for change, driven by a radical contestation of the Canadian federal government. This is not only change around the "projet de société," characterizing the Quebec political space, but also a change to a collective belonging constantly redefined in terms of the discussion above. The sov-ereignist movement continues through its constellation of organizations, political parties, and activists. In a sense, it appears less as a structure orga-nized around an electoral machine with a clear political choice and increas-ingly as a political space in which identity and the "projet de société" are widely debated.

REFERENCES AND FURTHER READING

Anderson, Benedict. 1991. *Imagined Communities: Reflections on the Origin and Spread of Nationalism*. Rev. ed. London: Verso.

André, Lecours, and François Rocher. 2003. "La "nation" ne tombe pas du ciel. Sur les' rapports structurants des nationalismes en concurrence. Les cas de la Belgique et du Canada." In *La nation en débat: Entre modernité et postmodernité*, ed. Raphaël Canet and Jules Duchastel, 111–33. Montreal: Athéna.

Beauchemin, Jacques. 2002. *L'histoire en trop. La mauvaise conscience des souver-ainistes québécois*. Montreal: VLB éditeur.

Bélanger, Éric, and Richard Nadeau. 2009. *Le comportement électoral des Québécois*. Montreal: Presses de l'Université de Montréal.

Belkhodja, Chedly, and Christophe Traisnel. 2012. "Une communauté nationale assiégée? Le constat des " nouveaux penseurs de sensibilité conservatrice » en France et au Québec." In *La communauté politique en question. Regards croisés sur l'immigration, la citoyenneté, la diversité et le pouvoir*, ed. Micheline Labelle, Jocelyne Couture, and Franck M. Remiggi, 121–44. Quebec: PUQ.

Bloc Québécois. 2004, *Le scandale des commandites*. Press release, Ottawa. http://www.blocquebecois.org/fr/default.asp (accessed September 12, 2005).

Bloc Québécois. 2004, *Paul Martin et les paradis fiscaux*. Press release, Ottawa. http://www.blocquebecois.org/fr/default.asp (accessed September 13, 2005).

Bloc Québécois. 2004, *Pour éliminer le déséquilibre fiscal*. Press release, Ottawa. http://www.blocquebecois.org/fr/default.asp (accessed September 12, 2005).

Bloc Québécois. 2004, *Pour faire le ménage à Ottawa*. Press release, Ottawa. http://www.blocquebecois.org/fr/default.asp (accessed September 12, 2005).

Bloc Québécois. 2004, *Pour protéger les intérêts économiques du Québec à Ottawa*. Press release, Ottawa. http://www.blocquebecois.org/fr/default.asp (accessed September 12, 2005).

Bock, Michel. 2004. *Quand la nation débordait les frontières: Les minorités françaises dans la pensée de Lionel Groulx*. Montreal: Éditions Hurtubise HMH.

Bock-Côté, Mathieu. 2007. *La dénationalisation tranquille*. Montreal: Boréal.

Bock-Côté, Mathieu. 2012. *Trudeau le séparatiste? Non merci*. http://blogues.jour naldemontreal.com/bock-cote/general/trudeau-le-separatiste-non-merci/ (accessed May 2, 2013).

Bouchard, Gérard. 2000. *Genèse des nations et cultures du Nouveau Monde*. Montreal: Boréal compact.

Bourque, Gilles, and Jules Duchastel. 1996. *L'identité fragmentée: Nation et citoyenneté dans les débats constitutionnels canadiens 1941–1992*. Montreal: Fides.

Bourque, Gilles and Anne Legaré. 1979. *Le Québec, La question nationale*. Paris: Petite collection Maspéro.

Cantin, Philippe. 1995. "Parizeau blame l'argent et le vote ethnique." *Le Devoir* (October 31: A4).

Chouinard, Tommy. 2007. "Marois devrait modifier son projet de loi, estime Landry." *Cyberpresse* (October 27).

Coleman, William D. 1984. *The Independence Movement in Quebec, 1945–1980*. Toronto: University of Toronto Press.

Collombat, Thomas, and Mona-Josée Gagnon. 2003. "Le syndicalisme québécois face à la résurgence d'une droite antisyndicale." *Chroniques internationales de l'IRES* 83 (July): 1–14.

Commission des États généraux sur la situation et l'avenir de la langue française au Québec. 2001. *Rapport*. Quebec: Gouvernement du Québec.

Commission on Fiscal Imbalance. 2001. *Fiscal Imbalance: Problems and Issues*. Quebec: Gouvernement du Québec.

Couture, Jocelyne, Kai Nielsen, and Michel Seymour, eds. 1996. *Rethinking Nationalism. Supplementary Volume, Canadian Journal of Philosophy*. Calgary: University of Calgary Press.

CROP. 2012a. "Évolution du climat politique au Québec: 17 au 22 octobre 2012. Politique provinciale et politique fédérale." Montreal: CROP.

CROP. 2012b. "Sondage annuel de l'Idée fédérale." Montreal: CROP, l'Idée fédérale.

David, Françoise. 2004. "Pour gouverner à gauche, il faut penser à gauche." *Le Devoir* (September 29: A7).

Dion-Viens, Daphnée. 2007. "Québec solidaire dénonce Dumont et Marois." *Le Soleil* (November 19: 6).

Dorion, Jean. 2012. "Charte de la laïcité—Quand un séparatiste se sépare." *Le Devoir* (September 22). http://www.ledevoir.com/politique/quebec/359768/quand-un-separatiste-se-separe (accessed November 13, 2012).

Dufour, Pascale. 2005. "L'adoption du projet de loi 112 au Québec: le produit d'une mobilisation ou une simple question de conjoncture politique?" *Politique et Sociétés* 23 (2/3): 159–82.

Dutrisac, Robert. 2006. "Malaise au PQ, qui perd deux dirigeants." *Le Devoir* (October 12: A3).

Dutrisac, Robert. 2007. "Louise Beaudoin se porte à la défense de Pauline Marois: "Il est nécessaire de réaffirmer la prédominance du français au Québec 30 ans après la loi 101." *Le Devoir* (November 1: A3).

Dutrisac, Robert. 2008. "Le PQ attise la colère des immigrants: Kippas, turbans et autres hijabs seraient interdits dans la fonction publique." *Le Devoir* (October 18: A1).

Fraser, Graham. 1984. *P.Q.: René Lévesque and the Parti Québécois in Power*. Toronto: Macmillan.

Gellner, Ernest. 1989. *Nations et nationalisme*. Paris: Payot.

Jenson, Jane. 1995. "What's in a Name?" In *Nationalist Movements and Public Discourse: Social Movements and Culture*, ed. H. Johnston and B. Klandermans, 107–26. Minneapolis: University of Minnesota Press.

Jenson, Jane. 1998. "Reconnaître les différences: sociétés distinctes, régimes de citoyenneté, partenariats." In *Sortir de l'impasse: les voies de la reconciliation*, ed. Guy Laforest and Roger Gibbins, 235–62. Montreal: IRPP.

Jenson, Jane. 1999. "La modernité pluraliste du Québec: De la nation à la citoyenneté. Un avenir construit sur le respect des droits, la reconnaissance de la contribution de tous à l'histoire et la participation aux institutions politiques." *Le Devoir* (July 31: A9).

Keating, Michael. 1997. *Les défis du nationalisme moderne: Québec, Catalogne, Écosse*. Montreal: Les Presses de l'Université de Montréal.

Kriesi, Hanspeter, Edgar Grande, Romain Lachat, Martin Dolezal, Simon Bornschier, and Timotheos Frey. 2006. "Globalization and the Transformation of the National Political Space: Six European Countries Compared." *European Journal of Political Research* 45 (6): 921–56.

Labelle, Micheline, Jocelyne Couture, and Frank W. Remiggi. 2012. *La communauté politique en question. Regards croisés sur l'immigration, la citoyenneté, la diversité et le pouvoir*. Quebec: PUQ.

Lacoursière, Benoit. 2007. *Le Mouvement étudiant au Québec de 1983 à 2006*. Montreal: Sabotart.

Laurendeau, André, Patricia Smart, and Dorothy Howard. 1991. *The Diary of André Laurendeau: Written during the Royal Commission on Bilingualism and Biculturalism 1964–1967*. Halifax: Lorimer.

Le Monde. 2012. *Les Québécois sont-ils toujours indépendantistes?* September 4. http://www.lemonde.fr/ameriques/article/2012/09/04/les-quebecois-sont-ils-toujours-independantistes_1755535_3222.html (accessed January 11, 2013).

Léger Marketing, Agence QMI. 2012. *Le Québec vu par le reste du Canada*. March 11. http://www.legermarketing.com/admin/upload/publi_pdf/Rapport_Sondage_AQMI_Quebec_vu_par_le_ROC_11mars2012.pdf.

Levine, Marc V. 1990. *The Reconquest of Montreal: Language Policy and Social Change in a Bilingual City*. Philadelphia: Temple University Press.

Lisée, Jean-François. 2005. "Des radicaux au P.Q.? Normal." *L'Actualité* 30 (12): 44.

Lisée, Jean-François. 2007. *Nous*. Montreal: Boréal.

Martel, Marcel. 1997. *Le deuil d'un pays imaginé: rêves, luttes et déroute du Canada français, les rapports entre le Québec et la francophonie canadienne (1867–1975)*. Ottawa: Presse de l'Université d'Ottawa.

McRoberts, Kenneth. 1988. *Quebec: Social Change and Political Crisis*. Toronto: McClelland and Stewart.

McRoberts, Kenneth. 1997. *Misconceiving Canada: The Struggle for National Unity*. Oxford: Oxford University Press.

Monière, Denis. 1981. *Ideologies in Quebec*. Toronto: University of Toronto Press.

Monière, Denis, and André Laurendeau. 1983. *Et le destin d'un peuple*. Montreal: Québec Amériques.

Montigny, Éric. 2011. *Leadership et militantisme au Parti Québécois*. Laval: Presses de l'Université Laval.

National Assembly of Quebec. 2003. http://www.saic.gouv.qc.ca/publications/resolutions/20031030.pdf (accessed May 2, 2013).

National Assembly of Quebec. 2007. Première session, 38e législature, *Projet de loi n.195, Loi sur l'identité québécoise, art. 10*. Quebec: Éditeur officiel du Québec.

Option citoyenne. 2005. Démarche d'option citoyenne sur la question nationale et constitutionnelle. Letter April 27, 2005. http://www.optioncitoyenne.ca/pivot/entry.php?id=215 (accessed June 2005).

Parti québécois. 2001. *Un pays pour le monde, Programme du Parti Québécois, version abrégée*. Montreal: Parti Québécois.

Parti québécois. 2012. "S'affirmer: Pauline Marois s'engage à adopter des règles claires pour encadrer les accommodements raisonnables." http://pq.org/actualite/communiques/saffirmer_pauline_marois_sengage_a_adopter_des_regles_claires_pour_encadrer_le (accessed November 13, 2012).

Pinard, Maurice, Robert Bernier, and Vincent Lemieux. 1997. *Un combat inachevé*. Quebec: Presses de l'Université du Québec.

Piotte, Jean-Marc, and Jean-Pierre Couture. 2012. *Les nouveaux visages du nationalisme conservateur au Québec*. Montreal: Québec-Amérique.

Rocher, François, and Guy Lecours. 2003. "La 'nation' ne tombe pas du ciel. Sur les rapports structurants des nationalismes en concurrence. Les cas de las Belgique et du Canada." In *La nation en débat. Entre modernité et postmodernité*, ed. Raphaël Canet and Jules Duchastel, 111–33. Montreal: Athéna.

Rumilly, Robert. 1975. *Histoire de la Société Saint-Jean-Baptiste de Montréal*. Montreal: L'Aurore.

Ryan, Claude. 2002. *Les Valeurs libérales et le Québec moderne, une perspective historique sur l'apport du Parti libéral du Québec à l'édification du Québec d'hier et d'aujourd'hui*. Quebec: Parti libéral du Québec.

Tessier, Benoît. 2008. *Espace politiques et positions partisanes: les plateformes électorales au Québec de 1994 à 2007*. Montreal: Université du Québec à Montréal.

Thiesse, Anne-Marie. 1999. *La création des identités nationales, Europe XVIIIe—XXe siècle*. Paris: Seuil.

Traisnel, Christophe. 2004. *Le nationalisme de contestation. Le rôle des mouvements nationalistes dans la construction politique des identités wallonne et québécoise en Belgique et au Canada*. Doctoral thesis, Université de Montréal, Université de Paris II.

Vallières, Pierre. 1968. *Nègres blancs d'Amérique*. Montreal: Parti pris.

Vallières, Pierre. 1971. *White Niggers of America*. Trans. Joan Pinkham. Toronto: McClelland and Stewart.

Vigile. 2005. http://www.vigile.net/ (accessed May 2, 2013).

Yale, François, and Claire Durand. 2011. "What did Quebeckers Want? Impact of Question Wording, Constitutional Proposal and Context on Support for Sovereignty, 1976—2008." *American Review of Canadian Studies* 41 (3): 242–58. http://dx.doi.org/10.1080/02722011.2011.594517 (accessed September 6, 2013).

Zabihiyan, Bahador. 2012. "Les souverainistes inspirés par la Catalogne." *Le Devoir* (November 26).

PART FOUR

Environment, Disability, and Health

TWELVE

The Canadian Environmental Movement: Remembering Who We Are

ROBERT PAEHLKE

Canadian history and culture reflects our vast land—its geography, climate, resource bounty, and beauty. Canada's rugged vastness and climate has always been challenging. In the long history of Canada's First Nations, the settlements with skilled hunters had the best chance of surviving the harshest winters, and only strong and determined voyageurs got to where they were going and back again. Just growing food in a cold country has always been challenging.

At the same time, life abounds in this land and resources are (or in some cases were) almost too bountiful. Clearing the forest for even a small farm was often a massive job, but there was wood for building and for warmth. At the time of Confederation, few imagined that much of the forest that stretched for thousands of kilometres could ever be harvested excessively. Fewer imagined that cod might someday be hard to find and that wild salmon stocks would be decimated by pollution, dams, overfishing, and clear-cutting. Yet, at the same time, the combination of harshness and bounty taught many Canadians to be mindful of and grateful to the land. Our culture—our paintings and our literature—is rooted in our landscape and climate. So too, to some extent at least, is our politics.

Seymour Martin Lipset, the noted American sociologist, observed that wheat farmers in the Canadian prairies were politically well to the left compared to most North Americans (Lipset, 1963). To explain this difference he argued that when growing wheat in Saskatchewan there is no pretending that success or failure is entirely within your control, that hard work is always rewarded, or that those that fail are either insufficiently bright or have made an inadequate effort. It is obvious that the outcome is simply not always in your hands alone, that everyone needs help sometimes, and that we all need to be ready to help others. It is not a long way from there to appreciating the need for government. Historically, Canadians in general have been more open to that possibility than Americans.

Slowly, Canadians have also learned to protect some resources. Canada is riddled with depleted and declining towns that have exhausted the resources that sustained them. Often they are so remote that there is no alternative source of jobs. Young people move on. Some of those towns have contaminated fishing as a result of mining, logging, or paper mills. Only a few lucky ones are able to convert themselves to retirement communities or tourist areas. These painful lessons were learned one community at a time, but, especially in the early years of the nation, such wisdom was lost in the vastness of Canada and its resources.

Early Canadians were mindful of the land and loved it but took time to realize that there were real limits to a dependence on extraction for economic survival. As the noted environmental activist Monte Hummel observed, "Americans were generally ahead of Canadians in concern for the conservation of resources. The concern probably resulted from the more extensive settlement in the US, which demonstrated the harm that civilization could do. In Canada a pioneer mentality of 'unlimited' forests, lakes and wildlife persisted longer" (cited in Paehlke 2009: 3). The US in the nineteenth century had intellectual giants who sensitized millions to the need to preserve nature. These included George Perkins Marsh, John James Audubon, Henry David Thoreau, and John Muir (Paehlke 1989).

The world's first national park, Yellowstone National Park in Wyoming, was created in 1872. Banff, Canada's first national park, was created in 1885. John Muir's public agitation pushed Yosemite National Park into existence in 1890. Interestingly though, it was not a push for conservation that created Banff but the push to build a railroad across the west and to the Pacific. Stunning destinations along the way were needed to justify the nation-building plans. Banff from its origin provided protection, but the core motivation was the acceleration of economic development.

There were, however, early conservation efforts in Canada. The first Canadian bird sanctuary was established in Saskatchewan in 1887. In 1907, Bernard E. Fernow, German-born first head of what was to become the U.C. Forest Service, was appointed first Dean of the School of Forestry at the University of Toronto; he was a strong advocate of scientific forestry and conservation. The International Joint Commission was created to protect US–Canadian boundary waters, including the Great Lakes, in 1909.

The Commission on Conservation, which advocated scientific forestry and careful resource management, was also established in 1909, but met its political demise in 1921. The 1920s, however, did see royal commissions to examine forest management practices, and in 1931 several Ontario community-based naturalist organizations banded together into the Federation of Ontario Naturalists, an organization that in time led to the creation of a conservation branch within Ontario's Planning and Development Department.

More recently, individual Canadians and several Canadian governments played a significant role in the post-1968 rise of the environmental movement. Greenpeace emerged as a globally influential environmental organization following protest of nuclear tests on Amchitka Island off Alaska in 1970. Canada has also played an important role in environmental diplomacy and with regard to global awareness and action regarding emerging environmental issues. These include climate change: one of the earliest high level gatherings on the issue was held in Toronto in 1988 when Brian Mulroney was prime minister. Regarding upper level ozone depletion, a 1987 global conference led to the signing of the very effective Montreal Protocol. In that same year, Canadians were instrumental in the publication of *Our Common Future*, also known as the Brundtland Report, the document that established the concept of sustainable development within global environmental discourse (World Commission on Environment and Development, 1987).

Canada, of course, has also had a long-standing history of multilateral action and has been a mainstay of peacekeeping and support for the UN. In this same tradition, Canada made a rare break with the US when Prime Minister Jean Chrétien signed the Kyoto Protocol on climate change while US President George W. Bush was walking away from it. Canada's environmental record has not always been exemplary, but its global reputation until recently has been one of a nation that protects its environment and cares about environmental protection globally. That reputation has declined under the Harper government. Canada is now considered a leading global opponent of effective steps to slow climate change.[1] The Canadian environmental movement has struggled to reverse this recent shift, but to understand the challenge it is facing we need to better understand that movement, its history, and its composition.

POLITICS, INTEREST GROUPS, AND SOCIAL MOVEMENTS

Social movements are amorphous and not easily fixed in time. A movement might have heroes and leaders, but no small group is singularly responsible for creating the movement or organizing it. Movements do not have a single headquarters or an address. They are comprised of large numbers of active individuals and passive supporters; a changing set of issues and many events, assertions, and media stories; a shifting roster of organizations; and, over time, an array of achievements and failures. The environmental movement, like the women's movement or the civil rights movement or the peace movement, emerge, surge and wane, and subside. They are about changing how people think, how they act, and what societies think is most important.

The organizations associated with a movement are primarily groups of citizens concerned about a particular set of issues. They endeavour to influence others, to rally them to support their cause. They also hope to influence what government or businesses do regarding the issues they care about. In this they are a type of interest group, though not necessarily one that has an economic interest in the outcome. They differ from a political party in that they do not necessarily address all public policy concerns and they seek to influence power rather than get elected or form a government.

Environmental groups address a wide range of issues including the protection of nature, biodiversity, ecology and habitat protection, air and water pollution, food quality, resource management, energy policy, climate, and the very broad concept of sustainability (which opens the way to many aspects of social and economic policy).

The environmental movement is usually said to date from the early 1960s, but its roots in the conservation movement stretch back into the nineteenth century or earlier. The conservation movement emphasized natural resource management, forestry, and wilderness protection (Paehlke, 1989). The environmental movement emphasized pollution, a concern that gained traction with the wider public following the publication of Rachel Carson's *Silent Spring* (1962), a book about pesticides and the effects of bioaccumulation on song birds (thus the book's title) and other species.

By this time, both the US and Canada had become urban societies, and while many were concerned with protecting wilderness, many more had an immediate response to issues regarding the air they were breathing in cities, the water they were drinking, and the food they were eating. The environmental movement had a broad political appeal, and large numbers of people became active very quickly. Citizen concern and media attention pushed governments all over North America to act. Environment Canada was created in 1971, and new environmental legislation, especially regarding air and water pollution, was passed throughout the late 1960s and early 1970s.

In 1972 and 1973, a new dimension was added: resource limits. The initial spark to this concern was the publication of the book *The Limits to Growth*, a publication that used computer modelling (then a very new thing) to predict future resource shortfalls (the predictions were not necessarily very precise, but they did get widespread attention) (Meadows et al., 1972). The reality of possible future resource limits was, however, brought home to those who had neither read it nor paid much attention. The Organization of Petroleum Exporting Countries (OPEC), following political tensions in the Middle East, sharply increased the price of oil. The age of cheap gas suddenly appeared to be over.

The environmental movement from that point forward had three inter-related core goals: 1) wilderness preservation and biodiversity, 2) air and water quality, and 3) sustainability. The first was the historic mission of the conservation movement. The second expanded to include the exposure of humans and nature to the impacts of pollutants and later to organic food, ozone depletion, acid rain, and climate change. Sustainability is all about the intelligent, long-term use of natural resources to fairly meet human needs, as well as the fairness associated with societal use of the wealth that derives from those resources.

This multi-dimensional approach to environmental politics broadened the base of political support for the environmental movement. It ultimately paved the way to the possibility of green political parties, starting in New Zealand, Australia, and Germany and eventually including the Green Party of Canada (GPC). Political parties that do not address all of the issues that citizens care about are not likely to be successful. The concept of sustainability opens the way to positions on a wide range of economic and social policy issues, as well as the full gamut of environmental issues. Environmentalism has become part of political life, much like liberalism, conservatism, and socialism but distinct in outlook from each of them.

THE ORGANIZATIONAL LANDSCAPE OF THE CANADIAN ENVIRONMENTAL MOVEMENT

There are at least nine kinds of environmentally oriented organizations and institutions that have emerged during the half-century of environmentalism in North America. There are two basic kinds of organizations within the environmental movement: ad hoc groups and larger, more permanent, often province-wide or national environmental organizations. Related is a third type of organization, an important Canadian variant of national environ-mental organization: the environmentally committed consulting firm. In Canada, there are also four types of environmentally focused governmental organizations (or organizations that are part of the governing process): royal commissions (or other public inquiries), green political parties, government ministries, and arm's-length government agencies such as the Science Council of Canada (1966–93) or the National Roundtable on the Environment and the Economy (NRTEE, 1993–2013). Finally, there are two other important kinds of organizations: university environmental studies and science programs and green businesses.

Citizen-based environmental organizations may arise in response to particular projects or issues. Early in the emergence of the Canadian environmental movement, one of the most successful examples of spontaneous activism, based in Toronto, arose in response to the construction of a freeway cutting through residential areas into the core of the city. The organization, Stop Spadina, achieved an early environmental movement victory. The partially constructed Spadina Expressway still today abruptly ends well short of its intended terminus. The defence of quiet residential neighbourhoods, opposition to air pollution, and support for public transit were massive and altered the shape of Canada's largest city from what it might have been.

Countless other ad hoc groups have arisen in response to commercial undertakings large and small—from municipal waste sites (dumps) to mines to other locally unwanted land uses (LULUs). Other campaigns have raised public awareness regarding ecologically important locations from small wetlands to vast wilderness tracts. Some defensive efforts have had a longer existence because protecting some sites requires extended vigilance (while destroying distinctive habitats need to succeed only once). A notable early protective group defended the Skagit Valley in northern British Columbia from a proposed dam (Perry, 1975). A longer-lived protective group is the Algonquin Wildlands League, which has striven to limit logging and mining in Algonquin Park. Another kind of ad hoc group opposes particular kinds of pollution. Notably successful in this regard was the Canadian Coalition on Acid Rain (CCAR), discussed below.

Other environmental organizations have a long history. Some of the oldest date back to the conservation era and began in the US. Some of these broadened the range of issues they address and operate independently within Canada. The most notable of these is the Sierra Club (founded in the US by John Muir in 1892), with the Sierra Club of Canada now based in Ottawa (Sierra Club Canada, 2013). Another important Canadian organization with US roots is Friends of the Earth. Greenpeace, on the other hand, began in Canada, now operates worldwide, and is particularly important in Europe.

Many Canadian environmental organizations began in the period 1968–72. Nearly every city of any size saw a new environmental group emerge during this period. Pollution Probe was established in Toronto by students and faculty at the University of Toronto (Pollution Probe, 2013). Very quickly there were Pollution Probes in most Ontario communities of any size. The Ecology Action Centre in Halifax and the Conservation Council of New Brunswick were two of the larger organizations in the Atlantic provinces; there were two groups in Montreal (STOP Montreal and SVP) (Ecology Action Centre, 2013); and in the west were SPEC, an early group in Vancouver, and STOP Edmonton. Most of these organizations emphasized pollution and excessive resource use, rather than wilderness protection, as their top priorities.

There were as well several environmental legally oriented organizations including the Canadian Environmental Law Association (CELA), West Coast Environmental Law (WCEL), and the Canadian Institute for Environmental Law and Policy (CIELAP) (Canadian Environmental Law Association, 2013). These organizations engaged in legal research, legal aid, and/or policy research and advocacy.

One of the earliest Canadian consulting firms with an environmental advocacy orientation was Middleton Associates, based in Toronto, with a client base that included governments, Crown corporations, private firms, and others. Marbek Associates was formed a bit later and operated in Ottawa, and in 1985 the Pembina Institute, perhaps today's leading Canadian firm, was established in Alberta.

Those who worked in these firms often had prior experience working for activist environmental organizations and by the mid-1970s were able to hire those who had earned degrees in environmental studies. These firms were an important part of a process of professionalization within the environmental movement—a shift from protest mode to getting environmental ideas inside government and business decision processes.

ENVIRONMENTAL ORGANIZATIONS AND GOVERNMENT

In Canada, there has been a long history of using public inquiries, including royal commissions, to address environmental concerns. Excessive logging led to the establishment of several public inquiries in the early part of the twentieth century. Especially notable among later environmentally oriented royal commissions was the Berger Inquiry regarding the construction of the Mackenzie Valley Pipeline. Mr. Justice Thomas Berger was appointed by the 1974 Liberal minority government in exchange for NDP support of the government. Berger's comprehensive study visited 35 remote northern communities and recommended a 10-year moratorium on construction of the pipeline (Berger, 1977). Other environmental inquiries during the 1970s included Ontario's Royal Commission on the Northern Environment regarding mercury pollution from pulp mills and the Royal Commission on Asbestos regarding workplace health.

Public inquiries appeal to governments because they may allow controversial decisions to be delayed until tempers cool. They also provide someone other than the government to share the blame for tough decisions, as well as time to sort through complicated and thorny questions. During the early days of the Canadian environmental movement, there were many such questions that aroused a great deal of public concern and challenged the interests of significant economic and political actors. Public inquiries were frequently part of the environmental policy decision process.

These public inquiries were not, of course, strictly speaking a part of the environmental movement, but they did contribute to its visibility and evolution. They provided forums within which Canadian environmental voices could be heard. These voices included citizen-based environmental organizations, individual citizens, and environmental professionals, including those based in environmental consulting firms as well as those working within or for First Nations, unions, or other civil society groups.

More recently, environmental ideas have come to be contested within the political process itself. The Green Party of Canada (GPC) was founded in 1983, with counterparts in each province following at various dates. The GPC did not have a significant electoral impact until 2004 when, under the leadership of Jim Harris, it ran candidates in every federal riding for the first time. In 2006, long-time environmental activist Elizabeth May was chosen as leader and the party participated in the leaders' debates and broke through to 6.8 per cent of the overall vote, getting about one million votes.

At that time, the party had 12,000 members and gained its first ever MP when Blair Wilson, a seated member, joined the party; however, he lost in the election later the same year. In 2011, the party lost ground (to 4 per cent of the vote) with some voters switching to the NDP in the hopes of preventing an electoral victory for the Harper government that was so hostile to environmental protection. Nonetheless, in that election, Party Leader Elizabeth May became the first federal member elected as a Green in the riding of Saanich-Gulf Islands in British Columbia.

Also important, of course, are environmental ministries themselves. They did not exist as such until the emergence in the late 1960s of the modern Canadian environmental movement. Environment Canada was created in 1971 when environmentally relevant functions of other ministries were transferred into it. Environment Canada's functions included parks, the weather service, endangered species, the regulation of air and water pollution, and eventually environmental assessment. Some environmental protection functions remained in other ministries: energy conservation was established within the Department of Energy, Mines and Resources (now Natural Resources Canada), and some aspects of environmental health were handled within Health Canada. Environment Canada has taken many initiatives, but the federal government has tended to defer to the provinces regarding this portfolio (Harrison, 1996).

Needless to say, environmental protection was not explicitly included within the allocation of powers between the federal and provincial governments as set out in the British North America Act of 1867. Environmental protection, in the modern sense of the term, did not exist at the time. The provinces were given powers regarding natural resources, but the federal government was responsible for "peace, order, and good government" as well as fisheries and matters related to interprovincial trade and commerce. An argument can be made both for and against decentralized environmental management, and in effect there is now in practice, as in many areas, shared jurisdiction.

Both the provincial and federal governments have been inconsistent regarding support of environmental protection. When public concern is high, both try to improve protection, but when the public mood cools, rollbacks are on the agenda. Legislation was passed in the 1970s and again in the late 1980s, but cutbacks were imposed in the mid-1990s when Ontario Premier Mike Harris cut environmental ministries by nearly half and privatized water testing, and, facing large deficits, the Chrétien government cut Environment Canada's budget by about 30 per cent (Winfield, 2012). In both cases, cuts to environmental protection were disproportionate compared to other government activities and services. With new cutbacks coming from the current Harper government, there are fewer lobbyists working on behalf of the environment compared to interests such as industry or agriculture. Without a strong expression of citizen concern, governments opt to reduce environmental protection.

Particularly vulnerable in such times are the arm's-length government agencies. They are not firmly embedded within a ministry and lack a minister to defend them in cabinet. Frequently, when the axes are wielded, these agencies face more than diminished budgets. They face oblivion. This is unfortunate because these organizations not only are sometimes a bit bolder than the larger bureaucracy, but they are both more visible to the public and less expensive. They cost less because they utilize experts who are employed elsewhere (in industry, universities, consulting firms, and environmental organizations) and are either unpaid or paid only for the limited number of hours that they work. They bring in new ideas and are less likely to need to curry favour within the governmental hierarchy.[2]

Another loss is that these organizations often provide a rare setting where business, governments, and environmental activists can exchange ideas. These interchanges are much more important than many realize. As we will see below, the environmental movement has changed greatly over time. Increasingly, green ideas are ideas that advance the economy as much as they challenge it. That is, environmental organizations may well still seek regulations that impose additional costs on some businesses, but they also now help to create many new businesses, including some that are now growing rapidly.

ENVIRONMENTAL ORGANIZATIONS, BUSINESS, AND UNIVERSITIES

Some businesses have always been green, though the expression "green products" only emerged in the late 1980s (e.g., Elkington and Hailes, 1988). Green businesses are politically important because they provide lobbying power that helps to offset those business lobbies that resist environmental protection. Green businesses that have existed for a very long time include producers of pollution abatement equipment, insulation, and environmentally benign energy sources including solar panels and windmills; producers of public transit equipment; tree nurseries; and bicycle manufacturers and those that manufacture products using recycled materials. Some of these businesses naturally favour legislation that leads to more pollution abatement or standards that increase the amount of insulation needed in new buildings.

Since the early 1990s there has been a huge surge in the variety of widely available green products. This began in earnest in Canada with Loblaw's extensive promotion of paper products from post-consumer waste paper, safer cleaning products and organic foods (Carson and Moulden, 1991). Organic foods have been available for decades to those willing to look, but more recently they have become available everywhere. This wide availability has been supplemented by the huge interest in locally produced food, products that are fresher and result in great transportation energy savings (Lappé, 2010). The food revolution has in many places been led by noted chefs.[3] More recently a wide array of more efficient lighting products and appliances has been introduced.

The construction of housing and other building has also been "greened." Lumber is certified as not having come from old growth forests. Many new buildings are built to what are called LEED standards, which take into account a variety of environmental concerns including the reuse of materials, toxicity, and energy efficiency.[4] In Canada in the 1970s, there were architects experimenting with super-efficient housing designs, including partially buried houses built on south-facing slopes. These houses took advantage of the fact that below several feet of earth winter temperatures are above freezing. Such houses need little heat other than passive solar and a small wood stove. Energy-efficient construction has been encouraged by government programs for experimental housing that have encouraged design innovation.

There are also products and businesses that have a greening effect, but are not always recognized as making a contribution. These include second-hand

and vintage goods, because there is no new resource or energy use or pollution resulting from resold and reused items. Also a green product (though often not seen as such) are cities themselves because energy use is far lower per capita than in rural and suburban locations where distances are longer and travel is almost always by car. In cities as well, each person's residential space is typically smaller, resulting in reduced energy use for heating and cooling. Also low in environmental impact are new communications technologies that also use less energy and material. Compare sending a text message to delivering a letter across the country or downloading music rather than producing, delivering, and playing CDs or vinyl recordings. These too are green even if they don't know it.

All these businesses, and others yet to emerge, provide opportunities for investors, employees, and consumers to do tangible things to reduce environmental impacts. Many large and small firms are involved. Some environmentalists argue, of course, that the greenest product is no product at all, and there is some truth to that. However desirable the avoidance of excessive consumerism, clearly we all must eat, cloth ourselves, travel at least some distance by some means, and have shelter and other indoor spaces. We cannot avoid all consumption; the challenge is to be mindful about it. Overall, the shift from doubting industrial society to working to reduce its impacts has significantly changed the character of the Canadian environmental movement.

Universities have also both influenced and adapted in response to the environmental movement. Universities do research relevant to environmental protection by, for example, studying the epidemiological impacts of pollutants, researching the pressures on species at risk, and undertaking a very large variety of other inquiries. Universities offer programs that prepare people for work in environmental protection and that help to create informed and active environmentally aware citizens. Finally, universities increasingly are undertaking cutting-edge efforts to reduce their own institutional impacts and make their own operations more sustainable.

Environmental ideas have affected the full spectrum of university research and teaching. Most disciplines have environmental sub-areas including environmental literature, economics, sociology, politics, philosophy, history, chemistry, and engineering. There are journals in each of these sub-areas to publish new research. Also notable are major university presses such as University of British Columbia Press and MIT Press that have helped to define environmentalism through the publication of environmental books. Most universities in Canada now have environmental studies or science degrees at both the undergraduate and graduate levels. A list of those degrees in Canada is published annually by *AJ: Canada's Environmental Voice*—a listing that is now nine pages long (*Alternatives Journal*, 2012).

More recently, many universities have reduced the environmental footprint of their own operations. They have made existing buildings more energy efficient and added LEED-standard new buildings; they have increased recycling of waste materials in residences, offices, and food operations; and they have improved land management practices. Some have university committees that include administrators, faculty, and students who work to continuously advance sustainability practices.

KEY EVENTS IN CANADIAN ENVIRONMENTAL HISTORY

Many of the events that spur public attention to the environment take place in distant locations. This has become increasingly the case since the 1960s. Previously, conservation advocates focused primarily on protecting and preserving wilderness sites familiar to people and species on which they depended for food, but almost always these were resources, settings, and species with which people were intimately familiar. Conservationists for the most part advocated for the wise use of resources and only sometimes for special, ecologically rich settings (in western Canada, for example).

The first concern of environmentalism, in contrast, was air and water quality and human exposures to toxic chemicals. Environmental activism thus centred on more immediate concerns—for the very air that people were breathing in their homes and neighbourhoods. These local concerns, however, were also pushed forward by distant events, which triggered more intense environmental concern here in Canada. These included, for example, the Love Canal toxic waste disaster in Buffalo, New York; the deadly release of toxic chemicals in Bhopal, India; the meltdown of the Chernobyl nuclear reactor in the Ukraine; the massive oil spill from the Exxon Valdez off Alaska; the Santa Barbara (California) oil well blowout; ongoing smog in Los Angeles; and the Cayahoga River fire near Cleveland, Ohio. Such events spurred core doubts regarding the long-term viability of industrial society and triggered the movement all around the world.

There were, of course, also many distinctively Canadian concerns and events. One of the first issues raised by the emerging Canadian environmental movement was that of phosphates from detergents in the Great Lakes, especially Lake Ontario. Others included the ecological impacts of the W.A.C. Bennett Dam in British Columbia, mercury pollution in Northern Ontario, and a series of Canadian energy mega-projects, especially the James Bay Hydroelectric Project and the Mackenzie Valley Pipeline. Also of great concern was pollution associated with other extractive and resource industries: aerial spraying by the forest industry in Nova Scotia, air pollution associated with the Trail Smelter in British Columbia, and the impacts of nickel smelting in Sudbury.

The aerial spraying of forests in Nova Scotia in the 1970s was an attempt to eradicate the gypsy moth, an invasive species that threatened forests. The spraying had health implications for people and wildlife living in or near the forests. Objections to specific chemicals and to the rules regarding spraying were led by Elizabeth May, who has remained an environmental activist and is today the leader of the GPC. Air pollution in Sudbury related to the processing of nickel ore dates to the early twentieth century when the ore was heated by fires set in huge open pits. The smoke was so thick that people used ropes strung along paths to find their way. Farmers brought legal cases against ore processing emissions in both Trail and Sudbury for crop losses, but even after settlements the pollution continued. Without an environmental movement and a public demanding action, governments rarely acted on pollution concerns.

Interest in Sudbury's sulfur pollution again emerged in the 1950s among scientists within the provincial bureaucracy but came to public attention only later with campaigns regarding acid precipitation led by environmental organizations in the 1970s and 1980s. Concern regarding the impacts of air pollution especially on plant life around Sudbury did, however, contribute to a decision to build the Inco high stack, a structure that approached the scale of the world's largest skyscrapers and that blew the sulfur oxides (and other pollutants) as far away as New England and the Atlantic provinces. Although Inco's emissions contributed to acid deposition in lakes and rivers, emissions controls were put in place only within the context of Canadian government demands regarding the acid rain impacts on Ontario lakes from coal-fired power plants in the US Midwest. An important Canadian environmental group, the Canadian Coalition on Acid Rain (CCAR) with the implicit support of the Canadian government, had been pressing Congress in Washington to take action, but that assertive effort was not an easy sell while Inco was broadcasting similar pollutants from Canada into New England and New York. The long saga of air pollution in Sudbury indicates how crucial it is that the public demand enforced regulations regarding pollution. Only a politically effective environmental movement can offset the political influence of affected industries to make that happen.

Many of the most important environmental issues of the 1970s arose in response to energy mega-projects. These proposed energy developments included the massive James Bay Hydroelectric Project, uranium mines in Saskatchewan, nuclear power plants in Ontario, and the Mackenzie Valley Pipeline. The latter was part of a plan to bring natural gas from Prudhoe Bay in Alaska and the Mackenzie Delta to Alberta and on to the continental US. All these projects were opposed by environmental organizations, and each generated widespread public debate.

However, sharp oil price increases in 1973 and 1979 and questions about supply stability created political counter-pressure from those who feared continued dependence on imported oil. Environmentalists appeared to stand against not only North American energy jobs but also most of the alternatives to dependency. However, an environmentalist response to these concerns came quickly and changed the trajectory of the movement more than could have been anticipated at the time.

Amory Lovins, at the time working for Friends of the Earth in England, coined the phrase "soft energy path" (SEP) to make the case that there are environmentally benign ways to produce the energy we need. He advocated using a combination of improved efficiency and small-scale, renewable energy sources. Also important at this time was the publication of an extensive "jobs and environment" literature that showed that environmentally preferable ways of doing things created more, not fewer jobs than more environmentally damaging economic alternatives. Detailed province-by-province studies of soft path possibilities were produced in Canada.[5]

As noted, Canadians also played an important role in the broader thinking regarding energy, environment, and economy beginning with the publication of *Canada as a Conserver Society* (Science Council of Canada, 1977). The Conserver Society was about "doing more with less," and the thinking behind it led to the World Commission on Environment and Development's *Our Common Future* and the concept of sustainable development. Both publications sought common ground between responsible environmental behaviour and economic growth. Not all environmentalists think that that is possible in the long term.

Another dimension in the evolution of environmentalism was a turn toward global issues. Canada played a role in this shift as well. A very early global conference on climate change was held in 1988 in Toronto, and the important global treaty on ozone depletion was signed in Montreal in 1987 (Benedick, 1991). In the late 1980s as well, there were massive celebrity influenced campaigns to protect tropical rainforests and the endangered species therein. Also important to the emerging shift was the widespread introduction of green products. The concluding sections of this chapter will assess where these changes have taken us.

THREE WAVES OF ENVIRONMENTAL OPINION AND ACTION

Concern for the environment surged in Canada in the late 1960s and has done so twice since. Each time, the level of concern has fallen back, and efforts to address environmental issues have slowed or faded. I have written about this pattern previously, but Mark Winfield in his history of environmental policy in Ontario has pinned the phenomenon down quite precisely, using detailed polling data and other information (Winfield, 2012; Paehlke, 2009). The first wave he places at roughly 1968–75, the second 1985–91, and the third 2004–08.

This pattern is visible in variations in media coverage of environmental issues, in open-ended polling regarding issues of greatest concern to Canadians, in the formation of new citizen environmental organizations or in the growth of established ones, and in the emergence of new environmental issues. Lagging the surges in public opinion by a few years are increased government action on environmental matters, new legislation, and increased environment ministry budgets. These surges also seem to correlate with rising and falling enrollments in environmental studies programs in Canadian universities.

The cycle is reasonably consistent in several regards. It lasts for less than a decade but usually for five or more years. The surge typically correlates with economic good times and declines when serious economic challenges and rising unemployment levels confront society. This only makes sense. People are concerned about the environment, but when their immediate economic situation is threatened and they are worried about feeding their families or meeting mortgage payments, wilderness protection, pollution, and long-term sustainability decline on their list of top priorities for public action or personal attention. The encouraging thing is that environment concerns typically return to high priority status once the economy stabilizes. The pattern is also similar in many countries at the same time.

During the first wave, pollution concerns were widespread, and many wealthy nations took legislative and regulatory action with regard to many chemicals previously released into the air and water. There are newer pollutants that are not yet adequately regulated, and there remain many nations, such as China, where pollution is a grave problem, but in Canada, Europe, and the US, considerable progress has been made. As well, first-wave environmentalists questioned the capacity of the earth to support perpetual growth in economic output and human population. The environmental movement still sought to protect wilderness, but it focused on the overall quality of life in, and durability of, industrial society.

First-wave environmentalists expressed doubts about big cities, about large-scale energy sources including coal, large hydroelectric dams, nuclear power, and offshore drilling, as well as mining, smelting, logging, pulp and paper, and oil refineries. In the 1970s, some environmental activists moved to remote low cost areas in rural British Columbia, northern Ontario, and the Atlantic provinces to live simply on the land. Some are still there. It was far from universal among early environmentalists, but there were undercurrents of doubt about both the capitalist system and industrial society.

The second wave was different in several ways. Its leadership was more professional, and well-established organizations used science and policy analysis. As noted, the second wave was also more oriented to global environmental issues, and the problems addressed increasingly could only be resolved by multilateral, even global action. This was true of acid precipitation, ozone depletion, persistent organic pollutants (POPs), and climate change. All these issues and others led to global environmental treaties, which by the late 1980s and 1990s had become numerous.

The second wave also emphasized policy solutions that encouraged new forms of energy production and new designs for both industrial processes and consumer products. Second-wave solutions de-emphasized "end-of-the-pipe" regulations that sought to keep toxic substances out of the environment. They tried rather to remove toxic substances from production processes and from products themselves or the use of products. Popular support during the second wave was at least as strong as during the first, but the orientation of the movement was less confrontational. The movement's access to power was far greater, and its relationship to industry evolved in many ways, including direct consulting with industry and providing advice to green investment funds.

The third wave has continued these trends. The most pressing issue by far during the third wave has been climate change, the most global of global issues both in terms of impacts and in terms of solutions. Many of the newer environmental organizations operate globally (the climate change group 350.org, for example, has organized *simultaneous* citizen actions in more than 100 countries). The environmental movement has moderated in many ways and has links to a wide array of new green businesses, yet—astonishingly—the government of Canada, of all places given the nation's history of environmental policy innovation and support for multilateralism, has become a leading opponent of effective global action on climate change, the most pressing environmental issue in recent years. It is a challenge to political analysis to assess these unexpected and seemingly contradictory developments.

THE UNEXPECTED EVOLUTION OF ENVIRONMENTALISM

Many Canadian environmental organizations have recently celebrated their fortieth anniversaries. Few people involved in their creation could have anticipated how the environmental movement would evolve. Especially in recent years, environmentalism is indeed very different, and the way it is seen is very different as well. Many 1970s environmentalists had doubts about industrial society, economic growth, cities, and capitalism. Astonishingly, today many see green energy, green infrastructure, and green products to be at the heart of the economy of the future. Most environmentalists also see cities as environmentally preferable places to live, given, for example, the availability of energy-efficient public transit. The days of back-to-the-land hippies appear to be over.

In 2008–09, when economic stimulus was urgently needed to restart economies, what did many governments adopt to fix the economic meltdown? Green stimulus was the order of the day in nations around the world. Few seem to have appreciated that this was one of the more amazing ironies of contemporary history. Nation after nation proposed green stimulus plans to restore economic growth and to build the economies of the future. The intellectual heirs of those who had expressed moral doubts about consumption and who were allegedly, and in some cases really, the enemies of industrial society, had become the most promising actors available to save economies from the errors of capitalism's leading lights (including investment bankers and Wall Street insurance companies whose dubious manoeuvres collapsed global markets).

In China, Japan, and Korea, investments in solar technologies have accelerated. In the US, public buildings have been made more energy efficient, and tax breaks for wind energy and direct federal funding of high speed rail have been offered. In Europe, already good transit systems have been further improved. In Canada, water and sewage systems have been upgraded; and in Ontario, less hostile to renewable energy than the Harper government, solar and wind energy projects have proliferated as a result of an innovative, German-style, feed-in-tariff policy. Even in Saudi Arabia (a nation not run by hippies or environmentalists), massive investments in renewable energy, especially solar, are now in place as a hedge against a future when the oil runs out.

In effect, the turn to green products of environmentalism's second wave has come of age. Environmentalism has become not so much a rejection of industrial society as a basis for the redesign of that economy's processes and products. In recent years, this shift has been particularly dramatic in the realm of food production, a transformation that is changing what we eat and how we grow it, deliver it, and prepare it. Green food initiatives include the "100-mile diet" (mindful of the energy and nutritional costs of long-distance food delivery), organic food, and vegetarian or reduced meat diets. Change has penetrated deeply: organic foods that might be found in small specialty stores during the first wave are today available in every supermarket, including Walmart.

A transformation of energy production is also emerging—especially in Europe, but also, for example, in Ontario and Iowa. As well, new LED lights that use a fraction of the electricity of incandescent bulbs and products made from recycled materials are widely available. More could be done, of course, but the point is that industrial society is adapting. There is a debate within green circles about whether what is being done is anything like enough and whether economic growth and environmental sustainability are in the end compatible (Victor, 2008). Nonetheless, it is a measure of the distance business has come that leading business schools now offer courses on sustainability, Google has invested a billion dollars in renewable energy, and Texas is a leading producer of wind energy.

Given the widening influence of environmentalism what is especially surprising is that today the Canadian federal government considers environmentalism a dirty word. The Harper government is rolling back environmental protection, has opposed action on climate change in international forums, and expresses open hostility to the very idea of environmental protection. This is not only out of step with the opinion of most Canadians but with Canadian history. While the environmental movement has moderated in its approach to business and government, Canada has a government that resists both environmental ideas and environmental science.

Canada has withdrawn from its commitment to the Kyoto Protocol after having consistently failed to comply with this central global agreement, one that it signed and ratified. The government has also undone federal protections for thousands of lakes and waterways and axed funding for a unique undertaking in environmental science, the Experimental Lakes Area (ELA) (Schindler, 2012). Federal ministers have asserted that environmental groups seeking to oppose pipeline projects are funded by foreign interests and are anti-Canadian.[6]

Even though most businesses are now open to environmental protection, there are others that strongly support this hardened attitude. The Harper government has done everything it can to support unlimited tar sands extraction in Alberta, the Conservative Party's core political base. The extraction of tar sands oil produces more greenhouse gases (GHGs) per barrel than conventional oil. Unlimited expansion there could seriously undermine all of the other things that Canadians do to reduce GHG emissions.

How has a government so hostile to protecting the environment gained power, given Canada's history of concern for its environment? One explanation lies in Canada's multi-party system wherein a majority government can be elected by a minority of voters. Regarding climate change, the four parties (NDP, Liberals, BQ, and Greens) that favour climate change action received 59 per cent of the votes in 2011 while the single party that opposes effective action received less than 40 per cent and formed a majority government.

Also limiting effective action on unlimited tar sands expansion in particular is the political reality of oil industry power within Alberta and the central role of provincial governments regarding natural resources (see the discussion in Paehlke, 2008). If Canada is to shift the government's opposition to effective action on climate change, the environmental movement will yet again need to arouse the Canadian public. Even with our historic inclinations on their side, it will not be easy.

CONCLUSIONS

Canadians have always been aware of their environment. Vast and at times harsh, it is not easy to miss. It also abundant in terms of resources, and that has left some Canadians unable to imagine that they could overexploit nature's bounty. Nonetheless, many Canadians came early to conservation concerns a century or more ago and early to the activist environmental movement in the late 1960s. The environmental movement had an urban, broad-based political appeal by adding a focus on pollution, sustainability, and energy policy to earlier concerns with the conservation of wilderness.

Early on, environmental activism was protest oriented. New groups pressed governments to regulate the activities of polluting and resource wasteful industries. Environmental organizations pressed their case continuously, but public concern regarding the environment has waned when economic times become difficult and unemployment increases. The result is a pattern of waves of strong public concern and several periods of environmental policy retrenchment by government. Through these cycles, though, the Canadian environmental movement has evolved continuously and become increasingly professionalized.

Today's environmental movement looks less to stopping emissions one work site at a time and more to encouraging changes in what industries produce and the processes they use to produce it. Some industries continue to resist change, but many have come to see that greener products can also find a large market and solid profits. These include products made from recycled materials, renewable energy installations, hybrid automobiles, transit, energy-efficient appliances, and perhaps most important local, organically grown food. Environmental activists began by picketing factories and objecting to industry, but they are now as likely to be imagining (or producing or buying) products that are changing how the industrial system operates. Forty years from its radical origins, the political side of environmental activism is still there, but the movement is also very much integrated into the fabric of Canada's economy and society.

NOTES

1   This was apparent in the news coverage of both the Copenhagen and Durban climate change conferences. See "Climate Change: 'Canada is the Dinosaur'" at http://www.ipsnews.net/2009/12/climate-change-canada-is-the-dinosaur (accessed January 17, 2013).

2   Such people might, of course, curry favour to get another contract, but often they are just offering their time for a token payment and earn their livings in full-time jobs elsewhere.

3   The best known of these and the founder of the movement is Alice Waters, a founder of California-style cooking. See one of her projects at http://www.edibleschoolyard.org (accessed October 1, 2013).

4   See the website of the Canada Green Building Council: http://www.cagbc.org (accessed February 18, 2013).

5   See Soft Energy Paths special issues of *Alternatives: Perspectives on Society and Environment* beginning with Volume 8 (Summer/Fall, 1978).

6   For a comment on this new pattern, see Paehlke 2013.

REFERENCES AND SUGGESTED READINGS

Alternatives Journal. 2012. *AJ: Canada's Environmental Voice.* 38:21–9.

Benedick, Richard Elliot. 1991. *Ozone Diplomacy*. Cambridge, MA: Harvard University Press.

Berger, Mr. Justice Thomas R. 1977. *Northern Frontier, Northern Homeland*. Ottawa: Ministry of Supply and Services.

Canadian Environmental Law Association. 2013. *Canadian Environmental Law Association: Equity Justice Health*. http://www.cela.ca (accessed February 1, 2013).

Carson, Patrick, and Julia Moulden. 1991. *Green is Gold*. Toronto: HarperBusiness.

Carson, Rachel. 1962. *Silent Spring*. Boston: Houghton Mifflin.

Dauvergne, Peter. 2010. *The Shadows of Consumption: Consequences for the Global Environment*. Cambridge, MA: MIT Press.

Ecology Action Centre. 2013. *Ecology Action Centre: Action is Our Middle Name*, http://www.ecologyaction.ca (accessed February 1, 2013).

Elkington, John, and Julia Hailes. 1988. *The Green Consumer Guide*. London: Victor Gollancz.

Harrison, Kathryn. 1996. *Passing the Buck: Federalism and Canadian Environmental Policy*. Vancouver: University of British Columbia Press.

Lappé, Anna. 2010. *Diet for a Hot Planet*. New York: Bloomsbury.

Leduc, Timothy B. 2010. *Climate Culture Change: Inuit and Western Dialogues with a Warming North*. Ottawa: University of Ottawa Press.

Lipset, Seymour Martin. 1963. *Political Man*. Garden City, NY: Doubleday.

Meadows, Donella H., et al. 1972. *Limits to Growth*. New York: Universe Books.

Paehlke, Robert. 1989. *Environmentalism and the Future of Progressive Politics*. New Haven: Yale University Press.

Paehlke, Robert. 2008. *Some Like It Cold: The Politics of Climate Change in Canada*. Toronto: Between the Lines.

Paehlke, Robert. 2009. "The Environmental Movement in Canada." In *Canadian Environmental Policy and Politics*, ed. Debora L. VanNijnatten and Robert Boardman, 2–13. Toronto: Oxford University Press.

Paehlke, Robert. 2013. "Environmental Protection under Siege." January 31. http://www.alternativesjournal.ca/blogs/aj-editorial-board/environmental-protection-under-siege (accessed January 19, 2013).

Parson, Edward A., ed. 2001. *Governing the Environment: Persistent Challenges, Uncertain Innovations*. Toronto: University of Toronto Press.

Perry, Jr., Thomas L. 1975. "The Skagit Valley Controversy." *Alternatives: Perspectives on Society and Environment* 4 (Spring): 7–11.

Pollution Probe. 2013. *Pollution Probe: Clean Air, Clean Water*. http://www.pollutionprobe.org (accessed January 31, 2013).

Powell, Douglas, and William Leiss. 1997. *Mad Cows and Mother's Milk: The Perils of Poor Risk Communication*. Montreal, Kingston: McGill-Queen's University Press.

Schindler, David. 2012. "Schindler's Pissed." *Alternatives* 38 (September/October): 19–23.

Science Council of Canada. 1977. *Canada as a Conserver Society*. Ottawa: Supply and Services Canada.

Sierra Club Canada. 2013. *Sierra Club Canada: One Earth One Chance*. http://www.sierraclub.ca (accessed January 31, 2013).

Toner, Glen, ed. 2006. *Sustainable Production: Building Canadian Capacity*. Vancouver: University of British Columbia Press.

Victor, Peter A. 2008. *Managing Without Growth: Slower by Design, Not Disaster*. Cheltenham, UK: Edward Elgar.

Wilson, Jeremy. 1998. *Talk and Log: Wilderness Politics in British Columbia*. Vancouver: University of British Columbia Press.

Winfield, Mark S. 2012. *Blue-Green Province*. Vancouver: University of British Columbia Press.

World Commission on Environment and Development. 1987. *Our Common Future*. New York: Oxford University Press.

THIRTEEN

Meaning Frames, Opportunity Structures, and Rights in the Canadian Disability Rights Movement[1]

LISA VANHALA

On November 3, 1980, members of the organization now known as the Council of Canadians with Disabilities (CCD) held a protest on Parliament Hill in Ottawa to assert their demands for recognition in a proposed new constitutional Charter of Rights and Freedoms (the Charter). The protest was the first time that people with a range of disabilities from across Canada gathered together to claim their right to disability equality loudly and publicly. The proposed Charter contained a section explicitly guaranteeing equality rights on some grounds, such as sex and race, but did not accord such protection to the rights of Canadians with disabilities. Previous calls by activists with disabilities to gain a voice in the constitutional process had failed, and the activists' frustration culminated in the demonstration. Yvonne Peters, a long-time activist and human rights lawyer who was present at the protest, stated: "People with disabilities were just beginning to experience the promise of rights, and we were resolved not to let the architects of the Charter diminish or undermine this potential by ignoring our claim to legally recognized equality" (Peters, 2003: 121). After a relentless lobbying effort on the part of these activists and their allies, "disability" as an enumerated ground was added at the eleventh hour to the list of grounds protected by the proposed Charter. Canadians with disabilities can now call on the promise of equality contained within the Charter to combat discrimination and marginalization. The equality promise in the Charter is both a cause and consequence of the emergence of a disability rights consciousness in Canada. It is also the battlefield on which subsequent wars for equality would be waged.

The disability movement has played a transformative role in Canadian society.[2] In the early days of the movement, exclusion of people with disabilities was the norm. An attitude of paternalism dominated disability issues (Neufeldt, 2003). On a societal level, this manifested itself through the existence of disability organizations that excluded persons with disabilities from leadership roles and that promoted a perception of persons with disabilities as helpless, defined by their impairment, and objects of pity or charity. On a policy level, disability was perceived as a health policy, welfare, or social security issue. There was no understanding of disability as an identity associated with human rights or citizenship claims (Peters, 2003; Vanhala, 2009).

Thirty years later the picture is very different. The voice of the disability rights movement is heard in public policy debates at all levels of governance. Disability activists have successfully shifted the policy discourse of disability from one of charity and paternalism to one of equality, dignity, and human rights (Fredman, 2002; Stienstra and Wight-Felske, 2003; Vanhala, 2011a). Inclusive education has become commonplace; public transportation is becoming increasingly accessible; facilities to enable independent living have in many cases replaced the role of segregated institutions; rights to physical integrity, voting rights, and the right to be accommodated in the workplace and in classrooms at all levels of education have been enshrined in law (Beachell, 2011).

Despite these advances, Canadians with disabilities continue to face a wide variety of barriers to inclusion, including physical barriers, prejudicial attitudes, and an unwillingness to accommodate difference. There has been growth in the population of people who have a disability as well as an increase in instances of discrimination based on disability. A Statistics Canada (2006) survey reveals that one out of every seven people in Canada now self-identifies as a person with a disability. There are also several indicators demonstrating that discrimination based on disability is a major problem within Canadian society. In 2010, 372 of the 853 complaints (44 per cent) accepted by the Canadian Human Rights Commission were related to disability, more than any other ground in the Canadian Human Rights Act. The picture at the respective provincial human rights commissions is similar (Vanhala, 2011a). Around the world, people with disabilities are more likely to have poorer health outcomes, lower educational achievements, higher rates of poverty, and higher rates of unemployment than people without disabilities (World Health Organization, 2011).

This chapter traces the evolution of disability rights mobilization in Canada since it first coalesced in the 1960s and 1970s. It explores the shift in the way disability has been conceptualized: from a bio-medical identity focused on an individual's impairment to the emergence of a political identity associated with equality and citizenship rights. I rely on the theoretical tools of frame analysis to trace this shift (Benford and Snow, 2000; Goffman, 1974). Framing refers to the signifying work or process of constructing meaning. A situation or event may be defined or perceived differently depending on the meanings attached to it. McAdam and Snow note that "applied to social movements, the concept of framing problematizes the meanings associated with relevant events, activities, places and actors, suggesting that those meanings are typically contestable and negotiable and thus open to debate and differential interpretation" (2010: 317). In this chapter, I explore the ways in which different frames shape social movement organizations and influence the types of strategies deployed and the issues on which they act (Vanhala, 2011a).

This explanation based on frame analysis is not incompatible with accounts that focus on resources or on "opportunity structures" (be they political or legal). However, two assumptions of opportunity structure theorists will be challenged. First, as Ellen Ann Andersen (2005) has pointed out, these "structures" are not objective features of the political and legal landscape: they must be perceived by activists to be deployed and access to them is often unequal. Some groups and classes of people are privileged by "opportunity structures" and others are excluded. Second, opportunity structure theorists have tended to see the relationship between "structures" and "agents" as unidirectional: the former impact on the choices and activities of the latter. However, agents can also influence the nature and shape of "opportunity structures." Structures and agents are dependent upon each other; they are recursively related or mutually constitutive (Giddens, 1984). A framing approach helps to account for why "political opportunity structures" or "legal opportunity structures" sometimes shape mobilizing behaviour, and why, at other times, they might be challenged or fundamentally transformed by social movements (Andersen, 2005; Vanhala, 2012).

Disability activism offers a rich case study of social movement mobilization. It illustrates many of the dynamics that have been theorized by new social movement scholars, and the literature in the field of disability studies can illuminate the emphases and lacunae of specific theoretical approaches in political science. Listening to the voices of disability activists can inform our broader understandings of the way Canadian politics functions. It helps to highlight which identities are taken for granted and which have been ignored for too long in the literature on social movements and group politics.

FROM THE MEDICAL MODEL TO THE SOCIAL MODEL OF DISABILITY

In Canada in the 1960s and 1970s, disability activists began to transform the idea of being a "person with a disability" from that of an individual's biomedical impairment to their identity as someone who is largely discriminated against by a society that is structurally and culturally biased against various forms of difference (Neufeldt, 2003; Peters, 2003). This has since come to be known as the "social (or rights) model of disability" and it is based on an understanding of "disability" as a socially constructed status. Instead of simply requiring conformity to the able-bodied norm, the social model requires some adjustment of that norm to afford genuine equality to people with disabilities. According to the social model, members of society (e.g., government, employers, and service providers) have a positive duty to make reasonable adjustments to accommodate people with disabilities to remedy these biases (Lepofsky, 1998; Malhotra, 2003). The goal of the disability movement under the social model is to influence public policy to achieve the inclusion of persons with disabilities in all spheres of life and to spread an understanding of the relevance of rights within the community.

The shift from a medical or charity model of disability to a rights-based understanding can be at least partially explained through social movement diffusion processes: for at least some activists, the emergence of a disability rights consciousness can be traced back to knowledge or participation in other anti-discrimination organizations, such as the women's movement, the consumer rights movement, the trade unionist movement, or the American civil rights movement (Vanhala, 2011a). Several activists commenting on the early period of the movement described the emergence of a rights-consciousness across the community and on a personal level:

> I think people with disabilities in Canada had to learn more generally that disabled people have rights. [And] that the Charter can have an impact on the quality of life for people with disabilities; that certain kinds of barriers and resistance or rejection can be understood as discriminatory acts that the Charter would prohibit . . . So we had a learning curve of re-understanding our disadvantaged position in society on a rights dimension. Because at one time, as a group, we largely accepted that the fault was in us, that we had to change, rather than social attitudes and institutional structures. (Cited in Vanhala, 2011a: 51)

> I was involved in some women's organizations before I got involved with disability issues . . . I have to say that it was a growth experience, while I really understood a feminist approach to issues in various aspects of life, it took me a while to come up with a disability analysis. That's partly because my experience was to persevere and overcome and to cope as an individual

and not make too much of a fuss about your disability. It took awhile for me to come to terms with [the fact that] it's not just me as an individual but it's also a societal issue and the barriers I'm encountering are not necessarily ones that I personally can solve . . . I put the two things together; my feminist experience and disability issues and realized they had many things in common. (Cited in Vanhala, 2011a: 52)

This process of consciousness-raising was the result of, and in turn fed into, a continual evolution in the paradigm of disability away from the medical and toward the social and political.

There are several implications to understanding disability through the social model. The first concerns the focus and understandings of "authority" among organizations and practitioners operating in the sphere of disability (Chivers, 2008). In the late 1970s and early 1980s, the primary concern of most impairment-specific charities was to fund and promote research to prevent disability or to offer interventions to "fix," "treat," or "cope" with it (Neufeldt, 2003). The "authorities" of disability within these organizations tended to be doctors, service providers, and/or parents or carers. In contrast, according to the social model, it is people with disabilities who best understand their own conditions, living situations, and needs. The social model promotes the idea that those with disabilities should make their own decisions. This approach does not preclude the provision of support within a context of autonomy (Chivers, 2008). Traci Walters of Independent Living Canada writes:

The Independent Living [IL] philosophy and movement were developed as a response to traditional models of service delivery. In general, society viewed disability as a deficit and people with disabilities were considered "sick" and in need of care. Unlike traditional paradigms, the IL model encourages people with disabilities to take control over their own lives, examine options, make their own decisions, take risks, and even to make mistakes in the learning process. The IL philosophy encourages self-determination and self-actualization and promotes disability pride. (Walters, 2011: 13)

A key mantra of the movement has been "a voice of our own." This refers to the right to autonomy at the individual level, in everyday decisions, and at the collective level, running disability organizations and exercising self-determination at the highest levels of decision-making across all policy sectors, including transport, health, welfare, education, foreign policy, and immigration.

The social model has also had an impact on the construction of the idea of "cross-disability membership" meaning frames (Vanhala, 2009). When disability was viewed through the lens of the medical model, impairment-specific organizations appeared to have little in common. Each individual's impairment—whether it be paralysis, blindness, deafness, cerebral palsy, obesity, or psychiatric illness—requires different medical or rehabilitative treatments, research, or services, so they were not perceived as a group; rather, they were seen as heterogeneous populations. With the shift to the social model of disability, however, the focus moved from curing or treating a myriad of impairments to the shared experience of exclusion. A more united voice of people with all types of disabilities began to be heard.

This re-articulation of disadvantage as shared discrimination has strengthened the third focus of the social model: the goal of removing barriers. These barriers may be physical—for example, the stairs to enter a building, narrow doorways, or seats that are too small—or they might be attitudinal, for example, prejudice, assumptions about capabilities, or pity (Chivers, 2008). This links to the associated concept of accommodation. The vision of creating a "barrier-free society" through the positive duty of accommodation creates an umbrella frame, one that addresses the discrimination faced by persons with different disabilities. The accommodations needed to break down barriers vary widely and could include the provision of braille or assistive technology for persons who are blind or visually impaired, access to sign-language interpretation for the deaf, or ramps for wheelchair users (Lepofsky and Bickenbach, 1985). Although these are all very different technologies and solutions, the language and vision of a "barrier-free society" plays a key role in uniting the disability community. One activist used this as a discursive tactic when lobbying for anti-discrimination legislation in Ontario: "I loved when my buddy who is deaf talked about braille. I loved when someone in a wheelchair talked about sign language. I, who am blind and can walk, would talk about ramps. It united us all together and it was very powerful" (cited in Vanhala, 2011a: 53).

THE EVOLUTION OF DISABILITY ORGANIZATIONS

Interpretive frames also influence, and in turn are influenced by, changes in social movement organizations. In the early 1970s, there were four large disability advocacy organizations in Canada: the Canadian National Institute for the Blind (CNIB), the Canadian Mental Health Association (CMHA), the Canadian Association for the Mentally Retarded (CAMR, now known as the Canadian Association for Community Living, CACL), and the Canadian Rehabilitation Council for the Disabled (CRCD). The "big four" dominated the policy agenda, developed community services, and became increasingly professionalized as the need for services (and hence funding) grew. Alfred Neufeldt argues that, as the services run by these organizations expanded, "the ability of these organizations to effectively advocate for change in public policy on behalf of their members was compromised" (2003: 23). These service or charity organizations all relied to some extent on a paradigm of "pity" and "sickness" to raise money from the public. While some of these organizations had an embryonic commitment to notions of equality, charitable and rehabilitation intentions remained the dominant drivers.

While there has been a long history of self-advocacy in disability organizations dating back to the 1920s—particularly among the deaf community and several consumer organizations of blind and visually impaired people—the 1970s saw an explosion in the number and memberships of grassroots organizations comprised of and led by persons with disabilities themselves (Watters, 2003). In Canada, the term "consumer organization" began (and continues) to be used to distinguish those organizations politically controlled and/or managed by people with disabilities from the older charity-minded organizations. An activist in Canada explained the use of the term: "we had adopted the word 'consumer' from [Ralph] Nader's movement in the States: a way to have power even though you are reliant on others to produce goods and services" (cited in Vanhala, 2011a: 55).

The consumer groups distinguished themselves from charity, service provision, and recreational organizations (which grassroots activists coined organizations "for" persons with disabilities) and claimed a voice of their own on the policy stage, instead of being spoken for by rehabilitation organizations. Through the 1980s, the principles of the social model of disability began to spread from these grassroots organizations; this diffusion led to the emergence of new organizations as well as changes to the governance and policies of some (but not all) of the old-guard charity groups. The first cross-disability self-advocacy organizations emerged in Manitoba, Alberta, and Saskatchewan between 1976 and 1978 and subsequently allied with each other (Driedger, 2011). It was within these groups that Canadians with disabilities began to challenge the then dominant view of disability as a medical defect or pathological limitation lying with the individual.

The emergence of provincial organizations led to the founding of one of the key organizations, known since 1994 as the Council of Canadians with Disabilities (CCD) but at the time called the Coalition of Provincial Organizations of the Handicapped (COPOH). COPOH grew through the 1970s and 1980s and brought together its member groups in national forums, which focused on issues such as the right to employment, transportation, and independent living (Armstrong, 2003). The organizations lobbied during the late 1970s for an amendment to the Canadian Human Rights Act to

include protection for people with disabilities. In 1981, COPOH also participated in the federal all-party Parliamentary Committee on the Disabled and
Handicapped, which was appointed during the International Year of Disabled
Persons to identify the challenges facing those with a disability and making
suggestions for reform. The parliamentary committee released its report,
Obstacles, and made recommendations on several important policy issues
including human rights, income security, employment, technical aids and devices, transportation, and communications (Torjman, 2011).

By the mid-1970s, the chasm between the ethos of advocacy and service
organizations was growing. Some service organizations also began to question the incompatibility between "pity" images used to raise funds, on one
hand, and attempts to change public attitudes toward disabled persons to
perceiving them as equally valued members of society on the other. CACL
was one of the first "old-guard" organizations to try a different approach
to fundraising: it explicitly rejected the use of the "pity" paradigm in its
strategic plan for the 1970s, began to campaign against institutionalization of
people with intellectual impairments, and promoted instead the idea of living
within the community (Neufeldt, 2003). According to Diane Richler, who
worked at CACL for 30 years, "[m]any families responded very positively to
the concept of community living, but others were fearful that if institutions
disappeared there would not be adequate care for their family members. Most
professionals were extremely critical of suggestions to dismantle the existing
system" (Richler, 2011). This resistance gradually lessened and, over the next
few years, the organization moved toward a social model understanding of
disability.

This mutability was rare at the time, and during the 1970s and 1980s, many
grassroots organizations emerged out of frustration with those traditional organizations that did not follow CACL's example (Stienstra and Wight-Felske,
2003). These new organizations began to lobby for, and received, government
funding instead of relying on charitable contributions, which they felt posed
certain ideological problems for the emerging movement. This rejection of
charitable funding is difficult to explain without reliance on an understanding
of meaning frames, that is, the growing importance of the rights model of
disability to disability activists. Turning back to theoretical explanations of
social movement mobilization, theorists working in the resource mobilization
tradition would have difficulty accounting for a rejection of funding from particular sources. Through the analysis of meaning frames, and a deconstruction
of the implications of the social model in particular, it is possible to account for
both the shifts in the universe of disability organizations as well as the changes
within particular organizations regarding their governance structures, service
delivery strategies, policy goals, and sources of resources. Only through

understanding the shifting of meaning frames in the construction of the concept of disability can this be logically explained (Vanhala, 2011a).

While CCD is, in many ways, considered the national voice on disability rights issues, the hegemony of its interpretive frames as representative of the disability community across Canada has not been unchallenged. Some women found that, in the early days of the movement, the diverse identities and differing agendas were less accommodated in the mainstream movement than they are today. In the mid-1980s, women with disabilities began organizing to identify and discuss the issues important in their lives. A feminist activist describes how she was pushed by her experience of exclusion in both the feminist sphere and the disability community to mobilize on the basis of that experience of exclusion in a different way.

> I had learned that most of the political work that I had done before was suddenly not accessible to me. I didn't stop being a feminist and a trade unionist, but I did start using a wheelchair; and my former world had too many stairs and was suddenly closed to me and beyond my reach. The women's movement didn't really "get it" about access and was suddenly also pretty much inaccessible to me. I turned to the disability community to do my political work and, soon after, I realized that the disability community just didn't "get it" around women's issues. I turned there because I figured that at least it would be accessible. It seemed that these organizations, which were mostly dominated by men weren't interested in doing—or didn't have enough time or money to do—anything about an issue like mothering as a woman with a disability or about the violence in our lives. (Meister, 2003: 227)

At an early meeting held in Ottawa in 1985, six areas of concern to women with disabilities were identified: self-image, employment, violence, health, sexuality, and mothering. This meeting, and a founding conference held in 1987, signified the birth of the DisAbled Women's Network Canada (DAWN-RAFH Canada) and the establishment of their mission to end the poverty, isolation, discrimination, and violence experienced by disabled women.

DISABILITY RIGHTS AND THE LAW

While there are several legal mechanisms providing protection from discrimination on grounds of mental and physical disability in Canada, arguably the most significant is the equality guarantee contained in section 15(1) of the

Charter: "Every individual is equal before and under the law and has the right to the equal protection and equal benefit of the law without discrimination and, in particular, without discrimination based on race, national or ethnic origin, colour, religion, sex, age or mental or physical disability." The equality guarantee came into effect in 1985 and its protections are meant to be interpreted in a purposive sense, that is, applied in a way that will serve to correct the injustices they were intended to rectify. For more than a decade, Canada remained the only state in the world that specifically granted equality protections to people with disabilities in its constitution.

The paradigm shift in the framing of disability occurred at roughly the same time as the Charter was being debated and developed by Canadian law makers (Armstrong, 2003). Yvonne Peters, who has been involved in the disability rights movement for 30 years, writes of the period:

> It is important to understand that the struggle to obtain constitutional recognition was more than just another political manoeuvre for people with disabilities. Indeed, it was a watershed event that occurred at a time when people with disabilities were just beginning to construct a new vision and analysis of the disability experience . . . The disability rights movement rejected the medical model of disability, and argued that it was social barriers and prejudices that created disabilities. The goal of the movement was to secure the right of persons with disabilities to self-determination, individual autonomy, and the opportunity to participate in society as full and equal citizens . . . This shift to a rights-based analysis therefore, represents a profound and decisive turning point in the history of persons with disabilities. (Peters, 2003: 122)

As discussed at the beginning of this chapter, when the text of section 15 was presented to Parliament in October 1980, "disability" was not listed as an enumerated ground meriting protection. The original draft of the provision did, however, include a list of other protected classes, for example race, national or ethnic origin, religion, age, or sex (Armstrong, 2003; Lepofsky and Bickenbach, 1985).

The disability movement applied constant pressure to consider disability rights a constitutional issue on the Trudeau government during the constitutional negotiations. The government was resistant to adding disability as an enumerated ground. Justice Minister Jean Chrétien argued against trying to solve "social problems" through constitutional amendment and argued that legislative flexibility could be better achieved through statutory human rights codes. The government was also concerned that the term "disability" was too vague and required further specification and elaboration, which it claimed was not appropriate at the constitutional level. Moreover, the government argued that the cost implications of including disability as a protected ground, and services this might entail, were a concern. Armstrong writes: "Rather than include disability as a prohibited ground of discrimination, the federal government decided that the list of grounds in the section should be open ended and that, at an appropriate time, the courts could read in disability as an analogous ground" (2003: 53).

COPOH, CAMR, and the CNIB challenged these claims. Many of these challenges lay in comparisons to other enumerated grounds. They argued that "disability" was no more difficult to define than other terms, such as "religion"; they held that there was little evidence to back up the cost argument and that disability was the only proposed ground of discrimination to which the cost-benefit analysis was being applied (Lepofsky and Bickenbach, 1985). Moreover, they argued that:

> Unless society's value of freedom from discrimination was itself equally applied, the handicapped would become a second-class minority, one for which discriminatory treatment as being seen to be of less significance, or less in need of prohibition, than [for] other minorities. (Lepofsky and Bickenbach, cited in Armstrong, 2003: 54)

The result of the protracted lobbying effort was the inclusion of "disability" as one of the enumerated grounds in section 15 of the Charter. Peters identifies three consequences of the successful disability charter lobby:

> First, it solidified the establishment of a national disability rights movement that remains active today. As Laurie Beachell puts it, "The Charter lobby was the coming of age for the disability rights movement." Second, it symbolized the shift from disability as a charity concept to legitimizing disability as a status entitled to rights. Third, it provided a legal framework and another mechanism to enable people with disabilities to continue to fight for justice and equality. (Peters, 2003: 134)

The evidence suggests that the process of developing and implementing the Charter accelerated the rights consciousness of disability groups (Peters 2003; Vanhala 2009, 2011a). The exclusion of "disability" as a facet of identity that is worthy of constitutional protection prompted outrage and action.

Once constitutional acknowledgment was achieved, this further bolstered the process of seeking equality. This highlights a recursive relationship between recognition within political and legal opportunity structures and the development of a rights-based identity (Vanhala, 2011a). Rights frames can simultaneously influence "opportunity structures" and collective identity by altering how individuals and groups perceive themselves and by changing how individuals and groups are perceived or treated by others (Smith, 1998; Engel and Munger, 2003).

The shift to the social model of disability, the corresponding emergence and empowerment of grassroots organizations led by people with disabilities, and the entrenchment of specific rights protections in the Constitution all paved the path for the movement's political strategies, including lobbying and strategic litigation. Of particular focus here is the mobilization of the legal framework established in the Charter. From the mid-1980s onward, several landmark legal cases taken by some of the key disability rights organizations continued to shape the equality landscape in Canada. But the influence was not unidirectional. In many ways these cases also played an important role in shaping the disability rights movement and the organizations that compose it. This discussion focuses on the campaigning around three issues—physical integrity rights, the right to vote, and the politics of disability and death—as representative of the types of multi-faceted activity the movement has undertaken.

Physical Integrity Rights

In 1986, a landmark early disability rights case was decided based not on Charter protections but with a substantive equality dimension nonetheless. The case of *E. (Mrs.) v. Eve*, which addressed the wish of a mother to sterilize her daughter who had an intellectual disability, had profound implications for the disability movement and for CAMR specifically. At the heart of the case was a group of people with intellectual disabilities. Through the early 1980s, CAMR was becoming more inclusive of the constituency for whom it spoke. Part of this involved the establishment of a body to advise the organization's board. This was known as the Consumer Advisory Committee and was composed of people with intellectual disabilities. When the *Eve* case came to CAMR's attention, the board, made up of parents and professionals, considered whether it should apply for leave to intervene before the Supreme Court. Despite a growing rights-consciousness within the organization in the early 1980s, the board was sharply divided on the issues in the *Eve* case, namely, whether consent over sterilization should be exercised by Eve herself or whether the power to make the decision should fall to her mother. In the face of indecision by the board, the Consumer Advisory Committee developed a strong rights-protection perspective on what should be argued in *Eve*, retained counsel, and applied for leave to intervene on their own behalf (Vanhala, 2011a: 73). Their participation and eventual victory had a profound effect on the organization and on the movement. A senior staff member described it in the following terms:

> I think that was a really important moment for the organization. First, to recognize that people with intellectual disabilities themselves had a clear voice and that voice should be supported right up to the Supreme Court of Canada. And also the idea that this isn't just about an organization; it's about a movement and there's a difference, and ultimately for the movement this was an important case and if this organization couldn't take the lead it could support another group to do that. (Cited in Vanhala, 2011a: 87)

The Supreme Court unanimously ruled in *E. (Mrs.) v. Eve* that a mother did not have the authority to consent to a non-therapeutic sterilization procedure for her daughter with an intellectual disability. The judgment stated:

> The importance of maintaining the physical integrity of a human being ranks high in our scale of values, particularly as it affects the privilege of giving life. I cannot agree that a court can deprive a woman of that privilege for purely social or other non-therapeutic purposes without her consent. The fact that others may suffer inconvenience or hardship from failure to do so cannot be taken into account. (*E.(Mrs.) v. Eve*)

It was also a significant case in terms of the politics of recognition: the law acknowledged that people who had been excluded and disenfranchised could speak for themselves in the nation's highest court (McCallum, 2011). Barbara Goode, then chair of the Consumer Advisory Committee, describes the victory and its importance:

> It was the first time ever that people with mental handicaps have taken a case to the highest court in Canada . . . Before people were just given the operation. We were not always given the choice. It is now against the law to be sterilized without you saying whether you want it or not. . . . The nine judges agreed with us that Eve should not be sterilized without her saying her own decision or choice . . . It was a great day for all of us. It

tells everyone that people with a mental handicap can make up
their minds given the proper information, and the information is
explained to them. (Barbara Goode, cited in Park et al., 2003: 191)

The *Eve* case had several radiating effects within CAMR and the disability rights movement more generally (Vanhala, 2009, 2011b). First, it
empowered people with disabilities within the organization and reinforced
the legitimacy of their voices within the governance processes. While the
consumers were developing their case in *Eve*, they also began pushing the
local, provincial, and national associations to change their names: they
found the name "Association for the Mentally Retarded" offensive and
wanted the organization to adopt a "non-labelling" name. The re-naming
was initially resisted, but at the annual general meeting in 1985, a group of
consumers and their allies walked out in protest and the name was changed
in 1986 to the Canadian Association for Community Living (Park et al.,
2003). The adoption of a new name was more than just a superficial change:
the ideology of the organization began to change as well. Second, there was
a broader impact on levels of rights and legal consciousness as new legal
battles emerged out of participation in the case. One of the members of the
Eve committee went on to be a leader in a legal battle in Alberta on behalf
of persons who had been sterilized against their will or knowledge under the
Sexual Sterilization Act of 1928. Third, there were multi-organizational field
effects: a group of self-advocates involved in the *Eve* intervention went on
to found People First, an organization made up of "people who have been
labelled intellectually disabled." (Park et al., 2003). The goals of People
First are to promote equality and to speak on behalf of others who have
been "labelled."

The lasting impact of the *Eve* case highlights how the results of actions
undertaken by social movement organizations are not always expected. The
process and results of lobbying and litigation can shape individual organizations and the movement more broadly in unanticipated ways. The *Eve* case
entrenched the principle of autonomy and self-determination and granted
legitimacy to the voices and choices of people with disabilities.[3] It also led to a
growing recognition among the movement that legal tactics could be used to
influence social change.

The Right to Vote

Participation in political life is a fundamental right of any citizen in a
democratic society, and, arguably, the most fundamental of the participation
rights is the right to vote. Laurie Beachell, the national coordinator of CCD,

highlighted this in a recent affidavit before the Canadian Human Rights Tribunal:

> Voting is a fundamentally important right in a free and demo-
> cratic society. For all Canadians, including Canadians with dis-
> abilities, voting is one of the most important ways to participate
> in the political process and have a voice in political, social and
> economic issues of the day. Voting is an essential act by which all
> Canadians, including Canadians with disabilities, exercise their
> rights and obligations as citizens of this country. Given the fun-
> damental importance of voting, barriers that people with disabili-
> ties encounter when they attempt to exercise their right to vote
> seriously undermine their status as equal citizens in Canadian
> society. (*Hughes v. Elections Canada*)

For Canadians with disabilities, access to the vote has not always been a given. In 1981, *Obstacles,* the report of the House of Commons Special Committee on the Disabled and Handicapped (see Torjman, 2011), showed that there were many barriers to voting. Since then, even as the franchise has been extended to some, barriers in the electoral process, be they physical or attitudinal forms of exclusion, continue to make it difficult or impractical for Canadians with disabilities to exercise their right to vote.

In the late 1980s and early 1990s, Canadian disability rights organizations played a pivotal role in pushing for legislative reform to enable full and equal access to all federal programs for people with disabilities. Until 1988, a mental capacity requirement meant that some people with mental health disabilities could not vote in federal elections. Hearings in the House of Commons in the early 1980s addressed the inaccessibility of polling stations and began a process of reform (Prince, 2004a). In October 1988, the Canadian Disability Rights Council (an organization devoted specifically to strategic litigation) won a landmark case against Elections Canada (the agency responsible for conducting federal elections) in the Federal Court (*Canadian Disability Rights Council v. Canada*). The organization challenged the provision in the Canada Elections Act that excluded from voting any person "restrained of his liberty of movement or deprived of the management of his property by reason of mental disease . . . ." Madam Justice Reed held that the provision was invalid because it conflicted with section 3 of the Charter, which guarantees the right to vote of "every citizen of Canada." Following the Federal Court decision, a Royal Commission on Electoral Reform was appointed to ensure that citizens are able to exercise their right to vote, to access their polling stations, and to be accommodated in the enumerating and voting process (Rioux and Frazee, 1999). Parliament then chose to repeal the portion of the Elections Act that violated the constitutional guarantee. Since 1992, mental capacity is no longer a basis for voter disqualification in Canada in federal elections. Bill C-78, An Act to Amend Certain Acts with Respect to Persons with Disabilities, effected reforms to several federal acts including those governing elections. The drafting of the legislation was based on direct consultation with the disability community, particularly the Canadian Disability Rights Council. It guaranteed full access to the franchise for persons with physical and sensory disabilities when the architectural accessibility of polling stations—for example, the requirement to provide level access—became mandatory (Vickers and Valentine, 1996).

In principle, voting rights for people with disabilities have been entrenched since this time. In practice, the picture is mixed. In 2008, Peter Hughes, who uses a walker, attempted to vote in two separate elections at a polling station that did not provide access to people with disabilities. He filed a formal complaint to Elections Canada and to the Canadian Human Rights Commission alleging that Elections Canada had discriminated against him by not ensuring that his polling station was accessible. The case was referred to the Canadian Human Rights Tribunal. CCD participated in the case of *Hughes v. Elections Canada* as an interested party. The tribunal found that Elections Canada did have adequate policies in place to ensure equal access to all polling stations and the right to accessible voting but that the policies had not been properly implemented. The decision set out an order that requires Elections Canada to undertake several activities to avoid similar rights violations. Prince has aptly termed this cycle of challenging, developing, and implementing a disability rights approach in policy "the déjà vu discourse of disability" (2004b: 66).

The Politics of Disability and Death

While the advancement of equality in law and in practice has been the focus of the disability rights movement's proactive work, the organizations discussed here have also had to devote significant resources and time to reactive campaigns. In particular, debates and legal cases addressing the right to die have been the focus of much of the Canadian disability rights movement's attention. The literature on "opportunity structures" is unable to account for this distinction between proactive and reactive campaigning activity (Vanhala, 2011a). A framing analysis approach takes us some way in accounting for why some frames evoke a strong defensive response by activists. Three legal cases discussed exemplify this dynamic.

In April 2011, the British Columbia Civil Liberties Association (BCCLA) filed a lawsuit to challenge the legislation that makes physician-assisted suicide by terminally ill individuals a criminal offence. The case involved, among others, Gloria Taylor, a woman with Lou Gehrig's disease or amyotrophic lateral sclerosis (ALS), who sought to have the option of choosing to end her own life. Many elements of the case parallel the constitutional challenge that Sue Rodriguez, who also had ALS, took to the Supreme Court of Canada unsuccessfully 20 years earlier.

In both cases, the Court and organizational interveners had to confront the issue of physician-assisted suicide. Both Rodriguez and Taylor wanted to control the circumstances of their deaths. However, by the time they would reach a point of no longer being able to enjoy their lives, they would not be able to end it without assistance. With the legal claim, each plaintiff hoped to be able to allow a medical practitioner to set up a means to end her life at a time of her choosing. While suicide is not prohibited by the relevant criminal statutes, providing assistance to commit suicide is. The logic underpinning the equality argument was that an able-bodied person would be able to control the manner of their death if they so choose and that a person who is disabled could not benefit from the same option.

The issue of assisted-death has proved difficult for the disability rights movement: it has led to divisions among and within organizations and resulted in changes to policy positions in some of the key organizations (Vanhala, 2011b). The challenge lies in the balancing of two conflicting issues, both of which can be understood to be compatible with a disability rights policy agenda. On one side is the issue of valuing people with disabilities and over-coming prejudices regarding quality of life. CCD and CACL's joint factum in the *Carter v. Canada (Attorney General)* case made this point:

> Both organizations have long championed the right of persons with disabilities to make decisions for themselves. It has only been with the most profound concern therefore, and following a thorough process of consideration, that they come before the Court to argue against striking down the Criminal Code prohibitions against assisted suicide and euthanasia . . . . The notion that "it is better to be dead than disabled" can be very powerful, particularly for someone who has not yet experienced disability or who is surrounded by persons who reinforce this negative stereotype. (Factum of the intervenors, CCD and CACL, in *Carter v. Canada [Attorney General]*)

On the other side were those, such as the British Columbia Council for People with Disabilities (BCCPD) in *Rodriguez* and the BCCLA in *Carter* that supported the plaintiffs' argument that denial of the right to assisted-suicide constitutes discrimination based on disability and denial of personal autonomy in making end-of-life decisions. An affidavit of Leslie LaForest in the *Carter* case argued:

> Who has the right to say when and how an ill individual dies? Should it be left to society, comprised mostly of people who are not dying? Or should it be left to the ill person who is, simply put, doing the actual dying? It is my fervent belief that no one has the right to tell me how, when and where my dying ought to occur. (Affidavit of Leslie LaForest in *Carter v. Canada* [*Attorney General*])

These cases dealt with vital questions of life, death, and freedom of choice and ignited public and social movement debate on the issues. The 1993 *Rodriguez* case had relatively little policy influence; the provisions in the Criminal Code that were at the heart of the case remained. Nonetheless, the case had an important influence on the disability movement; it created a space whereby the different rights-based arguments for and against physician-assisted suicide were articulated. In the *Carter* case, the British Columbia Supreme Court judgment declared the section of the Criminal Code that prevents physician-assisted death invalid and gave Parliament one year to draft new legislation on physician-assisted dying. However, before reading this as a fundamental shift in policy, it is worth noting that the *Carter* case is still in motion with the federal government appealing the decision of the British Columbia Supreme Court. It seems likely that the case will eventually be addressed by the Supreme Court of Canada. Also important to note is the fact that it was a civil liberties group rather than a disability rights one that was the driving force behind this case. This highlights again the reactive nature of the involvement of disability rights groups in these debates.

The series of *R. v. Latimer* cases also had the effect of pulling organizational attention toward rights surrounding death. Robert Latimer was charged with the first degree murder of Tracy, his 12-year-old daughter with cerebral palsy. He argued that he was driven to commit murder by his desire to spare his daughter from continued pain and suffering. In two cases that reached the Supreme Court, which dealt with various factual, legal, and procedural issues, Latimer unsuccessfully argued a "defence of necessity" and was convicted of second degree murder. The *Latimer* case thrust the issue of euthanasia on to the public agenda in an unprecedented way. The high-profile nature and subsequent public debate took the disability rights community by surprise. A CCD activist said:

> The public response to that murder astounded our community. We could not believe the ways in which Tracy was portrayed, as less than human, as having no rights. And the public seemed

> to portray Robert Latimer as the victim in this case, not Tracy. It was a real shock to our community that we had come such a little way . . . the *Latimer* case consumed us for about five years. I never thought we would have to spend that kind of energy on a case like that. And it still comes back every once and a while. (Cited in Vanhala, 2011a: 131)

After years of concerted campaigning for the right to live, work, and participate equally in society, disability rights activists were taken aback by the "relentless, passionate, public-wide debate on the fundamental issue of whether it is legally and morally acceptable for a father to take the life of his severely disabled daughter" (Peters, 2003: 22).

Disability rights activists, going against overwhelming public sympathy for Latimer's plight, lobbied intensively and intervened in the legal cases to encourage the Court to consider Latimer's actions and arguments in the light of the Charter's equality guarantees (Peters, 2003). From 1996 to 2002, CCD published an online newsletter called "Latimer Watch" that presented the movement's perspective on issues arising from the case. Interestingly, the *Latimer* case influenced CCD's position on the *Rodriguez* case discussed above. A long-time activist said:

> Half way through [the *Rodriguez* case] along came the murder of Tracy Latimer by Robert Latimer . . . and CCD reversed its position on Sue Rodriguez and basically said, people are so devalued and people are so vulnerable at certain points in their life that we cannot support assisted-suicide because we believe people will make choices for others in their life. (Cited in Vanhala, 2011a: 132)

The Court decision did not focus on the rights questions and, instead, strictly interpreted the "defence of necessity" provision to overturn Latimer's arguments. The Court found: "[t]he defence of necessity is narrow and of limited application in criminal law. In this case, there was no air of reality to that defence." *Latimer* reinforced the law and disability advocates lauded the Court's treatment of Tracy Latimer's murder like any other murder case (Armstrong, 2003). While many see the *Latimer* case as a victory, ultimately, like the *Rodriguez* case, it had few direct policy implications that really advanced the movement's agenda.

In the literature on social movements, there is much discussion of how social movement organizations can play a pivotal role as agenda-setters, influencing the topics to be debated in the public and policy sphere. In the area of the politics of death, however, disability organizations often have to respond in a reactive manner to national developments, spending resources dealing with issues they would rather not have to address. The term "opportunity" is a misnomer in these cases.

FIGHTING FOR EQUALITY ON OTHER FRONTS: PROVINCIAL LEGISLATION AND THE UNCRPD

While battles continue to be waged on the national stage, disability rights activists have also targeted the structures that shape access and equality on other levels of governance. Activists have to negotiate the realities of federalism and multi-level governance in policy areas that range from citizenship to education, from service provision to accommodation, from immigration to health. Campaigns for provincial legislation seeking to end exclusion in the public and private sectors have emerged at the local level. Provincial legislation focusing on disability equality was adopted in Ontario and Manitoba thanks in part to intensive lobbying campaigns by disability rights organizations. In Ontario in the 1990s, a group of disability rights activists began to advocate for a barrier-free society (Chivers, 2008). Largely as a result of lobbying by the Ontarians with Disabilities Act (ODA) committee over many years, the Ontario government adopted the Accessibility for Ontarians with Disabilities Act (AODA) 2005, which aims to develop and implement accessibility standards with respect to goods and services, facilities, buildings, and employment. The work of the movement did not end with the adoption of the act. The ODA committee reformed at that point and became the AODA Alliance; it continues to monitor and campaign on human rights issues and for strong effective implementation of the act. Manitoba also recently adopted disability equality legislation, the Accessibility Advisory Council Act 2011, which seeks to "enhance accessibility by identifying barriers that disable people and the ways in which those barriers can be prevented and removed" (Prince, 2011).

Canadian disability rights activists have also played an important role on the international stage, most significantly in the adoption of the UN Convention on the Rights of Persons with Disabilities (UNCRPD). Between 2002 and 2006, representatives from more than 100 countries and hundreds of NGOs worked to draft and negotiate a new UN treaty devoted to the human rights of people with disabilities (Estey, 2011). Dulcie McCallum (2011) writes that early in the negotiations a bone of contention arose regarding the intense involvement of civil society organizations. Some countries objected to the undermining of state supremacy in the development of international law. She describes the position of Canada:

> When some countries began to resist the idea of an inclusive
> process, Canada along with others took a firm stand on the

> involvement of civil society and supported their full participation: honouring their slogan *nothing about us without us*. This turned out to be the critical factor in the brilliant design of the *Convention's* text; it was conceived of and drafted largely by people who themselves have a disability. (McCallum, 2011: 149)

Canada played a particularly important role in promoting inclusive education and the notion of supported decision-making and promoting legal capacity. The Canadian delegation was given the lead by the chair on discussions on Article 12, which guarantees equal recognition before the law (McCallum, 2011). Article 12 mandates that an individual cannot lose his/her legal capacity to act simply because of a disability. It recognizes that some persons with disabilities require assistance to exercise this capacity and that states therefore have a duty to support those individuals and introduce safeguards against abuse of that support.

On December 13, 2006, the UN General Assembly adopted CRPD and an associated Optional Protocol. Eighty-one states as well as the European Union signed the CRPD when it was first opened for signature on March 30, 2007. This is the highest number of opening signatures recorded for any human rights treaty (Kayess and French, 2008). The UN High Commissioner for Human Rights, Louise Arbour (a former Canadian Supreme Court Justice), characterized the CRPD as a "catalyst for change" and a document that enshrines a paradigm shift in attitudes "that moves from a view of persons with disabilities as objects of charity, medical treatment and social protection to subjects of rights, able to claim those rights as active members of society" (UN Enable, 2006). The Canadian government ratified the CRPD on March 11, 2010. States have agreed that the promotion and implementation of CRPD will be carried out by "independent mechanisms," such as human rights agencies and commissions. CCD, CACL, and DAWN-RAFH Canada are working with the Canadian Association of Statutory Human Rights Agencies to ensure the implementation of appropriate monitoring processes (Nikias, 2012).

CONCLUSIONS

Social movement theorists have relied and developed the idea of "opportunity structures" to account for the opportunities and constraints that lie outside of a social movement. These theories show that in many ways the systems and support in place for voting, lobbying, and litigation help to channel a social movement's activities. While these theories tend to emphasize the positive notion of "opportunity," in many ways it is the "structural" dimension that has had a greater impact on the disability movement. These "structures" have served as barriers to disability rights activists. From the inaccessibility of the Houses of Parliament when disability rights activists first tried to lobby MPs in the early 1980s to the continuing challenges people with disabilities face when trying to vote, "opportunity structures" can at times be more nefarious and exclusionary than the terminology suggests. Political opportunity structures can serve to discriminate and marginalize without intending to.

However, despite the language used to describe these "structures," they are not immutable (Vanhala, 2012). The disability rights movement has fundamentally shaped the legal and political landscape and opened up opportunities for lobbying and legal mobilization in Canada. Over the past 30 years, the movement has significantly changed and broadened our understandings of what "disability" means and what "equality" looks like. The movement has pushed for "disability" to be included as a protected ground in the Charter and waged a series of political and legal campaigns to promote physical integrity rights, employment and educational equality, and positive perceptions of disability in debates about death. While this has always involved a range of tactics from insider lobbying to strategic litigation, it is worth emphasizing that rights-based legal mobilization has been a key tool for the disability movement compared to some other groups studied in this volume. This is in part due to the important legitimizing role that a group's presence in the courtroom can confer on identities, in particular, identities that have in the past been marginalized or even oppressed by the law and its interpretation (Vanhala 2009).

This chapter also underscores the ways in which disability rights organizations challenged and transformed "structures" at the provincial and, more recently, the international level. As Anna MacQuarrie (2011) points out, the adoption and ratification in the early years of the twenty-first century of an international agreement, the UNCRPD, embracing a rights-based understanding of disability, represents the next evolution of "nothing about us without us." While the real impact of this treaty in Canada remains to be seen, the participation and support of Canadian disability rights organizations within this process, particularly in promoting notions of inclusive education and equal recognition before the law, will have consequences for people with disabilities around the world.

NOTES

1   Members of the Canadian disability rights movement and its supporters have shared their time, stories, and experiences with me, and I am enormously grateful to them—this chapter would not be possible without their help. Some extracts of this chapter have appeared in *Making Rights a Reality: Disability Rights*

Activists and Legal Mobilization (2011), and I am grateful to Cambridge University Press for their permission to incorporate this material. Thanks are also due to the Canadian Political Science Association and Cambridge University Press for permission to use material from my article "Disability Rights Activists in the Supreme Court of Canada: Legal Mobilization Theory and Accommodating Social Movements" *Canadian Journal of Political Science* (2009). Finally, I would like to thank Rob Abercrombie and Corin Throsby for helpful comments on this chapter.

2   I offer several caveats here. First, the disability movement is, like many of the groups explored in this volume, remarkably heterogeneous and incorporates (and sometimes excludes) multiple identities. By using the term "disability rights movement," I do not want to suggest that this is a uniform or even a consensus-based movement. The disability sphere constitutes a wide variety of organizations, individual activists, and coalitions, many with differing or even conflicting goals, strategies, and identities. The organizations range from informal groups to disabilities studies scholars to professional lobbying organizations. Second, the focus in this chapter is on a small number of key social movement organizations. However, this clearly constitutes a decision-making and mobilizing elite within the broader community of people with disabilities in Canada, not all of whom will identify with the identities and concepts put forth here.

3   The legitimacy of this voice and the guarantee of equal access to justice was affirmed by the Supreme Court again in 2012. In the *D.A.I* case, the Court was asked to consider whether people with intellectual disabilities should be allowed to testify in court. CCD, CACL, DAWN Canada, People First, and LEAF were among the third-party interveners.

CASES CITED

Canadian Disability Rights Council v. Canada, [1988] 3 F.C. 622, 624.
Carter v. Canada (Attorney General), 2012 BCSC 886.
E. (Mrs.) v. Eve, [1986] 2 S.C.R. 388.
Hughes, James Peter v. Elections Canada [2010] CHRT 4.
R. v. D.A.I., 2012 SCC 5 [2012] 1 S.C.R. 149.
R. v. Latimer [1997] 1 S.C.R. 217.
R. v. Latimer [2001] 1 S.C.R. 3.
Rodriguez v. British Columbia (Attorney General) [1993] 3 S.C.R. 519.

REFERENCES AND FURTHER READING

Andersen, Ellen Ann. 2005. *Out of the Closets and Into the Courts: Legal Opportunity Structures and Gay Rights Litigation*. Ann Arbor: University of Michigan Press.

Armstrong, Sarah. 2003. "Disability Advocacy in the Charter Era." *Journal of Law and Equality* 2 (1): 33–91.

Beachell, Laurie. 2011. "Foreword. The Disability Rights Movement: The Agent of Change for Creating a More Inclusive Canada." In *Celebrating Our Accomplishments*, ed. Council of Canadians with Disabilities, 5–6. Winnipeg: CCD Online. http://www.ccdonline.ca/en/socialpolicy/poverty-citizen ship/income-security-reform/celebrating-our-accomplishments (accessed November 14, 2012).

Benford, Robert D., and David A. Snow. 2000. "Framing Processes and Social Movements: An Overview and Assessment." *Annual Review of Sociology* 26 (1): 611–39.

Chivers, Sally. 2008. "Barrier by Barrier: The Canadian Disability Movement and the Fight for Equal Rights." In *Group Politics and Social Movements in Canada*, 1st ed., ed. Miriam Smith, 307–28. Peterborough: Broadview.

Coalition of Provincial Organizations of the Handicapped. 1993a. "Factum of the Intervener." *Rodriguez v. British Columbia (Attorney General)* [1993] 3 S.C.R. 519.

Coalition of Provincial Organizations of the Handicapped. 1993b. "*Rodriguez:* Autonomy and Vulnerability Must Both Be Protected" *Abilities Magazine*. Fall (16): 77–78.

Driedger, Diane. 1989. *The Last Civil Rights Movement: Disabled People's International*. New York: St. Martin's Press.

Driedger, Diane. 2011. "A Voice Like No Other: Ours." In *Celebrating Our Accomplishments*, ed. Council of Canadians with Disabilities, 157–58. Winnipeg: Council of Canadians with Disabilities.

Elections Canada. 2007. *A History of the Vote in Canada*. 2nd ed. Ottawa: Office of the Chief Electoral Officer of Canada. http://www.elections.ca/content. aspx?section=res&dir=his&document=indexpdf&lang=e#al (accessed November 15, 2012).

Engel, David M., and Frank W. Munger. 2003. *Rights of Inclusion: Law and Identity in the Life Stories of Americans with Disabilities*. Chicago: University of Chicago Press.

Estey, Steve. 2011. "Disability Rights: Coming of Age at the United Nations." In *Celebrating our Accomplishments*, ed. Council of Canadians with Disabilities, 155–56. Winnipeg: Council of Canadians with Disabilities.

Fredman, Sandra. 2002. *Discrimination Law*. Oxford: Oxford University Press.

Giddens, Anthony. 1984. *The Constitution of Society: Outline of the Theory of Structuration*. Berkeley, CA: University of California Press.

Goffman, Erving. 1974. *Frame Analysis*. Boston: Northeastern University Press.

Kayess, Rosemary, and Phillip French. 2008. "Out of Darkness into Light? Introducing the Convention on the Rights of Persons with Disabilities." *Human Rights Law Review* 8 (1): 1–34.

Lepofsky, David. 1998. "Discussion: The Charter's Guarantee of Equality to People with Disabilities—How Well is it Working?" *Windsor Yearbook of Access to Justice* 16: 155–214.

Lepofsky, M. David and Jerome E. Bickenbach. 1985. "Equality Rights and the Physically Handicapped." In *Equality Rights and the Canadian Charter of Rights and Freedoms*, ed. Anne F. Bayefsky and Mary Eberts, 323. Toronto: Carswell.

MacQuarrie, Anna. 2011. "The UN Convention on the Rights of Persons with Disabilities: A New Era of Disability Rights." In *Celebrating Our Accomplishments*, ed. Council of Canadians with Disabilities Winnipeg: CCD Online. http://www.ccdonline.ca/en/socialpolicy/poverty-citizenship/income-security-reform/celebrating-our-accomplishments (accessed November 14, 2012).

Malhotra, Ravi A. 2003. "The Duty to Accommodate Unionized Workers with Disabilities in Canada and the United States: A Counter-Hegemonic Approach." *Journal of Law and Equality* 2 (1): 92–155.

McAdam, Doug, and David A. Snow. 2010. *Readings on Social Movements: Origins, Dynamics and Outcomes*. New York: Oxford University Press.

McCallum, Dulcie. 2011. "Up to the Basics: The Right to Decide." In *Celebrating Our Accomplishments*, ed. Council of Canadians with Disabilities , 148–49. Winnipeg: CCD Online. http://www.ccdonline.ca/en/socialpolicy/poverty-citizenship/income-security-reform/celebrating-our-accomplishments (accessed November 14, 2012).

Meister, Joan. 2003. "An Early DAWNing (1985–1994)." In *Making Equality: History of Advocacy and Persons with Disabilities in Canada*, ed. Deborah Stienstra and Aileen Wight-Felske, 221–43. Concord, ON: Captus Press.

Neufeldt, Alfred. 2003. "Growth and Evolution of Disability Advocacy in Canada." In *Making Equality: History of Advocacy and Persons with Disabilities in Canada*, ed. Deborah Stienstra and Aileen Wight-Felske, 11–32. Concord, ON: Captus Press.

Nikias, Vangelis. 2012. *Convention on the Rights of Persons with Disabilities: Overview and Next Steps for an Accessible and Inclusive Society*. (June 14). Winnipeg: Canadian Council of Disabilities. http://www.ccdonline.ca/en/international/un/canada/vangelis-nikias-June2012 (accessed December 4, 2012).

Park, Peter, Althea Monteiro, and Bruce Kappell. 2003. "People First: The History and the Dream." In *Making Equality: History of Advocacy and Persons with Disabilities in Canada*, ed. Deborah Stienstra and Aileen Wight-Felske, 183–96. Concord, ON: Captus Press.

Peters, Yvonne. 2003. "From Charity to Equality: Canadians with Disabilities take their Rightful Place in Canada's Constitution." In *Making Equality: History of Advocacy and Persons with Disabilities in Canada*, ed. Deborah Stienstra and Aileen Wight-Felske, 119–36. Concord, ON: Captus Press.

Prince, Michael. 2004a. "Persons with Disabilities and Canada's Electoral Systems: Gradually Advancing the Democratic Right to Vote." *Electoral Insight* (April). http://www.elections.ca/res/eim/article_search/article.asp?id=15&lang=e&frmPageSize (accessed November 14, 2012).

Prince, Michael. 2004b. "Canadian Disability Policy: Still a Hit and Miss Affair." *Canadian Journal of Sociology* 29 (1): 59–82.

Prince, Michael. 2011. "Legislative Reform." In *Celebrating our Accomplishments*, ed. Council of Canadians with Disabilities. 99–100. http://www.ccdonline.ca/en/socialpolicy/poverty-citizenship/income-security-reform/celebrating-our-accomplishments (accessed November 14, 2012).

Richler, Diane. 2011. "CACL's Deinstitutionalization Initiative: A Long Struggle." In *Celebrating Our Accomplishments*, ed. Council of Canadians with Disabilities, 15–16. Winnipeg: Council of Canadians with Disabilities. http://www.ccdonline.ca/en/socialpolicy/poverty-citizenship/income-security-reform/celebrating-our-accomplishments (accessed November 14, 2012).

Rioux, Marcia H., and Catherine L. Frazee. 1999. "The Canadian Framework for Disability Equality Rights." In *Disability, Divers-ability and Legal Change*, ed. M. Jones and L.A. Basser Marks, 171–88. London: Kluwer Law International.

Smith, Miriam. 1998. "Social Movements and Equality Seeking: The Case of Gay Liberation in Canada." *Canadian Journal of Political Science* 31 (2): 285–309.

Statistics Canada. 2006. *Participation and Activity Limitation Survey.* http://www.statcan.ca/cgibin/imdb/p2SV.pl?Function=getSurvey&SDDS=3251&lang=en&db=IMDB&dbg=f&adm=8&dis=2 (accessed December 3, 2007).

Stienstra, Deborah, and Aileen Wight-Felske, eds. 2003. *Making Equality: History of Advocacy and Persons with Disabilities in Canada*. Concord, ON: Captus Press.

Torjman, Sherri. 2011. "Special Parliamentary Committee on the Disabled and the Handicapped." In *Celebrating Our Accomplishments*, ed. Council of Canadians with Disabilities, 91–92. Winnipeg: Council of Canadians with Disabilities. http://www.ccdonline.ca/en/socialpolicy/poverty-citizenship/income-security-reform/celebrating-our-accomplishments (accessed November 14, 2012).

UN Enable. 2006. Statement by Louise Arbour, UN High Commissioner for Human Rights on the Ad Hoc Committee's adoption of the International Convention on the Rights of Persons with Disabilities, December 5, 2006.

http://www.un.org/esa/socdev/enable/rights/ahc8hrcmsg.htm (accessed November 14, 2012).

Vanhala, Lisa. 2009. "Disability Rights Activists in the Supreme Court of Canada: Legal Mobilization Theory and Accommodating Social Movements." *Canadian Journal of Political Science* 42 (4): 981–1002.

Vanhala, Lisa. 2011a. *Making Rights a Reality? Disability Rights Activists and Legal Mobilization.* New York: Cambridge University Press..

Vanhala, Lisa. 2011b. "Social Movements Lashing Back: Law, Social Change and Intra-Social Movement Backlash in Canada." *Studies in Law, Politics, and Society* 54:113–40.

Vanhala, Lisa. 2012. "Legal Opportunity Structures and the Paradox of Legal Mobilization by the Environmental Movement in the UK." *Law & Society Review* 46 (3): 523–56.

Vickers, Jill, and Fraser Valentine. 1996. "'Released from the Yoke of Paternalism and Charity': Citizenship and the Rights of Canadians with Disabilities." *International Journal of Canadian Studies* 14:155–78.

Walters, Traci. 2011. "A Revolution of the Mind—The Independent Living Philosophy." In *Celebrating Our Accomplishments*, ed. Council of Canadians with Disabilities, 13–14. Winnipeg: Council of Canadians with Disabilities. http://www.ccdonline.ca/en/socialpolicy/poverty-citizenship/income-security-reform/celebrating-our-accomplishments (accessed November 14, 2012).

Watters, Colleen. 2003. "History of Advocacy Organizations of the Blind in Canada." In *Making Equality: History of Advocacy and Persons with Disabilities in Canada*, ed. Deborah Stienstra and Aileen Wight-Felske, 163–82. Concord, ON: Captus Press.

World Health Organization. 2011. *World Report on Disability*. Geneva: World Health Organization.

FOURTEEN

Health Social Movements: The Next Wave in Contentious Politics?[1]

MICHAEL ORSINI

From breast cancer activism to the struggle of people with AIDS to the recent mobilization of persons suffering from environmental illness, the last few decades have been witness to a flurry of social movement activity targeting health. This chapter provides a glimpse into the brave new world of social movement politics through the lens of three health social movements: HIV/AIDS, environmental illness (specifically, Multiple Chemical Sensitivity), and asthma. I explore whether health social movements represent the next wave in contentious politics. While we have witnessed waves of protest organized around recognition struggles from, for instance, feminists, LGBT citizens, and racial minorities (see Hobson, 2005), and global counter movements against the deleterious effects of globalization and neo-liberal policies, I ask whether health is emerging as a "master frame" around which an array of movements is organizing or whether health might constitute yet another way to frame underlying questions of injustice.

Admittedly, this chapter can only begin to scratch the surface of these diverse and heterogeneous movements, each of which merits its own treatment. I have chosen these three to illustrate my contention that such movements throw up at least three new challenges not addressed by many traditional social movements. First, they simultaneously critique and engage with science, as is the case with people suffering from environmental illnesses and AIDS activists, and trouble our common understanding of expert knowledge (see Orsini and Smith, 2010). Second, they reflect, albeit in new ways, some of the traditional political cleavages that have animated the social movement

landscape for decades, namely, gender and racial oppression and class inequalities. To varying degrees, these movements work to reconstruct or reimagine
already existing grievances with respect to, for instance, racial oppression
or gender oppression through the lens of health. A good example of this is
"asthma activists" in the US, who have joined forces with civil rights leaders
and environmentalists in mobilizing racialized communities to take ownership
of asthma. Activists charge that members of minority communities are disproportionately affected by asthma because, among other things, their physical environment places them at greater risk of being exposed to pollutants,
especially in the inner cities of key American states. This debate is especially
charged as asthma is increasingly being diagnosed in children; at least 12 per
cent of Canadian children have asthma (Asthma Society of Canada, 2006).

A third unique feature of health social movements that is not common to
other social movements relates to the ability to engage in forms of contentious
politics in the first place. Social movement actors whose health is compromised by, for example, HIV infection may be limited in their ability to join
forces with others by reason of their physical health. In research on efforts by
people infected with HIV through the blood system, individuals living with
HIV and/or Hepatitis C spoke of the challenges associated with attending
demonstrations in the blazing heat of summer. Long-time US AIDS activist
Michael Callen once said, "My friends have their own theories about why
I've survived . . . They point to my political activism as Exhibit A. But I've
often wondered if they're right. The problem is, my AIDS activism has been
a double-edged sword. It has given me a reason to live, but it has also nearly
killed me" (Callen, 1990: 78). In the case of people suffering from environmental illness, the challenge is amplified since one of the main obstacles that
prevents their full participation in political life is the unsafe physical environment in the first place.

Not all of the movements mentioned here are necessarily active in the Canadian
context. Asthma activism, for instance, has taken root in major American urban
centres such as Detroit, which is marked by a large African-American underclass,
but has not taken hold in Canada—at least not yet. Other movements, however,
such as the one advocating on behalf of persons suffering from environmental
illness, have had surprising success in cities such as Halifax, which recently
instituted a scent-free policy to respond to demands from persons who claim
to be seriously affected by exposure to, among other chemicals, artificial
scents that are found in many products from household cleaners to soap to
perfumes.

As is the case with many social movements, contentious politics is marked
by its refusal to respect national borders (see Khagram et al., 2002; Tarrow,
2005). Therefore, what is occurring in different national contexts can, and

often does, have important effects on how other movements frame their demands and on how they adopt or adapt the templates or "master frames" present in other societies to shape their own collective responses. As outlined in the Introduction, social movement literature draws our attention to the importance of "political opportunity structures"—features of the external political environment that affect the ability of movements to challenge authorities (see Tarrow, 1994: 18). While much has been made of the domestic opportunity structures that influence movement politics, attention has turned recently to expanding this to contention that occurs outside of domestic or national contexts (see Tarrow, 2005). Movements in different territorial contexts may not only provide windows of opportunity for similar or like-minded movement activity to emerge, they may also provide important impetus to a host of challengers or counter movements (Meyer and Staggenborg, 1996).

The chapter begins by introducing the "health social movement" (HSM) concept, which is fairly recent in its formulation even though scholars have been studying such movements for several decades. I ask why HSMs should command the attention of scholars and students of Canadian politics and public policy and argue that they provide us with an opportunity to examine the cross-cutting issues of race, gender, and sexuality that have animated traditional social movements. In addition, they are particularly useful in locating debates about the use and dominance of expert knowledge in our society. Second, I provide brief vignettes of three HSMs, each of which reveals an important aspect of the new terrain of collective action. Third, I ask whether new theoretical tools and approaches are required to capture the dynamics of collective action in the field of health.

WHAT ARE HEALTH SOCIAL MOVEMENTS?

HSMs are "collective challenges to medical policy and politics, belief systems, research and practice that include an array of formal and informal organizations, supporters, networks of co-operation and media" (Brown et al., 2004: 52). They are particularly interested in contesting power and authority, be it in the realm of science, medicine, or politics. In addition, HSMs challenge how we understand individual and collective identity. While some might assume that the primary challenge for some HSMs, especially those representing persons living with stigmatizing conditions, might be to mobilize supporters in the first place, one of the more interesting features of such movements has been their ability not only to do so but also to include interested people who are not actually affected by the condition or illness. One important example of the latter has been the ability of the breast cancer movement, especially some of its radical offshoots that target the environmental causes of breast cancer, to mobilize women who are not living with breast cancer to get involved (see Klawiter, 2004). Moreover, it is important to stress here that in addition to the regular obstacles movement actors might face, many HSM activists face the added problem of being ill, which can compromise their ability to mobilize. Seemingly mundane things—such as attending a demonstration in blistering heat—can be especially taxing for someone who is ill.

It is also important to note that the processes of contestation are not uniform when one surveys a range of HSMs. For some movements, the primary struggle is to move scientifically legitimate conditions, which are not the subject of contestation within official circles, onto the political stage (Brown et al., 2004). Asthma is a useful example, since activists need not spend time convincing others that it is a legitimate condition; instead, asthma offers an opportunity to mount wider challenges around environmental issues such as transit pollution, which activists claim disproportionately affects people living with asthma. Asthma has also become racialized in the US, as it has become known that the overwhelming majority of new cases occur in economically disadvantaged urban communities in which there are significant numbers of African Americans. In addition, some members of HSMs face a greater uphill battle in convincing the public and authorities that their condition is legitimate in the first place, as is amply demonstrated by the case of environmental illness. Much energy is devoted to convincing naysayers that the symptoms they are experiencing are indeed real and that these symptoms can be linked directly to their exposure to consumer items that many of us take for granted.

Following Brown et al. (2004), I divide HSMs in three categories: *health access, constituency based,* and *embodied* health movements. First, health access movements, as their name implies, are primarily interested in "equitable access to health care and improved provision of health-care services" (Brown et al., 2004: 52). Constituency-based health movements are interested in redressing health inequalities that may be based on race, ethnicity, gender, class, and/or sexuality differences. The third type, embodied health movements, "address disease, disability or illness experience by challenging science on etiology, diagnosis, treatment and prevention" (Brown et al., 2004: 52).

Embodied health movements are identified by three characteristics (Brown et al., 2004). First, they place the "biological bodies" of people who are experiencing the disease at the centre of their efforts. Second, they often contest existing scientific or medical knowledge and practice. As Epstein (1991) has said of the AIDS movement, they challenge "science as industry" and "science as procedures." In the case of AIDS, for instance, activists have contested the role of the pharmaceutical industry with respect to the availability and affordability of AIDS drugs (science as industry), but they also insinuated themselves into debates about the appropriate conduct of science, including the use of clinical trials (science as procedures). Third, movement actors often find themselves collaborating with scientists and other health professionals in working to raise the profile of the disease/illness in question, whether that be advocating for increased funding for research, treatment issues, or prevention efforts. These three features, taken together, allow Brown et al. to position embodied health movements as "boundary movements." They use this term to underline their contention that these movements blur the lines between the state and civil society, between what is considered expert knowledge and experiential or lay knowledge (Brown et al., 2004: 54). Moreover, these movements borrow liberally from other social movements (e.g., the feminist and environmental movements), which complicates efforts to study them in isolation without paying attention to their forerunners.

Given the range of movements that merit scholarly attention, why, one might ask, is it useful to throw the spotlight on HSMs? First, the attainment of health is becoming a dominant theme in society and thus is on the minds of policy-makers interested in reflecting back citizens' priorities. Some scholars view this as part of a broader trend toward "healthism," a twenty-first-century ideology based on the primacy of health and wellness (Marsh, 2001). Why is health so important to us today? The answers are varied. One might argue, for instance, that rapid progress and the speed of changes associated with globalization have ushered in an era in which our environment, both physical and social, may be placing our collective health at risk. German sociologist Ulrich Beck famously coined the term "risk society" to characterize an era in which we are increasingly less capable of shielding ourselves from all manner of risk (Beck, 1992). Others speculate that health is emerging as an important political/social cleavage in its own right because people's sense of spiritual and material alienation forces them to find some comfort in assuming a "sick role"—they are able to find, as it were, an identity through illness. Sociologist Frank Furedi (2005: 2) has argued that society is becoming obsessed with sickness to the extent that "being ill is seen as a normal state, possibly even more normal than being healthy. We are all now seen as being potentially ill; that is the default state we live in today." One can claim a middle ground, however, between a focus on the individual and a broader focus on the external world; such a perspective would view health and contestation around health as inter-subjectively created and produced through subjects who make choices in a context that is not necessarily of their own making.

AIDS ACTIVISM AND THE SOCIAL CONSTRUCTION OF KNOWLEDGE

Although we are three decades into the AIDS epidemic, much has happened in the world of AIDS activism since the early 1980s when the disease first struck the gay community in North America. AIDS activism has moved from the very margins of society to occupying a central place in understanding the response to the epidemic. Kinsman was correct to suggest that the AIDS movement has become "one of the most profound social movements ever to emerge around health issues" (1998: 217). The biennial International Conference on AIDS attracts more than 15,000 of the world's leading researchers, scientists, and advocates in the field. After much agitation, this meeting of distinguished experts carved out an important space for the "other" experts: patients themselves and groups that represent their diverse interests.

When AIDS activists adopted the Holocaust slogan "Silence=Death" to characterize government inaction on AIDS, they probably had no idea how these simple words would burn in the memory of generations of activists. The slogan was the brainchild of ACT UP (AIDS Coalition to Unleash Power), one of the high profile AIDS activist organizations to emerge on the international scene. Formed in New York City in 1987, it retains only a few chapters in major North American and European cities. Two Canadian chapters, one in Montreal and another in Vancouver, had been in the forefront of radical AIDS activism in Canada but have since disbanded. ACT UP made an important splash at the International Conference on AIDS when it was held in Vancouver in 1996. Spurred on by ACT UP, thousands of delegates at the conference stood and turned their backs on then federal Health Minister David Dingwall for the duration of his speech to protest against the government's plan to cancel the National AIDS Strategy, a program that funds a range of community-based prevention initiatives across the country. This symbolic action, reported by the international media, illustrates the importance of the media in the framing of issues. Although many of the foreign delegates attending the conference were unaware of the controversy regarding the renewal of the National AIDS Strategy, the impression left by the "action" was that all AIDS activists and AIDS researchers were united in their opposition to the Canadian government's attempts to renege on its funding commitment to AIDS. (The federal government decided in the end not to cancel the strategy.) As Gusfield notes, "mass media do more than monitor: They dramatize. They create vivid images, impute leadership, and heighten the sense of conflict between movements and the institutions of society" (1994: 71).

ACT UP redefined public protest in several key respects. For example, it staged "die-ins," during which activists drew police-style chalk outlines around each other's dead bodies. Its most popular symbol, Silence=Death, is emblazoned beneath a pink triangle, the Nazi emblem for gay men. As Gamson explains, "ACT UP takes a symbol used to mark people for death and reclaims it. They reclaim, in fact, control over defining a cause of death; the banner connects gay action to gay survival, on the one hand, and homophobia to death from AIDS, on the other" (1989: 361). ACT UP's enemy, Gamson explains, is not the state per se, but is "invisible, disembodied, ubiquitous: it is the very process of normalization through labelling in which everyone except one's own community of the de-normalized (and its supporters) is involved" (1989: 357).

Much activist energy is spent trying to resist the language commonly summoned to explain disease, and the AIDS movement is no exception. One of its early demands was that the term "AIDS victim" be replaced by "people with AIDS." The Denver Principles, the manifesto of the National Association of People with AIDS in the US, opens with this statement regarding naming: "We condemn attempts to label us as 'victims,' which implies defeat, and we are only occasionally 'patients,' which implies passivity, helplessness, and dependence upon the care of others. We are 'people with AIDS'" (quoted in Navarre, 1993: 148). Of course, the legacy of this shift in thinking about illness has spread beyond AIDS. Radical breast cancer activists, for instance, have publicly acknowledged the AIDS movement as inspiring their unique brand of activism.

One of the more contentious issues with respect to AIDS activism relates to the ability of AIDS activists to maintain an autonomous voice in the face of increased reliance on state support and creeping bureaucratization. More than a decade ago, government funding of AIDS groups had "created rather than eliminated the room to generate radical criticism of state policies" (Rayside and Lindquist, 1992: 69). It is not clear, however, whether the same holds true today. Rayside and Lindquist suggested at the time that the general suspicion with which lesbian and gay activists viewed the state provided a healthy buffer against co-optation. That said, they did warn of the potential that AIDS issues might become overly institutionalized, "tailored to fit pre-existent bureaucratic policies and agendas, and distorted in a way that depoliticizes them" (Rayside and Lindquist, 1992: 70). Today, AIDS advocacy is channelled largely through institutionalized groups seeking public or community support for the delivery of programs and services, such as the Canadian AIDS Society, the national umbrella organization that represents about 125 community groups throughout the country.

While the radical activist politics associated with organizations such as ACT UP appears to have disappeared from the Canadian political landscape, traces of this in-your-face brand of activism can be found in AIDS Action Now! (AAN). The Toronto-based organization has been particularly active in the last few years with its PosterVirus campaign, which enlisted the support of well-known contemporary artists Allyson Mitchell and Kent Monkman, among others. As the group explains: "Through merging the worlds of art and activism we are intentionally evoking the history of creative responses to HIV. Our aim is to provoke discussion, controversy and dialogue in a way traditional activism cannot" (AIDS Action Now!, 2013). A recent issue that has mobilized many Canadian AIDS activists, including AAN, concerns the criminalization of HIV non-disclosure (Mykhalovskiy, 2011). Activists oppose the use of the criminal law to punish people who might expose their sexual partners to HIV infection, arguing that prosecuting people who expose others to HIV might frustrate public health efforts to encourage individuals to get tested for the virus, not to mention that it neglects the fact that in the majority of cases, individuals do not deliberately intend to infect others.

Finally, as alluded to earlier, much of the anger expressed by AIDS activists in general has been directed, not surprisingly, against the twin pillars of science and medicine. The case of the neglect of women is an important example in that it also illustrates how movements organized to challenge stigmatization (in this case, of gay men with AIDS) can reproduce stigma of their own. For more than a decade, the Centers for Disease Control (CDC) in the US (not to mention its Canadian counterpart, which often follows the CDC's lead) was loath to represent women in epidemiological understandings of AIDS. The CDC's original definition of AIDS, produced in 1987, required HIV infection along with specific opportunistic infections or cancers (such as *Pneumocystis carinii* pneumonia or Kaposi's sarcoma, a skin cancer). The list was developed when AIDS affected mainly gay males. In women, the early stages of HIV infection produce different symptoms (such as persistent gynecological infections and cervical cancer) than those in the CDC definition. The new, expanded definition includes HIV-positive people with CD4-counts of less than 200 per millilitre and, in response to pressure from women AIDS activists, a list of HIV-related illnesses, including the gynecological abnormalities and cancers from which women had suffered or died. Since the medical conditions experienced by many HIV-infected women were not included in the CDC's AIDS definition until late 1993, women often were diagnosed and treated later than men. This was connected to broader issues of treatment, since up until recently many women did not qualify for benefit payments because their symptoms differed from men's. The sentiment of women AIDS activists was best expressed in their placard: "Women don't get AIDS; they just die from it." While waging a war of recognition of women's unique experiences with HIV, activists for women with HIV nonetheless challenged the scientific establishment on a more pragmatic front to include more women in clinical trials—to, in other words, engage with science rather than solely criticize its gender-biased practices. Several reasons were offered to explain women's underrepresentation in clinical trials of AIDS drugs: (1) they may be excluded because they are either potentially or actually pregnant; (2) they are members of minority groups and lack access to the health care system in general and to research in particular; (3) they are drug users and are presumed to be noncompliant subjects; and (4) most of the trials focused on AIDS itself, not solely HIV infection, and many women did not fit the clinical definition of AIDS (Johnson, 1992: 3).

The AIDS movement is a potent example of how individual citizens can challenge society and the state to become credible experts in their own right and confront the stigma that surrounds an HIV diagnosis. The next movement we will examine, while still in its infancy, is also interested in challenging the dominance of science and medicine. Unlike the AIDS movement, however, the main challenge posed by people suffering from environmental illness involves getting others to take the disease seriously in the first place.

MULTIPLE CHEMICAL SENSITIVITY SYNDROME: SCENTS AND SENSIBILITIES

The number of people coming forward to claim that their health is being harmed by exposure to small amounts of chemicals and toxic products has been on the increase in the last few decades. Multiple Chemical Sensitivity (MCS) is also referred to more broadly as environmental illness. It usually denotes a reaction to chemical substances well below what would be considered normal. Those affected can be sensitive to several scented products—cleaning products, detergents, paints, pesticides, moulds, or food. Depending on the severity, a person may become isolated if they are unable to tolerate their workplace, school, or home. In extreme cases, this might require a visit to a "safe" place where an individual can restore their environmental health. Nova Scotia was the first province in the country to set up such a place, the Nova Scotia Environmental Health Centre. This self-described oasis provides shelter to the environmentally sensitive and acts as a place for patients seeking emotional support and various forms of treatment of their condition. The Centre takes its mission very seriously. Visitors are warned that they should arrive free of any scented products (deodorants, shampoos, perfumes, tobacco smoke) and free of clothing that has been dry-cleaned. If they are found to be in violation of this policy, they "will have the option of showering and changing into Centre scrubs or making another appointment" (Nova Scotia Environmental Health Centre, 2005).

It is, perhaps, not surprising, that those advocating on behalf of the environmentally ill are often dismissed as extreme, even Draconian, in their efforts to protect themselves from an environment they perceive as encroaching on their health and well-being. While one may quibble over the extent to which society should bend in accommodating their needs, it is evident that the experiences of the environmentally ill throw up a range of interesting policy challenges not always easily accommodated by policy-makers and society more broadly. At one level, they are demanding to be viewed as legitimately disabled, which can have repercussions for how we measure and compensate suffering. If MCS is not recognized by one's physician, how, for instance, can a patient rightfully claim to be disabled or to be unable to work and thus be eligible to receive social assistance or to request permission to be on paid sick leave from her/his employer? In addition, they are asking governments and societies more broadly to introduce policies banning the use of scented products in public bathrooms, regulating the use of certain chemicals in consumer products, etc. And, to press their case and potentially exaggerate their "injustice frame," activists often liken their experiences with their enemies in the chemical industry—including the manufacturers of pesticides, fragrances, cosmetics, and toiletries—to the tobacco industry's attempts to deny the link between smoking and cancer. The chemical lobby, they claim, devotes much of its efforts to questioning the existence of chemical sensitivity, attacking its sufferers as well as any sympathetic researchers who have studied its prevalence, instead of asking the tough questions about the links between these chemicals and a host of illnesses.

Not surprisingly, Halifax's decision to go scent-free has sparked a flurry of responses, from support to outright condemnation. Organizations supported by the fragrance industry, for instance, have attacked the scientific basis for the claim that scented products are the culprit. American conservative critic Michael Fumento, who once wrote about the "myth of heterosexual AIDS," has lashed out at the City of Halifax for caving in to the "fragrance fighters." In one article, he quotes a researcher who suggests that the overwhelming majority of people who claim to be environmentally ill are more than likely suffering from mental illness (Fumento, 2000).

As Kroll-Smith and Floyd (2000) explain, the challenges mounted by people who claim to be environmentally ill are not benign; they require those who are not affected to alter their behaviours to accommodate those who may be potentially harmed by exposure. Those who choose to ignore the plight of the environmentally ill are "implicated in the exacerbation" of their illness. Consider this revealing anecdote. Kroll-Smith and Floyd interviewed "Jack," who claimed to be suffering from environmental illness. The interviewer was seated 20 feet from the individual and came to the interview having respected the wishes of the interviewee: he showered without using soap, wore all cotton clothing, did not wear any scented products, and made sure his clothes were washed without the use of a fabric softener.

> Shortly after starting the interview, Jack became visibly agitated,
> lifting himself from side to side and up and down in his chair . . . He

explained that he was reacting to something new in his house . . .
His symptoms were increasing in severity. He looked at my pen
and asked if it contained a soy-based ink. I told him I bought it
at a bookstore without checking the chemical composition of the
ink. He smiled knowingly and asked me to put the ink pen outside. Within a few minutes his symptoms subsided. (Kroll-Smith
and Floyd, 2000: 83)

While such examples may seem extreme indeed, other groups suggest that
we should not underestimate the extent to which we are exposed to harmful
chemicals in our everyday lives. Environmental Defence, a Toronto-based
organization, released a much-publicized report in 2005 called *Toxic Nation*,
which revealed the results of testing 11 Canadians from across the country
for a range of chemicals. The study found that the participants tested positive for 60 of 88 chemicals, including 18 heavy metals and 14 PCBs (*Toxic
Nation*, 2006). What's more, a person's place of residence did not seem to
affect the level of exposure. Indeed, one of the study participants, a First
Nations leader from northern Quebec, which is fairly distant from most point
sources of pollution, showed the highest levels of mercury and persistent
organic pollutants in his system. Renowned wildlife artist Robert Bateman,
who lives on idyllic Salt Spring Island, British Columbia, was not spared,
either. He tested positive for 48 of the 88 chemicals, including 32 cancer-
causing chemicals. As the organization's executive director put it bluntly, "If
you can walk, talk and breathe, you're contaminated" (Environmental News
Service, 2005).

While there is greater acceptance of the health problems posed by our immediate environment, people suffering from environmental illness (especially
MCS) must confront suggestions that the source of their ill health resides
somewhere outside of their immediate environment. This, no doubt, frus-
trates their attempts to be seen as credible actors on the political stage. Despite
these challenges, individuals living with environmental sensitivities are now
recognized as disabled by the Canadian Human Rights Commission (CHRC)
and therefore protected under the Canadian Human Rights Act, which pro-
hibits discrimination on the basis of disability. The CHRC "will receive any
inquiry and process any complaint from any person who believes that he or
she has been discriminated against because of an environmental sensitivity"
(Canadian Human Rights Commission, 2007; see Sears, 2007 and Wilkie and
Baker, 2007).

The final movement we will discuss is also connected to the environment,
but it differs from environmental illness in that the main source of contestation
does not concern the legitimacy of the illness per se; rather, it focuses on the

intersection of environmental and justice concerns, specifically the claim that poverty and race place certain individuals at greater risk of developing asthma than others.

ASTHMA ACTIVISM: RACE, CLASS, AND THE POLITICS OF DISEASE

Asthma may seem to be an unlikely candidate for a discussion of HSMs. For the most part, it would seem, asthma advocates eschew the type of activities normally adopted by social movement adherents. People suffering from asthma are not typically marching in the streets or agitating governments for social change. Increasingly, however, asthma has become politicized. While organizations representing people with asthma are interested typically in raising awareness of the societal costs of this condition and of the need for prevention, greater attention is shifting to explaining the underlying environmental conditions that place people at greater risk of acquiring asthma in the first place or, at the very least, of triggering symptoms. While advocates for asthma have long emphasized a need to control indoor environmental triggers (e.g., pets in a home, mould, dust mites), increasingly they are focusing attention on outdoor triggers, such as air pollution. In the case of one's indoor environment, there is a greater focus on individual responsibility; parents, for instance, are cautioned to take greater care in ensuring that their child's home is as safe as possible. When one shifts the focus to the external environment, however, suddenly the field expands considerably. Not surprisingly, this new focus has found the agenda of asthma activists overlapping significantly with the concerns of the environmental justice movement. In the US, for instance, community organizations are mobilizing people with asthma not only to manage their condition, but to "see themselves as part of a collective of people with asthma who understand the importance of external factors beyond their individual homes" (Brown et al., 2003: 461). Such consciousness-raising teaches people with asthma to link their bodily experiences (wheezing, coughing) to factors in their immediate environment: "They cannot think about their inhalers without thinking about the excess of bus depots and trash incinerators located in their neighborhoods" (Brown et al., 2003: 461). One Boston-area organization that targets transit issues such as the idling of diesel buses has been successful in claiming that residents of the neighbourhoods in questions are victims of "transit racism" (Brown et al., 2003: 458). They argued that bus riders were being discriminated against when government money that could have gone to purchase newer, less pollution-causing buses was instead given over to a major highway project.

This "politicized illness experience" takes as its starting point the subjective experience of dealing with an illness and grafts that onto a wider critique

of society and politics. A key turning point for individuals, then, is to recognize that they are not helpless victims of an unfortunate condition but can
be active agents mobilizing fellow sufferers and policy-makers, as well as
community leaders, to take collective responsibility for health and environment issues. Viewing the importance of outdoor environmental factors has a
ricochet effect in that it allows people with asthma to recognize that the poor
quality of their indoor environment is not entirely within their control but
rather is linked to wider social structural problems, which force families to live
in squalid conditions that might exacerbate asthma triggers (e.g., cockroach-
infested quarters). Cleaning up one's own household is only part of the solution. In addition, for some activists, asthma is a master key that connects the
dots among several policy problems, from educational attainment to the role
of the pharmaceutical industry, which benefits from the large market demand
for prescription drugs (e.g., inhalers or "puffers") among asthmatics. As one
California activist explains, "Asthma is a hub in a large net of issues that bring
us together" (Winant, 2004: 1).

It is interesting to note, however, that in Canada, the main national
asthma advocacy organization, the Asthma Society of Canada, does not
offer much in the way of information on the social justice dimensions of
asthma. While the organization's website mentions that air pollution can
worsen the symptoms of asthmatic persons, it also notes that "air pollution
as a cause of asthma has not been verified" (see Asthma Society of Canada
2009). The major focus of the organization is on individual self-control—
asthma patients are counselled to take responsibility by limiting their
exposure to factors that might harm or trigger an asthmatic episode. Under
the heading, "Taking Control," patients are told that "Asthma doesn't have
to control your life. Instead, you can control your asthma . . ." (Asthma
Society of Canada, 2006). This hyper-individuality is not unique to asthma,
however. Under the guise of empowering the patient consumer, a range of
illnesses/conditions are reframed as challenges to be overcome through
proper lifestyle management, from diabetes to coronary heart disease to
obesity.

In contrast, the California chapter of the American Lung Association is
supporting clean air initiatives in low-income communities of colour and using
the language of the environmental justice movement to anchor its advocacy. It
is responding to the fact that in California many low-income families live near
refineries, petroleum tank farms, and hazardous waste disposal sites. In some
neighbourhoods, as many as one in six children has asthma (see American
Lung Association of California, 2013). Even the American Environmental
Protection Agency has entered the fray, calling for increased asthma education
and prevention to achieve environmental justice.

Having surveyed these three HSMs, each of which provides a distinctive prism through which to examine health-related contestation, I next ask whether we have the proper analytical tools to capture this newly emerging and dynamic field of social movement activism.

DESPERATELY SEEKING A THEORETICAL FRAMEWORK

There has been much debate in the social movement literature on the choice of theoretical approach; much of this debate, however, has generated more heat than light. While it is not necessary to replay the academic jousting matches that have occurred, it is important to summarize briefly the two paradigms normally summoned to explain social movement activity and ask whether we need to adapt these approaches to the new realities of social movements. As discussed in the Introduction of this book, the first approach, resource mobilization theory (RMT) is more state-centred in its approach and, hence, more akin to traditional notions of interest-group lobbying rooted in access to resources. It emphasizes the historical continuities of movements. The second, new social movement (NSM) theory, defines movements in a wider context and emphasizes goals such as identity and autonomy. Civil society, not the state, is the main unit of analysis. Of course, these strict categorizations do not sufficiently explain the processes of collective action. Identity and autonomy may be bound up with competition for resources; conversely, access to resources is often tied to larger political issues, such as autonomy. Each approach reveals only one part of the story, however. RMT theorists assert that "social movement activities are not spontaneous and disorganized and that social movement participants are not irrational" (Ferree, 1992: 29). Their strategic approach to the study of social movements is a direct response to previous theories of collective behaviour, which reduced political action to irrational outbursts of time and place (see Kornhauser, 1959; Smelser, 1962). Emerging in the US in the 1970s, RMT derived intellectual support from, among others, Mancur Olson's *The Logic of Collective Action* (1965). An economist, Olson challenged the notion that groups, much like individuals, act in their own self-interest. Indeed, according to Olson, the rational actor will pursue collective action only if the benefits of doing so outweigh the costs involved. The problem, however, is that individuals may reap the rewards of collective action regardless of their involvement—the so-called "free rider" problem.

RMT scholars have been accused of "normalizing" collective protest. Piven and Cloward assert that RMT's focus on the similarities between conventional and protest action muddies the understanding of social movement behaviour: "Blurring the distinction between normative and non-normative forms of collective action is the most fundamental expression of this tendency,

as if rule-conforming and rule-violating collective action are of a piece"
(Piven and Cloward, 1995: 137). They contend that RMT theorists mistakenly
lump together all collective action, regardless of whether it is in fact peaceful
or violent.

If RMT responds to the "how" of social movement action, NSM theory
stresses the "why"—meaning displaces structure as the foundational logic of
social movements. For NSM theorists, issues of collective identity are central
to the creation of social movement organizations. A key distinguishing feature of such movements is that they do not rally around class as a defining
issue: "new" social movements are presumably postmodern, postmaterial, or
uninterested in the economy or the state (Offe, 1985; Touraine, 1988; Cohen,
1985). It is argued that NSM actors enter the political arena to defend not their
economic interests but their collective identities. Collective identity is understood here as "nothing else than a shared definition of the field of opportunities and constraints offered to collective action: 'shared' means constructed
and negotiated through a repeated process of 'activation' of social relationships connecting through the actors" (Melucci, 1985: 793). Collective identity
formation is an all-encompassing process through which actors produce cognitive frameworks that enable them to survey their immediate environment
and to assess the costs and benefits of their actions. NSM theorists use the term
"framing" to refer to "the conscious strategic efforts by groups of people to
fashion shared understandings of the world and of themselves that legitimate
and motivate collective action" (McAdam et al., 1996: 6). As Goffman wrote
of framing, "There is a sense in which what is play for the golfer is work for
the caddy" (cited in Gusfield, 1997: 202). Movements frame the problems/is-
sues they seek to address and the nature/substance of their claims. Collective
action frames "underscore and embellish the seriousness and injustice of a
particular social condition or redefine as unjust and immoral what was previously seen as unfortunate but perhaps tolerable" (Benford, 1997: 416).

Several theorists assert that the two paradigms may actually complement
one another, that each can make important contributions to the study of social
movements. For McClurg Mueller (1992: 50), "one paradigm does not necessarily supersede the other, but rather affords a figure/ground shift in what is
considered problematic." Canel (1992) suggests that social movements must be
understood with reference to six factors, loosely grouped under two headings:
macro-processes and micro-processes. The first set of factors includes three
related concerns: systemic explanations of the rise of new social actors, an
elucidation of the relationship between the state and civil society, and the
process of collective identity formation. The second includes "the dynamics of
mobilization, organizational dynamics, and social networks" (Canel, 1992: 50).
For Canel, NSM theorists are well-equipped to address the first set of factors,

while RMT theorists are adequately placed to deal with the second. Cohen and Arato (1994: 509) stress that students of social movements should "view civil society as the target as well as the terrain of collective action" and examine the processes through which "collective actors create the identities and solidarities they defend."

While Tarrow's influential work on political opportunity structures has been helpful in informing debates about the ebb and flow of collective action, it has been less useful in probing issues related to collective identity formation. Moreover, the focus on structure has tended to exaggerate the differences between the state and society. Rather than thinking in terms of movements against states, it may be more useful to recognize that the two categories can bleed into one another. Protest and contention can move inside institutions (Katzenstein, 1998); organizations can work collaboratively with state actors to bring about policy change. The focus of social movement theorists on issues of collective identity, on the other hand, sheds necessary light on issues that transcend resource attainment. This is especially relevant in the case of HSMs, since although political battles ensue over funding of scientific and medical research, a significant component of HSM activism is devoted to overturning "meanings" affixed to disease/illness generally and the role of citizens in these processes.

In the last decade, two promising areas have emerged in the field of social movement theory. The first relates to the use of narrative approaches (see Polletta, 1998). There are important links, for instance, between the study of narrative in social movement theory and the study of narrative in the fields of medical sociology and medical anthropology that can be exploited. As Polletta explains, subsuming narrative under the broader category of frame, however, obscures some of the real differences between the two. What makes a frame successful "is clear specification not only of the injustice against which protest must be mounted but the agents and likely efficacy of the protest. People must be shown that deliberate action will have its intended effect." Narrative, on the other hand, succeeds by what it doesn't convey: "Narrative necessitates our interpretive participation, requires that we struggle to fill in the gaps and resolve the ambiguities. We struggle because the story's end is consequential—not only as the outcome but as the moral of the events which precede it" (Polletta, 1998: 141). Marrying narrative and social movement approaches to health can be useful in uncovering the embodied nature of illness; that is, understanding how people experience or make sense of illness in their everyday lives can shed light on potential strategies to reduce the incidence of disease and embrace prevention strategies. Moreover, a focus on the situated knowledge of persons living with illness can allow us to understand the dynamic processes of politicization that accompany some illnesses and not others. For instance, narratives of blame can partly help to explain why persons living with a stigmatizing illness might choose to suffer in silence; this may be compounded in instances where the ill person is already on the margins of society (see Orsini and Scala, 2006).

Second, social movement theorists are taking a closer look at the role of emotions in explaining the emergence, patterns, and outcomes of social movement protest. While sidelined in the past as unworthy and unreliable objects of analysis, there is a greater recognition that social movements in general operate in political environments that are deeply affective, as well. Movement actors make emotional appeals to potential members and mobilize deeply felt grievances in an effort to encourage authorities to respond. This is not, however, reducible "to tugging at heartstrings." A range of policy actors, from civil society groups to bureaucrats to "ordinary" citizens employ emotions in their everyday practices to influence policy and politics. The environment I alluded to earlier is often guided by a series of "feeling rules" through which these emotions can be regulated or managed. Feeling rules "guide emotional work by establishing the sense of entitlement or obligation that governs emotional exchanges" (Hochschild, 1983: 56). As applied to HSMs specifically, the notion of feeling rules can help us to explore the boundaries of appropriate emotional expression, including whether or not and to what extent movement actors are viewed as legitimate in their own right, as has been the case with people living with MCS who have been dismissed as suffering from emotional or psychological problems rather than authentic physiologic problems.

CONCLUSION

This chapter has introduced the reader to a range of HSMs that dot the Canadian political landscape—and beyond. The three movements chosen— HIV/AIDS, environmental illness, and asthma—are all engaged in efforts to deconstruct (and reconstruct) how we understand health. The AIDS movement has been instrumental in challenging the notion that the only credible experts on the epidemic are scientists or medical doctors. The lay expertise of people with AIDS has permanently marked our understanding of the disease and has influenced many HSMs formed in the wake of the epidemic. While it is fashionable to decry the mainstreaming of AIDS and the "selling out" of AIDS activists, they deserve credit for resurrecting the patient from his/ her sick role—and sick bed. An interesting question that flows from this idea is whether the image of the angry, defiant, placard-waving person with AIDS has become the standard by which all people with AIDS are judged and whether there is any discursive space for people with AIDS who eschew participation in activist organizations and who prefer to live out their illness behind closed doors.

The second movement, organized around the notion of environmental illness, is less mature in Canada, but there are indications that several disparate organizations are beginning to make their voices heard. I chose to feature MCS because it raises a set of perplexing questions for students of social movements centred on the notion of the body itself as a site of contestation. Persons claiming to be environmentally ill use their biological bodies to contest biomedicine's claims that there is no sound science demonstrating a causal link between MCS and environmental triggers. What is particularly interesting about these processes of contestation, however, is that victims are "linking their somatic disorders to rational explanations borrowed from the profession of biomedicine" (Kroll-Smith and Floyd, 2000: 83).

The third movement we examined, asthma activism, is useful in highlighting how hitherto depoliticized illnesses can acquire a contentious dimension, especially when movements can borrow from the scripts of other movements, including in this case the environmental justice and civil rights movements. It was noted, however, that in Canada, asthma advocacy remains tied to the notion of empowering the individual asthma sufferer to take charge of their condition.

Finally, I asked at the outset whether the proliferation of HSMs is reflective of a wider shift in the terrain of collective action. Is health emerging as a dominant cleavage in Canadian society, eclipsing other cleavages that have animated politics in the past? Is our health status becoming a currency we trade in the political marketplace, or is it, rather, another way of expressing deeply felt grievances related to other forms of oppression, such as those linked to race, gender, and sexuality? There are certainly examples of health social movements that are new, such as MCS, in the sense that they are viewed as the product of the proliferation of chemicals and toxins in our environment. In the case of asthma, there are increasing attempts to frame this public health problem in the language of social justice. It might be best, however, to heed Melucci's suggestion that "movements no longer operate as characters but as signs" (1988: 249). In challenging the dominant "cultural codes" in society, HSMs force us to rethink how we understand the connection between our bodies and our environments.

NOTE

1   This revised chapter benefited from research support offered through a Standard Research Grant from the Social Sciences and Humanities Research Council. In addition, part of this research was made possible by a grant from the Canadian Institutes of Health Research, which funded my research on Hepatitis C and allowed me to develop further my interest in health social movements.

A grant from the University of Ottawa's Faculty of Social Sciences allowed me to hire Lee Weiler, whose research assistance is gratefully acknowledged. My thanks to Miriam Smith and to the anonymous reviewers for helpful comments on earlier drafts.

REFERENCES AND FURTHER READING

AIDS Action Now!. 2013. http://www.aidsactionnow.org/?p=450 (accessed April 2, 2013).

American Lung Association of California. 2013. http://www.californialung.org (accessed April 2, 2013).

Aronowitz, Stanley. 1995. "Against the Liberal State: ACT-UP and the Emergence of Postmodern Politics." In *Social Postmodernism: Beyond Identity Politics*, ed. Linda Nicholson and Steven Seidman, 357–83. Cambridge: Cambridge University Press.

Asthma Society of Canada. 2006. Adults. http://www.asthma.ca (accessed April 2, 2013).

Banaszak-Holl, Jane C., Sandra R. Levitsky, and Mayer N. Zald. 2010. *Social Movements and the Transformation of American Health Care*. New York: Oxford University Press.

Beck, Ulrich. 1992. *Risk Society: Towards a New Modernity*. Trans. Mark Ritter. London: Sage Publications.

Benford, Robert. 1997. "An Insider's Critique of the Social Movement Framing Perspective." *Sociological Inquiry* 67: 409–30.

Brown, Phil, Rachel Morello-Frosch, and Stephen Zavestoski, eds. 2011. *Contested Illnesses: Citizens, Science, and Health Social Movements*. Berkeley, CA: University of California Press.

Brown, Phil, Brian Mayer, Stephen Zavestoski, Theo Luebke, Joshua Mandelbaum, and Sabrina McCormick. 2003. "The Health Politics of Asthma: Environmental Justice and the Collective Illness Experience in the United States." *Social Science & Medicine* 57 (3): 453–64.

Brown, Phil, Stephen Zavestoski, Sabrina McCormick, Brian Mayer, Rachel Morello-Frosch, and Rebecca Gasior Altman. 2004. "Embodied Health Movements: New Approaches to Social Movements in Health." *Sociology of Health & Illness* 26 (1): 50–80.

Callen, Michael. 1990. *Surviving AIDS*. New York: HarperCollins Publishers.

Canadian Human Rights Commission. 2007. "Policy on Environmental Sensitivities." http://www.chrc-ccdp.ca/legislation_policies/policy_environ_politique-eng.aspx? (accessed April 2, 2013).

Canel, Eduardo. 1992. "New Social Movement Theory and Resource Mobilization: The Need for Integration." In *Organizing Dissent: Contemporary Social

Movements in Theory and Practice, ed. William K. Carroll, 22–51. Toronto: Garamond.

Castells, Manuel. 2012. *Networks of Outrage and Hope: Social Movements in the Internet Age*. Cambridge: Polity Press.

Cohen, Jean L. 1985. "Strategy or Identity: New Theoretical Paradigms and Contemporary Social Movements." *Social Research* 52 (4, Winter): 663–716.

Cohen, Jean L., and Andrew Arato. 1994. *Civil Society and Political Theory*. Cambridge, MA: MIT Press.

Corburn, Jason. 2005. *Street Science: Community Knowledge and Environmental Health Justice*. Cambridge, MA: MIT Press.

Crimp, Douglas, and Adam Rolston. 1990. *AIDS Demo Graphics*. Seattle: Bay Press.

Della Porta, Donatella, and Sidney Tarrow, eds. 2005. *Transnational Protest and Global Activism*. New York: Rowman and Littlefield.

Donatella, Della Porta, Massimiliano Andretta, Lorenzo Mosca, and Herbert Reiter. 2006. *Globalization from Below: Transnational Activists and Protest Networks*. Minneapolis: University of Minnesota Press.

Environmental News Service. 2005. "Lab Tests Find 60 Toxic Chemicals in Canadians' Blood." November 15. http://earthhopenetwork.net/Lab_Tests_Find_60_Toxic_Chemicals_in_Canadians_Blood.htm (accessed April 2, 2013).

Epstein, Steven. 1991. "Democratic Science? AIDS Activism and the Contested Construction of Knowledge." *Socialist Review* 21 (2, April-June): 35–64.

Epstein, Steven. 1995. "The Construction of Lay Expertise: AIDS Activism and the Forging of Credibility in the Reform of Clinical Trials." *Science, Technology, and Human Values* 20 (4, Autumn): 408–37.

Epstein, Steven. 1996. *Impure Science: AIDS, Activism, and the Construction of Knowledge*. Berkeley, CA: University of California Press.

Epstein, Steven. 2008. "Patient Groups and Health Movements." In *The Handbook of Science and Technology Studies*, ed. Edward J. Hackett, Olga Amsterdamska, Michael Lynch, and Judy Wajcman, 499–539. Cambridge, MA: MIT Press.

Ferree, Myra Mark. 1992. "The Political Context of Rationality: Rational Choice Theory and Resource Mobilization." In *Frontiers in Social Movement Theory*, ed. Aldon D. Morris and Carol McClurg Mueller, 29–52. New Haven: Yale University Press.

Flam, Helen, and Debra King, eds. 2005. *Emotions and Social Movements*. New York: Routledge.

Fumento, Michael. 2000. "Scents and Senselessness." *The American Spectator* (April). http://www.fumento.com/scents.html (accessed April 2, 2013).

Furedi, Frank. 2005. "Our Unhealthy Obsession with Sickness." http://www.spiked-online.com/Articles/0000000CA958.htm (accessed April 2, 2013).

Gamson, Josh. 1989. "Silence, Death, and the Invisible Enemy: AIDS Activism and Social Movement 'Newness.'" *Social Problems* 36 (4): 351–67.

Gould, Deborah. 2009. *Moving Politics: Emotion and ACT UP's Fight Against AIDS*. Chicago: University of Chicago Press.

Gusfield, Joseph. 1994. "The Reflexivity of Social Movements: Collective Behavior and Mass Society Theory Revisited." In *New Social Movements: From Ideology to Identity*, ed. Enrique Laraña, Hank Johnston, and Joseph R. Gusfield, 201–28. Philadelphia: Temple University Press.

Gusfield, Joseph. 1997. "The Culture of Public Problems: Drinking-Driving and the Symbolic Order." In *Morality and Health*, ed. Allan M. Brandt and Paul Rozin, 201–30. New York: Routledge.

Hobson, Barbara, ed. 2005. *Recognition Struggles and Social Movements*. Cambridge: Cambridge University Press.

Hochschild, Arlie. 1979. "Emotion Work, Feeling Rules, and Social Structure." *American Journal of Sociology* 85 (3): 551–75.

Hochschild, Arlie. 1983. *The Managed Heart: The Commercialization of Human Feeling*. Berkeley, CA: University of California Press.

Jenson, Jane. 1995. "What's in a Name? Nationalist Movements and Public Discourse." In *Social Movements and Culture*, ed. Hank Johnston and Bert Klandermans, 107–26. London: UCL Press.

Johnson, Judith A. 1992. *Women With HIV Infection*. Washington, DC: Congressional Research Service, Library of Congress.

Katzenstein, Mary Fainsod. 1998. *Faithful and Fearless: Moving Feminist Protest inside the Church and Military*. Princeton: Princeton University Press.

Keck, Margaret, and Kathryn Sikkink. 1998. *Activists Beyond Borders: Advocacy Networks in International Politics*. Ithaca, NY: Cornell University Press.

Khagram, Sanjeev, James V. Riker, and Kathryn Sikkink, eds. 2002. *Restructuring World Politics, Transnational Social Movements, Networks, and Norms*. Minneapolis: University of Minnesota Press.

Kinsman, Gary. 1998. "Managing AIDS Organizing: 'Consultation,' 'Partnership,' and the National AIDS Strategy." In *Organizing Dissent: Contemporary Social Movements in Theory and Practice*, ed. William K. Carroll, 213–39. Toronto: Garamond.

Klawiter, Maren. 2004. "Breast Cancer in Two Regimes: The Impact of Social Movements on Illness Experience." *Sociology of Health & Illness* 26 (6): 845–74.

Kornhauser, William. 1959. *The Politics of Mass Society*. Glencoe, IL: The Free Press.

Kroll-Smith, Steve, and Hugh Floyd. 2000. "Environmental Illness as a Practical Epistemology and a Source of Professional Confusion." In *Illness and the Environment: A Reader in Contested Medicine*, ed. Steve Kroll-Smith, Phil Brown, and Valerie Gunter, 72–91. New York: New York University Press.

Marsh, Peter. 2001. "In Praise of Bad Habits." 22 November. http://www.spiked-online.com/Printable/00000002D2E7.htm (accessed April 2, 2013).

McAdam, Doug, John D. McCarthy, and Mayer N. Zald, eds. 1996. *Comparative Perspectives on Social Movements: Political Opportunities, Mobilizing Structures, and Cultural Framings.* Cambridge: Cambridge University Press.

McClurg Mueller, Carol. 1992. "Building Social Movement Theory." In *Frontiers in Social Movement Theory*, ed. Aldon D. Morris and Carol McClurg Mueller. 3–25. New Haven: Yale University Press.

McLaren, Leah. 2000. "Halifax Hysteria." *The Globe and Mail* (April 29).

Melucci, Alberto. 1985. "The Symbolic Challenge of Contemporary Movements." *Social Research* 52:789–816.

Melucci, Alberto. 1988. "Social Movements and the Democratization of Everyday Life." In *Civil Society and the State*, ed. J. Keane, 245–60. London: Verso.

Melucci, Alberto. 1996. *Challenging Codes: Collective Action in the Information Age.* Cambridge: Cambridge University Press.

Meyer, David, and Nancy Whittier. 1994. "Social Movement Spillover." *Social Problems* 41 (2): 277–98.

Meyer, David S., and Suzanne Staggenborg. 1996. "Movements, Countermovements, and the Structure of Political Opportunity." *American Journal of Sociology* 101 (6): 1628–60.

Mooers, Colin, and Alan Sears. 1992. "The 'New Social Movements' and the Withering Away of State Theory." In *Organizing Dissent: Contemporary Social Movements in Theory and Practice*, ed. William Carroll, 52–68. Toronto: Garamond.

Mykhalovskiy, Eric. 2011. "The Problem of 'Significant Risk': Exploring the Public Health Impact of Criminalizing HIV Non-disclosure." *Social Science & Medicine* 73 (5): 668–75.

Navarre, Max. 1993. "Fighting the Victim Label." In *AIDS: Cultural Analysis/Cultural Activism*, ed. Douglas Crimp, 143–47. Cambridge, MA: MIT Press.

Nova Scotia Environmental Health Centre. 2005. *Facilities.* http://www.cdha.nshealth.ca/integrated-chronic-care-service-iccs (accessed April 2, 2013).

Offe, Claus. 1985 "New Social Movements: Challenging the Boundaries of Institutional Politics." *Social Research* 52 (4): 817–68.

Olson, Mancur. 1965. *The Logic of Collective Action.* Cambridge, MA: Harvard University Press.

Orsini, Michael, and Francesca Scala. 2006. "Every Virus Tells A Story: Toward a Narrative Centred Approach to Health Policy." *Policy and Society* 25 (2): 109–30.

Orsini, Michael, and Miriam Smith. 2010. "Social Movements, Knowledge and Public Policy: The Case of Autism Activism in Canada and the U.S." *Critical Policy Studies* 4 (1): 38–57.

Orsini, Michael, and Sarah Wiebe. Forthcoming. "Between Hope and Fear: Comparing the Emotional Landscapes of Autism Activism in Canada and the U.S." In *Canada Compared*, ed. Luc Turgeon, Jennifer Wallner, Martin Papillon, and Stephen White. Vancouver: University of British Columbia Press.

Piven, Frances Fox, and Richard A. Cloward. 1995. "Collective Protest: A Critique of Resource-Mobilization Theory." In *Social Movements: Critiques, Concepts, Case-studies*, ed. Stanford A. Lyman, 137–67. New York: New York University Press.

Polletta, Francesca. 1998. "'It Was Like a Fever . . . ' Narrative and Identity in Social Protest." *Social Problems* 45 (2): 137–59.

Rayside, David M., and Evert A. Lindquist. 1992. "AIDS Activism and the State in Canada." *Studies in Political Economy* 39 (Autumn): 37–76.

Sears, Margaret E. 2007. *The Medical Perspective on Environmental Sensitivities*. Ottawa: Canadian Human Rights Commission.

Smelser, Neil J. 1962. *Theory of Collective Behavior*. New York: The Free Press.

Smith, Jackie. 2008. *Social Movements for Global Democracy*. Baltimore: The Johns Hopkins University Press.

Smith, Miriam. 2005. *A Civil Society? Collective Actors in Canadian Political Life*. Peterborough: Broadview.

Tarrow, Sidney. 1994. *Power in Movement: Social Movements, Collective Action, and Politics*. Cambridge: Cambridge University Press.

Tarrow, Sidney. 2005. *The New Transnational Activism*. New York: Cambridge University Press.

Touraine, Alain. 1988. *Return of the Actor: Social Theory in Postindustrial Society*. Minneapolis: University of Minnesota Press.

Weir, Lorna. 1993. "The Limitations of New Social Movement Analysis." *Studies in Political Economy* 40 (Spring): 73–103.

Wilkie, Cara, and David Baker. 2007. *Accommodation for Environmental Sensitivities: Legal Perspective*. Ottawa: Canadian Human Rights Commission.

Winant, Terry. 2004. "Reflections on Asthma Activism." Fresno Metro Ministry, News and Views, August.

Zavestoski, Stephen, Phil Brown, Sabrina McCormick, Brian Mayer, Maryhelen D'Ottavi, and Jaime Lucove. 2004. "Patient Activism and the Struggle for Diagnosis: Gulf War Illness and Other Medically Unexplained Physical Symptoms in the US." *Social Science & Medicine* 58 (1): 161–75.

Zavestoski, Stephen, Rachel Morello-Frosch, Phil Brown, Brian Mayer, Sabrina McCormick, and Rebecca Gasior Altman. 2004. "Embodied Health Movements and Challenges to the Dominant Epidemiological Paradigm." *Research in Social Movements, Conflicts and Change* 25:253–78.

Contributors

Peter Clancy is Professor in the Department of Political Science at St. Francis Xavier University. His areas of interest are natural resource politics, development in the Canadian north, and business politics and economic policy. He has recently published *Offshore Petroleum Politics: Regulation and Risk in the Scotian Basin* (UBC Press, 2011). He is also the author of *Micro-Politics and Canadian Business: Paper, Steel and the Airlines* (Broadview Press, 2004).

Amanda Coles recently completed her PhD in Comparative Public Policy at McMaster University. Her areas of interest include Canadian politics, unions, cultural policy, and feminist political economy. Her work has been published in the *Canadian Journal of Communication*, the European journal *Cultural Trends*, and for the Canadian Cultural Observatory, policy research branch. She is an Associate Researcher at the Interuniversity Research Centre on Globalization and Work (CRIMT) in Montreal, and started her position as a faculty member in the Department of Culture and Communication at the University of Melbourne in June 2013.

Alexandra Dobrowolsky is Professor in the Department of Political Science at Saint Mary's University. She works in the areas of Canadian, Comparative and Women, Gender and Politics on issues of representation, social policy, immigration and citizenship. She is the author of *The Politics of Pragmatism: Women, Representation and Constitutionalism in Canada* (Oxford, 2000); co-editor of *Women Making Constitutions: New Politics and Comparative Perspectives* (Palgrave, 2003); co-editor of *Women, Migration and Citizenship: Making Local, National and Transnational Connections* (Ashgate, 2006), as well as editor of *Women and Public Policy in Canada: Neoliberalism and After?* (Oxford, 2010).

Pascale Dufour is Associate Professor in the Department of Political Science at the University of Montreal. Her areas of interest include social movements and globalization and the politics of representation in Canada and France. She is the author of *Trois Espaces de protestation: France, Canada, Québec.* (PUM, 2013) and co-author of *Transnationalizing Women's Movements: Solidarities Without Borders*, (UBC, 2010). Her work has also appeared in the *Canadian Journal of Political Science*, the *Canadian Journal of Sociology and Politique et Sociétés*.

Jonathan Greene is Assistant Professor in the Department of Political Studies and the Department of Canadian Studies at Trent University. His interests include comparative political economy, social movements, and poverty and homelessness. His recent work has appeared in *Studies in Political Economy*.

Trevor W. Harrison is Professor of Sociology at the University of Lethbridge and Director of the Parkland Institute. His interests include Canadian society, political sociology, and public policy. He is author or editor of eight books on politics, notably *Of Passionate Intensity: Right-Wing Populism and the Reform Party of Canada* (University of Toronto Press, 1995), *The Return of the Trojan Horse: Alberta and the New World (Dis)Order* (Black Rose and the Parkland Institute, 2005), and (with Slobodan Drakulic) *Against Orthodoxy: Studies in Nationalism* (UBC, 2011).

Matt James is Associate Professor in the Department of Political Science at the University of Victoria. His areas of interest are social movements, reparations, political apologies, transitional justice, constitutionalism, and citizenship. He is the author of *Misrecognized Materialists: Social Movements in Canadian Constitutional Politics* (UBC, 2006) and several articles and chapters focusing particularly on social movements and historical injustices.

Audrey Kobayashi is Professor in the Department of Geography at Queen's University. Her work focuses on how processes of human differentiation—race, class, gender, ability, national identity—emerge in a range of landscapes and how these processes are shaped by public policy, legal and normative frameworks. She has a longstanding interest in the history of Japanese–Canadian communities. Among many others, her work has appeared in *Gender, Place and Culture*, *The Professional Geographer*, *Annals of the Association of American Geographers*, *The Canadian Geographer* and *Canadian Ethnic Studies*.

Kiera L. Ladner is Canada Research Chair in Indigenous Politics and in the Department of Political Studies at the University of Manitoba. Her areas of interest are indigenous politics, constitutional politics, social movements, and decolonization. Her work has appeared in *Studies in Political Economy* and the *Canadian Journal of Political Science*.

Michael Orsini is Associate Professor in the School of Political Studies and Chair, Institute of Women's Studies, at the University of Ottawa. His areas of interest are health politics and policy, social movements, and public policy. He is the co-editor of *Critical Policy Studies* (UBC, 2007) and his work has also appeared in the *Canadian Journal of Political Science*, *Social Policy and Administration*, *Social and Legal Studies*, and the *Canadian Journal of Urban Research*. He recently co-edited *Worlds of Autism: Across the Spectrum of Neurological Difference* (University of Minnesota Press, 2013).

Robert Paehlke is a political scientist and Professor Emeritus of Environmental and Resource Studies at Trent University. He was editor of the Canadian environmental journal/magazine *Alternatives* from its founding in 1971 until 1982. He is author of *Some Like It Cold: the Politics of Climate Change in Canada* (2008); *Democracy's Dilemma: Environment, Social Equity and the*

Global Economy (MIT Press, 2004); *Environmentalism and the Future Of Progressive Politics* (Yale University Press, 1991), and editor of *Conservation and Environmentalism: An Encyclopedia* (1995) and *Managing Leviathan: Environmental Politics and the Administrative State* (Broadview Press, 1990 and 2005).

Grace Skogstad is a Professor of Political Science at the University of Toronto and currently chair of the Department of Political Science at the University of Toronto Scarborough. Her research interests span Canadian politics and comparative public policy. She is the author of *Internationalization and Canadian Agriculture: Policy and Governing Paradigms* (University of Toronto Press, 2008); editor of *Policy Paradigms, Transnationalism, and Domestic Politics* (University of Toronto Press, 2011); and co-editor, with Herman Bakvis, of *Canadian Federalism: Performance, Effectiveness and Legitimacy* (Oxford University Press, 2012).

Miriam Smith is Professor in the Department of Social Science at York University. Her areas of interest are Canadian and comparative politics, social movements, and lesbian and gay politics. Among other works, she is the author of *Lesbian and Gay Rights in Canada: Social Movements and Equality-Seeking, 1971–1995* (University of Toronto Press, 1999); *A Civil Society? Collective Actors in Canadian Political Life* (Broadview Press, 2005); *Political Institutions and Lesbian and Gay Rights in the United States and Canada* (Routledge, 2008), and the co-editor of *Critical Policy Studies* (University of British Columbia Press, 2007).

Christophe Traisnel is Associate Professor in the Department of Political Science at the University of Moncton. His areas of interest are comparative politics, nationalism of protest in Canada and Belgium, social movements, political militancy, and French-speaking communities. His recent work has been published in *International Journal of Canadian Studies* (2012).

Lisa Vanhala is a Lecturer in the Department of Political Science and School of Public Policy at University College London. Her research explores the dynamics between social movements, law, and politics. Her current work focuses on environmental movements in Europe and North America. Her monograph *Making Rights a Reality? Disability Rights Activists and Legal Mobilization* (Cambridge University Press, 2011) won the Canadian Political Science Association Comparative Politics Prize (2012) and the Socio-Legal Studies Association Hart Early Career Prize (2012).

Charlotte Yates is Professor in the Department of Political Science and School of Labour Studies at McMaster University. Her areas of interest include union renewal and union organizing in the Anglo-American democracies; political economy of political parties and interest groups; organized labour and the state and globalization and social cohesion. She is the author of *From Plant to Politics: Autoworkers in Postwar Canada* (Temple University Press, 1993), co-editor of *Trade Unions in Renewal: A Comparative Study* (New York and London: Continuum Books, 2003) and co-author of *Negotiating Risk, Seeking Security, Eroding Solidarity: Life and Work on the Border* (Fernwood Books, 2013).

Index